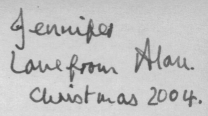

Jennifer
Love from Alan.
Christmas 2004.

PENGUIN BOOKS

TWO DEGREES WEST

P 251 - 255

'Outstanding . . . a thoughtful quest for the essence of England'
Sara Wheeler, *Daily Telegraph*

'Ironic, affectionate and curious, this was the most touching book I read
about England this year' Anthony Sattin, *Sunday Times*

'A mature, reflective, sometimes even poetic . . . celebration tinged with
an inevitable regret for the steady erosion of a rural way of life that took
thousands of years to evolve and only fifty to disappear . . . an original
and cultured mind writing about his native country, almost as if he were
explaining the mysteries of Indonesia to the folks back home. It is a
difficult trick to pull off, but he has done it' Paul Routledge, *Spectator*

'Wonderful social history' Barbara Trapido, *Observer*

'A unique guide to Britain . . . *Two Degrees West* is a creative mix of
academia, humourous anecdote and adventure . . . Writing with clarity
and patriotic compassion, Crane defines exactly what is extraordinary
about England and how in response to unavoidable change, she main-
tains her unique character' Sophie Ransom, *Geographical*

'Remarkable . . . a lively and instructive guide' *Literary Review*

'Fascinating . . . packed with amusing anecdotes' Val Hennessy,
Daily Mail

D1355102

P79!

ABOUT THE AUTHOR

Nicholas Crane's previous book, *Clear Waters Rising*, won the 1997 Thomas Cook/*Daily Telegraph* Travel Book Award. He lives in London with his wife and three children.

NICHOLAS CRANE

TWO DEGREES WEST

AN ENGLISH JOURNEY

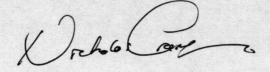

PENGUIN BOOKS

PENGUIN BOOKS

Published by the Penguin Group
Penguin Books Ltd, 27 Wrights Lane, London w8 5tz, England
Penguin Putnam Inc., 375 Hudson Street, New York, New York 10014, USA
Penguin Books Australia Ltd, Ringwood, Victoria, Australia
Penguin Books Canada Ltd, 10 Alcorn Avenue, Toronto, Ontario, Canada m4v 3b2
Penguin Books (NZ) Ltd, Private Bag 102902, NSMC, Auckland, New Zealand

Penguin Books Ltd, Registered Offices: Harmondsworth, Middlesex, England

First published by Viking 1999
Published in Penguin Books 2000
7

Set in Linotype Palatino
Printed in England by Clays Ltd, St Ives plc

For Imogen and Kit

Acknowledgements

I came across two degrees west during a chance encounter with J. B. Harley's *Ordnance Survey Maps a descriptive manual* (1975). To J. B. Harley, and to chance, I am indebted.

For their tireless interest, I am also indebted to Paula Langford-Smith, Elaine Owen and Richard Short at the Ordnance Survey.

To all those named in the text, I extend heartfelt thanks.

I would also like to thank the following:

Debbie Anderson, Revd Robert Atwell, Charles Crane, Roger Daynes, Dr Rita Gardner, Paul Gogarty, Andrea Hatcher, Francis Herbert, Tim Jasper, Simon Jenkins, Anthony Lambert, Anne Leuchars, Val Lowther, Hallam Murray, Mark Thackera, David Udberg and Nigel de N. Winser for contributions ranging from family history and cartography to locomotive nomenclature and the servicing of my ancient Olympus camera.

Chris Brasher, John Cleare and Peter Inglis for their excellent photographs and Tom Owen Edmunds for organizing the picture spreads with customary genius.

Reginald Piggott for his superb maps.

Derek Johns, Eleo Gordon, Lucy Capon, Caroline Sanderson, Keith Taylor, David Watson, Bela Cunha and all at Viking for their publishing skills and elastic patience.

Annabel, my wife, for encouragement, critical judgement and for the two children to whom this book is dedicated.

Illustrations

On the airfield at RAF Lyneham
Rush-hour on Chapperton Down, Salisbury Plain (John Cleare)
A final hurdle above the Dorset cliffs (John Cleare)
One of the burial mounds on Nine Barrow Down (John Cleare)
Swimming on the edge of Dancing Ledge (John Cleare)

All photographs without credits were taken by the author

Maps

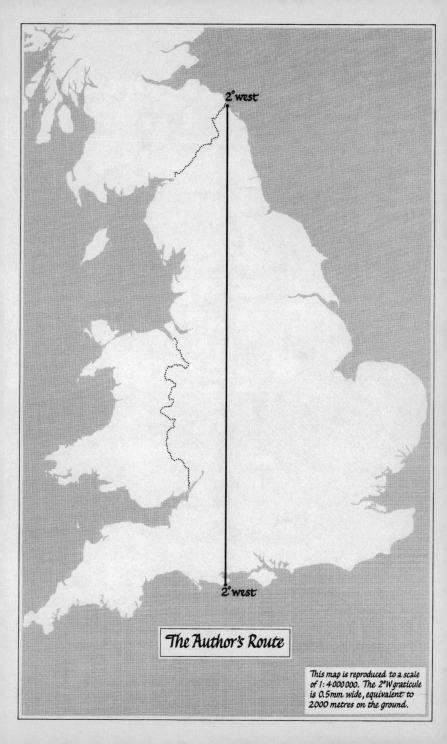

2° west

2° west

The Author's Route

This map is reproduced to a scale of 1:4 000 000. The 2°W graticule is 0.5mm wide, equivalent to 2000 metres on the ground.

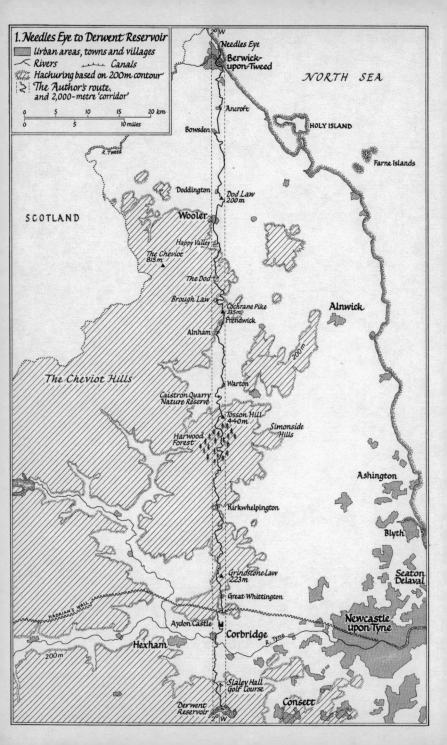

1. Needles Eye to Derwent Reservoir

Urban areas, towns and villages
Rivers   Canals
Hachuring based on 200m contour
The Author's route,
and 2,000-metre 'corridor'

0   5   10   15   20 km
0   5   10 miles

2°W

Needles Eye
Berwick-upon-Tweed

NORTH SEA

Ancroft

HOLY ISLAND

Bowsden

R. Tweed

Farne Islands

Doddington

Dod Law 200m

SCOTLAND

Wooler

Happy Valley

The Cheviot 815m

The Dod

Brough Law

Cochrane Pike 335m

Prendwick

Alnham

Alnwick

The Cheviot Hills

200m

Warton

Caistron Quarry Nature Reserve

Tosson Hill 440m

Simonside Hills

Harwood Forest

Ashington

Kirkwhelpington

Blyth

Grindstone Law 223m

Seaton Delaval

Great Whittington

HADRIAN'S WALL

200m

Aydon Castle

Corbridge

Newcastle upon Tyne

Hexham

R. Tyne

Slaley Hall Golf Course

Consett

Derwent Reservoir

2°W

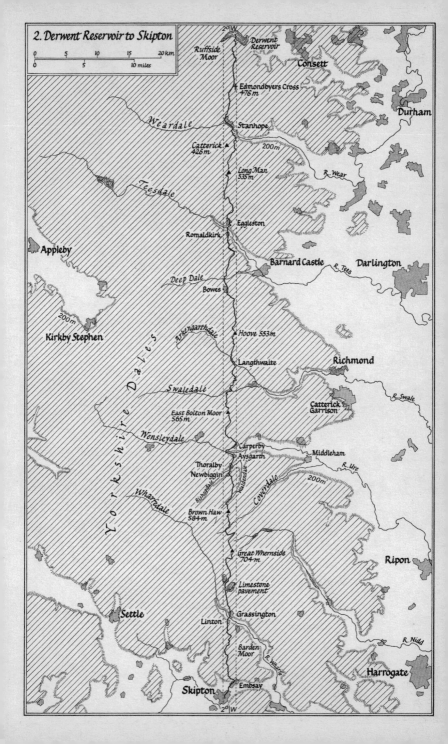

2. Derwent Reservoir to Skipton

2° W

0 5 10 15 20 km
0 5 10 miles

Ruffside
Moor

Derwent
Reservoir

Consett

Durham

Edmondbyers Cross
476 m

Weardale

Stanhope

200 m

Catterick
426 m

R. Wear

Long Man
535 m

Teesdale

Eggleston

Romaldkirk

Appleby

Barnard Castle

R. Tees

Darlington

Deep Dale

Bowes

200 m

Kirkby Stephen

Arkengarthdale

Hoove 553 m

Langthwaite

Richmond

Swaledale

R. Swale

East Bolton Moor
565 m

Catterick
Garrison

Wensleydale

Carperby
Aysgarth

Middleham

R. Ure

Thoralby
Newbiggin

Bishopdale

Walden

Coverdale

200 m

Wharfdale

Brown Haw
584 m

Great Whernside
704 m

Ripon

Limestone
pavement

Settle

Grassington

Linton

R. Nidd

Barden
Moor

R. Wharfe

Harrogate

Skipton

Embsay

2° W

Yorkshire Dales

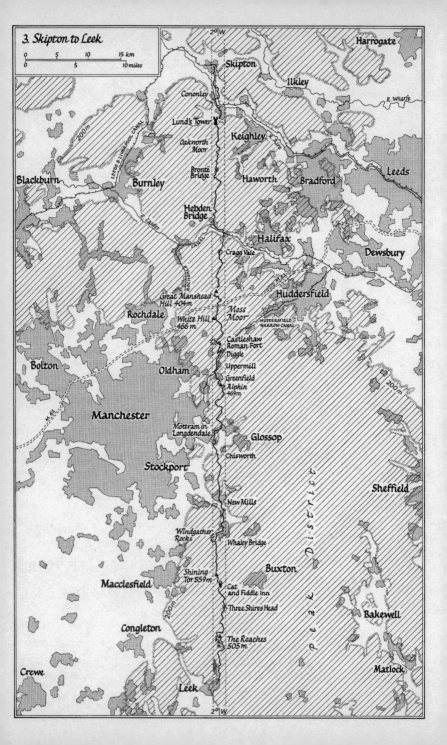

3. *Skipton to Leek*

0   5   10   15 km
0   5   10 miles

2° W

Harrogate

Skipton

Ilkley

Cononley

Lund's Tower

Oakworth Moor

Keighley

R. Wharfe

Leeds

LEEDS & LIVERPOOL CANAL

200 m

Brontë Bridge

Haworth

Bradford

Blackburn

Burnley

R. Calder

Hebden Bridge

Halifax

Dewsbury

ROCHDALE CANAL

Cragg Vale

R. Calder

Great Manshead Hill 404 m

Rochdale

White Hill 466 m

Moss Moor

Huddersfield

HUDDERSFIELD NARROW CANAL

Castleshaw Roman Fort

Diggle

Bolton

Oldham

Uppermill

Greenfield

Alphin 469 m

M62

Manchester

Mottram in Longdendale

Glossop

Chisworth

Stockport

Sheffield

New Mills

Windgather Rocks

Whaley Bridge

Buxton

Shining Tor 559 m

Macclesfield

Cat and Fiddle Inn

Three Shires Head

Bakewell

200 m

Congleton

The Roaches 505 m

Peak District

200 m

Crewe

Matlock

Leek

2° W

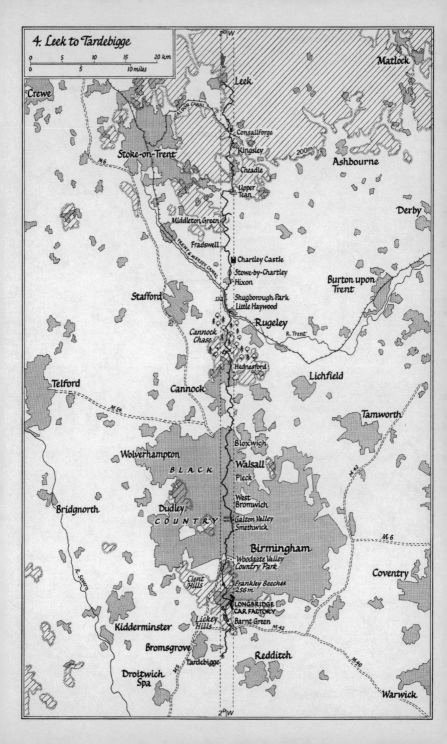

4. Leek to Tardebigge

0   5   10   15   20 km
0   5   10 miles

Matlock

Crewe

Leek

Consallforge

CALDON CANAL

Kingsley

Cheadle

200m

Ashbourne

Upper Tean

Stoke-on-Trent

M6

Derby

Middleton Green

Fradswell

TRENT & MERSEY CANAL

Chartley Castle

Stowe-by-Chartley

Hixon

Shugborough Park

Little Haywood

Burton upon Trent

Stafford

Rugeley

R. Trent

Cannock Chase

Hednesford

Lichfield

Telford

Cannock

M54

Tamworth

Bloxwich

Wolverhampton

Walsall

Pleck

West Bromwich

M42

BLACK

M6

Dudley

COUNTRY

Galton Valley

Smethwick

Birmingham

Coventry

Bridgnorth

Woodgate Valley

Country Park

Clent Hills

Frankley Beeches

256 m

LONGBRIDGE

CAR FACTORY

R. Severn

Lickey Hills

Barnt Green

M42

Kidderminster

M5

Bromsgrove

Tardebigge

Redditch

M50

Droitwich Spa

Warwick

2° W

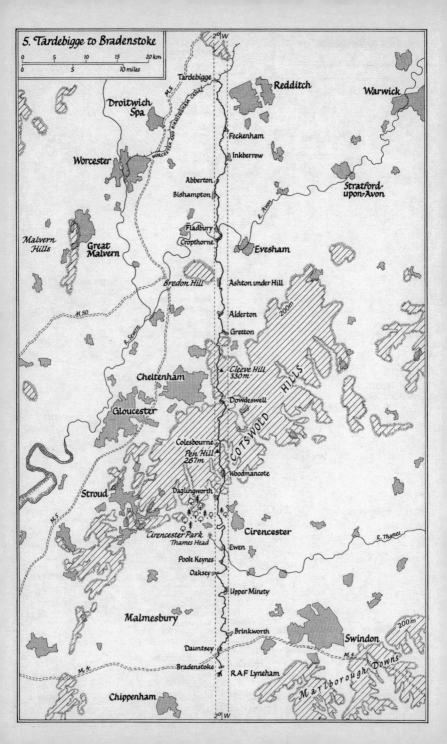

5. Tardebigge to Bradenstoke

0   5   10   15   20 km
0   5   10 miles

Tardebigge

Droitwich Spa

Redditch

Warwick

Feckenham

Inkberrow

Worcester

Abberton

Bishampton

Stratford-upon-Avon

R. Avon

Fladbury

Cropthorne

Malvern Hills

Great Malvern

Evesham

Bredon Hill

Ashton under Hill

Alderton

Gretton

200m

Cheltenham

Cleeve Hill
330m

Dowdeswell

COTSWOLD HILLS

Gloucester

Colesbourne
Pen Hill
267m

R. Severn

Woodmancote

Stroud

Daglingworth

Cirencester

R. Thames

Cirencester Park
Thames Head

Ewen

Poole Keynes

Oaksey

Upper Minety

Malmesbury

Brinkworth

Swindon

200m

Dauntsey

Bradenstoke

RAF Lyneham

M4

Marlborough Downs

Chippenham

WORCESTER AND BIRMINGHAM CANAL

2° W

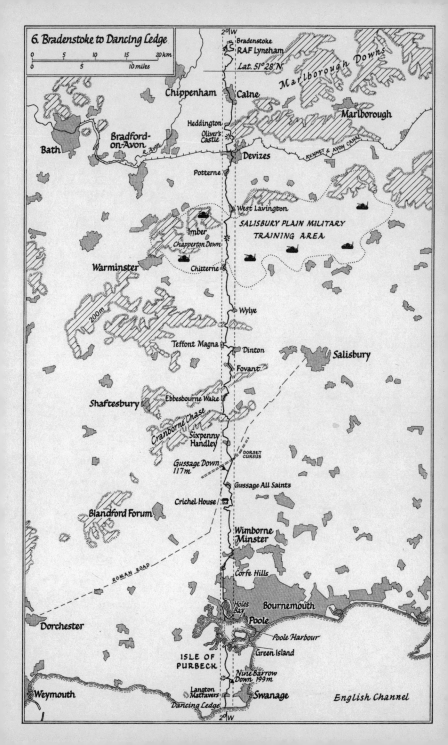

6. Bradenstoke to Dancing Ledge

0   5   10   15   20 km.
0   5   10 miles

2°W

Bradenstoke
RAF Lyneham
Lat. 51°28'N

Marlborough Downs

Chippenham   Calne

Marlborough

Heddington
Oliver's
Castle

Bath

Bradford-on-Avon

R. Avon

Devizes

KENNET & AVON CANAL

Potterne

West Lavington

SALISBURY PLAIN MILITARY
TRAINING AREA

Imber

Chapperton Down

Warminster

Chitterne

Wylye

200m

Teffont Magna   Dinton

Salisbury

Fovant

Shaftesbury   Ebbesbourne Wake

Cranborne Chase

Sixpenny
Handley

DORSET
CURSUS

Gussage Down
117m

Gussage All Saints

Crichel House

Blandford Forum

Wimborne
Minster

ROMAN ROAD

Corfe Hills

Holes
Bay

Bournemouth

Poole

Dorchester

Poole Harbour

Green Island

ISLE OF
PURBECK

Nine Barrow
Down 199m

Weymouth

Langton
Matravers

Swanage

English Channel

Dancing Ledge

2°W

Sea level: Northumberland   Between incoming waves, I hopscotched across the seaweed and brine and began to climb; a boot-jam in a wet cleft then a squirm to the dry rock of a tilted ledge, the rucksack catching. Three moves brought my nose level with land. One final heave, and I was on the cliff top, where I flipped open the compass and laid it on the map.

'Youse lost?' Beside me was a woman with two bulging plastic carrier bags.

'Not yet.'

'Wheres youse gannin?'

'Dorset. Down two degrees west.'

Unconventional behaviour requires an implausible explanation. Mine was that I was following a line of longitude.

The winkle collector scurried off along the cliff.

Two degrees west ran from one end of England to the other, from the North Sea by Berwick-upon-Tweed, to the Isle of Purbeck on the English Channel. It was the only line of longitude marked on the maps of the Ordnance Survey, who called it the Central Meridian, or the Line of Zero Convergence. For 577.96 kilometres, it cut an absolutely straight, logical course, up and down dale, through field and suburb, river and wood. The hundred or so villages and towns that it randomly selected did not include any leading tourist resorts, cultural hot spots or award-winning cities. As a route, it was counter-intuitive; a cross-section through England that would make me a stranger in my own land. I called it England's Meridian.

Off to the north-west of this Northumbrian breakwater reared Needles Eye, a great rock arch threaded with foam, besieged by wave-boom and screaming seabirds. Beyond, I could see Marshall

Meadows Point and the cliff that carried the Scottish border to the brink. South-east rose the hazy waterborne peak of Holy Island, St Aidan's sanctuary; the stepping-stone between a Judaean byre and England's adopted faith. Here was the beginning and the end of England. On this broken coast Dickens had seen his 'transcendent' rainbow.

It was mid-August: the Glorious 12th; the start of the grouse-shooting season. As I began to walk, salt spray rose in a sticky mist from one side of the path. On the other, the dark fuselage of the London train hissed through the humidity. Twenty-four hours earlier I'd been on that train, the countryside a blur.

It was one of those paths that should never end, but the coast wasn't going the way of the meridian and I had to turn inland. Before leaving the sea, I set the compass on north and peered up my line of longitude to its vanishing-point on the horizon. Beyond the intersection of sea and sky, two degrees west clipped the corner of Scotland, shaved the Shetlands and Jan Mayen Island then crossed the Arctic ice between Greenland and Spitsbergen to converge with the other longitudinal spokes at the silver hub of the North Pole.

Away from the cliffs the meridian crossed the fields of early cultivators, the ridge and furrow reflecting the swell on the receding sea. Ahead loomed massive stone ramparts, pierced by a cobbled tunnel through which I passed into Berwick-upon-Tweed.

Sandstell Point   In a guest-house overlooking the river I dumped my rucksack and walked unladen out to Sandstell Point, a peninsula of sand that at low tide reaches three-quarters of the way across the mouth of the Tweed.

On the edge of the sand were the two rowing-boats I'd seen from the guest-house window, drifting downriver on the ebb tide. The boats were cobles, the traditional wooden craft used by Tweed fishermen for netting salmon.

A crew of five, Duggie, Wally, Terry, Jason and Neil, stood beside the weathered blue boats, watching, chatting. They were all from Tweedmouth; a lean, cropped lot. Wally, the skipper, stood well clear of six foot and had the bristled skull of a squaddie; Neil, the stubbled redhead, wore a Newcastle United football shirt.

Their taciturn boss, Ralph Holmes, waited by his pick-up truck on the sand. These men were among the last survivors of an ancient Tweed industry that had once employed 300 fishermen who worked seventy-five cobles. Now, fourteen full-time fishermen worked the mouth of the Tweed, in three crews.

'No!' snapped Holmes, when I asked whether he was senti-mental about Berwick's historic association with salmon.

'This isn't a tradition. We're *working*.' His family had been in the business since 1834.

'What are the catches like?'

He shrugged, without taking his eyes off the water. 'It's not like it used to be. I've fished four hours for six fish. The fish just don't like the river any more. Probably it's the pollution.' There was a time when 300,000 fish were taken from the river in a single year.

Terry hobbled across the sand on a pair of aluminium crutches.

'Fishing accident?' I asked.

He shook his head. 'Karate. I kicked a wall. Ankle's broken in five places.'

Terry had made 850 free-fall parachute jumps. He also liked caving and climbing and was a qualified sub-aqua diver. He'd been fishing for twenty-four years and his father had been a foreman in the Berwick Salmon Fisheries Company. After the Second World War, the company had employed 150 men and had operated most of the fisheries on the river, but then catches fell and it passed into the hands of London businessmen who sold the netting rights in 1987 to the Atlantic Salmon Conservation Trust (Scotland). In 1988 the company ceased trading.

Stories circulated that the Atlantic Salmon Conservation Trust had turned the river into a private empire, with upstream beats being sold at £1,500 a day. The coble fishermen had been in the way, so they'd been bought off and their industry killed.

'This year has been terrible.' Terry shook his head. 'In the old days, one crew could get 900, 1,000 salmon on a tide. A lot of the problem is the factory ships out at sea, trawling. They get all the small salmon.'

Somebody yelled and Jason and Neil leapt towards their boat. Jason threw himself inboard and snatched at the oars while Neil leaned on the stern, pushing the boat into the current. The boat cut an arc across the river-mouth as the net unfolded off the stern, Jason's back arching as the blades chopped the water. Everybody stared. Had they netted the fish? A tail flipped behind the boat. Rowing comically fast, Jason brought the boat back to the sand and the five men threw themselves at the net, heaving it hand-over-hand on to the sand, heels skidding against the pull of the water and the thrashing fish. As the noose tightened, the water churned. The end of the net touched the sand bar. Silver fish flipped and tumbled in the green mesh. A salmon with its head rammed through the net stared wide-eyed while its body whipped like a rubber limb. Terry tossed aside his crutches and grabbed a felling stick. Neil and Terry's great arms rose and fell, thudding on to the fish with a frenzy of blows that threw up fountains of sea water and sand.

When they had finished, they stood back, panting. Holmes walked forward and picked up two of the fish, fingers hooked through gills, dipped them into the sea water, then walked briskly to the pick-up and slapped them into a blue plastic crate.

As the remaining eleven fish were rinsed, Neil folded the net on to the stern of the boat and turned it so that it was ready for the next launching.

The men went back to chatting, and waiting. After thirty minutes or so, Wally asked the time.

'Damn!' he swore. 'I'm missing *Emmerdale*.'

Berwick-upon-Tweed   That night the fish and chip shop in West Street was playing The Stranglers.

Tony and Maureen had been running the shop for thirty-five years. They were from Pompeii and their fish were from Andenes, Norway.

'What's the difference between a Neapolitan and a Northumbrian?' I wondered.

'What's the difference?' sputtered Tony. 'Day and night! Summer and winter! There's no way it can be described!'

There were four tribes on the mouth of the Tweed: Abyssinians, Twempies, Spittalers and Berwickers. Twempies came from Tweedmouth, and in Spittal the children took their mother's surname if their father wasn't a Spittaler. Abyssinians lived in the between-the-wars housing estate on the Scottish side of Berwick. When the houses were built, Abyssinia was an exotic lost cause, the Tibet of the thirties, and the estate came to be named after the only African country never to have been colonized.

'I'll be a bag of nerves,' laughed Karen as she laid bacon, egg, sausage, tomato, mushroom and fried bread on the table.

My landlady at the Walls Guest House was about to meet her mother for the first time.

Karen had been born in Torquay. Light-boned and dark-haired, she ran the guest-house with her husband Gordon. They had three young sons.

'I was adopted. A while ago I decided to try and find my mother. It was having kids that did it. I started wondering where I fitted in. Who I looked like. I've got my name now. I'm not Karen; I'm Shirley. The social worker keeps calling me Shirley, because that's who I am in the file.

'My mother was very young. I think she was fifteen. In those days the baby was taken off you. She must have wanted to keep me. It was 1970. The dark ages.'

Karen had put her name on a register. She was going to be given her file the following week.

'When I get it,' she laughed anxiously, 'I'll shut myself away in a dark corner. It's got everything about my mum. I only found out she was Cornish last week. I know her name now. I don't know what I'll say when I meet her. You can't just pick up the phone and say, "Hi! Remember me?"'

*

Above the town, seagulls scribbled in the clear sky and crapped with alacrity on pedestrians. (There'd been a letter in that week's *Berwick Advertiser* calling for gull cull.)

So many awnings lined the main street that it looked like a nomadic camp. The midweek market had brought Marygate to a clogged standstill. Acrylic slacks swung in the humid breeze above trays of fridge magnets and dog portraits. There were ready-to-wear spectacles, bath towels, waterproof trousers, Newcastle United T-shirts. (Entire families had come to town in the Toon Army strip.) Underneath the Town Hall, the Buttermarket had been set up with tables selling Peruvian cardigans, wooden toys, jewellery, aromatherapy oils.

Berwick's stalls yielded an item that I needed for future river crossings: an inflatable swimming aid. Made in China.

The warehouses of this port used to be treasure chests. In 1712 the merchant Josiah Thompson's stocklist included everything from fishing hooks and gunpowder to cloves and awl-blades.

Three centuries on, I was directed up an alley to E. F. McNeil's warehouse and an incredible cornucopia of miscellaneous junk. It was as if the good ship *England* had hit a reef and been looted by wreckers. Inside were Victorian sinks, a lifejacket, oars, black-and-white TVs, wooden carpentry tools, scuffed golf clubs, sad beds, velveteen stools, folding Formica tables, a print of 'The Haywain' rendered in fluorescent toothpaste, fogged sherry glasses, a hurricane lamp, *The Woman's Day Encyclopaedia of Cookery*. In a cardboard box of imports was a 1959 pressing of Kenneth McKellar's 'Roamin' in the Gloamin'' and Klaus Wunderlich's improbable *Organ Rhythm*. I left with Volume 1 of *The Geographical Magazine* and a rare copy of the single *Música Popular Portuguesa por Artur Andrade em Orgão Electrónico*, with Artur on the sleeve wearing an accountant's suit, heavy black specs, a yard-brush moustache and a psychopathic grin. Back at the Walls Guest House, I prised the black vinyl out of its cardboard sleeve, and found that I hadn't got Artur at all, but 'Geraldine' by the Rattles.

Volume 1 of *The Geographical Magazine* was a better deal, and contained the first six issues, from May till October 1935. In the Foreword of the first issue, the editor, Michael Huxley, rallied his readers with the Castilian apophthegm: *Geografía manda*, 'Geography dictates'. The same could be said for two degrees west.

From the walls above the Tweed, Berwick's three bridges form a trialogue of meshing spans; the fifteen sandstone arches of the pack-horse bridge superimposed upon the concrete hoops of the road bridge and Robert Stephenson's giraffe-legged viaduct.

Berwick's history is piled layer upon layer in a hot and cold geology of border misadventure. Sackings, sieges and a yo-yo economy periodically razed the streetscape and stunted architectural dreams. Seldom was there an opportunity to create or to nurture great civic building. The town changed hands thirteen times in 300 years, and there were weeks when blood and ash fell more frequently than rain.

Since 1482, when Berwick finally became English, the town has been a border outpost with a frequently ambiguous status. For a while, English-owned Berwick was the county town of Scottish Berwickshire, which led to the rumour that the town was still at war with Russia because its name had been omitted from a treaty.

Marooned on the furthest tip of England, an hour's train ride beyond Newcastle, England's most northern town teeters between the edge of the map and obscurity. Perhaps it was self-preservation that had encouraged every able-minded scribbler in town to turn out a Berwick book. In the corner shop behind the Town Hall, there were volumes on Berwick's history, on the barracks, the lifeboat, on Berwick at war, on Berwick's postcards, its salmon fishing and on the local crash sites of wartime aircraft.

The town's unofficial historian is Francis Cowe, who runs a wholesale shop at the end of Bridge Street. In his tweed jacket, khaki tie and silver hair, Francis cut a donnish caricature amid the brown cardboard boxes of confectionery, Cheeselets and lavatory rolls. He has an English degree from Durham University.

'Who writes all these books?' I asked.

'In the old days,' replied Francis sagely, 'everyone who went to Holy Island wanted to write a book about it. Unfortunately some of them did. And now the same thing is happening to Berwick.'

Against a wall of crisp boxes, Francis' wife Janet, a retired historian, was debating joint stock companies and the South Sea Bubble with Dr Tony Barrow, who had worked with Francis on a couple of local walking guides. Dr Barrow (whose PhD had dissected the local whaling industry) had dropped in at the shop to pick up ideas for *Corn, Carriers and Coastal Shipping*, an article he was writing for a transport journal.

Two minutes away in the Town Hall – where Queen Elizabeth gazed majestically down upon pensioners hunched over teacups and flapjacks – a man with a grey pony-tail was launching yet another book on Berwick. 'It's my first,' said the author, David Brenchley, from behind his trestle table. *A Place by Itself: Berwick-upon-Tweed in the Eighteenth Century* had taken four years to write, drawing on libraries as far off as Chicago and New York. It is a microscopic examination of the century that transformed a remote run-down garrison town into a bustling port with a doubled population, an academy, town hall and the first purpose-built barracks in the country, designed by Wren's old clerk of works, Nicholas Hawksmoor. The event that turned Berwick around was the Act of Union in 1707, which united the two enemies and abolished cross-border trading restrictions. The following hundred years, states Brenchley, were Berwick's 'golden century'.

Back at the wholesale shop in Bridge Street, Francis Cowe shook his head. 'The *real* golden century was the thirteenth, up to March 29th 1296. A terrific period of growth. It was a Scottish town then, heaving with people. Berwick had foreign merchants' houses. It was exporting wool to Flanders. The Guild statutes show that Berwick was Scotland's principal port. There were five friaries in Berwick. There was no other Scottish town that had that many. The friars went where the money was.'

'What happened on March 29th?'

'That was the day the rivers ran with blood,' replied Francis.

'Edward brought in the armed warhorses. It was like the Nazi panzers arriving.'

It is one of Berwick's many pleasures that every encounter can spark a controversy, and there is no better place to cool off than to take a turn around the town's Elizabethan walls. They are turfed on top and laid with paths and benches with enormous views over the sea, the Tweed and the hills.

'The utmost town in *England* and the strongest hold in all *Britaine* is *Barwicke*,' wrote John Speed in his seventeenth-century atlas. Speed depicted Berwick as an armoured knuckleduster thrust provocatively towards Scotland. Modern maps of Berwick look much the same, except that the town has spilled over the walls. These great grey bulwarks of stone rose during the Anglo-Scots arms race of the 1500s, under the influence of shadowy Italians fresh from the Tuscan war zones, who used Renaissance mathematics to manipulate angles, scales, ranges, ballistics and a host of cutting-edge measures necessary to counter modern artillery. For the Tudors, Berwick and the Tweed were the front line.

From Meg's Mount, the highest point on the town walls, I could look out to sea and across the river to Spittal, with its incongruous chimney on the foreshore. South down the meridian the Cheviots beckoned, big and blue. It was time to leave.

That night I spread the maps.

Two degrees west was marked as the line oo. To avoid climbing over roofs, I'd widened the definition of England's Meridian to a 2,000-metre band bordered by the grid lines 99 and 01. For the duration of the journey, I would walk, eat and sleep within these two lines.

In Berwick I'd been protected from the rigours of the line because this was one of only three towns on the meridian that lay entirely within my allowable corridor. I'd been able to roam with impunity. Apart from New Mills in the Pennines and Calne in

Wiltshire, all the towns on my route were only partially accessible. The narrowness of the 2,000-metre band presented other difficulties too: a motorway with no bridge, rivers, an artillery firing range. I would be trespassing daily.

Straight-line walking required specialized equipment. I had large-scale maps, an especially accurate compass, lightweight watertight Brasher Boots, clothing that would dry quickly after fording rivers and canals and a camouflaged umbrella.

'Que Chova', the umbrella that had accompanied me on my earlier walk across Europe, had reached pensionable status and so, before leaving London I'd made a pilgrimage to James Smith & Sons, purveyors of umbrellas, walking sticks and whips ('used all over the world') since 1830. Satisfied customers included Gladstone, J. B. Priestley and Steed of *The Avengers*. Steed it was who admonished a manically twirling Russian agent, Ivanov: 'Not so aggressive with the umbrella. Sprightly, not eager. Eagerness is the next worst thing to enthusiasm.'

The uncompromising nature of my line demanded a versatile umbrella that could be used for pole-vaulting rivers, deterring bulls and, in the event of injury, as a walking-stick. Since half the route crossed high moorland, the umbrella also needed to be resistant to heavy rain and wind.

Discussions with Mr Arnold Rosen, Mr Jonathan Wardle and the owner of Smith & Sons, Mr Robert Harvey, confirmed that I needed a stick-umbrella, that is a walking-stick on to which are mounted the spokes and cover of an umbrella.

'You need hazel,' thought Mr Wardle. 'It's light and it has a degree of "give" which will absorb shocks. And of course it is what shepherds use for their crooks.'

'Does the hazel come in camouflage, for trespassing?'

'You can have it in green. It is,' said Mr Rosen, 'what you might call a *discreet* green.'

We debated the pros and cons of ten or eight spokes. Ten made a stronger, but heavier umbrella; I chose eight. Mr Wardle measured me and cut the stick to suit my height, then tipped it with a brass and steel ferrule.

My receipt for £79.50 was written out by hand on a cash-sales docket from the 1940s. 'Back in the war,' explained Mr Rosen, 'someone over-ordered, and we're still using them.'

As I left the shop, Mr Wardle handed me a booklet. Inside were instructions for opening, closing and rolling an umbrella, and the following note of caution:

> The rain it raineth on the just
> and also on the unjust fella,
> But chiefly on the just because
> The unjust has the just's umbrella.

The Devil's Causeway   The sun was sailing low on the water when I turned my back on Berwick and walked southbound over the old pink bridge. By the time I reached the lifeboat station the town had shrunk to a partially remembered huddle of distant roofs behind its pale Elizabethan girdle. Ahead stretched the taut thread of two degrees west, mapped but untrodden.

For the first hour of that mid-August day I was the luckiest man alive. I had new boots, a full stomach and an open sky.

As I walked through the stone streets of Spittal, I could feel the opposing pulls of meridian and instinct, one telling me to turn right into a nondescript housing estate, the other wanting to walk on to the end of the street and the sea, then down the coast path to Holy Island and Bamburgh's Norman keep, Embleton Bay and kippers for supper at Craster. Cow Road climbed steeply away from the water, up to the crest of the hill where I could look for a last time across the blue ribbon of the Tweed to England's furthest sea cliffs.

Already the meridian was beginning to give a larger-than-life sense of the landscape. Instead of going around the lumps and dips, it went up and down them. Walking this unique line of longitude would create a journey in raised relief, full of surprises and con-forming to no predetermined themes. Except for fractional instances where the meridian coincided for a kilometre or so with the course of a Roman Road, or a canal towpath, or a hill crest, it neither followed the flow of the land nor the currents of culture and history that habitually steer the writer and traveller.

At the top of the hill, my plan was to locate the site of a Roman fortlet and the terminus of the Devil's Causeway, the Roman Road that was built from Hadrian's Wall to the Tweed after Emperor Antonius Pius ordered the reoccupation of Scotland. According to the map, the Causeway ran with the meridian for seven kilometres until it crossed the 01 grid line.

But instead of a Roman fortlet I found a telecommunications mast for mobile phones, and where a public footpath should have cut across a field to the Devil's Causeway, there was a high wire fence. Fretting mildly, I tried another public footpath, 300 metres to the south. This one was not blocked but neither was it visible. Unwalked and unmarked, it turned round a field into the thigh-high undergrowth of an old open-cast coal pit, then set off through a second field of cattle. Two barbed wire fences later I gave up trying to follow the right of way and set the compass on south. Clearly, the depiction of a public right of way on a map was no indication that the route was either open to the public or technically a 'way'.

Ten minutes later I was on the verge of the new Berwick bypass being wind-blasted by careering trucks. South from here for a while there were no public rights of way, or indeed any paths. There was, however, the line of the Devil's Causeway, which I'd imagined from the map to be a kind of antique freeway along which I could tramp, trespassing admittedly, but unconstrained by fences and walls. In other parts of England, the 'agger', or embankment, that the Romans used to lay as the foundation for their roads was often a solid, dry, raised footpath that was ideal for long-distance walking despite 2,000 years of neglect.

The air began to sweat. The sun burned. Blundering along the field edges in the gutter between crops and hedges I was soon stung, scratched and sticky. I saw no sign of the Devil's Causeway.

It was a translation glitch; a problem of interpretation. On my maps, public footpaths existed as green pecked lines; the Devil's Causeway existed as a grey pecked line. But that didn't mean either existed as a physical entity on the ground. Maps could mark things that had once existed, or which ought to exist.

At the heart of the problem was scale. The maps I had were scale models on which the landscape was reduced to the barest bones. Many of the details that I would have found useful (such as the location of barbed wire fences, aggressive farmers and streams with drinkable water) were omitted because my interests were not those of the majority of map-users and because the cost of mapping is proportional to the frequency with which features are liable to change.

Yet maps were the closest I could get to picturing my linear world. Maps defined the line.

My transect was too early for cyber maps and telegeography, the fractal sons of William Speed, so I had sheets of paper. In these I could not have been better served, for the Ordnance Survey publish the best maps in the world. OS maps are meticulously surveyed, showing methodically selected detail that is appropriately projected on to precisely drawn sheets which are coloured and lettered to make them descriptive, explicit and legible in a wind-torn rainstorm. Nobody could ask for more, but they're still miniatures of the real world.

OS maps come in many scales, but there is none better for walking than the 1:25 000, where 1 centimetre on the map is the equivalent of 250 metres on the ground. Born in 1914 as $2\frac{1}{2}$ inch-to-the-mile military maps covering East Anglia, the series became the army's preferred scale for tactical manoeuvres. The leap from military to civil use was largely due to the enthusiasm of the OS director general of 1935, a man who'd spent the First World War in the 4th Field Survey Company, mapping battlefields for foot-soldiers. Major General Malcolm MacLeod argued that the limited editions of 1:25 000 maps should be extended to cover the whole country, adding that they would 'undoubtedly have considerable civil value and ... enjoy a good sale'. MacLeod's tenure at the Ordnance Survey coincided with a cartographic revolution whose story would unfold as I walked down two degrees west. It was his foresight regarding the 1:25 000 maps that provided me with the key to unlocking the meridian. Metricated, updated and overlaid with the 1,000-metre squares of the national grid, these maps marked all rights of way and a plethora of incidental detail such as triangulation pillars, boundary posts and bogs. Contours occurred at five-metre intervals and – equally important for micro-navigation – field boundaries and ditches were marked. As a rule, I reckoned that anything not shown on this map could be jumped over. Later, I'd find exceptions to the rule.

For an overview of my route, I also carried a home-made strip map created by gluing together six of the small-scale OS 1:250 000 maps then cutting out the strip containing the meridian. To make it portable, I folded the two-metre strip into a concertina.

Carrying the large-scale 1:25 000 maps was more of a problem. There were over seventy of them. With confounding logic, the Ordnance Survey had chosen two degrees west as the map edge for almost every sheet along the line. The cutting and gluing took my father-in-law Colin and me two painstaking days. Accuracy was essential. A slight overlap or misalignment between two glued sheets would introduce deviations to compass bearings that crossed the meridian; a slip of the scissors could lead to a five-degree error on a Yorkshire moorland and the chance of getting lost or – much worse – breaking the bounds of my permissible corridor. We produced thirty-six separate maps, numbered and folded so that each would fit in my trouser pocket.

Three hours after leaving Berwick I had managed to cover five kilometres, at an average speed of 1.7kph. At this rate, the English Channel would take nearly five months to reach.

Ancroft   The road to Wooler rose and fell over the swell of the Border hills. Insects hummed in the hedgerows, a buzzard turned on a thermal.

The morning's cross-country battle abruptly ended when the meridian converged with the B6525. The first village was Ancroft. There was nothing left. The pub had closed. The post office had closed. The vicarage had become 'The Old Parsonage' and the school 'The Old Schoolhouse'. A notice outside the church instructed visitors to obtain the keys from Mrs Turner or Mrs Youngman. Both were out. Across the road, the dappled grey stone of Ancroft Manor stood silently in its copse, defended by an intruder alarm. All human life appeared to have fled the village.

Only the cattle and sheep moved, browsing the hummocked field beside Dean Burn. Under the crumples lay medieval Ancroft, abandoned in 1667 when the plague struck. A leaflet in the church porch told of the survivors carrying dying victims into a field downwind of the village where they erected crude shelters of broom, which became funeral pyres as each incumbent died. The field is still known as 'Broomie Huts'.

Ancroft's cottages were burned too. The stubs of the walls could still be traced in the turf, divided by the intermittent channel of the old main street. After the plague, Ancroft recovered and within half a century had a population of over 1,000 and a reputation for clog- and shoe-making that secured it sales to the navy and army. Ancroft's boots marched against Napoleon. On a bank behind the field stood a row of sycamores. Once there were one hundred, one for each of Ancroft's cobblers.

Thwarted by the locked door, I lay on the bench beneath the church tower, a squat, square three-storey affair that had once been a border pele, a defensive parsonage for the priest of Ancroft and Tweedmouth. Had I been able to borrow the key and climb the tower, I might have been able to see Holy Island, twelve kilometres to the east.

The hill out of Ancroft was marked on the map as Bride's Brae, after the local girl who was fatally thrown from her horse on her wedding day and who now haunts this lonely road on moonlit nights.

Bowsden The long deserted road led south under the hovering sun until a sign solidified out of the heat shimmer. The sign promised a pub in Bowsden, and gave the distance as a quarter of a mile.

After covering twice that distance and still walking, I was drawing perilously close to the 99 grid line when the Black Bull appeared at the far end of the village.

'That's a hell of a long quarter mile!'

The man dead-heading petunias outside the pub looked up and laughed. 'Aye! It's a tactical quarter mile. A slip of the paintbrush!' It was, he added, difficult to get motorists to divert far from the main road.

David Webster waved me around the back. The Black Bull was a low-eaved building with cosy gabled windows and a front door at the rear. It had once been a farmhouse. The bar was empty.

'We get about eight regular customers a week.' David filled my glass. 'Twenty at weekends. They're lucky I'm still here.'

'How much longer are you going to hang on?'

He shrugged. 'It's the driving that's killed country pubs. People who used to come to Sunday lunch, go to the Metro Centre in Newcastle now, and shop all day. The quoits league's folded, though the darts struggles on. The Lamb at Ancroft's gone.'

David's wife Christine made me a large ploughman's and I sat in the cool of the bar rehydrating on pints of shandy.

Bowsden has fewer than one hundred inhabitants, mainly retirees and commuters. A century earlier, the grassy valley I'd passed on the way into the village had been busy with men quarrying limestone. Then, Bowsden supported a postmaster, a school (closed in 1963), a provisions merchant, a poulterer and grocer, four cobblers, two blacksmiths, a joiner and two inns. The Black Bull used to get a lot of custom from passing miners, on their way home from the open-cast pits. The pits were filled now; the miners gone to work elsewhere. Or out of work. Mining had been rubbed from the map, literally; a pub I'd passed earlier in the day had been marked on one of my maps as 'Miners' Arms'; now it was 'The Three Bridges'.

The Websters were running out of options: they bought the Black Bull with $5\frac{1}{2}$ acres, then sold two plots for houses. That left half an acre for David's 'little sideline'. 'It's a dental-floss packing factory,' he grinned. Behind the Black Bull was a shed where four full-time workers and two part-timers fitted bobbins of dental floss into plastic cartridges, then attached self-adhesive labels and packed the finished products into boxes. 'We're turning out 60,000 a week,' said David. 'It keeps the pub going.'

Barmoor Mill Farm   From Bowsden I took a public footpath across the fields to Barmoor Mill Farm and a remote bungalow that had been marked on my map in Berwick by Gavin Douglas.

This rangy, hyperbolic stranger had leapt from the audience of the Edinburgh Book Festival the night before I began walking. Gavin was to appear more than once on the meridian. The day I walked into Berwick, he was there, with a car full of perspiring bottles of beer and wine. 'Drink, drink! Drink it all!' he'd yelled, throwing open coolers.

Gavin had once worked as a sheep shearer in Italy, and his current job as an ovine consultant entailed visiting remote farms across the north of England.

'Get out the maps!' he'd urged. We'd stretched my strip map across Berwick's quayside.

He'd run his finger down the meridian, reciting names of friends and relations. When his finger reached the bottom end, where two degrees west fell into the English Channel, he'd yelped, 'No!'

Gavin Douglas, the first man I'd met on two degrees, had learned to swim in the sea-water rock pool on Dorset's Dancing Ledge, the last point on my line.

One of the people Gavin knew who lived on the meridian was Tim Smalley, of Barmoor Mill Farm. 'You'll like him,' Gavin had insisted. 'He's completely fearless. He started a business making horse sileage in bags. He's got a trebuchet.' Such was the stream of incredible information that poured forth from Gavin that I forgot to ask why a sileage manufacturer needed a medieval siege catapult. Home deliveries? Repelling trespassers?

When I reached the bungalow, I found a message hanging from a rope across the drive: 'NICHOLAS CRANE', it read, 'THIS IS 2° WEST.' (Actually, it wasn't quite; it was at least 100 metres west of the meridian.) The message continued: 'Tim Smalley sadly making hay. Hope to picnic with you at the Dod tomorrow. GAVIN.'

Beneath the message were a bottle of water and an apple. Sadly, there was no sign of the trebuchet.

Dod Law   By the time I climbed the bracken of Dod Law, the shadows were reclining lazily against the pillowed hill.

Five thousand years ago Neolithic men armed with stone tools came to this hill and chipped enigmatic patterns into the rock out-crops. Steered by a book I'd bought in Berwick, I quickly found two of the carvings cut into the surface of a table-sized, horizontal rock near the foot of the hill. Each was the size of a big dinner plate and took the form of diminishing rings with a 'cup' in the centre. The rings were broken at one point, and all the breaks were aligned to form a 'channel' or path from the outside to the centre. 'Cup and ring' marks like this have been found in their hundreds across southern Scotland and northern England. Sometimes there are other shapes too: spirals and ovoids, with the cups appearing singly or in clusters; odd keyhole shapes; circles with fringes and extended serpentine grooves which run like miniature river-beds through the rock. Rarely are angular shapes such as squares and triangles found, which is significant since these would have been easier to carve.

As I stood on the hillside high above the valley of the Till, the sinking sun deepened the shadows on the cup and rings so that they appeared to grow younger with every minute that passed. I was taken back two months to the Côa Valley of northern Portugal, where I'd seen aurochs, horses and ibex cut into the warm rock of the world's largest collection of outdoor Paleolithic figures. But the most recent of Côa's extraordinary carvings were 10,000 years old, at least twice the age of Northumberland's cup and rings.

So what had inspired the ancient Britons to favour symbolism over representation? The expert in the subject was the late Ronald Morris, who unearthed over a hundred different theories concerning the origins of cup-and-ring marks, ranging from messages from outer space, to records of a chief's sexual conquests. Morris favoured a religious explanation, and hypothesized that the cup and ring had the same kind of symbolic significance that was later ascribed to the cross. He also thought that a correlation between cup-and-ring sites and sources of copper ore and gold, suggested a possible role for the carvings as 'prospectors' magic'. Alternatively, since many of the alignments corresponded with sunrise and sunset at particular times of year, they may have been megalithic calendars.

As the shadows rose up Dod Law I climbed with the sunlight until I stood on the summit.

Dod Law is exactly 200 metres high, an appropriate decimal distinction for the site of the most northerly Ordnance Survey triangulation pillar on the meridian.

'Trig' pillars have become a part of the British landscape, like humpback bridges and red phone boxes. On summits from Sutherland to Sussex they stand cast in concrete to uniform dimensions: 4 foot high, tapering from a 2 foot square at the base to a 1 foot 2 inch square top fitted with a brass plate to take the feet of a theodolite. Each pillar is intervisible with at least two neighbouring pillars, covering the rural and urban landscape with hundreds of measured triangles whose corners act as reference points for the cartographers who draw the maps.

Construction of the pillars began in 1935, when the Ordnance Survey decided to replace the earlier piecemeal triangulation of 1852 with a unified national triangulation. (Along with problems of inaccuracy, many of the nineteenth-century stations – which were buried rather than free-standing – had been built over or had disappeared, including one that was removed by a policeman under the impression that he had discovered a Zeppelin bomb.) MacLeod, the OS director general who'd put his weight behind 1:25 000 maps, appointed Captain Martin Hotine of the Royal Engineers to be head of the Trigonometrical and Levelling Division, and it was Hotine who masterminded the great retriangulation that put 6,173 trig pillars on the country's highpoints.

Erection of the pillars was undertaken by small teams who often worked in appalling weather, digging three-foot foundations by spade and then carrying sand, gravel and cement to remote summits using locally hired pack horses. Dod Law's pillar went up in May 1946 at a cost of £6 14s 6d. The public were mystified by the sudden appearance of these concrete emplacements, and rumours spread that they were sundials, or mountings for anti-aircraft guns, or oil wells or Jubilee memorials.

Once a pillar's cement had set, the surveying team arrived with its fifteen-kilogram 'Geodetic Tavistock' theodolite to measure the angles and distances to the surrounding pillars. These were manned by solitary 'lightkeepers' living in tents and communicating with their colleagues by Morse Code. Lightkeepers would often cycle for miles to the nearest garage to recharge the six-volt car batteries that powered their lamps. Between the trig pillars were intermediate sighting-points that brought the total number of survey stations to 22,000. With a break for the Second World War, the retriangulation of England, Scotland and Wales took seventeen years.

The ugliness of trig pillars has long since been submerged by sentimentality. Few who have spent time in British hills have not stumbled on a compass bearing through a whiteout praying for one of the Ordnance Survey's pale waymarks to materialize from the mist. Today, a government body intent on desecrating the country's high tops with concrete bollards would face marches and the explosions of 'direct action'. Even the OS have called them 'concrete monstrosities'. Yet when they announced in 1992 that most triangulation pillars had been made redundant by satellites that could fix a point on the ground to within one centimetre, there was such an outcry that the OS had to invent an adoption scheme for members of the public unable to bear the loss of a treasured friend. There is a new breed of 'bagger' (usually male and unmarried), who hikes between summits collecting the numbers stamped on to the brass brackets on the sides of the pillars. The number on the Dod Law pillar incidentally is S3695.

Cuddy's Cave   The moor where St Cuthbert tended sheep has become a golf course. As evening laid a calming hand on the ruffled tops, I looked from the triangulation pillar to the faraway dot of Holy Island. Near where I stood were the rumples of an Iron Age hill-fort. In the valley, Wooler was a vulnerable smudge underneath the purple bulwark of the Cheviots.

The rim of Fell Sandstone led me along Dod Law's southern crest, then I dropped down to cross a dry valley on to a lower hill, and in coming off this stumbled upon the entrance of Cuddy's Cave, a black eye peering down at the bridge over the River Till. Cuddy's Cave was one of St Cuthbert's refuges.

The cave would have made a passable bivouac site, but it was competing with the Tankerville Arms Hotel (English Tourist Board: four crowns) in Wooler, which I reached in time to sit down to local smoked salmon and lemon, lettuce and stottie cake (a circular Northumberland granary bread), followed by fresh Eyemouth cod mornay. As I drained the last of the Chablis, I had an uneasy feeling that the meridian was being far too benign.

Wooler   In Hamish Dunn ('Antiques, Curios, Collectors' Items & Books') I bought the *Official Guide to Wooler* (1925) and learned that the town was one of the best health resorts in the country and that it was 351 miles from London, had a population of 1,328, and had recently benefited from the North Eastern Railway branch line from Alnwick. The town had gas lighting, up-to-date hotels for the increasing numbers of char-à-banc trippers, two picture palaces (the one in the old Drill Hall had plush tip-up chairs), a lending library run by the postmaster and sanitation that was 'almost perfect'.

In those days, Wooler's shops sold everything from pickled beef to tennis frocks, and Hamish Dunn's premises were the Pringle & Co. shoe shop ('Latest Shapes Keenest Prices'). The telephones still had single digit numbers and the air was recommended by doctors for its invigorating qualities.

A century earlier, Wooler was known only for its wool, its goats-whey cures and its lack of accommodation; when Sir Walter Scott visited in 1791, he had been obliged to take a room at a farm in Langleeford (where he'd shot a crow to make a quill). But by the 1920s, Muirhead's *Blue Guide* – the bible for between-the-wars travellers – listed the Black Bull (Telephone No. 9), the Wheatsheaf, Henderson's Temperance and the Cottage Hotel – which then charged 4 shillings a night for a room. The Cottage became the Tankerville Arms Hotel.

Today, the town's population has crept up to 2,000, the railway has gone and so has Wooler's claim to be on the main motor road from London to Edinburgh; all through-traffic is now deflected over the Carter Bar road to the south, or the A1 to the north. Wooler has dropped its 'Capital of Glendale' label in favour of 'The Gateway to the Cheviots', shifting the emphasis from the town's role as the focal point of the local economy, to its anticipated future as a recreational service centre.

Unkindly dismissed by Muirhead as 'a small, grey market town', Wooler is not overwhelmed with tourist attractions. The weekly Thursday market disappeared over a century ago (although an annual market for farm servants lingered on for a while) and the castle ruins would fit in a builder's skip. Wooler is also short of famous sons and daughters, though Grace Darling stayed here once, and John Cunliffe, author of the *Postman Pat* stories, lived in Glendale Road while he was working as a mobile librarian.

The High Street had most of the services you'd expect to find in a traditional, unspoiled English market town, from a family butcher to a chemist, stationer/bookseller (who sold maps and miniature Agas) and Stormin' Norman's Chippy.

'Why Stormin'?' I asked the girl behind the counter.

'Because 'e's wild and woolly.'

She was very beautiful (all Wooler's girls were beautiful), a flaxen-maned bequest from the Viking oarsmen who used to harass Northumberland's coast.

There was also a shop hung with hiking equipment called Hillfolk, run by John and Hilary Thompson. John, breezy and fit, had spent twenty years flying helicopters in the Army Air Corps. 'I called at the shop during an exercise, and they hadn't got what I wanted . . . so I bought it.'

He had a choice of plastic water bottles. I'd planned to save weight by not carrying water, but had come to the unwelcome conclusion that if the August heatwave continued I'd die of thirst.

A second pass through Hamish Dunn's packed emporium yielded, for 75p, a copy of George du Maurier's *Trilby*, the book that gave my walking hat part of its name.

Trilby O'Ferrall, that 'very tall and fully-developed young female', walks into the novel dressed in a French infantry greatcoat, a striped petticoat and a pair of gigantic male slippers. She's broad-cheeked, with a bony nose and big white teeth ('Himmel!' exclaims Svengali memorably. 'The roof of your mouth is like the dome of the Panthéon'). The soft felt hat with the indented crown was a later affectation.

My hat was a trilby-balaclava hybrid – a *trilbava* – invented by the man who designed the boots on my feet, the Olympic runner and outdoor clothing innovator Chris Brasher. Intended for use on windy mountains, the trilbava had the conventional brim and tapered crown of a trilby, but secreted within its interior was a retractable gusset that could be pulled down over the ears and the nape of the neck, clamping the hat to the head. Tests that I'd undertaken by leaning out of a car window at 50kph with my gusset down failed to dislodge the trilbava. The trilbava made the conceptual leap between the aesthetic and the practical: the broad brim was impenetrable to ultra-violet rays and prevented ocular injury on bright days, while it was also impervious to rain and snow. The trilbava's drawback was that in extended-gusset mode it made the wearer look like the victim of botched cranial surgery.

In a supermarket on the High Street I crammed sardines, cheese and Highland oatcakes into the rucksack. After Wooler, I reckoned that I wouldn't pass a shop on the meridian for seven days, until I reached Corbridge. Even then, I'd only be able to visit the outskirts of the town. The next shop after Corbridge would be Stanhope, two days (and a reservoir crossing) further south.

Happy Valley　The way to Happy Valley rose out of Wooler like a wish made real; the empty strand of tar and stone lifted skyward by birdsong and the promissory hills.

Through the 100-metre contour climbed the road, to the ford at Coldgate Water and the stile that opened the door to Happy Valley.

In the twenties, this had been the classic ramble for Wooler's visitors, made possible by Mr Hughes of Middleton Hall, who'd allowed the public to cross his land. Today, the Tynesiders come by car to the picnic site and public conveniences at Cresswell Bog, then take the public footpath. Freckled with sunlight, the path tunnelled through woods beside a small ravine that tinkled with cataracts and splashing children. Families picnicked on water-worn boulders, or stood pale-skinned in the current between the banks of nodding ferns. A rope tied to a bough dangled like a liana from which skinny-ribbed kids swung and dropped, falling with pedalling limbs to meet the river in mushrooms of spray. Ten minutes along the path another stile stood between the woods and a blaze of white light. Out here, the river twisted through stones at the foot of a broad sweep of open turf that led the eye up to the hills.

This was the first time I'd seen the Cheviots close up; close enough to hear the wind bounding roundly over the bracken; close enough to smell the resin in the slope-foot conifers. Burped into being 300 million years ago as an erupting volcano on the sea-floor, the Cheviots rose as a mass of ash and lava that cooled into pink andesite. Ice and water took off the sharp edges, and the height. In the geological blink since the last ice sheets melted, the Cheviots had known a time of plenty, when wild boar and deer roamed oak forests and Bronze Age farmers cut barley on upland plots. Now these slopes looked old and tired, shorn of trees and showing their wrinkles, the thin skin of vegetation kept alive by the warmth of the Gulf Stream – a whimsical ocean current that travels half-way around the globe to warm the shores of the north Atlantic. The Cheviots occupy the same latitude as Ketchikan in Alaska.

Happy Valley was a dead end, blocked off by grid line 99. To reach the Cheviots, I had to return down the path and take the narrow road south through the hamlets of North Middleton and South Middleton. Between the two was the site of Middleton Old Town, Medelmost Medelton, and before that Medil Wong Tun, the Town of the General Assembly. Now it was gone.

The Dod   Moorland tussock grass rose each side of the path between Dod Hill and Heddon Hill. At South Middleton the road had ended and I'd followed the fingerpost that read 'The Dod 3' towards the rising ground of the Northumberland National Park.

It was good to be high. Where the path hopped over a burn on a wooden bridge, a clump of alders tickled the dying breeze and I dropped the pack again and dawdled, not wanting time to pass.

Since leaving Wooler, I'd been conscious that I was climbing to a place that promised something special. Already it was early evening. I had food and a sleeping-bag and nowhere to stay. Not knowing where to lay my head always turns the end of the day into some kind of climax. No journey starts until the last prearranged pillow is left behind.

Beyond the burn, the path rose a little, and I could look down into the valley that hid the Dod. The cottage and outbuildings that took their name from the hill that was on my right, Dod Hill – Rounded Hill – shared the same linguistic roots as the Dod Law that I'd climbed the previous evening (law is the Old English *hlaw*: hill or mountain).

The Dod was a meagre sanctuary: just a shallow scrape in the mid-slopes of the Cheviots, run through by a burn and laid with a few fields. The cottage stood at the west end of the valley, slightly raised and protected from the prevailing wind by a bastion of conifers.

In the furthest field the low sun glinted on a windscreen. As I walked down the track, a familiar figure wearing a broad-brimmed Akubra strode towards me waving a map. 'You're hungry! We've got food waiting on two degrees!'

Gavin Douglas led the way down the track to his Toyota. It was parked astride the meridian.

We sat at the table Gavin had erected on the grass. He had brought his daughter Charlotte, who seemed quite used to her father's picnics. Condensation misted the chilled glasses of wine as the sun subsided towards the dome of Hedgehope Hill and Gavin ranted about the injustice of the Cheltenham races moving to Channel 4 ('It's unbelievable ... I'm going to *Nova Scotia*!'). The table, three chairs and car stood alone in the vast moorland bowl, placed with precision upon the invisible line. Incongruity is a high order of pleasure.

As dusk settled and Charlotte handed out insect repellent, we had a couple of visitors. The first arrived by tractor. A very thin man with a lopsided grin in grimy jeans and leather boots slithered to the ground and held out a hand to Gavin. Barry Brown owned the land, 1,800 acres of it, grazed by 1,000 ewes and 40 cattle. He had spent the day cutting hay on two of the Dod's fields.

Ten minutes later, Barry's shepherd arrived on a Suzuki 200 trail bike. A shepherd's crook poked from a holster made from a length of plastic tubing bolted to the motorcycle frame. Robin Mathewson smiled shyly from beneath a flat cap and politely declined Gavin's offer of a drink.

For Barry and Robin, the Dod was home. Robin had worked for Barry's father, and could remember Barry as a fifteen-month-old baby. In those days they had all lived together in the cottage. The valley had no electricity and their power came from a generator. Barry used to ride to school on a pony. After Barry's family moved from the Dod to Wooler, Robin had stayed on. He'd been in the cottage for forty-two years.

In the last of the light the others left; Barry on his tractor, Robin on his trail bike, and finally Gavin and Charlotte in the Toyota, bumping up the switchback track until their tail-lights were a pair of red eyes blinking against the blackening night.

Earlier, I'd wondered whether Robin would offer me shelter for the night in the cottage, but he was a private man for whom unexpected visitations would – I thought – be disturbing. So I was relieved when he suggested that I sleep in the hay barn up by the sheepfold on the hill.

The barn was the size of a big garden shed, cosy and half-full of hay bales. I shifted bales to make a mattress, then took one of Gavin's apples and sat on a rock, leaning against the rough stones of the sheepfold. A kilometre up the valley, a solitary yellow light marked an uncurtained window in Robin's cottage. There was no sound, or movement.

The stars thickened. Where I live in London there is a hill which I stand on at night. If I look up, I see nothing; if I look down, I see galaxies of twinkling lights. London's night is upside down.

Here in the Cheviots, I was as close as it is possible to get in England to measurable tranquillity.

In 1995 I'd been sent a file by the Council for the Protection of Rural England. The CPRE and Countryside Commission had

commissioned a series of 'tranquillity' maps which plotted the topography of disturbance. 'Tranquil areas' had to be more than four
kilometres from the largest power stations; three kilometres from
busy roads, large towns and industrial areas; two kilometres from
less busy roads and smaller towns; one kilometre from 'medium
disturbance' roads (more than 10,000 vehicles a day) and main-line
railways. Tranquil areas had to be beyond audible range of airfield/
airport noise and open-cast mining. The maps also showed areas
subject to lower levels of disturbance caused by other roads and
railways, power lines, windpower sites, settlements of over 2,500
inhabitants and industrial sites.

The tranquillity maps showed that England is chronically dis-
turbed. Only three extensive areas of tranquillity remained: north
Devon, the Marches of Shropshire and upland Northumberland,
the largest of the three tranquillity sanctuaries, with the Cheviots at
its heart.

At 5.30 a.m. I heard Robin kick-starting his bike at the other end of
the valley.

A thin blade of sunlight had found a way through the barn
wall, and as I stirred in my sleeping-bag it glistened with motes of
haydust that drifted and swirled on unseen eddies like coral sand
flicked by a fish tail.

The bike engine muttered and faded. Robin would be going
out to check the sheep. Twenty minutes later I heard him return.
Under a clean sky I walked down the slope and pushed my face in
the burn, then continued up the track to the cottage.

The door was ajar. 'G'morning Nicholas!' called Robin as I
unlaced my boots on the doorstep. In my sleep I'd been somewhere
else, London perhaps, and the harmonies of lowland Scots and
Geordie froze me into a silent smile; apart perhaps from a Celtic-
speaking Cornish sailor, it would be hard in England to find somebody as foreign to a Home Counties screen-slave as a Cheviot
shepherd.

'You'd like porridge. Some breakfast,' continued Robin. 'Sausage, bacon, aye. I'll be mekin' the porridge.'

He moved inaudibly from the kitchen, taking short quick steps in his slippers. I wanted to chat in the kitchen, but he led me through to the sofa in the sitting room and handed me the autumn issue of *The Northumbrian*. The sofa was part of a three-piece suite in a brown-and-grey check. In the corner stood a Samsung colour TV. On the wall was a framed long-service certificate from the National Farmers Union awarded to Robin for 'having served the Agricultural Industry in this County for 44 years continuously'. Also on the wall was a barometer presented to Robin in the same year, by the Brown family, and a clock in the shape of Africa, sent to him by his brother who worked there as a mechanic. The cottage was spotless and smelled lightly of disinfectant.

We ate at the kitchen table.

Robin had a routine. He started work at 4.45 each morning. 'I always take my main meal at twelve o'clock. You call that lunch. We call it dinner. Then in the evening I have supper, which you call dinner.'

The *Newcastle Journal* was delivered daily unless the culvert carrying the burn had flooded. 'Sometimes it's a week till they get through, then I get all the papers at once.'

On Fridays he went shopping in Wooler, but if he needed clothes, he sent away to J. D. Williams in Manchester. On Sundays he drove over the border, past his birthplace near Jedburgh, to Melrose where his 87-year-old father was in a nursing home. His father had been a gardener. It was a routine that only the weather could interrupt. The track to the Dod could be cut by snow from December through till March.

Robin hadn't been on holiday for twenty years and had never travelled further north than Edinburgh, or further south than Newcastle.

'What did you think of Edinburgh?'

'Glad to get out of it. Bloody noise. I couldn't live in the town.'

'So you've never been to London?'

'I've not got time to see London. There's nothing in London for me.'

'What d'you think of flying?'

'I wouldn't go in an aeroplane.'

Robin had always drunk water from the burn. He'd always been healthy and had never had an injection.

After breakfast I pulled on my boots and we stood at the corner of the windbreak. Robin remembered the spruce being no higher than the fence. Across the rough moorland before the cottage were dotted his black-face sheep.

'A good shepherd is a good "kenner",' nodded Robin. 'He knows his sheep. Each sheep knows its bit of hill; they don't just go anywhere. It's called "heft"; that's the bit of the hill the sheep stays on.'

He pointed to a hawk – which he pronounced 'hark' – hovering up on Hare Law and I asked about the dead owl that I'd found in the barn. 'Notty lotty owls now.'

He'd seen so many changes in these hills. 'I used to help the shepherds when I was at school. At clipping time all the farms joined together and we'd have twenty men clipping by hand. It's different now.'

Before Robin worked for the Browns, he had worked at Langleeford, where Sir Walter Scott had taken goats-whey over a century earlier ('My uncle drinks the whey here as I do ever since I understood it was brought to his bedside at six every morning by a very pretty chambermaid').

When Robin was at Langleeford, there had been six shepherds. 'In the old days the older shepherds used to pass their knowledge on to the new shepherds. Now you need certificates an' all.' They used to bring in the hay with horses.

Robin had spent his twenty-first birthday lambing, and his sixtieth birthday lambing. 'Both birthdays,' he said with no hint of surprise, 'I was in the same spot on the same hill.'

Reaveley Hill From the Dod I followed Robin's arm towards Reaveley Hill.

Beyond the second burn, or 'sike', where the slope began to steepen, I stopped and looked back. All about me, bees were working the purple heather. A curlew cried. In the middle distance, a few black-face sheep lifted their heads, then returned to their foraging. Beyond them, the Dod was already miniaturized by distance; cottage and barns hunkered down before their block of defensive conifers. I could see no sign of Robin; he had been swallowed by the heaving ocean.

On Reaveley Hill I came to the ruined shepherds' cottage that Doug Goodfellow had lived in until the late 1950s. Robin had remembered the postie making the daily journey past the Dod and up Reaveley Hill with his bicycle, a round trip from Wooler of fifteen miles, half of it off-road. After Doug left, the cottage remained empty. In the 1980s, a young shepherd hung himself with baler twine in the hay barn. It was just before lambing time. Robin said that it had been a bad winter.

The Breamish Valley   From Reaveley Hill I followed a spur that curled down to the haphazard stones of a hill-fort on Ewe Hill, one of the truncated buttresses that looms over the Breamish valley.

A couple of hundred metres below my boots, the cars were beginning to gather on the floodplain. It was a Sunday morning and by noon the valley road would be in spate. The Breamish is famous for its August migration. Upstream, the river and the road ran together along the green baize of the 'haughland' till I lost sight of both beneath Brough Law.

No paths led off Ewe Hill and so I slithered down the cleft of Shivers Cleugh, then forded the Breamish and threaded my way through the broom and gorse of the haugh to the car park at Bulby's Wood.

John Steele, senior park ranger, was sitting at the wheel of his white Land Rover. With his suntan and platinum hair, binoculars and patch-pocket shirt, he could have been cast by Hollywood in a Greens-against-Armageddon film. His Land Rover was so clean that it might have come to the Breamish on the back of a trailer, wrapped in clingfilm.

John was one of a team of seven full-time and six seasonal rangers. He knew the Northumberland National Park as well as his own garden. 'It's a crazy shape,' he laughed, pointing to a map of its long, contorted outline, seventy kilometres from north to south, thinning to six kilometres at its waist, yet covering 1,030 square kilometres. It was one of the largest National Parks in the country, but it had the smallest population: only 2,000 people, or two per square kilometre, one-quarter of the figure for the Highlands of Scotland. 'Another thing,' added John. 'It's the largest block of land in the country which is not crossed by B-roads. All the Cheviot valleys are "blind". Apart from the Carter Bar road, there are no main through-routes. We're remote. Very remote.'

After Hadrian's Wall, the Breamish was the park's busiest hot spot. 'Last weekend we had 600 cars here in one day,' said John. 'That's about 2,000 people.'

Two hundred thousand visited the Breamish each year. For the mining towns north of the Tyne, like Ashington, Newbiggin, Seaton Delaval, Blythe, 'going to the haugh' was a ritual. Families had their own spot and woe betide a different family who unfurled a rug on hereditary territory. Some of the families were fourth-generation visitors, coming fifteen, twenty times a year, year after year, to 'their' bit of the haugh, like salmon to the same part of the river, and sheep to their personal 'heft'. According to John, only 15 per cent of visitors to the Breamish were first-timers. For the men who worked shifts in the hot, black depths of the earth, the sunlit pools and glades of the Breamish were a paradise. In the early seventies, 900 cars a day would crawl bumper to bumper up the valley. People would roll their eyes and cry, 'The haughs are hotchin'.' The numbers fell when the mines closed.

To the park rangers, the seasonal human migration up the Breamish was another facet of the valley's complicated ecosystem. Because there was no natural niche in the valley for such an overwhelming volume of a single species, the humans needed help: access agreements with landowners to open up a wider habitat, and environmental education in the form of ranger-led tours, leaflets and a background presence from the rangers themselves.

Some visitors complained to park rangers about the bumps in Bulby's Wood car park, unaware that the 'bumps' were the ridge and furrow of the medieval field system.

Sometimes there were species clashes; if Easter fell early, the humans could overlap with the egg-laying of the oyster-catchers. A common sandpiper could fly from West Africa to the Breamish only to find that its breeding place was occupied by a barbecue. (Like the miners, the sandpipers always returned to the same spot of river.) Sea trout swimming upstream sometimes found their way barred by dams built by children to create bathing pools. Every week the rangers pulled down the dams; every weekend they re-appeared.

The humans were, however, adapting to the habitat of the Breamish. The fire-lighting and camping that were features of the seventies migrations, had virtually died out, and littering had become so rare that the rangers found it hard to fill three sacks at the end of a day.

It is an access agreement between the National Park and the Duke of Northumberland and his tenant farmer, John Wilson, which opens the haugh – and fifteen kilometres of 'permissive paths' on the surrounding hills – to the public.

'It works,' smiled John. 'People don't feel intimidated on the Breamish. Often they're fearful of irate landowners. It's all about conflict management,' he continued. 'Visitors feel relaxed here, away from the boss, on their haugh.'

We went on safari upstream. By now the haugh was clogged with cars. The river chuckled with children, paddling and netting, building dams, lobbing pebbles. Barbecue smoke drifted over the bubbling water. I asked John what wildlife I might meet on the Breamish.

'We've got Caddis Fly larvae!' he replied excitedly. 'They're about an inch long and about the thickness of a matchstick. And we've got Mayfly larvae too, which are nice. They have three tails.'

A few minutes later, we paused where the river had exposed a bank of pebbles. 'Arctosa!' yelped John. 'The wolf-spider! He's probably been in the Cheviots since the Ice Age; he's only found in dry gravelly beds that have yet to be vegetated. He likes heat. When the vegetation colonizes the rock, it cools down and Arctosa has to move on. He can only exist on rivers that are in spate. He's huge-bodied and sits in his burrow with his legs poking out, waiting for unsuspecting flies. He's *brilliant*! Absolutely *superb*!'

We found a wolf-spider, and the larvae, and a fresh-water shrimp called Gammarus. Then John spotted Paul Frodsham.

Brough Law   Northumberland National Park's archaeologist was moving slowly along the road in a well-used estate car.

Paul's ecstatic, unshaven face had been splashed across a month-old copy of *The Berwick Advertiser* I'd seen three days earlier. *The Journal* had run the same story under the headline: 'Dig finds stun archaeologists'. I'd got Paul's number from the tourist office and he'd offered to meet me in the Breamish.

Paul was thirty-three, born in Cambridge, with a degree from Durham. He'd been working in the Park for five years when his team unearthed a 4,000-year-old Bronze Age food vessel from a cist – a stone tomb – on a hill called Turf Knowe. The exquisitely decorated pot, and the several contemporary burials from the site, came as a plaintive cry from our forgotten roots: the period of history leading up to Rome's invasion.

'Like to see a hill-fort?' said Paul, pulling a rucksack from the back of the car.

A well-trodden path sliced up the contours towards the crest of Brough Law. As I panted in his slipstream, my guide fumed in indignant bursts. 'It's like cowboys and Indians. People grow up thinking that the Romans were the "goodies". It's a bizarre situation. We've got about fifty Iron Age hill-forts in the National Park and we've just done a survey of them all and found that only about half a dozen have been even partially excavated. I'd argue that you can't explain the Roman period until you've found out what happened to the native sites.'

The fort sat like a crown of stones on the hilltop. In its circular dishevelment the wall had resumed some of the hill's shape, soft and curved, a great 'O' on the top of the earth, symbolically sensuous and at one with the shape of the summit on which it had evolved. All about us were other hills, also crowned with forts.

'These indigenous native Iron Age hill-forts feel natural, feel right in the landscape,' continued Paul. 'They're great big structures. They add to the sense of place. The Roman forts don't fit.' He pointed to a segment of 2,000-year-old wall that remained as upright blocks. 'All this rock is andesite. When it's broken it is pink, and it stays that colour for thirty or forty years. All these hill-forts would have been bright pink.'

Paul's excitement reminded me of another archaeologist, Professor Ion Glodariu of the University of Cluj, standing on a similar hilltop in Transylvania, sweeping his arm over excavated walls and a solar clock that had once stood in the capital of the Dacians, wiped out too by the Romans.

The hills around Brough Law were scattered with the remains of other ages: hut circles, ridge-and-furrow cultivation strips, burial cairns, mysterious walls. Every angle of the massive view was rich with the relics of lost civilizations.

'There's nowhere else in England,' continued Paul, 'where so much archaeology from such a wide span of history is so clearly visible: up here there's everything from the Neolithic to Bronze Age cairns, Iron Age hill-forts, Romano-British settlements and a medieval village. Brough Law is the only hill-fort in the valley which has been dated using radiocarbon. It's 230 BC. There's no proof that anyone lived up here permanently. Yeavering Bell has 130 hut circles. Brough Law has three or four. The key to understanding these sites is *prestige*; being able to say, "This is our hill-fort." They were used perhaps for gatherings and ceremonial activities. Brough Law's walls would have been visible for miles.'

We moved on, down the back-slope of the hill, through a ring of stone stubs protruding from the turf.

'I'd say this is a Bronze Age cremation cemetery,' nodded Paul. Further on there was a rocky mound ('That is *definitely* a Bronze Age burial cairn') and various walls that started and stopped for no apparent reason. 'It's all up here. There's lots of it. But we don't yet know what it is because there have never been the resources to investigate.' The topic of budgets rekindled Paul's *cri de coeur*. 'People are happy to spend *thousands* to find out whether a Roman fort was abandoned in 100 or 101, but not a *penny* to find out what happened here over the previous 10,000 years. I've been here five years and I've barely scratched the surface.'

Paul led us off the main ridge, down a spur to the left. Ahead, balanced on a promontory overlooking the lowlands that rolled away towards the coast, was the brown stain of an archaeological dig.

'Turf Knowe,' pointed Paul. 'That's where we found the food vessel. We excavated two Bronze Age burial cairns. There were several cremations in the left cairn. Some with pots. One in a beautiful burial urn. We found it at five in the evening and pressed on till seven or eight to get it out and it proved to contain a baby. My daughter had just been born and it had a strange effect on me. Anyone with young children who looks at that urn just has to ask *why?* The right-hand cairn had a burial with an iron spearhead, so the cairn must have been re-used later. Maybe a reinforcement of dynasty by burial in an ancestral place.'

Paul turned and looked back up the slope to Brough Law's rounded Iron Age crown. 'The *joy* – the *complete* joy – of this project is that there is *nothing* Roman here. Hadrian's Wall is in serious danger of becoming a theme park. I could take you on a midsummer's day to fifty of these hill-forts, all with fabulous views, and at forty-five of them you wouldn't see any other people. Roman sites look and feel alien in the landscape – and they are – they're the remains of an alien occupying force who dropped by for 300 years then buggered off.'

Cochrane Pike   In the last of the sunlight I climbed Cochrane Pike and took a final backward glance across the Cheviots, back over the Breamish and Reaveley Hill, to beyond the Dod.

Off to the east, the dark rim of Fell Sandstone that forms a breakwater between the sea and the Cheviots, swept south from Berwick then turned inland and rose to the Simonside Hills and England's Meridian. The sandstone came from a river bigger than the Ganges which used to pour across the part of the globe now occupied by north-west Europe. For the rivers searching for the sea as they rushed from the Cheviots, the Fell Sandstone had always been an awkward obstacle. The Breamish had been obliged to turn north, parallel to the sea, until it met the Till, which headed north too, until the Tweed showed the way around the northern rump of the hills to the gap by Berwick.

Inland from Cochrane Pike, the Cheviots themselves were a brooding presence, massive and colourless against the dying sun. Off to the north-west I could see the flattened dome of the Cheviot, the highest point on the range, with the English-Scottish border crossing its lower slopes.

The loftiest tower of England's northern rampart was hijacked by Daniel Defoe for the dramatic climax of *A Tour Through the Whole Island of Great Britain*, the travelogue-cum-guidebook that the author of *Robinson Crusoe* published in three volumes between 1724 and 1726. Defoe would be one of the more consistent literary visitors to the meridian, intercepting two degrees west all the way from Northumberland to Dorset. He was also the least reliable. Much of his information was gathered on spying assignments for the Whigs undertaken years earlier, and many of the places he described he had not visited. In Berwick-upon-Tweed, for example, he failed to mention the Elizabethan walls, and many of his entries are clearly invented, none more baldly than his account of climbing Cheviot. The wily fabulist's description of his ascent by horse to the summit of 'the Pico or Master-Hill' is one of the most inspired fabrications in mountaineering literature, yet Defoe concocted a tale that delivered accuracy and exaggeration in just the proportions necessary to make his story credible. Enough of his description fits the topography for him to have researched in some detail the route up Cheviot.

In Defoe's account, guides led his party to a place on the hill where in winter 'great rivers came pouring down'. These could be the twin ravines of Hawsen Burn and New Burn, both of which must be wild when in spate. Defoe then described how they rode up one of these burns (Hawsen Burn still carries a bridleway) to a point where 'the main hill seemed still to be but beginning'. This is the impression a climber would get looking upward from the saddle between Broadhope Hill and Scald Hill towards the main summit. He then writes of the gradient steepening and their nerves failing.

First they dismount (to the derision of the guides) and then refuse to take another step 'because we all had a notion, that when we came to the top, we should be just as upon a pinnacle, that the hill narrowed to a point, and we should have only room enough to stand, with a precipice every way round us'. Already Defoe had compared a distant view of 816-metre Cheviot to 'the Pico-Teneriffe at the Canaries', presumably meaning Pico del Teide, the 3,718-metre peak on the island of Tenerife, which Herodotus likened to 'a column in the sky'.

Such was the author's terror at the unseen summit that his party sat on the ground and refused to go further. It was only when the guide had convinced the shuddering visitors that there was room enough on the top of Cheviot to 'run a race' that they continued to the summit and found 'a most pleasant plain, of at least half a mile in diameter'. Shortly afterwards, Defoe's party were joined by a guide leading a clergyman, his male companion and two ladies, all on horseback.

It was a cheeky deceit. Conceiving that a Matterhorn of rock projected from the Cheviot was a clumsy but effective method of upgrading a rounded peat bog in an age when few of Defoe's readers would have been aware that the Alps stopped some way short of Northumberland.

In May 1936 the Ordnance Survey had a genuine drama trying to place their triangulation pillar on top of Cheviot. To get to his workplace, the constructor, Mr H. Court, had to cycle six miles from Wooler then climb for nearly three miles. With five hired men and horses from local farms, Mr Court shifted two tons of sand and fifteen hundredweight of cement to the top of Cheviot, where, having suffered torrential rain and several threatened walkouts by the horsemen, he erected the pillar after seventeen days of effort – a feat which puts Mr Defoe's mountaineering epic in the shade. The day Mr Court finished, he set off to build the next pillar on Dun Rig. The bill he submitted to the OS for building Cheviot's pillar came to £49 16s 8d, seven times the cost of putting a triangulation pillar on top of Dod Law ten years later.

Blackchester Hill   A fence line through bog and knee-high grass led me off the Cheviots to a track which angled down to the deserted hamlet of Prendwick and the road for Alnham. Except for a fox quick-stepping for Churchbrae Plantation, I saw nobody for the rest of the day.

Dusk was settling as I walked into the hamlet of Alnham: 'home of the River Aln'. It lay just below the springs that fed the stream that had exploited a fault line in the Fell Sandstone and broken through the hills to Alnwick and the sea at Alnmouth. Like Prendwick, Alnham was silent; cottages that had once been smallholdings or the homes of the cobbler or blacksmith, now had the half-dead attitude of holiday homes. The church was full of bird droppings and its graveyard thigh-high with grass. Beside it, the pele tower that had once been a youth hostel had been converted back into a private house. The pub had gone, and the school, and the population. On the other side of the road, cattle strolled across the turfed undulations of the castle and long-buried homes.

There was nowhere obvious to sleep in Alnham, apart from the graveyard, and I've been off graveyards ever since opening my eyes one dawn in a French *cimetière* and seeing a pair of black-cowled eyes peering over a gravestone. I'd left the cemetery at speed, sleeping-bag flying like a wind-sock.

From Alnham a fence ran through moon-gilded corn over Blackchester Hill. A light night-time breeze blew fleets of silver clouds between the upturned rim of the Cheviots and Simonside Hills. No light showed on the great bowl of the earth. On the south side of Blackchester Hill I unrolled my sleeping-bag at the field edge and drifted off under the eye of the moon, winking from behind fleecy lids.

I woke wet with dew and continued walking, down the hill into a valley mist that hid a trespass past a farmhouse I had to make in order to stay with the meridian.

After a short section of road, I was back in fields full of lambs bleating pitifully at the white-out. Somewhere close by, a motorbike or quad bike burbled in the mist; a shepherd probably, out before breakfast.

At the foot of the fields, the public footpath turned along the valley of Wreigh Burn where, after splashing through calf-deep bogs, I came to Low Trewhitt, a remote farm tenanted by Tom and Boo Chrisp, names given to me by Gavin Douglas. The meridian passed within 300 metres of their back door.

Low Trewhitt   Tom Chrisp was leaving for the fields as I walked damply to the door of Low Trewhitt. 'Boo's inside,' he waved. 'You'd better have some breakfast.'

It was a farm kitchen: Aga, high ceiling, large wooden table, big mugs. I was wet and muddy from the knees down.

'Breakfast first. Or a bath?' asked Boo, as if noxious itinerants dropped by every morning.

From the old pantry, Boo ran the most northern safari company in England. Bushbuck Safaris catered for small groups of discerning Americans and Europeans with $3,500–$4,500 to spend on a two-week tailor-made itinerary. They'd stay in walk-in tents with bathrooms, viewing game from the backs of elephants, or from canoes or on their own feet. Once a year, Boo went to Africa on a recce. Low Trewhitt was well connected: the pantry had a computer, fax and e-mail, and London was only four hours from the back door, using the car and the Newcastle train.

'You can run a company from anywhere nowadays,' said Boo, handing me a shivering hill of scrambled eggs. Now that Anna and Kitty were starting school, Bushbuck was about to produce a new brochure and change up a gear.

Boo and Tom had studied at Aberdeen University; she'd been reading Gaelic, he was a land economist. They had married in a gale on a November day in 1991, at the church I'd passed in Alnham. Boo's veil had blown over the hills. The hounds of the West Percy Hunt were at the reception and afterwards eighty guests took off across the fields on horseback. Boo still hunted with the West Percy, every Tuesday and Saturday, from October. It was a 'farmers' hunt' with riders drawn from every social orbit: there was an insurance salesman, a milkman, a dentist, an air hostess. Boo and Tom had marched in London against the bill to ban fox-hunting.

After breakfast I went out to the fields to find Tom. He was standing on the edge of the corn, wearing a wide-brimmed panama, with his hands stuffed in his pockets. In front of him, a gigantic green mechanical locust was chewing its way through the winter oats. The combine was struggling; taking a few gobbles, choking, then reversing and trying again.

'It's a disaster,' said Tom, shaking his head grimly. 'It's too wet.'

Back Field covered thirty acres. If the price held – which looked unlikely – and Tom got £70 a ton, he'd be able to sell his eighty tons of oats from Back Field for £5,600, to which he could add a European Community subsidy of £100 per acre, making a total of £8,600. His costs – rent, planting, fertilizer, the combine and so on – came to about £180 an acre, or £5,400 for the field. So, in theory, he would make a net profit for a year's work on one field of £3,200. Since the subsidy on Back Field amounted to £3,000, the real profit was £200.

Over a snatched lunch, Tom talked about Low Trewhitt and the hazards of farming. 'The last two years we had good harvests. This one is being more difficult. More normal.' Rain in June and July had flattened the crops. 'People always say, "Poor farmers; always complaining", but we're producing food which they can eat whatever the weather.'

Tom had 900 acres: 400 down to corn, the rest grass for sheep and cattle. His father Jock and grandfather Jack had farmed this land as tenants of Lord Armstrong, before Low Trewhitt passed to the National Trust. In Jack's time, thirty men and women worked on the farm. 'Now there are two,' Tom added. 'We can't afford any more.'

Low Trewhitt still bore the reminders of Lord Armstrong's enthusiasms for science. After he had created Cragside – the first house in the world to be lit by hydro-electricity – Armstrong had excavated a lake at Low Trewhitt and installed an ingenious turbine system to power the farm machinery. From one of his bookshelves, Tom handed me a prized copy of David Dippie Dixon's *Upper Coquetdale*, published in 1903. In Dippie Dixon's day, Trewhitt Lake was a 'fine sheet of water eight acres in extent', stocked with 'splendid trout', rich in coot and wild duck and fringed by a luxurious growth of rushes and sedges. But the dam broke and the lake is now full of grass.

Tom spent the afternoon bringing in the oats from Back Field. An operation further removed from the romantic notions of harvesting would be hard to imagine: from the combine out in the field, a casually employed tractor-driver brought trailerloads of oats back to the barn and emptied them into one corner. Tom, driving a second tractor, shovelled the oats into a hopper, from where they were lifted by conveyor to the top of a tall cylindrical gas-fed hot-air dryer, driven by the power takeoff of a third tractor. When the drum had filled to the top, and the oats inside were dry, Tom pulled a lever and the dry oats cascaded on to the concrete. Then he got back on to his tractor and shovelled them into a heap at the other end of the barn, ready for collection.

The thunderous dryer and revving tractors, the dust and heat filled the day with a sticky reverberating din. If you'd taken away the daylight, the inside of that barn would have been indistinguishable from a coal mine.

When it was too dark for the combine to cut, Tom came back to the house and we sat down at the kitchen table to a supper of grouse and woodcock. For the first time that day, he leaned back in a chair. He was worried about rain in the night; the combine hadn't managed to cut half of Back Field and rain would stop it dead.

Having watched Tom for much of the day, I could almost grasp the scale of his physical endeavour. More difficult to appreciate was the perennial weight of uncertainty that could turn months of effort to nothing.

That night the clouds sneaked back into Coquetdale and blacked out the moon.

Tom and Boo had given me a room which faced a stone wall into which was set a small fourteenth-century window from the pele tower that once stood at Low Trewhitt. When I had a roof over my bed I usually willed the night rains to clear the skies for the morning but on this night I prayed that the clouds would bear their burdens beyond the oats of Coquetdale.

*

The rain stayed away and in the morning Tom resumed his battle with Back Field.

As I was leaving Low Trewhitt I passed Tom's shepherd, John Bradbury, a big man in braces and a battered straw hat. He was stock-marking sheep with splashes of red dye on their right shoulders. 'Our neighbour has blue in the middle of the back. Windyside use black.'

It was John I'd heard the previous morning, out in the mist putting his lambs on the 'fog' – the young freshly cut grass. John had been born in Derbyshire but had moved to Northumberland thirty-six years ago. 'This is the finest country in the land,' he said, wiping his brow with a red kerchief. 'It's got everything: coast, inbye land, castles.'

He and his wife Margaret had been at Low Trewhitt for six years. He had three dogs, Moss, Kylie and Bud, and a couple of puppies. 'You want names that are short and sweet', said John, echoing the advice of Junius Moderatus Columella in 60 BC. 'Like Ness, Lass, Pip, Floss, Ben, Cap. You need a name you can get out of your mouth quick.'

'What makes a good sheepdog?'

'You're looking for a dog with a nice outrun, and then you want them to be able to come in behind the sheep with a little bit of eye. Then bring them straight back down the field. And when you tell him to stop, he must stop. A lot of things can go wrong if he doesn't stop.' John looked at his dogs. 'Then you must always use the same commands: "Come by!" is left; "Away to me!" is right. Young shepherds use "Away to me" for left. It doesn't matter as long as you always use the same command.' The previous October John had been invited to Vancouver Island to judge the West Canadian Sheepdog Championships.

John's calendar was a constantly shifting routine. 'In winter at about eight o'clock in the morning I go and check that the sheep have got hay and sileage. At lambing we fetch them into the sheds. We used to lamb in the open with everything the sky throws at you. Now you don't lose the lambs. After tea I go round and catch the lambs that have got separated. If a lamb is away two nights, the ewe will try not to take it back. Before clipping we have to check the ewes twice a day; after clipping it's once a day. At six weeks the lambs get a mineral drench and injection. They go to market in September, next month.'

The life of a shepherd had changed. 'In my young days you walked with your stick and your dog and a bag with penicillin and a syringe and a bit of tar in case a sheep had a bad head or foot. It was more traditional farming then. A lot of sheep are now put on the fields that can't be ploughed or are too steep. So the sheep don't get the best fields and the lambs don't fatten so quickly. When I was young it was quite a nice lifestyle. But there is more stock now. It's more work. And you get more money. There are plenty of young shepherds about, but not enough work. The family farms are using their own family; they take the shepherd's cottage and turn it into a holiday let. And shepherds don't come cheap any more. Also they've got the four-wheeler bikes, which allow one shepherd to do the work of two.'

John's own quad bike was an extraordinary contraption that he'd customized by adding a weather-proof cab made from pieces of a cut-up caravan. With its sheepskin seat and dog box on the back it looked like an all-terrain ice-cream van.

'The only time it frightened me was in a gale,' grinned John. 'It got to lean a bit.'

Another change that John had seen was the return to the borders of sheep rustling. Low Trewhitt had lost forty sheep the previous year. 'Then,' added John, 'Nick Foster who's nearby lost ninety last October.'

The sheep were usually being stolen in batches of forty, suggesting that the rustlers were limited to the capacity of one truck. Quad bikes were going missing too. 'They were putting them in forty-ton lorries and covering them in grain,' shrugged John. 'Then taking them to Ireland.'

I'd meant to start walking after breakfast, but John suggested that we went back to his cottage for tea. As he walked, he limped. 'I was tagging a calf, and as I pushed the tag through its ear the calf blared and its mother came up behind me and tossed me. Eight times it tossed me, until it tossed me over the wall into a wood. I lay there till it cleared off. I still have to go to the osteopath four times a year.'

'I didn't know that a cow could be dangerous,' I said.

'Aye,' laughed John. 'You do now.'

Over tea, John talked of his stick-making. 'I always use hazel sticks. I've got a friend who sends them to me from Wales. Then I dry them for two years. Then I get a thorn head out of a hawthorn bush and dry that for two years. You can splice the head on or use a piece of copper tube. Then you file and sand it, play about with it on winter's nights.'

Dippie Dixon writes of a hill shepherd who'd been given a stick by a famous stick-dresser. After scrutinizing the new stick he muttered, 'Heavy! Heavy! Heavy!' and threw it aside with the comment, 'A'll nivvor wear it!'

John continued. 'The first thing you do if you see a branch or a tree down is to look for the curves. If you're with a hillman you can swap the neck for a good piece of horn. The hillmen like a neck stick for the blackies.'

'Which stick-makers do you admire?' I asked.

'Norman Tulip is the great stick-dresser in Northumberland, but the fella who learned *him* was George Snaith.'

John had a curious relationship with George Snaith. 'When I was in Derbyshire I used to get the *Scottish Farmer* and I wrote to them asking for information on how to make a horn-headed stick. Six months later I get a letter from this old man, George Snaith. Well, when we moved to Northumberland, to South Sharperton, it was very wet one day and the old lady from the post office, Lizzie Robinson, came by and she said, "I didn't know you can make sticks, John." Then she said, "Who learned you?"

'"That man," I says, pointing to the letter from George Snaith.

'"D'you know who this is?" said Miss Robinson. "He lived across the road from where you are now, but he died a few weeks before you moved in."

'Miss Robinson told me she didn't know anyone who George would've written a letter like that to. He was a strong man, a hard man to know. Miss Robinson said he 'ad hands like shovels, yet he could mek such delicate things: a pocket knife out of a reaper's blade; a ladies' necklace out of horse hair. I was sad to have missed him,' mused John. ''E learned me 'ow to mek sticks by letter.'

The morning was running away but I couldn't bring myself to leave. John's enthusiasms were those of another world.

He talked for a while about the bantams which he lost to a mink and about the sixty birds he still had, entering the best for poultry shows ('I done quite well with ma Anconas'). Then he mentioned the Roman axe-head and I knew I'd have to sit this one out too.

'It was in the potatoes: bronze,' recalled John. 'I put it in the garage. Then I was talkin' to a local doctor. A police pathologist, Harvey McTaggart. He's retired and lives in the blacksmith's cottage. Harvey says, "Where d'you find it?"

' "In the potato drills," I said.

' "Could you tek me to the spot?" says Harvey.

'When I found it, I'd lined up the spot on an ash tree and a thorn. Harvey spent two days quartering the spot with string and posts and a metal detector and he finds nothing and so he says, "Come back with me." So we went back to the spot and I kicked the soil and said, "There's one!"

'It was probably an old lookout post, up on the hill. I knew what I'd found because there's a picture in Dippie Dixon's book.'

Reluctantly, I left Low Trewhitt.

Wreigh Burn   One field before Snitter Windyside I left the road and followed a track down to the ford through Wreigh Burn.

The Tam boys were camping by the ford. Tommy, Stephen, Mark, Anthony and David, pale, skinny lads from a Newcastle suburb. They had a tent against the fence and a keep-net full of Coca Cola hanging in the burn. The embers of the previous evening's fire smouldered in the centre of a circle of ash. Minnows swarmed in a fish tank cut from the bottom of a green plastic barrel.

I told them I'd seen a heron the previous morning as I wallowed through bog further upstream.

'Saw'n otter lass night,' volunteered Tommy.

They were very excited about the otter. They'd watched it swimming where the burn passes the woods.

Like the migrating families of the Breamish, the Tams' August camp on Wreigh Burn went back further than they could remember.

Warton The tall man with the small dogs and Edinburgh brogue whom I met at the gate at the end of the track into Warton turned out to be Harvey McTaggart, the man who'd helped the shepherd John Bradbury find his second Roman axe-head.

Harvey's old blacksmith's cottage stood beside Warton Farm. Like Low Trewhitt, it had once been part of Lord Armstrong's estate. (There was a rumour that the gateposts of Warton Farm were so far apart because they had to accommodate the width of Lord Armstrong's carriage when he came visiting his mistress.)

Harvey had spent twenty-four years in Hartlepool working as a forensic pathologist for the police. 'Just nasty, a lot of it. Boyfriends killing their partners and so on.' But he'd enjoyed his work. 'It wasn't just gore; I got the chance to be involved with interesting people: policemen, barristers, judges, forensic scientists. I liked the science.'

One of Harvey's clients had made it on to the TV programme *Crimewatch*. There had been a series of robberies in the Cleveland–Darlington area and the police suspected that the culprit was a man who had shot a police sergeant in Leeds nine years earlier. The suspect was being watched by plainclothes police when he took flight into the centre of Stockton. Waving a shotgun, he hijacked a police car. There was a chase and the robber crashed the car with a loud bang into a pedestrian walkway.

'He was sitting on a bench in the police station,' continued Harvey, 'when he suddenly keeled over, dead!'

The shotgun had been lying on the passenger seat of the stolen police car and the impact of the crash had tripped the hammer.

'It was only when police officers opened his anorak that they saw the hole in his side. The liver had moved up and the shot had hit the back of his abdominal cavity. It was,' sighed Harvey, 'a *lovely* bit of natural justice!'

Flotterton   Ten minutes after Harvey had waved me off, I was in the kitchen of Flotterton Hall with Frank and Heppy Warton.

In one of my encounters with Gavin Douglas, he had thrust a piece of paper into my hand which read: '2° Frank Walton 85yrs Farmer/Racehorses. Flotterton.'

In fact Frank was seventy-one, but Gavin was right about the racehorses. Frank owned 'about twenty' of them. Mighty Mack, who won the Scottish Grand National in 1988, was one of Frank's. Cups, trophies and paintings lined the walls beneath the exquisite cornices of Flotterton Hall's dining room. One of the pictures showed Frank's son riding Desert Orchid at the Percy Hunt point-to-point.

Frank's family had a lot of land: 20,000 acres; 10,000 sheep and 500 cows. They had bought Flotterton Hall in 1952. From the lawn they could look over a silver curl of the Coquet to the purple wall of the Simonside Hills.

'You'll be staying for lunch?' said Heppy.

They drove, I walked, down the B road to the bungalow that had recently become their home now that Flotterton was too large.

Over coffee, I wondered what had made Frank and Heppy's marriage so long and happy.

'Give and take,' said Frank quickly. 'Same as breaking draught horses.'

Caistron   In his battered panama, Frank led me to the short cut over the fields to the quarry road.

The quarry had been skilfully hidden by a curtain of conifers on the bank of the River Coquet. Where the public view of the Coquet still resembled Dippie Dixon's enchanted vale, the place behind the trees looked as if it had been hit by an earthquake: instead of a natural palette of dappled greens, there were hues of raw stone, ruptured, piled and prowled by roaring yellow machines.

The quarry manager was a charming 26-year-old called Darren Stell. In his punning 'Hard Rock' baseball cap, earring and boiler suit with the arms ripped off, Darren could have been a post-apocalyptic cab-driver out of an urban horror movie. His toys were *big*: a Liebherr 912 tracked excavator, Volvo 5350 dump trucks, a Kuken crusher as tall as a house. Darren could dig 500 tons a day.

He liked his work. 'There's nothing to it, really,' he said, heaving a lever to spew gravel into a shuddering truck. The Kuken had screens that sifted the gravel into 10mm and 20mm sizes, and a gigantic wash barrel. The sand would be used for pavements; the stones would end up in garden centres and driveways.

There were no bridges marked on the map between 99 and 01, so I'd expected to wade the Coquet.

'No need!' yelled Darren, over the rattle of falling stones. The quarry company had thrown a steel bridge over the river and Darren said that I'd find Neil in the trees on the far side.

Neil Telfer was building an ornithological hide with Joe Williamson, a retired production director from Ryton Sand and Gravel Group. The Group had been recipients of the Sand and Gravel Association Cooper-Heyman Trophy For The Most Outstanding Restoration During 1991. The Nobel Prize for hole-filling had been awarded to Ryton Group for creating Caistron Nature Reserve from the mess they'd made of the Coquet.

In contrast to Darren's ripped-up world across the water, the south bank was decorated with woodland walks and twinkling lakes singing with wildlife.

Neil had been part of Caistron Reserve since its conception in 1969. Thousands of trees had been planted, shorelines landscaped and hides built. 'It's the only job I've had which I look forward to coming back to,' he smiled. 'It's very rewarding. You've got to be patient. If you create a habitat, you may have to wait a year or two for it to develop. I've been here twenty-eight years.' His voice was drowned by the mewings from a flotilla of lapwings. Behind him the tail of an upended coot bobbed like a sinking canoe.

In each of the hides was a score-sheet for visiting birdwatchers. The previous month, Ponteland Women's Institute had spotted a Chilean flamingo from Hide No. 8, whose tally for the year already stood at eighty-two species that included wigeon, a kestrel, two goldeneye, kingfishers, wrens, a pair of redpolls and spotted flycatchers, 154 Greylag geese and, on 5 July, 1,000 starlings. Since the reserve opened, a total of 194 different species had been recorded.

'You should have seen it when we started,' said Neil. 'It was just diggings. Very bleak.'

At Caistron I saw more birdlife than I'd seen since leaving Berwick. Yet the effect of this resurrected habitat reached way beyond these cosmeticized pits: the bittern that Tom Chrisp once saw on the river at Low Trewhitt had probably flown up from Caistron looking for a mate. To the birds who'd learned its location, Caistron was now a migration stopover; to schools and ornithologists (who could visit the site at no charge) Caistron was a window on a vanishing world.

Some of my prejudices were under siege; not only about quarrying, but about hunting and fishing too. Tom Chrisp had told me that, three years earlier, he and Boo had heard a corncrake feeding in a crop that was being grown for pheasants and partridge ('One in the eye for the RSPB!' Tom had said). He argued that controlled shooting created niches for new species, and rural income. Even John Steele, the park ranger I'd met back in the Cheviots, had been in favour of grouse-shooting, pointing out that grouse fed off heather shoots, and a well-managed heather moorland supported a more diverse habitat than grass for grazing. It was a measure of the dire state of hill-farming that six to ten days' grouse-shooting a year, at a charge of £1,000 per gun, provided the same income as 1,500 sheep for a year.

It all made economic and ecological sense, but in removing the sheep a diversity of human activity had gone too. Dippie Dixon reckoned that in Coquetdale, the big changes in the lives of the shepherds occurred in the last quarter of the nineteenth century, as the inventions of the Industrial Revolution migrated from the manufacturing heartland of the West Midlands. The spinning wheel and piles of cardings (wool ready for spinning) had disappeared from shepherds' cottages, replaced by the sewing machine. The cheese-press and 'chesfit' (the vessel containing curd) had gone too, as cheese-making became an urban industry. The patent roller mangle had replaced the wooden 'bittle' that had once been used for beating flax and linen. In Dippie Dixon's day a few elements of the shepherd's life were still intact: they still ate Northumberland 'crowdy', an oatmeal porridge, and a shepherd's cottage still smelled of 'peat-reek' from burning peat for heat and cooking.

Change was inevitable. Since the meridian was about to begin its long cross-section through grouse country, I'd have a chance to see what kind of culture had replaced the shepherds.

The Simonside Hills Coquetdale quickly fell away as I climbed the sandstone scarp that had been shadowing the meridian all the way from Berwick.

At Bickerton Wood – an enchanting wedge of old England filled with oak, ash and alder – I took a breather beside a row of crows who'd been strung from the barbed wire having paid the price for pilfering seed. Bluebottles fizzed about their beaks. A hare rose on its hind legs, paws bunched into furry fists.

Above the wood, where arable gave way to grazing, I came upon a cup-and-ring stone. Unusually, the Ordnance Survey – who marked even the most diminutive cups on the map – had failed to register this great carved stone. It lay as long as my umbrella, with four good cups connected by channels, and two offset cups, one of them cross-hatched with striae. One corner of the boulder had deep scratches and what appeared to be a bevel. I stumbled excitedly around the block as if it were unmarked treasure.

'My theory,' Paul Frodsham had told me as he drew in my notebook the three principal variations of cup-and-ring designs, 'is that they all have the same meaning: they're depicting life as a journey. To heaven. To Valhalla. Or back to the beginnings of time, to the place of their ancestors.'

Looking about the hillside, there were other signs. Close by was the dip and rise of ridge and furrow, left by medieval cultivators who'd pushed the limits of agriculture far above the valley floor. There were hints too of transhumance. A thousand metres to the north-east was a building called Wolfershiel, recalling the time when 'shiels' were the seasonal homes of shepherds who would move up from their winter quarters in the valleys to spend the summer on the high pastures with their flocks – an echo of the transhumance that still clings to the uplands of continental Europe.

The notion that Northumbrian shepherds conformed to the migratory patterns of their southern cousins is supported by Cox in his *Magna Britannia* of 1720, who wrote of the more 'mountainous' parts of Northumbria having 'ancient Nomades, a martial sort of People, that from April to August lie in little Huttes (which they call Sheals, or Shealings) here and there dispersed among their Flocks'.

The circular timber and turf shiels would have had an adjacent 'stell', or fold, for the sheep, like the one I'd slept beside in the Cheviots. From where I stood part-way up the Simonside Hills, I could see a stell behind a wall above the cup-and-ring stone. Then there was the name of the range itself: Simonside (like Gunnerside and Ambleside) took its name from the Old Norse term *saetr*, the summer pasture that Scandinavian farmers used for their flocks and herds once the snows had melted in spring.

John Bradbury, the shepherd at Low Trewhitt, was convinced that we underestimated sheep. 'There was this old fella from Netherton,' he said, 'who told me he brought some black-face ewes from Peebles and they found their way back from Northumberland to Peebles. Sometimes sheep know better than you do.'

John's story took me back to the Cévennes, where shepherds still talk of the time, thousands of years ago, when sheep made their own seasonal migrations. It was the men who began following the sheep, not vice versa.

Above the carved stone, the angle of the Simonside scarp steepened, and grass changed to heather. There were no paths and so I set my eye on the highest point on the skyline and started pulling myself upward. As Coquetdale blurred into a soft-focus haze, the brow of the Simonsides sharpened. Rocks began to appear in the heather, and hidden holes, into which I frequently fell.

By chance the meridian struck the Simonside Hills at their highest point, so that I emerged on to a dramatic crest – Tosson Hill

– that was piled with great stacks of weathered sandstone, eaten into plasticine curves by wind and rain. The big blue view was made for gliding, for tilting away from the summit rocks and riding the updraught along the face of the Simonsides towards the sea, a slippery gleam on the horizon. This would be my last sight of salt-water until I trod the back-slope of a Dorset down at the other end of the meridian.

Casting my mind back over the eight days since I'd climbed from the North Sea, I could already sense that straight-lining was a fascinatingly inefficient method of travelling from A to B. In just over a week, I'd covered a straight-line distance of only fifty-five kilometres, an average of seven kilometres a day. Tosson Hill was, however, one-tenth of the way to the English Channel. I lingered up here, savouring the seclusion of this isolated summit and remembering Paul Frodsham's expression when I told him that the meridian ran over the Simonsides. The fact that there were so many burial monuments up here, but no settlements, suggested that this distinctive eminence may have been a sacred mountain. One of the local legends that Paul and his team had discovered was a continuing belief that people should never climb to the top of the Simonsides, because of 'nasty little men' who live there.

On Tosson Hill's uppermost point rose triangulation pillar 91551, erected by the Ordnance Survey in May 1936. This was one of the rare 'First Order' pillars, built at the corners of the 'primary triangles' – those with sides that averaged thirty miles in length and which formed the skeleton on which the smaller triangles were attached. Of the total of over 6,000 trig pillars in England, Scotland and Wales, fewer than 500 were First Order, and just three stood on my meridian. They were placed on my line with a pleasing symmetry: the most northerly peered down on the North Sea; the most southerly overlooked the English Channel; and the one in the centre not only occupied the highest point on the meridian, but lay close to its mid-point. The Ordnance Survey's truncated obelisks stood like shrines on the Way of St James, marking the beginning, the middle and the end of my pilgrimage.

From Tosson Hill I saw my first grouse moor, and it was not pretty. For the full width of my 2,000-metre band, the gentle back-slope of the Simonside Hills was covered with dull monochrome heather that had been burned into precise rectangles. From here, grouse moors stretched intermittently to the journey's mid-point at the southern tip of the Pennines, 240 kilometres to the south. Nearly every ten-kilometre grid square on the map was stitched with the black bullet holes of grouse butts. The first butts were visible from the top of Tosson Hill, a line of gun-pits obliquely across the meridian where it traversed Boddle Moss.

Climbing the wild heather up the front of Tosson Hill had been like wading through deep snow, with periodic plunges into unseen crevasses. On Boddle Moss the managed heather was less deep because it had been burned off by the gamekeeper, but it camouflaged water-filled draining ditches.

It was 7 p.m. by the time I'd crossed Boddle Moss and found the gap in the fence and a fingerpost pointing into the conifers.

Harwood Forest   The largest forest on the meridian was shown on the map as a vast green block, divided by logging tracks. There were no views and virtually no landmarks. At each track junction I had to take compass bearings to eliminate the risk of straying too far east or west. Periodically the low rumble of machinery carried through the ranks of conifers, and more than once I stood aside to wait for a logging truck which passed unseen on some alternative track.

Apart from deer, springing like phantoms across firebreaks, I met nobody.

Night fell and I was still in the forest.

Unlike a natural forest, with its glades and bowers for beds, a plantation impedes the casual dosser; every tree had a bog beneath it or a spiked entanglement of fallen branches.

After ten kilometres in the trees, the ranks of trunks thinned and turned to silhouettes and I came to the southern border of the forest. Unable to see clearly, I unrolled my sleeping-mat on the least uneven ground, waking at first light to find myself lying on the verge of a road.

Dew rolled off the bivouac bag. A pine spangled the lightening sky, and I turned my head in time to catch a fox in mid-stride. The road ran between the black forest and the undulating khaki moor, a ruler-straight divide between dark and light.

For breakfast, I tipped into the steel mug the last of my food: a sachet of muesli and a sachet of powdered chocolate drink from the Tankerville Arms, crumbs from the bag of Women's Institute shortcake bought in Berwick Town Hall, and water. It looked like mud and sawdust and was the best breakfast I've ever tasted – although I'd probably send it back if I was served it in the Savoy.

The compass led me off across the moor under a suffused bleary sun. Dew sparkled; rabbits bolted. I was picturing the pub lunch I'd have in Kirkwhelpington when the sky splintered and dark wings tilted at my head. As I ducked, a jet fighter turned so low above the moor that I could see the pilot's face. The sound followed: an explosive roar that pulverized the boggy ground then tailed away like a fading meteorite.

Catcherside That morning I came to a field gate that had been widened to accommodate modern farm machinery. The gateposts were two massive standing stones that must have been in that place for over a century, hauled upright by a draught horse before the days of steam. One of the posts now lay flat, still wrapped in the heavy chain that had dragged it behind a tractor from its socket at the end of its wall. I took it as a bad omen for the day.

It seems to be the nature of journeys that there comes a point (usually after a fortnight or so) when flaws begin to appear in the plan. On this walk it happened on the ninth day, when the entire project began to be threatened by under-performing underpants.

What I had initially dismissed as a quirk of mis-dressing had, over the kilometres, revealed itself to be a manufacturer's fault in the underwear that I'd bought in Berwick to replace my own Marks and Spencer boxer shorts after cotton fatigue caused them to rip from top to bottom. Oddly, the M & S boxers self-destructed on the same day that the *Sun* reported – under the headline 'Sparks Flew

Out of My Marks Knicks' – that the Marks and Spencer underwear of a Co-op check-out operator had spontaneously combusted. 'It was terrible,' said Melanie Thompson. 'I pulled my uniform down and my knickers were burning.' For a happy moment I thought I had stumbled upon another promising example of two-degree connectivity, for Melanie's Co-op was in Greater Manchester, through which the meridian passed, and we wore the same brand of underwear and both of us had suffered comparable misfortunes on the same day. Sadly, scrutiny of my map revealed that Melanie's supermarket lay more than 1,000 metres from two degrees. Equally sadly – and unlike Melanie – I had no replacement underwear. I always walk in Marks and Spencer cotton boxer shorts, which are quick-drying and cut for unconstrained exertion. In Berwick, all I could find was a garment patterned on an Edwardian bathing costume, made from striped tent fabric with an absurd button fly that took ten minutes and several broken fingernails to open. More grievously, the replacements had the irritating habit of 'slotting', which – in the manner of seemingly minor irritations – was beginning to undermine my morale. In a further twist of meridional complicity, the next town centre on my line was Skipton, the birthplace of Mr Thomas Spencer, co-founder of Marks and Spencer. Unfortunately, Skipton was a month's walk away, and even when I reached it, I would only have access to one half of the town, since the grid line 99 ran down the centre of the High Street. Which side of the line Skipton's underwear specialist lay became a subject of increasingly emotional speculation.

Kirkwhelpington   The village emerged from the edge of the moor with the promise of a lost oasis.

It wasn't a big village, but it was the first I'd been through since leaving Wooler four days earlier. Kirkwhelpington had no pub or shop but it had a church and it had Eileen Rogerson.

'Churchpupington, my grandfather used to call it,' said Eileen, recalling the time when this was the homestead of someone whose nickname was 'The Puppy'. Puppy became whelp. The church came later. Eileen had squeezed the post office into the back half of her council house dining room. It was the smallest post office I'd ever seen, and its walls were stacked tight with rural essentials from tomato soup to tinned peaches.

Kirkwhelpington's previous postmaster had been Jack Creighton.

'He was coming up to seventy,' recalled Eileen, 'and he said to me, "D'you fancy running the post office?" My little one was two and the other was starting school. Well, Jack put in his notice and I came home to Ken, my husband – he's a fitter at the quarry – and Ken said, "Well, you probably *could* run the post office . . ."'

That was 1988. The debt took five years to clear.

'It ticks over,' she laughed. 'It provides a service for the community. This is the main focus of the village. We've a lot of old people living on their own. They totter down for a bar of chocolate and a chat. You get everybody's problems; you've got to be a good listener, and sympathetic.'

Kirkwhelpington was virtually cut off for those without a car. Hexham, Ponteland, Morpeth and Rothbury had the closest shopping streets, but they were all twenty kilometres away as the crow flew; only Ponteland (and Newcastle beyond it) had a daily bus link to Kirkwhelpington.

'Many of the old people don't drive,' said Eileen, 'and those that do find that the roads are too icy in winter. It can get desperate.'

There had never been a pub in Kirkwhelpington, but there was once a library and reading room, a blacksmith and a cobbler. The school had closed when Eileen was a child. She'd been sent to boarding school in Wooler.

'The sad thing is,' continued the postmistress, 'that the commuters who are moving into the village now are bringing children, but there's no school for them.'

New arrivals were expected to be good gardeners. Kirkwhelpington was a showpiece of blooms and lawns that had been shaved to billiard-table felt for the National Gardens Scheme open day. Capability Brown was born just outside the village and would have known these gardens when they were vegetable plots and pig runs.

Eileen put me in a chair in the sun by the door and brought sandwiches and a mug of tea. I sat with *The Times* as a healthy trickle of customers came to the back door of a council house where an ex-secretary and mother – open six days a week for newspapers, groceries, pensions and conversation – ran a one-woman life-support system.

Boggle Hole   It must have been a very long time since anyone had tried to walk from Kirkwhelpington to Boggle Hole. Beyond the village, there were no rights of way and the map was divided into a mosaic of fields surrounded by stone walls, hedges, barbed wire and ditches.

My first attempt to leave the village was unsuccessful. Down by the river, I was about to pass through a gate on to a public footpath that crossed a garden, when the owner appeared in a green Rover saloon. 'Can I help you?' he said in a get-lost tone.

'I'm following the public footpath.'

'The footpath goes nowhere.'

'It goes to the river, and Copping Crag.'

'You can't get across the river.'

'I'll wade.'

He thought for a moment.

'Copping Crag has fallen down. Covered with trees. Gone. There's no point in you going to look.'

On the way back up the lane I passed a cottage called 'Wits End'.

My second attempt to leave Kirkwhelpington took me past the Old Temperance Hotel – now a private house – and down to a humpback bridge and a green lane strangled by nettle and thistle and lined by old-man beeches with twisted arthritic limbs – an ancient drove road perhaps, from the outbye pastures to the village.

Before the green lane petered out I turned down a side track to Harelaw farmhouse to ask permission to cross the fields. Two combine harvesters were parked in the yard, and I was met at the garden gate by a harassed young woman. 'Terrible harvest,' she said, shaking her head, 'a disaster. The ground's too wet, and this humidity is keeping the corn damp.'

She was soon to marry the tenant of the farm and she must have been wondering what the future held.

By now, the day's intense humidity was contributing to the slotting problem. Furthermore, the fields south of Harelaw farm were barricaded with barbed wire and nettles. At Boggle Hole (a feature I never identified, but which must have been associated with the ditch I was trying to cross) I snagged the seat of my trousers on a galvanized steel barb and ripped a hole big enough to post a small dog. Henceforth being 'boggle-holed' was synonymous with wrongly thinking that things could not possibly get worse; a false nadir.

The next village south was still ten kilometres away, most of it trackless. There were burns to jump, more barbed wire, hedges that stung and clawed, and then the rain came down in vertical bars while I tried to sort out compass bearings in a huge off-square field. An ambush by a bull was followed by a more serious encounter on the back-slope of Grindstone Law.

Wet, ragged, muddy and tired, I forgot John Bradbury's cautionary tale and followed the line of a public bridleway across the centre of a field of bullocks, rather than taking the long route around the edge. Led by one brazen beast, the bullocks trotted after me, huffing and snorting. The far side of the field was at least 200 metres away – too far for me to beat them in a sprint. I unsheathed the umbrella and increased my pace towards the distant gate. As they came up to my shoulder I turned. There were at least thirty of them and they could sniff the apprehension on the wind. Rapier thrusts with the umbrella kept them beyond reach as I hastened towards the gate, but then they began an encircling movement, cutting me off from my only means of escape. I feinted to the right, but they knew that the wall was too high for me to jump. Reasoning with them was out of the question, as was killing them with the umbrella. I ran. They ran.

What stayed with me for days afterwards was not the bovine halitosis, or the wall of quivering black beef, but the sound of 120 hooves drumming on hard turf.

Fifteen yards from the gate, I knew that they were going to win the race. With a swipe of my left hand, I unlocked the waist-strap on the rucksack and – still sprinting – shrugged it off and slung it high over the wall. Twenty pounds lighter I surged forward just as the first muzzle collided with my backside and nudged me head first over the gate. My fall was softened by a tumulus of cow dung from which I slithered screaming, 'It's a bridleway, you *bastards!*'

Fifteen minutes later, in sight of the lights of Great Whittington, and with one last field to cross, I was walking along another bridleway, reassuring myself that milch cows were a breeze compared to bullocks, when the entire herd went berserk. Some ran at me, others jumped fences. Unlike the bullocks, this wasn't a coordinated military manoeuvre, but hysterical panic. The danger came from inadvertent collision.

Sprinting and weaving for the edge of the field, I found that someone had bulldozed a two-metre-high mudbank across the bridleway.

Panting, I fell into the village of Great Whittington.

Great Whittington Less than thirty minutes' driving time from Newcastle upon Tyne, Great Whittington had fallen to the commuters.

Drawn by a clink of wine glasses and tinkling laughter, I came to a converted schoolhouse, where a short-haired woman with beatific eyes and a white blouse had taken advantage of a gap between evening showers to take an outdoor drink with two neighbours. What she saw was a turd totem-pole propped on an umbrella. My trousers were ripped and brown with slime; I was unshaven, limping, and suffering from mild post-traumatic stress.

'Good evening,' she said sweetly. 'Can I help you?'

'Is there a bed and breakfast in Great Whittington?'

There wasn't, but she would drive me to one. I didn't travel in cars, and a look at my map under the street light revealed that she had in mind a place east of 01.

'Then you could try the pub,' she suggested. 'If you get stuck, do come back here.'

In the Queen's Head Inn I bought a pint of Guinness and asked the barman whether the landlord had rooms for the night.

'No,' he replied, smugly.

'That's a pity.'

'What're you going to do?'

'Sleep outside, I guess.'

'You *poor* bugger. On a night like this.'

Hadrian's Wall   Anaesthetized by Irish stout, I marched through drizzle until midnight, when I came to a stile at the foot of Milecastle 21 and fell into the vallum.

The bivouac site I selected lay near the crest of Down Hill, the home 2,000 years ago of Roman auxiliaries from one of the continent's conquered provinces east of the Danube. By day they'd checked the credentials of drovers and traders as they passed through the Wall; by night they stared north towards the misted hills of the ungovernable Selgovae. Lying in my sleeping-bag I could see how the land fell away in front of the Wall, towards the distant glow of Corbridge. Away from the town, in the deep black vale, solitary specks of light marked the spots where families slept and farm dogs lay with an ear to the wind.

Five years earlier I'd watched the moon sink into the ruins of Colonia Ulpia Traiana Augusta Dacica Sarmizegetusa, the fabulous capital that Trajan founded beneath the Retezat Mountains after his campaigns smashed the Transylvanian 'barbarians'. The cost of defeating Decebalus and his scythe-wielding Dacians was felt in Scotland, where Trajan was forced to pull back from the Clyde–Forth line to a new fortification that followed the only defined break in Britain's Pennine backbone: the coast-to-coast gap between the Tyne and Solway and the future course of Hadrian's Wall.

Separating the Brigantes from the Selgovae meant shifting 2,000,000 tons of rock and soil by hand. The five-metre-high wall was eighty Roman miles (117 kilometres) long. Fortlets were built at one-mile intervals, with two watch-turrets between each mile-castle and sixteen other forts. On the north side of the wall legion-aries dug a ditch eight metres wide and three metres deep; on the south side there was a vallum, a ditch seven metres wide and three metres deep and two banks of earth.

On waking, I found that my milecastle was little more than scar tissue in the turf and the vallum into which I'd slipped the night before had become a benign scoop in the side of Down Hill.

A wall of mist filled the valley; Hadrian's great divide between the Romans and the barbarians had been superseded by a gently billowing net curtain.

Aydon Castle In a stream called Hollywell Dene, I bathed in the rain and washed my trousers. I'd stitched the rips while sitting in my sleeping-bag at dawn on the Wall, but in effecting a draught-proof repair I'd bunched the material into several disconcerting pleats.

Sartorially compromised, I splashed down the lane in sodden trousers and teeming rain, umbrella thrumming. My boots, maps and my umbrella were my most important pieces of kit. I could have lost everything else and still completed the journey. Practicality was only half the story. To an Englishman, an umbrella is a surrogate side-arm, a replacement for the rapier, the Home Counties Colt .45. It's the parodic weapon, the symbol of English insouciance – guile with style. Schwarzenegger's industrial machine-gun was Steed's brolly, tilted five degrees from the vertical. For the Egyptians, who invented umbrellas, they represented the universe: the curved cover symbolized the arched body of the celestial goddess Nut; the stick and spokes were the god Shu, holding Nut aloft with a hand to thigh and breast. We took to them late. The first Englishman to sport an umbrella was the philanthropist and traveller Jonas Hanway, in the 1750s, after his return from Russia and Persia. A century later, in 1852, it was, however, an Englishman (Samuel Fox) who invented the slimline frame that propelled the nation to the forefront of umbrella manufacture. I fretted as much about losing the brolly as losing the way.

The lane ran down to the edge of a tight wooded ravine and Aydon Castle. Despite the claim by English Heritage that this was 'one of the finest examples in England of a thirteenth-century manor house', the castle was deserted.

'Maybe it's the weather?' said the custodian.

Aydon was one of English Heritage's less popular attractions, netting 18,000 visitors a year, one-fortieth of the figure for their top property, Stonehenge.

'They filmed *Ivanhoe* here,' added the custodian.

Aydon Castle was built on the shatter-zone between Scotland and England, and its story is one of overcoming fortitude rather than a steady ascendancy to architectural merit. One of Aydon's earliest victims was the Suffolk merchant Robert de Reymes, who took advantage of a lull in the Border troubles to move from East Anglia to Northumberland in about 1296. As he was settling in, hostilities flared between Scotland and England, land values collapsed and Aydon, along with Hexham and Corbridge, was burned. De Reymes spent his life fighting his neighbours and patching up his increasingly fortified home. By the time he died, his income had dwindled to a mere 14s 7d a year. Over the following centuries the house suffered cycles of ruin and rebuilding as successive owners struggled with Aydon's marginal geography. When the house was entrusted to the Ministry of Works in 1966, it was a dilapidated farm.

In the slanting rain, Aydon was a disconsolate shell. Walls and battlements ran with water, hoodmoulds dripped. The great hall had withdrawn into gloom. A little sun would have made a great difference, but that is what Robert de Reymes must have thought too.

The rain was heavier still by the time I left the flooded courtyard and descended into the wooded ravine that defends Aydon on three sides.

Fat leaves tapped beneath the barrage as I followed the old

bridleway to Corbridge, up the bank of the ravine to a field where a glowering bull sent me on a detour to Gallow Hill. Up here the rain eased, revealing a well-washed panorama of the Tyne valley. Light reflected off Hexham further upstream and directly below, the roofs of the town the Romans called Coriosopitum glistened wetly among the trees.

Among the house names I passed on the way into Corbridge were 'Belvido', 'Rumbles', 'Stavros' and a bungalow called 'The Bungalow'.

Corbridge   The constraints of the meridian meant that the centre of town was out of bounds, but I could visit an osteopathic clinic, a car showroom, a residential care home, a chartered surveyor, a dental practice, a Methodist church, an upholsterer and lino layer, the Tynedale Friends of Multiple Sclerosis Charity Shop, a Shell garage and a bed and breakfast.

Wondering whether they had a second-hand inflatable boat on the bric-à-brac shelf, I called at the charity shop. They didn't, but I did buy a jar of sugared apricots for supper. 'We're a little bit posher than Geordies,' said Olive, who ran the shop.

Then I walked down Spoutwell Lane to look at the river.

In the dark, all I could see was a wide black expanse of muscled water sliding alarmingly fast towards the North Sea. With some trouble, I identified a finger of shingle where I could enter the water gradually, rather than dropping straight from the bank into unfathomable depths.

Just upstream (but 100 metres the wrong side of the grid line 99), I could see the outline of the road bridge that was just twenty-four years old when Celia Fiennes rode over it on her 'Great Journey' of 1698. Of the travellers whose paths would continue to intersect with the meridian, this indefatigable colonel's daughter was the most inspiring. She seems to have been a compulsive wanderer, making her first journey when she was no more than twenty, then extending her itineraries until she was riding for months at a time to the furthest corners of England. The 'Great Journey' was undertaken when she was thirty-six and took her from London to Hadrian's Wall, then back to the capital by way of Cornwall. Well-born Celia was two years younger than the butcher's son who went on to write *Robinson Crusoe*, and of an entirely different sensibility. Where Defoe talked up (or invented) his laddish adventures, Fiennes underplayed the everyday trials of the road: a brush with highwaymen, falls from her horse, appalling roads and dodgy inns were given less space than descriptions of textiles, food, gardens and domestic architecture. Had Defoe been fording the Tyne in *A Tour Through the Whole Island of Great Britain*, the river would have been as wide as the Mississippi and twice as deep. My next meeting with Celia was scheduled for a road over the Pennines that squeezed from her the most dramatic passage in her diaries.

Back at the bed and breakfast, I washed my clothes in the sink, ate sugared apricots till I was reeling with hyperglycaemia, then stayed up till midnight working with the ball of string, plastic footballs and carrier bags I'd bought in the Shell garage.

The Tyne At first light I walked through the silent streets of Corbridge and back down Spoutwell Lane to the riverside.

Just upstream, traffic was beginning to flow over the road bridge. I undressed. Above my Edwardian underpants I wore the black inflatable ring I'd bought in Berwick with its white inscription: WARNING! ONLY TO BE USED IN WATER, IN WHICH THE CHILD IS WITHIN ITS DEPTH AND ONLY UNDER ADULT SUPERVISION. Lashed to the top of the rucksack was my bivouac bag, inflated and looking like a dead cow, and slung down the side of the rucksack were the carrier bags containing the footballs. In one hand I held my umbrella – tightly bound with string into a fluvially streamlined pole – which I intended to use as a stabilizer during the crossing. In the other hand I held one end of a luggage-strap which was attached to the rucksack. If I felt the rucksack dragging me under the surface, I planned to release it and drag it behind me as I struck out for the far shore. On my feet I wore boot insoles inside a pair of green mountaineering socks; the insoles would protect my feet from broken glass and sharp stones, the socks would permit a sounder purchase on slippery rocks. I had thought of everything.

Running through a final equipment-check prior to immersion, I heard voices.

Preferring not to be seen, I stepped beneath the branches overhanging the river bank. The voices came closer. 'This way,' said a male.

Feet scrabbled on the steep bank and a man appeared beside me. Four other people followed: a woman, two girls and a boy. They stood and stared.

'Good morning,' I said.

The man began to shepherd his family backwards across the shingle.

'It's OK,' I called. 'I'm only crossing the river.'

The man looked at the bridge, over my right shoulder.

'I can't use the bridge,' I said.

'Mmmmmm,' he intoned.

The Sullivan family were on their way back from a holiday in Scotland to their home in Dorset.

'Where in Dorset?' I asked, wondering whether they lived anywhere near the meridian.

'Hamworthy.'

'Hamworthy!' It was right *on* the meridian; the point on the northern shore of Poole harbour where I'd be searching for some kind of vessel to carry me over the water to the Isle of Purbeck.

Mr Sullivan had a camera around his neck and offered to take photographs of the Tyne crossing. As I took the first tentative steps into the river, I wondered how much the *Sun* would pay for authentic drowning shots.

The water did not reach my thighs.

Since it was so shallow, I waded back across the Tyne to leave the footballs with the Sullivans, then returned to the south bank, got dressed, deflated my bivouac bag and Chinese swimming aid (which I anticipated needing again) and set off towards a much larger body of water. Ten kilometres south of the Tyne, the meridian was blocked by a reservoir.

Slaley Hall   A road with Alpine switchbacks zigzagged steeply out of the Tyne valley past a signpost drilled neatly with a pair of bullet holes, then plunged into an empty land of forests and sheep pastures.

The rain of the previous day had left the air as clear and brittle as glass, cut with chills and balmy hot spots. A public bridleway I would never have walked had I not been wedded to the meridian led me down to a glittering burn where the polished poles of beeches reached for the sun from a bed of dappled fern. Twenty minutes later I had my back to barbed wire as a bull with boulders for bollocks eyed me from the bridleway, wondering whether to toss me over the trees or tear up more turf.

For the final four kilometres to Derwent Reservoir there were no public rights of way, and so I was forced to resort to 'TT' – tactical trespassing. In this case, it meant passing through a plantation, then crossing Slaley Hall golf course and finally Espershields Farm, which overlooked the reservoir.

There were no security cameras at the imposing entrance to Slaley Hall, and so I dropped into line behind a Mercedes and a Ferrari and walked confidently through the landscaped entrance. Once inside, I'd planned to slip through the dead ground between greens and emerge 1,500 metres further south on the road by Espershields Farm. But curiosity took me to the bungalow that was the headquarters of the Slaley Hall security team.

'We had Tina Turner here,' one of them said. 'Called herself Miss Nash and took the whole third floor. Seven thousand five hundred pounds a night. And Ian Botham! He almost *lives* here.'

We opened the map and they showed me how to get through to the road.

Espershields Farm occupied a wide south-facing slope of a hill called Hairy Side that descended for nearly two kilometres to the shore of the reservoir. After Wolfershiel on the Simonsides, and Merry Shiels (*maer* is the Old English for boundary) which I'd passed the following morning, this was to be the most southern reminder on the meridian of our nomadic heritage. All three had been high: Wolfershiel at 140 metres; Merry Shiels at 199 metres and Espershields at 290 metres.

When I walked down to Espershields farmhouse, the last person Neville Stevenson wanted to meet was a hiker intent on trespass. Everything had gone wrong that day. Even the bull had escaped.

'Did you know,' I asked, 'that your farm lies right on two degrees of longitude?'

'Yes,' he said.

It wasn't the reply I'd expected. Nobody ever had the faintest idea what longitude they lived on. But Neville had a relative in Canada, and they had been comparing their respective latitudes and longitudes.

Derwent Reservoir   Stare at a map for long enough and it leaves a mental imprint that turns a first visit into a nostalgic reunion. That is what happened with Derwent Reservoir. I felt that I'd been there before.

When planning the walk months earlier on 1:250 000 scale maps, I'd imagined leaving Corbridge equipped with a variety of locally acquired buoyancy aids: lorry inner-tubes, plastic drinks bottles, expanded polystyrene packing chips, hot-water bottles, condoms; anything that could be inflated or floated. At the shore of the reservoir, I would bag up all the buoyancy aids in dustbin sacks, build them into the substructure of a raft made from dead wood scavenged from nearby forests, then wait for a favourable wind (or make a mast and sail) and float across to the southern shore.

The drawback to this plan was that it was life-threatening.

Later, when I examined the larger scale, 1:25 000 maps, I made an extraordinary discovery: 600 metres east of the meridian, on the northern shore of the reservoir, was a feature marked as 'Sailing Club'. It stood out on the map like a drink dispenser in a desert.

A phone call to the Northumbria Tourist Board produced the number of the Business Development and Marketing Officer at the Economic Development and Regeneration Unit of Derwentside

District Council, who put me in touch with the Honorary Member-ship Secretary of the Derwent Reservoir Sailing Club, who asked me to put my request in writing to the Council of Management for the sailing club, which resulted in a phone conversation with the officer in charge of the club's safety boat, a farmer called John Hull.

John told me on the phone that I could have a lift over the water so long as I arrived on a Wednesday afternoon, Friday afternoon, or at a weekend. 'On the other side of the reservoir it's barren,' he warned. 'Once you leave us you need food and water. Anything could happen.'

Life would indeed be different over the water, for the reservoir separated the woods and pastures of southern Northumberland, from the Pennines. For the next 190 kilometres the meridian took a roller-coaster ride against the grain of moor and dale.

As I came down the slope from Espershields I could see the belts of conifers wrapped around the footings of Ruffside Moor on the far shore. Somewhere over there was my father.

In Corbridge I'd telephoned Hol and learned that he was going to attempt a rendezvous with me on the meridian, an ambitious challenge since my progress down the line was so unpredictable. I was also unwilling to commit myself to anything that hinted of a schedule.

'Doesn't matter,' rationalized Hol. 'There are several places at the beginning of the Pennines where I can guess which route you'll take.'

He planned to identify the bottlenecks in the 2,000-metre cor-ridor, then choose one and wait for me to pass by.

The Sailing Club was deserted, the trailers empty on the slip. It was perfect sailing weather: under an aquamarine ceiling, a steady breeze pushed isosceles sails across a broad blue smile of water framed by the Pennines.

When the boats came in, John Hull joined me on the clubhouse balcony. He had grown up in Kip Hill; two rows of sixteen houses each. 'I had ambition,' he said. 'I wanted to go down the pits. Everybody did. We used to walk along the Black Path, the track past the pit heaps to the mine. It was automatic that you got a job in those days.'

John met Sylvia when he was sixteen. 'Sylvia's father was a miner. I was very happy. She had a lot more finesse than I ever thought I had; eating with a knife and fork, instead of fingers. She's one in a million. We've been married twenty-nine years.' They wanted to move to the Norfolk Broads.

As the wind dropped and the last boats were rolled on trailers up the slip, the clubhouse began to fill with families, singles, children, pensioners.

'There's no class here,' grinned John. 'You could be sitting in the bar next to a farm-worker or a heart surgeon. No one knows. It costs about £130 a year to keep a boat here and get twelve months' sailing; you couldn't get a season ticket to Newcastle United for that. A bus driver could keep a boat here.'

Buying a round, I found myself beside the club secretary, a biochemist called Bill who sailed a Laser ('Very exciting; very easy to capsize') and rode a Yamaha XJ600S motorbike. He worked at Newcastle's Royal Victoria Infirmary, and was trying to get a plaque erected to commemorate the infirmary's most famous laboratory technician, Ludwig Wittgenstein.

After the Chernobyl fire, the Rotary Club brought twenty-six Ukrainian children to the sailing club for the day. The local police took them for rides on their motorbikes, they sailed and in the evening there was a party with a spinnaker sail full of balloons.

'We'd had a sponsored sail to raise money and each child received at least ten presents,' remembered John. 'The water company gave them a Walkman each, the police gave them £5 each. When they left, they hugged me. Some of them were crying.'

When I pulled back the clubhouse curtains at dawn, rain was smearing the windows and the view was one of universal drabness; sky, water and hills had assumed tones beyond the end of the depressive spectrum; not colours at all, but degrees of lightlessness.

A long plastic bench by the bar had been my bed and the flicking of water drops on the glass in the night heightened the sense of stolen contentment; were it not for the bizarre chance that the largest body of fresh water blocking my route came equipped with a cooperative boat club on the appropriate shore, within 1,000 metres of the meridian, I'd have been lying in a wet sleeping-bag under a tree drafting raft designs.

Mike Collier had volunteered to sail me to the far shore. 'He's straight down the line,' John Hull had told me the night before. 'A true Geordie.'

'The thing with these boats,' said Mike, as we rolled his trailer down the slip, 'is that you must always remember to put in the bung.'

Mike took his sailing seriously and was concerned that the paint job he had planned for his Series II GP14 would add too much weight to the boat.

With my rucksack stowed by the centre board, we slid silently through the rain. On my knee I had my map in a plastic bag and beside it, the plastic card marking the buoys on the reservoir. I'd identified a possible landing place on the south shore, where a public bridleway emerged at a small bay; a tricky landfall because a headland projected to within 150 metres of 01 and the surrounding water was shallow.

We glided over the county line from Northumberland to Durham, then Mike pulled the tiller over and we tacked back towards Overwater buoy, turning quickly again to take two tight tacks into the bay. The crossing had lasted only ten minutes; in my home-made raft (I was going to use my boots as paddles if I could find nothing better) the voyage would have taken at least two hours and consumed prodigious quantities of adrenalin.

I slid off the foredeck into the water, shook hands with my ferryman and turned to the Pennines.

Ruffside Moor The compass pointed confidently upward through a forest of waist-high, waterlogged bracken, into seeping mist.

Higher up, heather and bog shifted in and out of focus through the unsteady lens of the cloud. Ruffside Moor's upper parts were undistinguished by any features that could be related to the map, so I was climbing on a timed bearing, changing course at the 340-metre contour and holding 180 degrees until I sensed the ground beginning to fall to Burnhope Burn.

As I dropped from the floor of the cloud, I saw a small red figure rising from the furred form of the dale below. I stopped and watched as the figure made height through the heather. It was Hol. 'Ah,' he called upward with a laugh, 'I estimated you'd be here by 1100 hours.' He pulled back the sleeve of his dripping jacket and peered at his wrist. 'Ten fifty-nine. One minute early!'

Hol had hitchhiked from Norwich to Derwent Reservoir the previous day. While I had been sunning myself on the balcony of the sailing club, my father had been making a reconnaissance of the landing places between 99 and 01, and identified the point at which I would probably come ashore. Knowing that I would take breakfast before sailing, he then guessed (correctly again) the course I would take over Ruffside Moor. Using figures he'd adapted from trials he'd run on Kinder Scout, which had demonstrated that a reasonably fit loaded man in no particular hurry can negotiate peat bogs of this kind at an average of 2.4kph, he'd estimated that I'd be crossing the 300-metre contour line on the south side of the moor at 1100 hours.

Estimating precise arrival times for making a rendezvous has always been a family game. My father and mother had once driven their twenty-year-old Land Rover to southern Greece via Yugoslavia, while I had ridden a bicycle via Italy. On that occasion the margin of error for making the rendezvous at the post office on the island of Levkás was greater than usual: thirteen minutes.

As we joined the road, Hol was already calculating when we'd reach Stanhope, on the far side of the next moor.

B6278   The B6278 shadowed the meridian over the moors towards Weardale, climbing to 476 metres at Edmondbyers Cross, where we trod through wet curtains of mist on a black strip glistening with runoff.

Hol's trousers were held up by seven metres of nylon cord, doubled back several times and then tied at the waist with a quick-release bow and a half-hitch.

'Why,' I wondered, 'don't you save weight by shortening the cord?'

'Ah,' said Hol. 'This is more than a belt. It's for hauling people from bogs.'

'Won't the cord break?'

'That is a possibility that cannot be ruled out. You wouldn't care to fall in a bog, would you, so that I can find out?'

Before leaving home, Hol had not had time to test the breaking-strain of the cord. Neither had he estimated how many seconds it took to pull the tail of the bow, unlock the half-hitch, withdraw the doubled-over cord from the seven belt loops in his trousers and throw one end of the cord to the sinking victim while holding the other end with the same hand that was preventing his unsupported trousers slipping to his ankles and interfering with his ability to probe for and select a stance on the lip of a life-threatening bog. The speed with which the prototype bog-belt could be released was further affected by being wound round in two places with strips of electrical insulating tape in order to keep the doubled-over strands from separating and digging into his waist. Since Hol carried no knife, he would have to borrow one – which might take some time on a remote moor.

'The belt,' conceded Hol, 'is still in the early stages of development. At present it's more of a *spur-of-the-moment* idea.'

The road dropped off the moor through an industrial necropolis, ghosted by mist and eerily still. By the road were the burial mounds of old footings, quarry scars, the banks of abandoned railways and reservoirs, loading docks and the brick mausoleums of engine sheds.

For a while we walked on the track-bed of the Weatherhill Incline, passing a stone post carved with the letters S & D R – the shorthand used by the world's first steam-worked public railway, the Stockton & Darlington.

The incline we were descending was once a part of the highest public railway in England; the 34-mile line from Weardale over the Durham moors to the mouth of the Tyne. In an episode that anticipated the trials of the Channel Tunnel link at the end of the following century, the original operating company – the Stanhope & Tyne Railway – found itself hamstrung by increasingly canny landowners who raised the stakes as the line progressed over the Durham moors. Wayleaves rose from a modest £35 per annum for a 1¾-mile stretch over Stanhope Fell to £300 per mile as the line closed on the Tyne. A farmer at Boldon charged £30 per annum for the line to cross a mere 66yds of his land. The engineering was a triumph: to drag the wagons up to the moor from Weardale, two inclined planes were built. A 50 horsepower Stephenson engine pulled two wagons at a time up the 1 in 12 and 1 in 8 Crawley incline out of Stanhope, and a second engine hauled the wagons up the 1 in 12 Weatherhill incline to the moor. An inventive combination of horses, engines, locomotives, sixty-eight miles of rope and gravity lifted wagons of lime, coal, lead and stone over the moors to the wharves on the Tyne. But the cost bled the Stanhope & Tyne Railway and in 1840 – eight years after construction began – the company folded with debts of £300,000. Within a year, the Stockton & Darlington Railway had the line running again.

The consulting engineer for the Stanhope & Tyne Railway had been the young Robert Stephenson. Through his early years, Robert had watched his father George co-invent with Davy the colliery safety lamp, construct a 6mph locomotive (which George called 'My Lord'), invent the blastpipe and begin work on the Stockton & Darlington mineral railway. Robert began work on the Stanhope & Tyne Railway three years after his father had hit the headlines with his 30mph locomotive, *Rocket*.

By the time George Stephenson died, twenty years later, Robert had emerged from the shadow of his famous father as an accomplished engineer and builder of bridges; among them the Royal

Border Bridge, beside whose elegant arches I'd walked at the top end of the meridian.

As I followed Hol's familiar back down the long railroad gradient into Weardale, the rain bore down upon the rumpled imprint of Robert Stephenson's ingenious dream. One of the last to use the line was a battery-powered car in 1925, conveying grouse guns up to the moor. The track was lifted in 1943 although the Crawley incline lasted until 1951. The original Weatherhill beam engine was replaced in 1919 and is now exhibited in the National Railway Museum, York.

Higher in the mist, I'd noticed the coded label 'C2C' painted on to the wet tarmac beside an arrow. Now I realized what it was: we'd just crossed the National Cycle Network's 'Sea to Sea' route. In a nod towards wheeled continuity, Sustrans had routed C2C along one of the disused mining lines.

Stanhope   Up on the moors we'd crossed a tribal border: in the capital of Weardale the boys were wearing the red-and-white of Sunderland rather than the black-and-white of Newcastle.

Stanhope's cobbles once clattered with iron-bound wheels and quarrymen's clogs; its air carried the smuts of steam trains and smelters; its men broke limestone at a shilling a ton with 16lb flat hammers; its eight-year-olds wore soldiers' cast-off red-coats in lead mines; its ore was cast into cannon-balls fired in Crimea; its paths were trodden by Bronze Age armourers, Roman boar-hunters and cattle-driving Scots.

'That'll be 95p thank you!' smiled the woman serving hot chocolate in the Durham Dales Centre, a glass and stone complex housing a tea-room, tourist information desk and a business centre with a conference room, desk-top publishing and all the backup required to achieve the Centre's stated aim of 'economic regeneration within the Durham Dales'.

Situated between the seductively sold Yorkshire Dales to the south and Hadrian's Wall to the north, Weardale has a problem hooking tourists. Further upstream there are a couple of mining museums, but the dale has no stupendous castles or cliffs or water-falls or dinosaur parks. Stanhope's main sights were a 300-million-year-old fossilized tree stump in the churchyard wall and an altar in the church, inscribed by a Roman prefect called Caius Tetius Micianus of the Sebosian wing, commemorating a giant boar he captured 2,000 years ago on Bollihope Common. Stanhope's best-known inhabitant was Bishop Joseph Butler (the author of *Analogy of Religion*), who doesn't have quite the pulling power of Herriot and the Brontës.

Stanhope's only chance to erect a brown heritage signpost slipped through its fingers over a century ago when a cave above the village yielded the Heathery Burn Hoard, a fantastic stash of Bronze Age metalware that had lain in the dark since a sudden flood inundated the valley and its occupants 3,000 years ago. Quarrymen hacking out a tramway shortly after the opening of the Stanhope & Tyne Railway in 1843 came across eight bronze rings and then, as the cave was eaten into over the following years, spearheads, socketed axes (and a mould for casting the axes), tongs, a gold armlet, a bronze cauldron and necklaces of teeth and shells which must have been worn by the spouses of the metal-workers. Six bronze cylinders which could have been nave-bands off wheels excited speculation that the cave contained the earliest evidence in Britain of a wheeled cart. The hoard was claimed by the British Museum, but over a century later, when the Dales Centre opened in 1991, staff made an exploratory enquiry about their treasure.

'We accept,' wrote back a curator from the Department of Pre-historic and Romano-British Antiquities, 'that the Heathery Burn find is extremely important for the Weardale region, as it is nationally.' The curator continued that the museum 'cannot contem-plate' a loan of any of the objects since they were either in permanent displays or were 'crucial research material'. The British Museum did however offer to sell the Dales Centre colour prints of the objects for £36.80 each, or black-and-white prints for £12.80 each. Plus post and packing. Plus VAT.

*

April and Dale Fawthrop were enjoying their second night behind the pumps at the Pack Horse Inn, and I was their first paying guest. They'd just bought a sixteen-year lease on the pub.

'As soon as I opened the door,' recalled April, 'it felt right.'

'If it does well and we make plenty of money,' added Dale, 'we may buy a pub of our own.'

Across the front of the Pack Horse they had hung a banner which read UNDER NEW MANAGEMENT.

April was thirty-two, Dale twenty-six. They had three daughters. Dale's father had been a publican over at Burnhope, but Dale, a bearded chunk of muscle wearing gold earrings and a gold neck-chain, had gone into hydro-demolition. 'It gives you such a lovely feeling,' he sighed. 'You can cut concrete. It'll chop you in half if you get in the way. There was a kid who had one go through his chest when the hose broke.'

His most interesting job had been jetting a waste-burning plant in the West Midlands. 'It's such a buzz to see things come clean. All the rust coming off.'

'What's it like working in a pub, after all that excitement?'

'I'm enjoying it,' Dale replied, adding wistfully: 'But there's a difference between pulling a beer pump and firing a water-hose at 12,000 pounds per square inch.'

To save money, and because he said he would get a better night's rest, Hol hitchhiked back over the moors to sleep at a youth hostel in Edmundbyers.

In the Pack Horse, April and Dale had booked the Orpheus Road Show. It was a Saturday night, and everyone old enough to rip a ring-pull rolled into Stanhope and spent the evening ricocheting between the Bonny Moor Hen and the Pack Horse disco. I hung on till late, waiting for the climax I'd once witnessed in a cowboy bar in Wyoming, when empties spun through the cheroot smoke and where enemies were sometimes hurled down the stairs. But nothing happened. Potential protagonists swayed away into the wet night, the Orpheus Road Show packed their deck and I drifted to sleep in my room above the bar while a solitary car spun its tyres round and round the Market Place, burning excess fuel.

Mary was cleaning the previous evening's debris from the bar as I ate my fried breakfast. 'She's three days older than the grass,' laughed Dale affectionately as he passed through the bar.

Mary had been born in Stanhope and was talking with Pat, who worked in the kitchen, about Eddie the Ghost.

'David, the previous landlord, saw Eddie go across the corridor and through the wall,' said Pat. 'And David had *never* seen anything before. Another time David was in the cellar and someone tapped him on the back.'

'What's Eddie look like?'

'Well,' said Pat. 'One day I'm working in the kitchen and there he was leaning on the doorway. Trousers. White shirt. Just stood there. When you turn to look again, there's nobody there.'

Mary chipped in: 'Clare heard three knocks on the wall once, and I heard someone coming up the stairs when the pub was empty. Another day the door opened and suddenly all the tea-bags fell on the floor.'

'Why's the Pack Horse so full of ghosts?'

'In the old days,' said Mary quietly, 'when they held public executions in the Market Place, this was where the executioner slept.'

At that moment, Hol appeared in the doorway with his ruck-sack and an envelope. 'I've been doing some work on calories,' he said, peering over his glasses at the envelope. It was covered with figures.

South of Weardale there were no settlements bigger than Stanhope until Skipton, ninety kilometres down the meridian. I was reluctant to bear the weight of more than a couple of days' food, since I was fairly sure that some of the dales villages hid post offices which might also stock groceries. As a fall-back I was prepared to knock on doors and negotiate a mutually acceptable price for any surplus food a householder might have lurking in a larder or anorak pocket.

Hol's approach to victualling has always been more expedition-ary. He calculates the probable number of days until the next resup-ply, multiplies that figure by the number of expeditioners involved, and multiplies the resultant sum by the daily calorific requirement. After that come several hours in a shop assessing the small-print on every packet and tin, then, accounting for net weights, energy conversion rates, carbohydrate/fat/protein ratios and price, he commits himself to a purchase. On the rare occasions that he has been deputized to shop for the family, he uses the same method of product selection.

For several years, Hol's winter climbing expeditions in Scotland were fed entirely on a substance called 'Protoveg' which he had found being wholesaled from a mysterious warehouse. Protoveg was soya disguised as dehydrated minced beef. In every aspect except taste, Protoveg was the perfect food: it was incredibly light-weight, it was fat free and one sack could feed ten people for a fortnight. For years we ate this stuff, while rotas of chefs tried increasingly extreme methods of altering its taste. We fried it, baked it, turned it into curry and porridge, made it into pancakes and dumplings; marinaded it in claret, seasoned it with herbs and tinned marmalade. But it always tasted like cardboard that had matured in a damp loft for a decade then been shredded and rehydrated in pond water. It was the soya experience that made everything I've eaten since register high on the scale of deliciousness.

Long Man   We left Stanhope too late in the day to reach Teesdale before dark.

Our way out of Weardale was an obstacle course of quarries, fields of cattle, barbed wire and in one place a re-routing of the public right of way where the path had slipped over a cliff. When we reached the moorland above the fields we found that the game-keeper had mown a path through the heather, all the way to Bolli-hope. I could have kissed him.

We struck Bollihope's valley in its mid-reaches, where the river switchbacked briskly under the road bridge. In thickening dusk, we

The walk began with wet feet and a rock climb up a cliff on the Northumberland coast.

The seventeenth-century stone bridge over the Tweed was on the meridian, which saved a swim. One week's walk to the south lay the River Tyne, and no bridge.

One of the few remaining teams of salmon fishermen working the mouth of the Tweed. After the net is hauled in by hand, the salmon are killed with sharp blows from wooden 'felling sticks'.

The mysterious 'cup and ring' marks carved at least 3,000 years ago on to an outcrop on Dod Law. Archaeologists regard them as religious symbols. Others have claimed them to be megalithic calendars, or the records of a tribal chief's sexual conquests, or messages from outer space.

A storm brewing over the Cheviots, which are scattered with Iron Age hill-forts and the Bronze Age burial cairns of cremated infants. Nearby, a young shepherd had hanged himself in a barn.

Shepherd Robin Mathewson, with his crook holstered, on the track to the remote Cheviot cottage that has been his home for forty-two years.

Farming the hard way, 350 metres above sea level on the edge of a windswept moor. Ken Allinson's 120 acres of grazing are the highest in this part of Teesdale.

Not a military prototype, but the customized quad bike that Northumbrian shepherd John Bradbury built from bits of a wrecked caravan. The box on the back carries his sheepdogs, Moss, Kylie and Bud.

To cross Derwent Reservoir, the largest body of fresh water blocking the meridian, I had made plans to build a raft. For emergency buoyancy, I carried an inflatable children's swimming ring. The hills on the far side mark the start of the Pennines.

My father Hol at the Ordnance Survey triangulation pillar on Hoove, whose bleak summit had to be located by compass. We slept that night under the stars in the bracken above Arkengarthdale.

The summit of Great Whernside and the highest point on the meridian.
Erection of this triangulation pillar in 1935 aroused intense local controversy.

Hol crossing the summit of Brown Haw, with Great Whernside at last appearing
above the horizon. Around his waist Hol wore a belt of nylon line which he
could unravel and use for rescues from bogs and disused mine shafts.

The limestone pavement above Wharfedale. Extraction for wall-building, garden rockeries and industry means that only 3 per cent of Britain's pavement remains intact.

Tony Schindler and his son John, across whose land I was trespassing when I met them on the edge of Barden Moor. Later, I encountered landowners who were less sympathetic. Tony's grandfather had emigrated to Yorkshire from the Swiss Alps.

Over 6,000 Ordnance Survey triangulation pillars project from the high points of Great Britain. When satellites made most of them redundant, their proposed demolition was greeted with such dismay that the OS offered individual pillars for 'adoption'.

Dropping off the end of the Pennines towards
Three Shires Head and the half-way point in the journey.

climbed a rib of moor which angled up above the turfed ruts and scoops of old quarries and mines to a steep-sided sike that drained the bogs on the northern slope of Long Man. Up here, on a bleak levelling just above the 400-metre contour, we lay down as the sky sucked the last of the light from the moors.

It was a bed with a view. Lying with the sleeping-bag up to my neck, and my head on my jacket, I could see headlights as small as insect eyes creeping across the moor twelve kilometres to the north, up by Edmundbyers Cross where we'd snacked on sardines in the mist during the wet walk from Derwent Reservoir. About 800 metres to the west of our bivouac was another road, and now and again a late commuter's headlights silently strobed the empty slopes. As I lay waiting for the next lights, I saw that Hol was out of his tent, standing with one arm outstretched and a single finger raised skyward. Then, like a crane with its boom at full extension, he raised four fingers and revolved slowly through ninety degrees.

'*Dad!* What are you *doing*?'

'Ah,' he replied. 'I'm confirming something I was thinking about last night. It's a method for estimating distance based on the thickness of a human finger.'

These are the formulae which Hol wrote in my notebook by torchlight on the side of Long Man:

If θ is in radians

$$\left.\begin{array}{l} \theta = \sin \theta \\ \\ \theta = \tan \theta \end{array}\right\} \text{ for very small angles}$$

If $\theta = 1° = \dfrac{1}{57.3}$ radians

$$\sin \theta = \frac{b}{a}$$

$$a = \frac{b}{\sin \theta} = \frac{b}{\theta} = b \times 57.3 \text{ (basic formula)}$$

At one kilometre

If $a = 1000$ metres, $b \times 57.3 = 1000$

$$\text{Therefore } b = \frac{1000}{57.3} \simeq 17$$

For a larger finger, e.g. Hol's,
         b = approx 25 metres
         4 fingers = approx 100 metres

'In simple terms,' he explained, 'the width of a human finger is such that, if held at an easy arm's length in front of the face, its two sides subtend an angle at the eye of almost exactly one degree, as do two points about seventeen metres apart at a distance of one kilometre.'

I tried to remember what 'subtend' meant as Hol continued, 'My fingers are a bit above average size, so for me a convenient rule of thumb is that one finger-thickness is twenty-five metres at a distance of one kilometre.'

Hol paused to take a sighting on the next headlights. 'I was holding my finger width beside a car on that road to calculate how far we are from it.'

'So what were you doing turning around with four fingers held up?'

'Checking that I was holding my hand the correct distance in front of my eye. When I've got the correct distance, sixteen four-finger-widths take me through ninety degrees.'

'Dad. Is this your idea?'

'Hardly. It can't be a coincidence that the word "degree" bears such a similarity to the word "digit".'

Episodes like this convince me that my dad is a genius.

Quizzical sheep stood in Long Man's wet heather.

Three metres away, there was no sign of movement from Hol's tent, a long, low ridge of nylon just big enough to accommodate one prone man and his luggage. The tent had been made to Hol's specifications for his most recent traverse of the Pyrenees and he'd designed it for minimal weight and optimal comfort. At its lower end, the tent tapered to a height of only fifty centimetres, just sufficient for a pair of feet in a down-filled sleeping-bag.

We ate breakfast by throwing a loaf back and forth between the two of us.

As I was pulling on my trousers the silhouette of a quad bike crossed the horizon and cut down the bog and heather.

'Gamekeeper,' I warned Hol, who was rolling up his tent.

The keeper brought the bike to a halt, but stayed astride his saddle with the engine running. Across the bike's rack was strapped a rifle case.

'Have you been lighting fires?' he accused.

He was concerned about the peat catching fire and smouldering underground. On the 12th, saboteurs had disrupted the first day's shooting over at Bowes and a Land Rover had been damaged. Gamekeepers up and down the Pennines were on full alert. We'd been spotted on Long Man just before dark, by another game-keeper passing down the road in his Land Rover. He'd phoned the keeper whose land we were on, and he'd set off at dawn to intercept us.

He was a good-natured man whose livelihood depended upon the success of twelve days' shooting a year. He wouldn't disclose who owned the estate ('Londoners. That's all I'll say'), and when I brought out my camera and asked if he would mind posing on the bike for a photograph, he yelped 'No no no!', gunned the engine, and quickly dwindled to a bouncing dot, leaving the tang of four-stroke hanging in the damp air and the impression that we'd just encountered another endangered species.

Teesdale   We climbed from the bivouac to the top of Long Man and saw the line of the Roman Road that ran over the moors from Weardale to Teesdale, a pale gap in the dark swell of heather eight kilometres to the south. After so many centuries, the road was still there, as straight and pale as a grass stalk.

We had trouble reaching the Roman Road. From afar, these moors looked smooth and rounded, but at close range they were horrible obstacle courses of ankle-turning heather and hidden holes. Also, I was having trouble with a leg. Six days earlier I'd dropped into a thigh-deep hole lined with rocks while climbing the Simonside Hills, and what had seemed a mere graze at the time had developed into a sharp pain and a swollen muscle. While I lagged and whinged, Hol (seventy the month before) was getting fitter and faster with every passing day.

Geography dealt us a joker that morning. Just as the Roman Road was about to dive into Teesdale, it crossed the 99 grid line and our way forward was blocked by the walls of Laverock Hall, so we had to climb back up to the moors on a detour that added another two kilometres of tiresome heather to the day.

The descent into Teesdale was painful but beautiful. As we came off the moor, the sun broke cover and caught the clouds of pollen kicked from the heather by our boots. Unlike the gloomy gulf of Weardale, Teesdale was wide and bathed in brilliant light, with gentle fields separated by pencilled walls and sprinkled with parkland trees. Diamonds sparkled on a distant reservoir, insects buzzed, butterflies tumbled.

By the time we reached the dams that had once held the water for the lead smelters along Blackton Beck, I was struggling to keep up with Hol.

Eggleston   It was Eggleston Fun Day and the villagers were selling jellies and running three-legged races on the playground of the derelict school.

Hol elected to sleep in his tent on the moor above the village. I checked into the Moorcock Inn where the publican ferried plastic carrier bags of ice-cubes to my room as I lay on the bed with a view up Teesdale to Great Dun Fell, thirty kilometres away on the crest of the Pennines.

Rainer Zacharias had grown up in the old Hanseatic port of Lübeck, on the neck of the Baltic, and had met his wife Heather on board the 35,000-ton *Olau Hollandia* sailing from Sheerness to Flushing. Rainer was purser; Heather was in charge of cleaning. They had bought the pub with their redundancy pay, but it wasn't until they moved in that they discovered that Eggleston was a 'dry' village. 'They're Methodist,' laughed the publican gamely. 'They don't drink.'

Mr Bainbridge, who ran the post office, was a Methodist and thought there were about fifty or so left in the village. Wesley himself had brought Methodism to the miners of Teesdale, and a chapel was built at the top of the green in 1828, over forty years before the village got a church.

A year after Wesley's death, Eggleston was visited by a man who despised most aspects of his changing world, from the destruction of the countryside by mining, smelting and mill-building, to evangelists and bad port. The Hon. John Byng was an opinionated ex-lieutenant colonel of the Foot Guards who was making a 'Grand Tour' of northern England. Although his journals are preoccupied with the twin obsessions of the eighteenth-century mounted traveller – stabling and the stomach – he seldom missed a chance to slander the 'lean unwashed artificer' of modern industry or to praise the 'clean, jolly husbandmen' in the fields. By the time he rode into Eggleston, he was already hydrophobic after fording the River Ure, and he found Teesdale a 'wild, bleak country, only inhabited by miners, or visited by grouse shooters'. What did inspire him was the taming of the moors. 'I observe, with pleasure,' he noted, 'the demolition of the heath by the progress of the plough up the hills.'

Byng's travels coincided with the most frenzied period of parliamentary enclosure; between 1760 and 1801 over 500 Acts of Enclosure converted three-quarters of a million acres (an area four times the size of the Yorkshire Dales National Park) of 'waste' into agricultural land as the demands of war pushed the field boundaries into increasingly marginal terrain.

In Eggleston, I was told of a farm close to the village that was rumoured to have no water or electricity. The farmer had been seen on the moor fetching water in a milk churn and smoke was said to ooze from the farmhouse roof because the chimney had collapsed.

In torrential rain, I found the place up by the moor. At 350 metres above sea level, it was the highest building in the neighbourhood and its sloping draughty fields could well have been the same plots that Byng had seen being cut from the heather 200 years earlier. The house looked a partial ruin and stood on the edge of a quagmire grazed by cows. The chimney appeared to have fallen through the roof. Dogs howled. Farm debris lay rotting in puddles; sileage oozed from a sagging barn.

From behind a shed a man appeared, wearing a stained jacket and a flat cap, unshaven, with a septic growth the size of a raspberry obscuring one eye. Unkempt hair sprouted from the cap. He was too suspicious to engage in more than a cursory exchange. He had, he said, 120 acres, 500 sheep and 40 'suckers': shorthorn crosses and other breeds. He agreed that his farm was high up, but said that the grass was good.

'Father bought it fifty summat years ago.'

'Have you got children? Who'll inherit the farm?'

He shook his head. 'Most people got more sense than to bother with farming.'

Today, Eggleston is well into its third age.

The village that began as Ecgel's Farm in the twelfth century, grew into an agricultural community strung along the banks of a stream that fell to the Tees. The industrial age began in the 1770s, when the London Lead Company built Teesdale's smelting works on Blackton Beck. Eggleston's population trebled to 800 over the next hundred years, then fell back to 300 when the lead industry died. Now it's a friendly, unimposing place, with its green, the post office and a grouse dependency.

'There was this Venezuelan,' I was told by a drinker in the Moorcock's bar. 'He flew by private jet to Teesside, then he hired a Range Rover to drive up Teesdale, shot 200 brace of grouse at £110 a brace then flew out the same evening.'

'We live on the grouse,' said another. 'The local economy depends on it.'

Once a year, the owner of Eggleston Moor threw a party at the Moorcock for his gamekeeper and beaters, with food and unlimited drink.

Eggleston was still getting used to its post-industrial age of commuters, retirees and 'incomers'.

'The village is changing,' said Debbie, a mother of three who worked at the Moorcock. 'There's more people coming in. But I can't complain. I'm an incomer myself, from Stoke-on-Trent. I love it here.' She paused. 'But I'm still learning. I found out about gossip when I was separating from my husband. What they can't find out, they make up.'

Romaldkirk After two nights at the Moorcock, I limped fifteen minutes south across the old county boundary of the Tees to Romaldkirk where I checked into a bed and breakfast whose most conspicuous residents were a kilted major and nine spitting llamas.

'They're disgusting!' grimaced Wendy Harper, who had inherited the animals with the property. The major came each September for the grouse-shooting.

'I was more harassed in this village by barking curs,' wrote the Hon. John Byng, 'than I ever remember.' He noted in his *Journals* that Romaldkirk was 'a goodish village with sash-windowed houses and a well-built church'.

The church had been reduced to services on three Sundays a month, with a congregation that couldn't match the thirty or forty who showed up at Eggleston's Holy Trinity, but it did have a functioning Sunday school which was sponsoring the education of a six-year-old boy in the Philippines. In St Romald's was hewn the history of Romaldkirk: Saxon footings, Norman chancel, fourteenth-century vestry, fifteenth-century tower, Italian inlaid floor, Victorian restoration, and a peculiar asymmetric window whose tracery didn't fit. Lying in one of the transepts, dressed in chain-mail and grasping his sword, was Hugh Fitz Henry, lord of Bedale, Ravensworth and Cotherstone, who died in Berwick-upon-Tweed fighting the Scots for Edward I.

In the churchyard were the shin-high gravestones of two boys, Richard Blogendon Watkins from Ramsgate, who died at winter's end in 1810, and Thomas East from Shoreham. They had been pupils at the school whose buildings still stand on the banks of the Tees outside Romaldkirk. Woden Croft was one of the notorious 'Yorkshire Schools', whose tales of Gothic cruelty ultimately led to their downfall. Malnourished and beaten, boys supplemented their headmasters' incomes by working on local farms. One of the boys who survived was Richard Cobden, who'd been sent north in 1814 when his father had to sell the family farm in Sussex, and who returned south to become a politician and the 'Apostle of Free Trade'. Later, Cobden wrote that he 'could never afterwards endure to speak' of his incarceration on the Tees.

While the rain poured down, I gave my leg another day off and pottered about Romaldkirk leaning geriatrically on my umbrella and getting a wet head. It was the only moment on the walk when I could have done with two umbrellas.

Where Eggleston – the County Durham lead-mining village – had stretched untidily up the moorside from the north bank of the Tees with its pair of pubs, shop and boisterous Fun Day, its close neighbour Romaldkirk – the old Yorkshire farming village – was clutched self-consciously and silently around a village green on the south bank.

Like Eggleston, Romaldkirk had spent the last century shrinking: down from five inns to two and reduced from a peak population of 380 in 1831, to around 150.

'We're mainly retired professionals who like to dust the green,' said Derrick Herdman, who used to teach music in Croydon. 'We've come here to get away from it all; there's no triple parking and in the evenings all you hear is the hoot of an owl.'

Romaldkirk's residents included the youngest man in the Foreign Office to be awarded the OBE; a Fellow of the Royal College of Organists, who had written a book about 'time and space'; and the son of a secret agent.

Hugh Becker had been cast from the mould of his father: blue eyes, fair hair, the classic triangulation of cheek and jaw. And the charm, of course. Above him, the cross of St George hung damply from the flagpole of Romaldkirk Hall.

Captain John Becker, British Military Intelligence, had been murdered in his Singapore office on 24 August 1948, four days before the birth of his son. John Becker worked as a rubber planter and then a merchant before the war, and his linguistic skills and passion for Thai and Malayan nationalism brought him to the attention of the British intelligence services. Like Lawrence of Arabia, he was a romantic patriot who won the respect and love of those whose struggles he supported. He dressed in native clothes and there were rumours of a child by a Thai princess. In 1941 Becker was masterminding a Thai uprising that would trigger an 'intervention' by British troops and thus disrupt Japanese invasion plans. As the Japanese forces gathered, Becker wrote a warning memorandum to General Percival, who – for unexplained reasons – destroyed it. In odd circumstances, Becker was arrested by the British and shipped out of Singapore four months before Percival surrendered the island to General Yamashita. But Becker wasn't able to forget the Far East, and when the war ended he returned to his old haunts, where Communism had become the new enemy. Shortly after meeting a Russian agent, he was shot by a deranged Chinaman whose motives and eventual fate have never been clarified.

'What you don't know, you don't miss,' concluded Hugh, of the father he had never met.

John Becker's passion for oppressed minorities had translated into his son's drive to reinvigorate rural Durham. Hugh's chairmanships included local training projects, tourism, economic development, conservation and fishing. The countryside, he said, perceives itself to be disadvantaged by the urban block vote; the only thing to unite a rural population was a common enemy, such as an intrusive planning application or an attack on blood sports.

'What d'you think of grouse-shooting?' I asked.

'It's a significant contribution to the economy.' He described how the sport propped up the accommodation industry and its suppliers. One of his wife's pubs, the Old Well Inn in Barnard Castle, ran a 'Meals in Fields' service for grouse parties; Romaldkirk's inn, the Rose and Crown, was full that night with visiting 'guns'. To Hugh Becker, the alternative to grouse-shooting was 'white maggots' and wind-farms; take away the grouse, and subsidized sheep would overgraze and erode the moors, and every skyline would be disfigured by the flailing arms of wind turbines.

The urban–rural divide, said Hugh, would broaden as soon as rural communities found a focus. 'I believe in setting a solution in motion and allowing it to evolve. Give an idea a life and it will grow.'

The bar of the Rose and Crown was a cross between a London gentleman's club and a traditional Pennine pub. Two stuffed grouse stood with horse brasses, a hunting horn and framed prints of the inn's early days.

To the tick of a grandfather clock, a group of guns spun yarns. One of them knew of a gun who'd just bagged 1,000 in four days.

'I'm absolutely tired,' complained another, with a central European accent. 'I've been shooting four days a week since the 12th.'

That, at a grand a day, was £12,000 for the privilege of hanging around in the wind and rain on a bleak moor.

At the bar the guns had turned to a subject that had been obsessing the letters page of the *Daily Telegraph*: hanging baskets.

Deep Dale   The following morning, Hol and I walked out of Romaldkirk on the Tees Rail Way, a leafy, level walkers' highway that snaked south along the track-bed of the railway line that once carried Eggleston's lead pigs down the dale to Barnard Castle. With most of Britain's branch lines, it closed in 1964 when Richard Beeching's axe fell.

The grassy track-bed curved past the hamlet of Hunderthwaite and over the River Balder on the slender legs of a viaduct. 'A good spot for rope-work,' we hypothesized before spotting a red warning sign erected by Durham County Council warning that climbing, abseiling and 'similar activities' were not permitted.

With the roofs of Cotherstone in view but out of bounds, and perilously close to 01, we spent twenty minutes making paced measurements and taking back bearings with the compass in order to locate an invisible public footpath. Hol's compass was somewhat superior to mine: a Silva Type 4/54 with a prism set into the bezel that allowed him to take a fix to within half a degree. Huffing with impatience while he pinpointed our location to the nearest blade of grass reminded me of mountaineering in Scotland and long waits in flying snow while he held a heavy brass prismatic compass to his eye. As soon as I was old enough to own a compass, he'd let me lead us in the wrong direction without correcting me. When I eventually realized my mistake and was absolutely lost, he'd made me work out where I'd gone wrong.

With the maps open on the grass, and reassured by a good fix on a distant radio mast, we eventually isolated the correct hedge and climbed into the fields that led to Crook Beck and the long high road over the moors to Bowes.

It was a wild walk, with squalls of wind and rain slashing out of the west between ray-bursts of sun. We could see the squalls from so far off that I had time to erect the umbrella and point it into each incoming cloud burst. Beside the road stretched undulating moor, a military firing range and bleak farms with names like Nova Scotia and Low Crag.

Directly ahead, blocking the meridian, rose the black wall of Scargill High Moor, the gateway to the Yorkshire Dales.

Bowes   Midway between Scotch Corner and Brough on the most important trans-Pennine route in northern England, this small, grey coach halt sits hunkered down on the bank of the Greta just below the 300-metre contour.

The Romans built a fort here, called Lavatris, which was robbed of its stone in 1170 to build a great castle which eventually lost much of *its* stone to the village houses. Nowadays the traffic has left the main street, and the sounds are those of the wind and the A66 whining over the roofs. It was a strange place, still functioning with a post office, shop and coaching inn, but isolated from its original reason for being at such a remote spot on the moors.

Charles Dickens had used Dotheboys Hall in Bowes for the

school ruled by the repugnant Wackford Squeers in *Nicholas Nickleby*. Like Woden Croft outside Romaldkirk, Dotheboys was one of the ghastly 'Yorkshire Schools' whose record of maltreatment gave Dickens the device he needed to send Nicholas and his fugitive friend – the dim-witted brutalized Smike – on the long odyssey that would end with Smike's death through consumption and Nicholas's marriage to Madeline.

Beyond the castle and Roman banks I found Dotheboys, still recognizable as 'a long, cold-looking house, one storey high, with a few straggling outbuildings behind'. The slate roof sagged a little now, but the wind still called like a sad phantom. The school closed soon after Dickens visited in 1838, and William Shaw, the headmaster of Shaw's Academy (as Dotheboys Hall was then known) and model for Wackford Squeers, lies buried in the churchyard of · St Giles, along with one of the boys who died at the school.

Standing before the wind-chilled stone of Dotheboys triggered a flashback to my own school, a boarding penitentiary converted from a Second World War USAAF hospital in bleakest Norfolk, where the White Lady showed up at midnight dormitory séances and a Luftwaffe officer was regularly seen with a scalpel stuck in one eye (the surgeon's elbow had been jogged by the German's Alsatian who thought that his injured master was about to be mutilated by a Britisher *Doktor*). The school came straight from the pages of *Nicholas Nickleby*. Discipline was in the hands of sixth-formers, who amused themselves by punishing the 'plebs'. Tortures ranged from simple crucifixions (suspending the victim by coat hooks beneath the armpits) to having one's head flushed down the lavatory (always a downer before breakfast). My defence was a manic grin which eventually convinced my tormentors that I was a waste of time. Revenge came at the end of the football season as the sixth-formers sat down at the television to enjoy the FA Cup Final. In a dormitory upstairs, my friend (whose father had worked during the war at Bletchley Park) and I plugged a clandestine TV jammer made from a doctored electric motor into the mains and fuzzed the screen as the players ran on to the pitch.

*

On the wall of one of the houses near Bowes post office was a flaked and faded 'Winged Wheel', the plate-sized emblem of the Cyclists' Touring Club that used to be awarded to the proprietors of bed and breakfasts whose service was judged to match the exacting standards of CTC members. Midway between industrial Teesside and the Lake District, Bowes was on the weekend run for the fleets of twinkling cycles bound for the mountains.

The CTC had given me – a geography graduate born a century too late to be an explorer – my first job. They put me to work designing a national network of cycling routes. I'd been riding a bike for nearly as many years as I'd been walking: riding to school, riding around the county boundary of Norfolk at fourteen, and then to Greece at nineteen, Africa at twenty. The bike had been my escape vehicle. At the CTC I met people who rode bicycles around the world; dragged them over the Sahara and through the swamps of Darien. A few of the CTC's 40,000 members were certifiably eccentric. I remember a retired RAF type rolling up one morning with a swordstick clipped to his handlebars, bound for Australia.

The Bicycle Touring Club (the name was soon changed to the Cyclists' Touring Club in order to accommodate the new fashion for tricycling) was born in Harrogate in 1878 with an annual subscription of half-a-crown and an optional uniform of dark green Devonshire serge jackets, knickerbockers and peaked Stanley helmets. The club's objectives were 'to promote touring by bicycle, to help tourists to secure companions, and to protect its members'. The CTC was the first touring club in the world. 'Bicyclists are become a power,' declared *The Times* later the same year. 'They have attained the speed of a horse.' Indeed, bicycles had *outstripped* the horse; within twelve months of the CTC being formed, the mile had been ridden in under three minutes while the record pedalled in one day had crept up to an incredible 250 miles. In 1884, the year that Thomas Stevens of Berkhamsted accomplished the first bicycle crossing of the USA, Gladstone took the view that 'physically, morally, and socially, the benefits cycling confers on the men of the present day are almost unbounded'. At the time, his First Lord of the Treasury, Arthur Balfour, was riding a bike to work.

In these early days, products flooded the market from the

cheap, conventional Mazeppa No. 2 to the sophisticated cross-framed Starley 'Psycho'. *Sturmey's Indispensable Handbook to the Safety Bicycle* of 1885 listed over sixty current models that had been named to appeal to every level of society, from Imperialists (Victoria, Regent, Empress, Club); to regionalists (Manchester, Northern, London); tearaways (Invincible, Xtraordinary, Challenge, Champion); technos (Rocket, Propeller, Pilot); anthropomorphs (Kangaroo, Antelope, Fox, Racoon) and tyros (Facile, Safety, Balance, Cogent). The wide range of prices – from £8 to £25 – encouraged the universality of the new craze. One decade later, in 1895, the cycle factories of England manufactured over 800,000 machines. In Russia, Leo Tolstoy noted in his diary that 'There is nothing wrong in enjoying oneself simply, like a boy.' The 67-year-old writer had just been given a bicycle by the Moscow Society of Velocipede Lovers. By 1899, CTC membership had mushroomed to 60,000.

Pioneering enthusiasts included Mark Twain ('Get a bicycle. You will not regret it if you live'), Hilaire Belloc, who went to France in 1889 as the cycling correspondent of the *Pall Mall Gazette*, and Jerome K. Jerome, who noted in *Humours of Cycling* (1897) that 'Every woman in London apparently is learning to ride the bicycle.'

Arnold Bennett was an enthusiast, and so were Henry James and George Gissing, who had been taught to ride by H. G. Wells.

Thomas Hardy criss-crossed Wessex on his bicycle and in 1898 took a tour with Kipling. Two years earlier, H. G. Wells had created fiction's first cycling hero, the 'generously, opulently' pedalling Mr Hoopdriver in *The Wheels of Chance*.

The ultimate getaway vehicle liberated and mobilized an entire generation. The bicycle hastened the passage of women down the road to sartorial emancipation by encouraging the switch from petticoats to long knickers. A bicycle was cheaper than grooms and stabling and it could be parked in small premises.

To the educated men of modest means who were pouring from the new schools and universities, the bicycle was adventurous, affordable and doubled the daily range of a horse. Daredevilry and spectacular crashes were the narrative of the road: Kipling and his wife crashed the tandem he called a 'devil's toast-rack' or the 'Hell-Spider' and in 1897 Renoir skidded in a puddle and broke his right arm, obliging him to paint with his left while his mother stood by with the turpentine and cloth. Balfour once appeared on the Treasury bench with his arm in a sling and a slipper on one foot.

Of the many celebrities from the golden age of pedalling none meant more to the Cyclists' Touring Club than their 621st member, George Bernard Shaw. Shaw, who reckoned bicycling 'a capital thing for a literary man', was particularly reckless. He learned the skill in 1895 at the age of thirty-nine: 'My God, the stiffness, the blisters, the bruises, the pains in every twisted muscle, the crashes against the chalk road that I have endured . . . But I shall come like gold from the furnace: I will not be beaten by that hellish machine.' Later that year he crashed into a ditch while riding in the dark without a lamp in Wales and lay for some time pinned by the bike watching the moon through the spokes. A fortnight later, he had such a colossal collision with Bertrand Russell that Russell's knicker-bockers were 'demolished' and his bike smashed while Shaw (according to Russell) 'was hurled through the air and landed on his back twenty feet from the place of the collision'. The following year Shaw wrote off his bike in a head-on collision with a horse. By 1897 he was writing, 'I have been taking my annual bicycle accident; and the left side of my face is temporarily obliterated . . .'

Within a year of this letter, bicycling suffered a catastrophic reversal of fortune. Instead of ruling the road, the bike was nudged into the gutter by the success of a new invention by Daimler Benz. For a while, bike and car ran neck-and-neck; in Surrey, the Chief Constable supplied his highway patrol with 125 Singer bicycles to overtake and apprehend motorists exceeding the 12mph limit.

But in 1908, George Bernard Shaw hung up his Stanley helmet and became a petrol-head. The golden age of self-drive, when bicycles spun star-cogged through a virtuous universe, was over.

Hoove For two days we hiked south over map squares littered with quarries, 'hushes', 'levels', shooting-boxes, butts and more ominous mantraps like shake holes, swallow holes, 'Shafts (dis)' and 'Mines (dis)'.

The artificial chequerboard of managed heather overlying the older industrial acne completed the picture of a wilderness that had been felled, burrowed and burned into patterns entirely removed from the original. Landforms seldom rose above knee-height, which gave the rare interruptions to the poxed contours a monumental presence. One of these was a lonely rock outcrop on the county boundary between Durham and Yorkshire, where a flat rock indented with a curious hollow and channel that might have been the eroded outline of a cup and ring, projected like a speaking platform over the moor. Above the Fryingpan Stone, on a vast and formless hill called Hoove (a name which may have derived from the Old English *hufe*, a hill shaped like a hood), one of the Ordnance Survey's pale triangulation pillars glowed above the bogs as if lit with a hidden light source.

Arkengarthdale   We slept in the bracken above Arkengarthdale and walked before breakfast down to Arkle Beck where sheep were being funnelled over a low stone bridge by a whistling farmer.

A public footpath by the coruscant stream led to a steep little wood that brought us to the back entrance of Scar House, where beaters and keepers were gathering for a shoot.

'The Duke of Norfolk's son,' someone said when I asked who was shooting.

'They're still in the house, having breakfast.' Eleven guns were expected.

More beaters arrived, until thirty or so had gathered, each bearing a stick with a white flag.

A man from Darlington parked a trailerload of Labradors for recovering the downed grouse.

'Enjoy it?' I asked one of the boys with the flags.

'S'great!' he said.

They were paid £20 a day.

Ten minutes down the valley, outside Langthwaite's village shop, we sat on a bench in the sun sucking Victoria plums. Langthwaite was barely big enough to be a village; a snuggle of stone cottages beside a tight little bridge. Without cars the village would have had a crooked charm, but every nook glinted with autoglass.

So rarely had I seen an English landscape unaffected by cars that I no longer had the imaginary muscle to see a village, or a bridge, or a pub, as a function of place rather than transit. Langthwaite's stone walls were no longer the rock-hard structures familiar to the lead-miners who spent a thousand years hacking at the bedding planes of Arkengarthdale, but the artificial backdrops for *All Creatures Great and Small*.

Cringley Hill We left Arkengarthdale on the old miners' track to Swaledale, climbing above the hamlet of Arkle Town to a precise little pass suspended airily between the two dales. It was an enchanting spot, rare in the moors for its angularity, and set below musical Cringley Hill.

Since leaving the Tees the meridian had penetrated Norse country, the crescent of Pennine upland that was colonized after Vikings from Ireland swarmed eastward over the moors and took York under Ragnall mac Bicloch in 919. The legacies of their back-door attack are the strings of Norse place names along the dales that they used as their lines of communication between Ireland and the frontline. So *dalr*, a valley, added to *garthr*, an enclosure, and *Arkil*, became Arkengarthdale, the valley where Arkil had his enclosure. Arkle Town is Arkil's farmstead. Langthwaite is a hybrid, adding the Old Norse for a clearing, *thveit*, on to *lang*, the Old English for long. Swaledale probably comes from the Old Norse *svirla*, which mutated into the Old English word *swillain*, to swirl. Arkengarthdale also gives us the part-Norse hamlet of Booze, the house on the curve (of the hill) and CB, the only place name in England that consists of initial letters, called after Oliver Cromwell's physician's grandson, Charles Bathurst, who bought the Manor of Arkengarthdale in 1656 and who would probably have passed into obscurity if his family had not taken the precaution of appending his abbreviated name to a huddle of houses they'd built to exploit the local lead mines.

We lay on the warm dry turf of the pass eating 'Bainbridge cakes' from Eggleston's post office while volleys of popping gunfire drifted across Mossy Thorn. Where Vikings once shepherded their flocks, a line of beaters was stretched over a kilometre of heather, flagging the grouse towards the spouting butts.

Swaledale   Below the sombre moors, Swaledale shone in tones of green that seemed to spill into the fecund air itself.

Sprinkled across the scalloped valley were toylike field barns, 'laithes', that had once stored hay and given cattle shelter through the winter. Like the cattle-barns of the Basque Country that are still in use today, those of the Yorkshire Dales evolved as an organic response to the rhythms of animal, man and season. By building the barns in hay meadows, the distance farmers had to move their crop was minimized. Twice a day during the winter, the farmer would walk from barn to barn feeding and milking his cattle, and spreading the dung on to the adjacent field. Inside the barns, the cattle were separated by 'boskins' of timber or stone and tethered to posts known as 'rudsters'. Slits or scaffolding-holes in the walls provided ventilation. With subsidies and agricultural mechanization after the Second World War, farmers abandoned their seventeenth-century barns for massive prefabricated sheds that sit along the dale floor like aircraft hangars.

A footpath dropped past a ruined barn to the floor of Swaledale and Scabba Wath Bridge, where we passed a signpost to Reeth and Grinton.

'I've seen that sign before,' laughed Hol, 'through the windscreen of an Auster.'

Fifty years earlier, he had been acting as an 'Air OP' in an artillery exercise and the army pilot (or 'driver' as the army called its flyers) had flown him from the airfield at Leeming, up the Great North Road to Catterick, where they had buzzed Richmond then turned left up Swaledale and lost their way.

'Let's read a signpost,' announced the driver, as the plane dived to the treetops. Earlier, the same driver had flown between a pair of 12-foot radio aerials projecting from the roofs of two army trucks.

East Bolton Moor   To bridge the moors between Swaledale and Wensleydale within the meridional corridor required an eleven-kilometre sequence of compass bearings that took us up the track-bed of a long gone narrow-gauge railway, along old miners' paths and grouse-shooting tracks to an interminable dogleg through bog and heather stippled with spoil heaps and disused shafts.

The shafts were difficult to spot.

'If you go into one, you stay in,' Hugh Becker had warned me in Romaldkirk. The risk to ramblers of dropping into the under-world was the reason that he saw little conflict between grouse-shooting and recreational walking.

Crossing Whitaside Moor, the grouse were lifting with klaxon calls, flying fast and low, jinking left and right in pairs, threes and fours, like dogfighting aeroplanes.

'It doesn't seem entirely fair on the grouse,' observed Hol as we peered over the lip of a butt built like a military bunker. 'All this ack-ack coming up at them. It's not as if they've got anything to hit back with.'

'Bombs?'

'Laser-guided bombs.'

'AWACS grouse.'

'Rapid-fire guano.'

'Stealth grouse.'

'Got it!' said Hol. 'What they need are *tweed-seeking missiles*.'

The spectacle of smouldering guns lurching from their butts wreathed in the vapour trails of *Lagopus lagopus* kept us occupied all the way up to the highest point on East Bolton Moor, where we could see for fifty kilometres over the Vale of York to the North York Moors and Roseberry Topping, the scarred rock that Norsemen knew as Othenesberg, Othin's Hill, the throne of the war god Odin. Roseberry Topping seemed an appropriately symbolic airbase from which grouse could launch their *reconquista*.

From East Bolton Moor, we could also see the truncated plateau of Pen Hill: 'Ther standithe the ruine of a Castlet or *pill*, in the top of an hill, and it is called Penhill,' wrote the sixteenth-century antiquarian John Leland of the Dales landmark that was to be one of the beacons lit for the Spanish Armada. Penhill flamed again to call dalesmen to Masham when Napoleon threatened invasion, and again for Queen Victoria's Jubilee.

From our own lookout at 565 metres, Pen Hill was dwarfed by the neighbouring black whaleback of Great Whernside. The loftiest summit in Yorkshire was also the highpoint of England's Meridian and the only instance of two degrees west breaking above the 2,000-foot threshold that separates a 'hill' from a protuberance that might almost be called a 'mountain'.

At the edge of Carperby Moor our track dropped through a dry valley beside Wegber Scar and passed an old quarryman's hut which looked suitable for a night's shelter.

I pushed open the stiff wooden door and squelched into the carcass of a sheep.

'Shall we sleep somewhere else?'

The sweet stench of decomposing meat stuck with us as if the wind itself had gone rotten.

Sheep, it seemed to me, didn't receive the rights of disposal afforded to larger animals; a sheep could be discreetly dumped in agricultural crannies that wouldn't take a cow or a horse. In Northumberland, I'd jumped over a wall to have a crap and landed on a dead sheep which had gone off like a rubber cushion.

Below the scar, the walled track we were following crossed one of the 'jagger roads' that were used by cattle drovers and the packmen who shipped coal, lead and corn across the high country before the floors of the dales were felled and drained. This one made its way past lonely field barns on the 500-metre-wide shelf on the northern wall of Wensleydale between Castle Bolton and Askrigg.

Just below the jagger road, where our track cut a hairpin down Ponderledge Scar, we unrolled our sleeping mats on a table-top of turf overlooking the dale. It was a glorious spot, but by the fall of dusk, dark clouds were piling.

An eerie wind blew down the scar beside our airy lawn, promising rain before dawn.

Some time beyond midnight, I sat up in the bivouac bag and gazed past the silent triangle of Hol's tent to the floor of Wensleydale, a black plain meagrely sprinkled with isolated lights.

Sleep came and went and then Hol was calling that it was raining and did I want to come into his tent? I couldn't get my whole body inside, and while Hol drifted back to sleep I lay waiting for dawn.

Sunrise arrived as a beautiful mandarin burst over the grey Vale of York. Less than a minute later it was snuffed out by a raincloud.

Hol woke from a nightmare: he'd been in his first vehicle, bought on a student grant in the 1950s when secondhand cars were rare and expensive. 'Dodo' was an old Morris van that was past its extinction date. Rain was falling, the windscreen wipers were not working, the battery was flat and the brakes were erratic. I was in the passenger seat with my cousin Jeremy, leaning from the window telling Hol which way to steer the van, which eventually left the road and rolled to a halt on a weighbridge.

'A true nightmare,' added Hol.

'What's the problem with weighbridges?' I wondered from my damp sleeping-bag.

'First, they're manned by officials who have an interest in the roadworthiness of vehicles. Second, a weighbridge is by definition absolutely level, and you can't bump-start a car on anything but a slope.'

Hol's nightmares fell into three categories: 1. being in mechanically unsound vehicles which might attract the attention of the police; 2. being back in the army; 3. being with my mother when the logic of his reasoning did not appeal to her.

'Which is worst?' I asked as we stuffed our wet gear into rucksacks.

Hol shuddered. 'The army.'

The rain was still falling as we splashed down the stone track to Carperby.

Aysgarth 'A Yorkshire Arcady', wrote Edmund Bogg.

The romantic biographer of England's uplands had already written three books about Wensleydale when *The Green Dale of Wensley* was published in 1909. Bogg's book included portraits of dalesmen Simon Scrope and Aaron Knaggs, and the longaeval local women, 106-year-old Betty Webster and Hannah Mason, who died aged 105 in 1812.

About Carperby Bogg was uncharacteristically mute. The village took its name from one of the Irish Norsemen, Cairpre, who built his farm here. Before Bogg's time it was an outpost of Quakerism and one of its residents had achieved local fame as a bird-stuffer whose victims included one of the last pairs of breeding merlins on Carperby Moor, trapped in 1884 by a gamekeeper called Cherry.

It was a Sunday morning, still early, and still raining. Hol and I passed through the village without seeing a soul. A footbridge by the old ford took us over the Ure into Aysgarth, where we turned from the weather into the George and Dragon Inn thinking of hot chocolate. In the bar a man on a stool was staring at a television.

As I shrugged off my sodden rucksack and jacket I caught snatches of a disembodied voice: '. . . tributes are pouring in . . . her great humanitarian work.'

'Someone's died,' I said to Hol, as he dumped his pack in the pub's porch.

'It's Princess Diana,' said the man on the stool. He looked accusingly at the screen. 'A car crash.' The ugliness was incomprehensible.

We took our hot drinks to a table, and one or two hours later I suggested to Hol that we stay the night in Aysgarth and hope for better weather.

Unconstrained by the meridian, Hol was able to use Aysgarth

youth hostel, which lay a few metres east of 01. On the village green, I found a bed and breakfast with a sign upstairs that read: BATHS 25P UNLESS YOU ARE STAYING AT LEAST 2 NIGHTS. In view of the tragedy, my bathing fee was waived.

Sheila and Wilson Jones spent the day at the TV.

They'd moved to the Dales from Sunderland in 1987 after Wilson lost his job as foreman engineer when the shipyard closed. He'd been in the yards for thirty-seven years.

'We came here and set up a b & b,' smiled Sheila, handing me a tray of tea and biscuits. Wilson rattled the coal fire with a poker. He'd been out in the rain and was still wearing his flat cap.

'Sunderland was known around the world for shipbuilding.' He'd worked at Austin & Pickersgill. 'I'm bitter about it. The Conservative government spent £26½ million refurbishing the yard and then it got pulled down. All the heavy industry's gone now. Shipbuilding, steel, coal. All gone. Everything's gone.'

Tom Dinsdale had gone too. He'd died three months earlier. Tom had been Aysgarth's village elder. He made walking sticks. Once he'd been at a fair up at Garsdale Head and Prince Charles had bought one of his thumb sticks. Tom had made a stick with a sheep's horn head for Sheila and Wilson's ruby wedding anniversary.

I'd just missed Ron and Wig too. Ron Tonstall had died a year earlier. Ron used to tell a story from the days when he worked at the army camp at Catterick. The buses used to collect the workers from Aysgarth, and one winter's day when the drifts were leaning against the walls, Ron saw a flat cap lying on the snow. 'Pull up!' he called to the driver. 'There's a new cap out there!' Ron jumped down on to the snow and, as he picked up the cap, a muffled voice yelled, 'D'you mind! I'm under 'ere on me bike!'

'And d'you know,' Ron used to say, 'I knew that man. He was Mr Prescott.'

William 'Wig' Metcalfe died the year before Ron, and like Ron, he knew everything there was to know about the village.

Ron and Wig had gone to the village school. It was now a

doctor's surgery. Wig used to talk of the days when the doctor held his surgery in the pub. Another local doctor, Will Pickles, became the first president of the Royal College of General Practitioners. According to Sheila, Dr Pickles died of gangrene in 1969.

All through that grey Sunday the rain hung from Aysgarth's roofs like a heavy shroud. The main street was deserted. Everyone was watching television, wide-eyed with remote-controlled grief. My scope for 'doing' Aysgarth was constrained by 01, which put the village's famous waterfalls out of bounds. Visiting Aysgarth without calling at the falls was like turning back twenty steps before the brink of the Grand Canyon. Everyone from Leland to Turner knew the falls. Dr Pococke, who led an expedition of Englishmen to Chamonix in 1741, compared Aysgarth Falls to the cataracts of Egypt; the Hon. John Byng, my eccentric companion in Teesdale, thought the falls 'delicious'.

The village must once have been lovely. The Vikings who named it 'enclosure among the rocks' would have known a Scandinavian torrent that dashed through stands of woodland. Now the village sits ordinarily along the verges of the A684 500 metres upstream of the falls, insufficiently gorgeous to have been overrun by second-homers and therefore still functioning as a community. Between the end of the tourist season and the beginning of lambing in March, the Village Institute runs evening classes, badminton and whist drives and the George and Dragon competes at darts, dominoes and quoits in the Wensleydale pub leagues. Nigel, the landlord, holds parties through the year and his Christmas dinner was already fully booked. The previous Mothering Sunday he had given each of his women customers a box of chocolates.

The village depended on traffic crossing the Pennines between the A1 and M6 and on tourists breaking their journey on the long drive to Scotland. Each September, Sheila and Wilson put up farmers driving their one-year-old sheep in triple-decker trucks to the 'gimmer' sales at Hawes.

*

From a phone box in the rain, I learned from my mother, who is a retired physiotherapist, that I'd damaged my *extensor digitorum longus* and that it would heal quicker if I took shorter strides.

Bishopdale Starting the day with a 'Full English Breakfast' is like setting off on holiday in the family car: the tank's full of juice, everything in sight has been packed in, the bodywork's bursting at the seams, and there will be catastrophe before lunch.

The FEB that Sheila laid beside the muttering coal fire in the morning included thick-sliced bacon from West Burton, sausages from Hawes, tomatoes, eggs and fried bread. Then toast, butter and marmalade. Powered by this slow-burning grease feast, I climbed with Hol out of Wensleydale through weeping cloud to Bishopdale and its capital Thoralby, a straggle of stone houses on a T-junction first settled by a Norseman called Thorald who'd hacked out a farm on the dale's fertile alluvium.

Bishopdale was once filled with the icy water of a vast glacial lake whose sediments sank and formed a rich, level bed of silt. Long after Thorald's time, the dale became the hunting preserve of Middleham Castle – the lair of Warwick the Kingmaker and a bolt-hole of Richard III. After that, the yeoman farmers moved in to make good livings and build fine stone houses. Reminders of those times are still chiselled into Thoralby's lintels; above one door is the date 1653.

Thoralby clung to other relics from its past: the pinfold still stood, a ragged stone pen that was once the livestock pound before enclosures gobbled up the common land. The Methodist chapel – dated 1889 – was in good repair and so was the village's Sir Giles Gilbert Scott phone box. There was a pub, the George Inn, and a post office run by Elaine Miller, who'd taken over from George Sadler after his thirty-six years' service.

Elaine's post office was also an off-licence, a mountainbike hire centre, a grocery, a newsagent and a drop-in centre, providing anything from nappies to postcards, eggs, pensions, cigarettes and the *Daily Telegraph*. To the village's population of around 200, she could add the inhabitants of neighbouring Newbiggin, which had no shop, and those of Bishopdale. She was open seven days a week, from 7 a.m. to 6 p.m.

'I enjoy it,' she laughed. 'I always wanted to work for myself.'

On Tuesdays a bus bound for the weekly market at Hawes called, and on Fridays there was a bus to the market at Leyburn.

Newbiggin was a ten-minute walk south over Bishopdale Beck.

Unlikely Thoralby, which was on the through-route from Wensleydale to Wharfedale, Newbiggin was on a road to nowhere but itself. The bed and breakfast was for sale and the gentrified cottages silent. On a trailer labelled 'D. Hawkins – Shearing & Shepherding', a spray-paint poet had added 'Billy Bollock Chops'.

Swallows were gathering on the wires. It was the first day of September.

Wasset Fell From Newbiggin we climbed again in bright rain through hoof-sockets of mud to the crest of Wasset Fell and stepped into a vast, dripping plantation floored with a soft, rusty bed of pine needles.

We emerged as if from the leaking hold of a sinking ship and slithered in flooded ruts down to the mid-reaches of Waldendale where grey farms hunched amid the drystone walls in the bed of the rain-smudged valley.

Waldendale At Hill Top Farm we called for water. Pat Globe was at home with her two children, two cats, dog, goldfish, eight sheep and two hamsters, Otis and Horace. They had moved to Waldendale five years earlier, from Keighley. Pat and her husband Rob, a general sales manager for a company in Knaresborough that made plastic bearings, had been looking for a place in Cumbria, and came upon the dale by chance. The house had twelve acres and a barn which had been adapted by the previous owner to sleep eighteen indoor campers. Regulars included a school from Bradford and a troupe of lady clog-dancers from Halifax who came twice a year to rest after the performing season.

The big warm kitchen had quarry tiles and a stone fireplace. We sat cuddling mugs while the rain lashed ineffectually against the window.

Rob drove eighty kilometres to work in the morning and eighty kilometres back in the evening. 'You accept that whatever you do, you drive,' shrugged Pat.

'There's a little shop and a butcher in West Burton. Usually I do one big shop in Northallerton, once a fortnight. Then I stock up in October and November for the winter. The road's always clear because the milk tanker comes every day. One of the farmers on the other side of the dale has a snow-plough contract.'

'How did the dale take to you, as incomers?'

'They're all on your side. Ready to help out. There's no hostility. We didn't have difficulty as incomers, though we trod carefully. The local farmer dips and shears our sheep, and in return he sometimes comes and asks if he can plug in his welding kit or whatever; it's barter really. It's funny; when you move into a place like Waldendale, everyone instantly knows you're here. They know what time your husband goes to work. Having children makes it easier, it gets you introduced to the community.

'It might be harder for the children when they're older. The village hall committee makes a big effort, with barn dances, plays, dominoes, bowls, discos, and on May Day and Harvest Festival. At the moment the hall's burned down. An electrical fault. But they're rebuilding it.'

Rachael was nine, Thomas seven. During term time they were taken down by school taxi to the Church of England school in West Burton. There were forty-seven pupils at the school.

'There's a chap in the village who's a potter and he does clay work with the children. The children also have pen friends in a big city school in Hull, which shows them the wider world. Living in the country needn't hold you back. The three sons who lived in this house before us did well: one stayed to farm, the second is an architect in London and the third is a high-flyer with NASA.'

'D'you miss the town?'

'I don't think we regret leaving it, though sometimes when you run out of something you think it would be nice just to nip out. But on a cold winter's day, when there's an indigo sky outside, we get all the coal fires going and it's popping hot and we turn out the lights and put a match to the candles and it's wonderful.'

Great Whernside The cloud had lifted while we'd been drinking tea in Pat Globe's kitchen and the wet forest we'd walked through that morning was now a distant square of bright velvet. Field barns littered the dale like blocks of rock left by the Ice Age.

There were no paths between Waldendale and Coverdale.

Above the last drystone wall we climbed a round moor called Brown Haw while RAF fighters ripped strips from the sky. From the top of Brown Haw, Great Whernside – the apex of two degrees west – was suddenly close, bathed in inexplicable sunlight. So we came off the moor at a gallop, through sucking bog and tussocks the size of urchins' heads, down into Coverdale – our fourth dale of the day – to wade the river where a brown spout of water thundered from a tight chasm.

Whernside's long ridge rose southward, into the dusk and then darkness. As we climbed, the night sky filled with stars and then electric lights, set in an arc of shivering constellations from the north-east to the south: Darlington, Northallerton, Thirsk, Ripon, York, Knaresborough, Harrogate, Leeds, Bradford, Keighley and – straight down the meridian – the glow of Skipton. The other arc, where the Pennines and Bowland Forest formed a light-absorbent wall, was absolutely dark.

We slept up here, where two degrees west touched the sky.

We woke on an island in the clouds.

Silvery waves lapped at the sunlit grass below our bivouac site. A pair of military jets wheeled overhead and as the bog squelched beneath my elbow I thought of the pilots peeling off flying-suits and tucking into volcanic breakfasts.

'Bread?' called Hol, tossing a damp loaf across from his tent.

The lie-in was a mistake because our idyllic atoll was over-whelmed before we'd packed the rucksacks. Great Whernside slowly sank from sight.

In shifting vapours we climbed to a trig pillar and a monumen-tal cairn, humped like a Bronze Age barrow.

Cairn and pillar were uncomfortable companions: when Martin Hotine – now a major – dispatched his Ordnance Survey triangula-tion team to Yorkshire in 1935, the locals got wind of an imminent desecration. The OS insisted that the cairn be removed because its location on the highest point of Great Whernside was precisely where they needed to build the trig pillar. Inspired by the outrage of Yorkshire novelist, Mr C. J. Cutliffe-Hyne, the *Telegraph and Argus* ran the headline 'Indignation of Dales Dwellers', followed by the sub-head 'Stone-age Link Removed – And Replaced by Concrete Pillar'. Removal of cairns, the article claimed, would sever Yorkshire's link with its primitive past. Cutliffe-Hyne's protestation that the Dales would be disfigured by 'concrete Cleo-patra's Needles' was supported by the Court of the Manor of Kettlewell, of which he was chairman. 'We do not want spikes on top of our hills,' wrote the lords of the manor to the Ordnance Survey, suggesting instead that the surveyors cut a 'wedge' like a slice of cake from the cairn, then carefully insert their pillar and replace the wedge. Deferentially, the OS replied that their records suggested that the cairn was not Stone Age, but had been built in 1840 by the Ordnance Survey to protect the centre-mark that they'd cut into the underlying bedrock during their original triangulation. In a classic English compromise, the Ordnance Survey dismantled the cairn, erected their concrete trig pillar, then rebuilt the cairn a few feet distant.

Great Whernside's Cleopatran needle was the central of the three First Order pillars on the meridian. A fortnight earlier on Tosson Hill, I'd lost sight of the North Sea; in a month or more to the south the third of the trio would reveal the sea again.

With the compass set on 198°, we found the fence line dropping to Sweet Hill, where a change of bearing to 172° took us down through the cloud.

Several sharp explosions split the mist.

The butts were on the map. I'd ignored them. Guns would not be up in the mist before breakfast, surely?

We swerved to the right out of range, and I swivelled the compass bezel through ninety degrees so that we could track our new course, a two-kilometre detour through bogs and heather, out of the floor of the cloud, to the long drystone wall that ran along the upper limit of Wharfedale's fields.

Capplestone Gate, from the Norse words *kappall* and *stein*, the stony place where horses gather, was marked now by another OS triangulation pillar, and here our path hurdled the wall and dropped as the 'Conistone Turf Road' into an upland garden.

Conistone Old Pasture Snow-white rock shone above rich green grass that might have been trimmed with scissors. Here was the landscape compared by Auden to faultless love.

Formed when warm oceans teemed with primitive creatures, then compressed, lifted and scraped by ice, 300-million-year-old limestone now lay beneath the open sky like the bleached skeletal fragments of mythical giants.

Limestone has formed the continent's most spectacular ranges, like Spain's Picos de Europa and the Alpine Dolomites where fanged massifs are riddled with caves and fraught with cliffs. Rivers run underground. England's limestone is different, and deals in the subtleties of evocation rather than magnificence of scale. Neatly, the meridian began and ended on limestone, for Berwick and Purbeck shared the same rock, and so did the Cotswolds.

The Conistone Turf Road pivoted downhill around wall corners and past a ruined kiln, as tall as two men, where farmers once burned limestone between layers of coal, then raked the lime from the 'eye' of the kiln on to carts which would be tipped on to their fields to improve the grass.

Beyond the kiln the path ducked through a slot in a scar whose upper surface had been bevelled by ice into a limestone 'pavement', flat to the eye from a low perspective but a nightmarish crevasse-field when peered at from above, the great blocks or 'clints' separated by knee-deep fissures or 'grikes'. It is a devil's pavement; to run across grikes would be to break both legs in the first stride.

A few stunted trees rose from the pavement, their roots miraculously finding succour in a pocket of captured soil. The grikes hide a world of secretive species, from the minute Whorl snail to rare butterflies like the High Brown and Pearl-bordered Fritillaries, and tiny birds such as the wheatear and *Troglodytes troglodytes* – the foraging wren. Deep in the grikes on thimblefuls of moist soil lurked alpine cinquefoil and mountain melick.

So much colour and form, after days of interminable moors, told of a welcome transition.

We ate a picnic lunch by the pavement. Sardines.

The pavement had been 'notified' by the Nature Conservancy Council and the Countryside Commission under Section 34 of the Wildlife and Countryside Act 1981. It was also subject to a proposed Limestone Protection Order, and protected under the European Habitats and Species Directive 1992. Further protection came from its inclusion in a Site of Special Scientific Interest. In concert with this statutory protection, a body called the Limestone Pavement Action Group had joined forces with the Biodiversity Working Group, who were acting on the Costed Habitat Action Plan which arose from Volume II of the UK Biodiversity Action Plan (Government Steering Group Report). This stupendous bureaucratic armour-cladding had been caused by centuries of limestone exploitation, from agricultural lime-burners to gardeners who like to buy bits of limestone pavement for their rockeries.

If we are to believe the figures, only 2,600 hectares of Britain's limestone pavement remain, and only 3 per cent is undamaged.

Wharfedale We left this precious fragment of paradise on a section of the Dales Way, a 135-kilometre walking route from the Lake District to Ilkley. For the first time I found myself queuing at a stile and sharing a path with ramblers equipped with swinging map cases and no-nonsense knees.

For three kilometres we lost height into Wharfedale. Not since the Cheviots had the meridian crossed a landscape bearing relics of such continuous occupation.

About 10,000 BC, when the ice finally eased its grip on the dales, the tundra took root and grazing reindeer and wolves moved up from the south during the short summers. Mesolithic hunter-gatherers followed, living off the land as aborigines, leaving their harpoons in caves. For a while, between the growth of the forests and the arrival of Neolithic colonists, environmentally sound Meso-lithic man ate what he needed and left what he didn't. Around 4,000 BC the desecrators showed up, hacking down the forests of oak, ash and hazel that covered the dale's slopes and ploughing the better soils until erosion forced the pioneers to move on. Some of the limestone pavements that are now regarded as priceless examples of natural wonder are bedrock exposed by intensive Neolithic ploughing. By the Bronze Age, about 1,000 BC, most of the trees around Wharfedale had gone. Today, less than 1.5 per cent of the dales has the coverage of broad-leaved woodland.

The activities of the last 3,000 years lay thick on the ground each side of our path as it sloped down towards Grassington. We passed the walls of a group of Romano-British farmsteads and a great cairn that was rifled in the 1890s for its bronze. Later Iron Age burials had also been found at the cairn.

Lead workings lay by the path, and the high stone walls built after the parliamentary enclosures of 1792. They were long, thin fields tapering towards the village so that each owner had a share of better and worse grazing.

Off to our left were the ribs of field borders dug by the Romano-British farmers for their cereals, and a cairn where in 1892 the Reverend Harker had found five human skeletons, flint spearheads and a pottery vessel not dissimilar to the one that came out of Turf Knowe at the top end of the meridian.

The slope from the foot of Great Whernside down to Wharfe-dale was a mass of scar tissue: tombs, walls, farms, kilns, tracks, ridge and furrow, grouse butts, shafts, cairns, tips and, beside the end of our track, the imprint of an entire medieval village. Yet to many this is an intact landscape, unspoiled by human interference and invested with the qualities of a wilderness. Which is an understandable view from the suburbs of Bradford or Burnley.

To Bradford-born J. B. Priestley, Wharfedale was a golden Arcadia. In his classic, *English Journey*, described by its subtitle as a 'rambling but truthful account of what one man saw and heard and felt and thought during a journey through England during the autumn of the year 1933', the playwright, novelist and critic made a return pilgrimage up the valley after a reunion in Bradford with survivors of the platoon he'd served with in the trenches.

'The trees dripped gold,' he eulogized. 'If we had been ten years in a dark cell and newly released, we would not have stared at a world that seemed more extravagantly but exquisitely dyed.'

Grassington   The only mainstream tourist centre on the meridian was set around a sloping cobbled square five minutes' walk from the Wharfe. The previous month, August, 26,000 had passed through the National Park and Tourist Information Centre, overwhelming Grassington's population of 1,300.

Having been granted a charter for a market and fair in 1282, Grassington is technically a town. For me it was a metropolis. I hadn't seen so many shops since Wooler. Grassington had everything from tea-rooms and delicatessens, to a supermarket and a hiking shop.

Unfortunately I had no money.

The last bank I'd passed on the meridian had been in Berwick-upon-Tweed and the stash of cash in my pocket had finally run out. There were two banks in Grassington but I had an account at neither, and, despite pleadings and a fan of plastic cards, there was no method of extracting money from either bank without paying an outrageous fee.

'What about the Spar supermarket?' suggested Hol after I'd wasted an hour. 'Cash back.'

It cost nothing, took sixty seconds and got me fifty quid. Something odd was happening with merchandizing: much of my food on the meridian had come from petrol stations and post offices and now I'd found a supermarket better equipped to dish out cash than a bank.

'Grassington was at its best ten years ago,' said the man selling stationery and maps from a shop above the Square. 'There's too many visitor-type shops now.'

David Helm had been Grassington's postmaster until he reached sixty.

'People used to come to Grassington to shop. Now they go to the supermarkets in Skipton.' David said that half of his custom came from visitors. 'We couldn't survive on locals alone. For fifteen weeks in winter this shop runs at a loss.'

A few steps up the hill, Sandra Jenkins was closing her hardware shop. 'It's the recession, and the coal mines closing, a general lack of trade. And my husband's seriously ill. It'll be the end of Grassington having a hardware store.'

Sandra came from Barnsley, and her husband from Surrey. To locals they had once been 'offcumdens', incomers. 'We're not offcumdens now,' laughed Sandra. 'We've been here seven years. We've been accepted. There's a lovely community spirit here.'

Indeed there was. Grassington was one of those places that welcomes a stranger on a mission. After a few hours, I had a list of local names and phone numbers that would have kept me busy for a month.

One of the names which kept cropping up was Chris Baker. He lived with his Breton wife Jacquie and her daughter in a cottage that had been converted from a seventeenth-century barn near the end of the cobbled street known as Chamber End Fold. Born in Bradford, Chris was the managing director of a small family company that made most of the country's uniforms and billiard-table cloth.

'If you live in this village,' said Chris, showing me to an armchair, 'there's so much going on that you can be out every night of the week, whether you're a ten-year-old Brownie or a 65-year-old third-ager.'

A genial giant, Chris was a churchwarden and chorister at St Michael and All Angels, and had been chairman or secretary of the Wharfedale Rugby Union Football Club for forty-four years.

The club was in Division Three of the Jewson's League.

'We play all over the country,' chuckled Chris. 'It's amazing. Flying to Redruth, Exeter, Southampton. Incredible. Not like it was. There never used to be enough people in the dale to put together a team. We'd be waiting for the Skipton bus to see who could wear a pair of shorts.'

Chris Baker was also the chairman and controller of the Upper Wharfedale Fell Rescue Association. He'd been involved in the Mossdale Caverns call-out of 24 June 1967.

Britain's worst caving accident drew over 200 rescuers up to the moor to work day and night in appalling conditions. The call-out had come at 11.10 p.m. on the Saturday night after a day of torrential rain, and within an hour the rescue team were racing through the darkness towards the remote cliff six kilometres north of Grassington. At 1.15 a.m. they arrived at the cliff and found the cave entrance under a metre of water. Frantic efforts were made to divert the water and by 2.25 a.m. they managed to penetrate the first section of the cave.

'The rescue went on for six days,' said Chris, 'until it was decided that no one could be got out. Not even the bodies. Six of them, there were, drowned by floodwater.'

Mossdale was the most tragic call-out the team had faced. Typically they could expect ten to twenty incidents a year, ranging from lambs down shake holes to overdue cavers and people dropping down lead mines.

The rewards could be unexpected. 'I was watching the Cup Final,' remembered Chris, 'and I got a call that a fisherman had broken a leg up near Buckden and had to be carried off. Well, I missed the end of that match but after we got him down the guy fished in his back pocket and pulled out a tenner and said, "This is what I was going to spend in the pub. You'd better spend it."'

He showed me the annual report for the previous year. It

had been a quiet twelve months: two lambs down a pothole at Yockenthwaite; a body to recover from the Wharfe, and another from a pool at Buckden; several stretcher rescues off the moors and a call to Ilkley Moor to search for a man lost in a blizzard.

On page 3 the chairman updated the association's history:

'48 years on we have attended 587 operations involving 629 Males, 113 Females, 3 Horses, 74 Cows, 6 Calves, 402 Sheep, 149 Lambs, 23 Dogs, 2 Cats, 3 Goats & 17 miscellaneous calls including 1 Bloody Parrot.'

The Upper Wharfedale Museum occupied two eighteenth-century miners' cottages overlooking the Square. Inside, were intimate, bizarre artefacts that would never win gallery space in larger museums: a box of human gallstones, an iron dibble (for making holes in fields for planting), two halberds taken to the Battle of Flodden, castrating tools, a teacup with a special lip on the inside to prevent the drinker's moustache dipping in the tea, the Kalee carbon-arc film projector which stood in Grassington Town Hall, a peat barrow, ration books, a glass nasal douche and sixteenth-century hunting horns once used by the foresters of the Langstrothdale Chase. An enema syringe.

Hol stayed in the museum for the rest of the day, then went to the home of a retired physicist he'd met. The physicist had worked on Concorde's flight trials. I settled down in a tea shop with the newspapers and learned that a couple in Punjab had named their daughter Diana and that the Buckingham Palace website had recorded 4 million hits since its obituary on Sunday. Scotland Yard were expecting 1 million mourners to fill London in three days' time.

Linton   We stayed two nights, not in Grassington, but in its twin village, Linton, on the other bank of the river.

The two villages occupy either end of a glacial moraine that reaches across the dale and which is cut in half by the Wharfe.

Grassington, 'The farm among the pastures', has the tourists and shops; Linton, 'The farm where flax is grown', has the youth hostel.

Youth hostels are cheap but you have to sleep in dormitories with strangers. After lights out the darkness fills with alarming glottal gurgles and whistling exhalations. In foreign youth hostels (and climbing huts, which are far worse), dormitory windows are kept tightly closed to prevent any ingress of fresh air. If you creep from your bed and slyly open the window, a figure throws itself across the dorm and scrabbles to shut it. I have spent nights in perpetual motion, opening windows. Because hot fumes rise, it is essential to sleep on a bottom bunk. At Linton, I slept beside a cyclist from Rhyl who spent the nights making bicycle-pump noises with his nose.

The hostel occupied a seventeenth-century rectory just off Linton village green, a verdant rectangle with a little stream crossed by a packhorse bridge, a clapper bridge, a road bridge, stepping stones and a ford. In 1949 Linton was elected winner of the 'loveliest village in the north' contest by the readers of the *News Chronicle*, who erected a commemorative stone column with a tilted globe on the green in front of Fountaine's Hospital, a set of extravagantly baroque almshouses built by the man who was the timber merchant to the architect of Castle Howard, Sir John Vanbrugh.

The parish church for Grassington and Linton lay midway between the two villages, on the river bank. St Michael and All Angels squats with its stubby bell tower wrapped on three sides by the tightest bend in this section of the Wharfe.

There are those who think that the serpent's strangling coil about the church is Ruskin's 'divine hieroglyph of the demoniac power of the earth'. The symbolism of the serpent in heathen worship, and the practice of using dedications to St Michael for churches that occupied old pagan sites on low-lying ground, has led to speculation that Wharfedale's pre-Christian inhabitants congregated here long before the Bishop of York attended the Council at Arles in AD 314. Inside the church, Green Men spewing foliage stare down from fifteenth-century roof-bosses reminding visitors how Roman fertility rites were handed down to medieval Christians.

The most extraordinary treasure owned by the church is a small brass crucifix with a crude, emaciated Christ, dating from the tenth century, possibly earlier. It was stolen in 1980.

There used to be a sundial in the graveyard, but that was stolen too.

Barden Moor South of Linton the Ordnance Survey had ringed the Duke of Devonshire's grouse moor in purple to denote its new designation as 'Access Land', open to the public by permission of the owners.

A list on the wall of the National Park and Tourist Information Centre in Grassington advised that September was tricky: we could cross the moor on the 4th, 6th, 7th or 8th, but after that we'd have to kick our heels in Wharfedale until the 14th or 20th. Or crawl over the heather fending off grapeshot with dustbin lids. We'd be crossing on the 4th.

There was a difficulty: to gain access to the Access Land, members of the public had to use designated Access Points, of which there were only four along the fifteen kilometres of the moor's northern border. None of the four fell within 1,000 metres of the meridian. Neither could I reach the Access Land without trespassing first; apart from the routes to the inaccessible Access Points, there were no public rights of way to the northern edge of the moor. The hoi polloi were never intended to reach the heights.

My usual tactic for crossing private land was to stride boldly through in a straight line and to discuss terms if I was intercepted. In cases where the landowner lay within the 2,000-metre corridor, I usually asked first. If for some reason I felt that access might be a problem, or that I might be removed forcibly from the meridional band (by, say, a farmer's shotgun), I relied on the 3Cs of trespassing: camouflage, concealment and confession. My umbrella and hat were green; my rucksack black; my trousers and shirt night-time blue; my compass (designed for the escape kits fitted to the ejector seats of RAF fighters) had a non-reflective matt-black casing. Using contours, walls, barns and woods I could string together sequences of dead ground. If confronted by a landowner, I could smile, apologize and explain the methodology behind two degrees west in less than twelve seconds.

When I'd walked across Europe four years earlier, I'd had none of these problems, in part because I wasn't trying to walk in a straight line, and in part because continental landowners are not as covetous of their land. In England, the enclosures that accelerated from the 1750s, parcelled the countryside into small blocks that are now wired, hedged and ditched. Most of the land on the meridian that wasn't cultivated was zealously patrolled grouse moor. Across this antisocial landscape were the public rights of way, most of which were too devious or obstructed to be of use to anyone but myself, forced to walk them as legal interludes on a line of longitude. Excluding the honeypots of the Cheviots and Grassington, I'd passed no more than five people using public rights of way in 200 kilometres of straight-lining.

Part-way through a trespass, on the way to the Duke's Access Land, we met the landowner. Tony Schindler was curious, then amused. He and his son John were mending a drystone wall high on the side of Stebden Hill. 'Aye,' laughed Tony as his son passed him another rock. 'We've got nine miles of drystone walls. It keeps us out of mischief.'

Below them, the fertile trough of Wharfedale was latticed with the lines of generations of stone-shifters; hundreds, thousands of kilometres of stone walls. Were you to put an electric current into a Wharfedale wall, it would run all the way up the Pennines to the bastions of Berwick-upon-Tweed.

The Schindlers lived in Thorpe, an old Viking settlement which took its name from the Norse for an outlying farm or hamlet. To Tony it was the 'hidden village'. 'When the Scots came down, the people in the dale would take their children and animals up there. It's surrounded by trees and hidden from below.'

In Burnsall, where the wives of Tony and John worked, St Wilfrid's had a pair of Viking hogsback tombs.

Father and son rose each day at 6 a.m., worked a couple of hours, took breakfast at eight and were out again by nine.

'This is the easiest time of the year,' grunted Tony, clunking a rock on to the wall. 'No lambing until April. We've finished siloing. All the grass is in. We got one crop in July, and the second in August. The cows come in at the end of October. It's a good time of year. Good working weather.'

Tony's grandfather had been born in Rüti in the Bernese Oberland. Being the eldest child he'd had to go out and find work. He'd come to Yorkshire and started a wool business.

Tony knew he'd be a farmer. He'd started as a tenant, thirty years ago. The best moment of his farming life was the purchase of his first field. 'It was just ten acres. To stand in it was quite something. I thought, *Yes!* It's all *ours*!'

Tony now had 270 acres, 45 Friesians, 220 sheep, a son. Grandsons.

'I'll be looking to expand the farm even more,' said John, straightening his back and glancing at his father. 'You end up with nothing as a farmer. You leave it all to your sons.'

Above Tony's walls the steep face of Barden Moor rose up to a skyline scattered with weathered rock. We walked along the edge of the moor, climbing steadily to 500 metres and the obelisk on top of Cracoe Fell.

There were thirteen names from the First World War; three from the Second. They were old names from old regiments: Tom Swales and Rhodes Spence, both privates in the West Riding regiment; Fred Nelson from the South Staffs, Gerald and Michael Maude, both captains in the Yorks. On the first day of the Somme, Yorkshire lost 9,000 men, more than any other part of the country.

Southward stretched the uneven surface of the duke's grouse moor, a war zone itself, littered with butts and peat pits, disused shafts, coal pits, shake holes and quarries, patched and burned heather.

From the obelisk I could look up and down the meridian, at the rounded misshapen Pennine moors, seeing them as the worn-out, battle-scarred vertebrae of England's backbone.

Embsay We came off the back of Cracoe Fell to Yethersgill Head
where the duke had used Celtic architects to build a shooting shelter
with rounded drystone walls and a tapered thatched roof, miniatures of the Stone Age *pallozas* that can still be found in the valley-
heads of Spain's Sierra de Ancares.

The meridian was about to leave the Yorkshire Dales. Our track
began to dip into Airedale, out of the National Park. We passed the
quarry that supplied the stone for Skipton Castle and the reservoir
that provided Skipton's water, and then we were entering the
suburb of Embsay, past the chimney of the water-powered spindle
mill that made bayonets during the Crimean War, and the still
stinking tannery, to the railway yard.

'My loco,' said Colin Davies tapping the side of *Wheldale*, a
48-ton, Hunslet J94 Austerity o-6-o saddle tank. 'Made in Leeds,' he
added. 'Nineteen forty-four.' Colin was one of the drivers on the
Embsay & Bolton Abbey Steam Railway, whose operator, the charity
Yorkshire Dales Railway Museum Trust, runs rides over part of the
old line from Skipton to Ilkley.

In one of those circularities of life, this tank engine was the
same locomotive that Colin had driven fifteen years earlier as a
working man at Wheldale colliery near Castleford. He'd been on
Wheldale's footplate on 24 September 1982, the colliery's last day of
steam.

'It's a very strong engine,' he said toothlessly. 'Very reliable.
Keep it oiled, full of water, with a nice steady fire and it'll do
anything you want. My engine,' he said again. 'Now it's come home
to me.'

Before working at Wheldale colliery, Colin had driven steam
engines at Glass Houghton coking plant and at Newmarket colliery
near Wakefield, hauling fifteen wagons at a time.

'Shunting for the Coal Board. Continuous shifts. There was no
fireman, so the driver shovelled coal. Oh aye, drive and fire.' He
glanced up at the curve of *Wheldale*'s boiler. 'It's my life. It's all I
do. Drive steam locomotives.'

We thanked Colin and crossed the tracks to browse for a while
through the bookshop, where *BR Locomotive Numbering* rubbed

spines with *Russian Locomotives Vol. II* and *Bogie Carriages of the London, Brighton & South Coast Railway*.

Hol wanted to visit the signal-box.

'We're all trying to hang on to the past,' said our guide as he led us past a rusting NCB platelayers' van and a black Barclay 0-4-0 saddle tank that had been rescued from a County Durham coking plant.

Matthew, a stick-thin 25-year-old in Doc Martens and jeans, worked as a volunteer on the railway. He unlocked the lower floor of the signal-box to reveal a cats' cradle of wires, levers and cranks which he explained concisely and unfathomably. Then we mounted the wooden steps to see the levers.

Hol's excitement reminded me of the time that he'd shown me a spark-retard lever on the steering-wheel of a Rolls-Royce. But signal-box levers have more than a mechanical evocation. Of the many black-and-white films to have used the slam of one of these chest-high levers to imply a fateful swerve towards a cinematic denouement, the most dramatic was Jiri Menzel's *Closely Observed Trains*, in which the Damoclean metal arm lifts the signal to clear the line for the ammunition train that will carry away the body of young Miloš, lurking on the gantry with the box of dynamite given to him by the beautiful trapeze artist who solved what the subtitles coyly called his *ejaculatio praecox*.

The black levers were the points, explained Matthew, blue were 'facing point locks'; red were the stop signals.

Hol asked whether he might be allowed to move one of the black levers.

Peering through the window, he released the spring catch and sighed. 'That's the pinnacle of a lifetime's ambition. Something I've wanted to do since I was a boy: to pull the lever in a signal-box and *see the points move!*'

Skipton In 1990 Princess Diana had come to Skipton to open the new auction mart. Now the Cross of St George hung at half-mast above the High Street.

The Princess was being buried the following day and Skipton was mourning. People walked with their eyes averted. Even the traffic seemed muted. Inside the church a steady trickle of townspeople came to sign the book of condolence.

A 'nasty, filthily-inhabited town, for I never saw more slatterns, or dirtier houses,' spat the Hon. John Byng in 1792. Byng didn't like Skipton. The church, he wrote, was 'very damp and very dirty', and he described the New Inn as 'a gawky, dismal, ill-contrived thing built by and resembling the Duke of Devonshire'. The colonel's supper had been 'vile' and he'd been forced to stop up his inn window with a towel.

Allowances have to be made for the fact that the old soldier was unwell on the day he rode up the Aire, but even by Byng's intemperate standards, he was harsh on a town that the Etonian poet Thomas Gray had described thirty years earlier as 'pretty'. Today, Gray would still recognize Skipton as a 'large market town in a valley, with one very broad street gently sloping downwards from the Castle'. The town has a market three days a week and, as the self-elected 'Gateway to the Dales', it gets some passing trade from tourists.

But Skipton, like the other towns on the meridian, is not an A-list tourist sight. Apart from the vituperative Byng, literary travellers had skipped Skipton in favour of the neighbouring dales and in particular Malham Tarn, used by Charles Kingsley for *The Water Babies*. Rudyard Kipling's visits to his aunts in Otley Street are not enough to turn Skipton and its environs into Kipling Country.

So Skipton has remained a typical English market town, conspicuously free of wine bars, heritage trails and souvenir shops, and well-served by traditional English eateries such as Chico's Pizza and Pasta, Efe's Kebab House, the Tung Po House and Mughal Tandoori.

The splendid castle ('inconvenient, miserable, tattered' – Byng) was almost empty when I visited, as was the museum whose excellent collection included a hogsback tombstone from Burnsall, a horn once used on the Grassington mail coach and stone charms that were hung above shippen doors to ward off the evil eye.

We slept in Middle Town, a triangle of mill-workers' terraces on the downwind side of Skipton, wedged into the sloping triangle bounded by the gully of Skibeden Beck, the steepening moorland and the canal.

Half of Middle Town's terraces had cobbled back alleys and front doors opening on to the street; the other half were slightly larger, with low front walls. In Bourne House, we ate our fried breakfast with a travelling salesman while Simon and Garfunkel sang 'The Sound of Silence' on Radio 2.

Hol was wearing a tie. 'It's a lightweight tie,' he said as he buttered his toast. 'Only 26 grams.'

My father always wears a tie when hitchhiking. He claims that respectability reduces journey time. He was hitchhiking back home to Norfolk that morning.

We walked together up the east side of the High Street. Grid line 99 ran down the centre of the road, so I had access to the church, town hall, museum and castle, but not to the bank, supermarket, tourist information office or post office. Or to Marks and Spencer.

It was Friday, market day, but the stalls were subdued and the heaped produce looked more like votive offerings than market wares. Beyond the crockery, socks and doorknobs, a man stood silently by stacks of cheeses: Wensleydales with apricots; Wensleydales with cranberries; with blueberries; Wensleydales smoked, or blue, or both; Coverdale laced with ginger; cheeses from Swaledale and Emmerdale.

At the top of the High Street, Hol stepped over 99 and disappeared from sight.

Rain was forecast. In a hardware shop in Newmarket Street I bought two metres of polythene sheet for improving future bivouacs.

The Leeds and Liverpool Canal   At Airedale, the Pennines changed. Skipton marked the end of big moors and generous green dales. The map showed that the meridian's remaining ninety kilometres of Pennines would become progressively pinched between cities, the valleys clogged with houses and mills, and plaited with roads, canals and railways.

A bridge over the disused railway at the top of Middle Town led into a listless semicircle of crescents and culs-de-sac. Somebody had named their home AR OUSE; a caravan rested on jacks; a boy kicked a ball.

At the far side of Horse Close Estate the meridian met its first canal.

Of the three trans-Pennine canals, the Leeds and Liverpool was the only one still open to through traffic. It bore the signature of James Brindley, the greatest British canal-builder. A crofter's son, born in the High Peak of Derbyshire in 1716, he was apprenticed to a millwright and quickly showed a flair for engineering, establishing himself as a millwright in Leek and experimenting with steam engines. His reputation brought him to the notice of the man responsible for starting canal construction in Britain, the Duke of Bridgewater, who employed him to build a canal between Worsley and Manchester. Brindley was forty-three. By the time he died, he'd built 365 miles of canals. Brindley remained illiterate through his life, once noting that he had made an 'ochilor servey or a ricconitoring'. His plans were created largely without written words and drawings, and when confronted by a knotty problem he habitually repaired to bed. I was to cross his path several times on my passage through the heart of England.

Completed in 1816, the Leeds and Liverpool was an epic project: the first of the trans-Pennine canals to be started and the last to be completed. It was also the longest single canal in the country. The cost, after forty-six years of intermittent construction, was a colossal £1,200,000, nearly four times the original budget. To link the North Sea with the Irish Sea, the Leeds and Liverpool took advantage of the only major breach in the Pennine spine, joining the Aire valley with the Calder in a great northward kink which doubled the straight-line distance between the two cities to 127 miles. As well as the canal itself, the 'navvies' (as the navigators came to be known) had to excavate ninety-one locks and a 1,640-yard tunnel. (The tunnel was the scene in 1912 of the greatest bovine feat of the century, when a cow fell in and swam from one end of the bore to the other; it survived, despite being revived with brandy.) The completed canal reduced a three-week trip by road to three days by water. Industrial costs dropped. Skipton's mills began to import cotton in place of Pennine wool and the local limestone quarries suddenly found new markets.

As I joined the towpath a narrowboat registered in Watford puttered towards Skipton and I sensed a tingle of connectivity with my ultimate destination; arterial waterways once wriggled all the way from Skipton to the English Channel. The Macclesfield, Trent & Mersey, the Grand Union, the Thames, the Wey and Arun, were all segments of a national network that once touched the three coasts of England. Today, only the blocked Wey and Arun prevents a narrowboat leaving Skipton and docking several weeks later at Littlehampton on the south coast. Enthusiasts aim to open the Wey and Arun by 2010; maybe 2020.

For three kilometres I followed the Leeds and Liverpool along the bed of Airedale. After the moors, walking on the level, smoothly curved towpath was as effortless as loitering on a travolator. A mill drifted by. A heron hung in the headwind, its pterodactyl wings tilting and quivering before it side-slipped to the rushes and took up station, as grey and still as stone.

The temptation to follow the water was overwhelming. This towpath would lead to others which would take me by various deviations to the Kennet & Avon in Wiltshire, where I could rejoin the meridian. But two degrees west dictated that I leave the Leeds and Liverpool at Farnhill Bridge and climb back to the moors.

Back on the road again, I walked through Cononley, where a chimney like a bare flagpole rose from three floors of glass and grimy stone on the edge of the floodplain, then climbed out of the Aire and down again to Glusburn, where more mills rose from Holme Beck.

In Sutton-in-Craven, old men in flat caps and cardigans were playing bowls in the shadow of a mill that had been converted into office suites. Then I was climbing again, towards the stone finger of Lund's Tower on Keighley Moor.

As I pulled myself up the final rock outcrop to the foot of the tower, a figure rose above the battlements, balancing on the crenellations in the tearing wind, arms outstretched as if taking flight.

Earl Crag Jon Tinker is one of Britain's leading mountaineers, a specialist at winter routes in the Himalayas, with a reputation for superhuman levels of physical and mental stamina.

'Me, mate?' laughed Jon, jumping down from the battlement into the top of the tower. 'I've got the breaking-strain of a soggy Kit Kat.'

Such are the self-deprecatory nuances of the inverted English ego that a man who has tackled K2 and the Rupal Face of Nanga Parbat, in winter, and who reached the top of Mount Everest from the north must insist that he is no more than a spineless confection well past its sell-by date.

We sat in the top of the tower while the wind gusted through the crenellations and Jon handed me a can. 'Ginger beer. The Famous Five's favourite drink.'

He'd driven across from his home in York to do some 'bouldering' on Earl Crag. Over the years I'd followed Jon's career with a bystander's awe. He'd reached places I could never see; more people have been into space than have slept in the ice-cave half-way up Mount Kenya. A couple of times the *Daily Telegraph* had sent me out to interview Jon, once on the roof of Canary Wharf railway station, where he was working in a team of roped access technicians (RATs), fixing the glazing. Then one February they'd sent me to Ben Nevis, to Number 2 Gully, a near-vertical gutter of ice across which Jon had wafted in his crampons, relaxed, confident and completely at home.

Between expeditions he worked as a professional mountain guide for Sheffield-based OTT Expeditions, leading trips to the Himalayas, Alaska and the Pamirs. The previous week he had been standing on the summit of Europe's highest mountain, Elbrus, with six ecstatic clients.

'What sort of advice do you give your clients, when they're half-way up and suffering?'

'Climbing a mountain is like eating an elephant,' replied Jon. 'One bite at a time.'

Oakworth Moor   South of the tower a road ran over the moors to Near Slippery Ford where it veered east and I had to take to rough country.

More than 300 metres above sea level, a gamekeeper's house stood alone beneath Black Hill at the end of a long track.

Kevin Benson had just collected his children from school, their red uniforms blazing against the drab moor.

Kevin looked after 2,000 acres, from Earl Crag in the north to Oakworth Moor in the south. His father was keeper on the next-door moor. 'I always wanted to be a gamekeeper,' said the son. One day a week he had help from a part-timer. 'Basically I'm on my own. I love it.'

He'd had a mixed season. 'It's been OK, but not brilliant. There was a late fall of snow in May that killed the young birds. In a good year we get nine or ten days' shooting; in a poor year one or two days. Some years we don't shoot at all.'

Nine guns were shooting next day. The gamekeeper had checked that the turf around the top of the butts was tidy. He'd make the packed lunches in the morning.

'What're the guns like?'

'They're not your landed gentry. The days of bowing and scraping are gone. We get very ordinary people. Arable farmers. Barristers.'

'What about the opposition?'

'It's changed for the worse. There's more anti feeling about it now. A lot of them are misinformed and don't know what they're talking about. Most come from towns. By shooting we're culling every year and keeping the stock healthy. If grouse-shooting was stopped, the population would explode and strongyloidiasis disease would go through them like the plague. It's a worm that gets into their guts. They die a horrible death.'

The Old Silent Inn   Kevin pointed out on the map the easiest route through the heather to the far side of Oakworth Moor.

The afternoon was wild and windy, with stacks of black clouds threatening a wet night. On Kiln Hill I lost the route and floundered in spitting rain to a deep valley mapped in tiny fields bounded by drystone walls. Down here was an isolated inn.

A leaflet at the bar claimed that the inn's name came from the silence forced upon locals when Bonnie Prince Charlie hid there. Scotland's most famous fugitive would have been even more surprised to read that he'd stayed 'for several weeks'. The Old Silent Inn was also home to the ghost of a headless soldier. I was the only guest.

After breakfast I joined Marj, the cleaning lady, who was sitting with a bucket and mop before the TV. Crowds stood ten-deep as a gun-carriage drawn by six horses rolled towards Westminster Abbey.

'She was well liked,' said Marj. 'It was the touching that did it.' Marj had tears in her eyes. 'As soon as I've finished the vacuuming I'm off home to watch telly. My husband'll be in the kitchen listening to the football on the radio.'

Marj had seen the inn's ghost. 'The first time, I saw it in the dining room. The second time, it walked right through the wall of the ladies' toilet. It's a nice ghost, mind.'

The cortège crept closer to the Abbey; the bell tolled.

Outside the inn windows, the wind blustered at the lead-coloured sky, tossing the coarse grass that rose to the black silhouette of a stone cottage.

Harry's card on the wreath read 'Mummy'. There can't have been a parent in the land who didn't crack when that came on the screen.

Later, when the big black car was leaving London for its journey up the motorway, two Yorkshiremen came in for a pint. 'Never seen anything like it,' said one. 'I always says there's no such thing as a good funeral, but this one is summat else.'

I left for the moor when the hearse reached the Luton turnoff.

Brontë Bridge   The tempest gathered force as I crossed the dam of Ponden Reservoir into Brontë Country.

Lines of spume whispered over the choppy water towards the grey buildings of Ponden Hall, alone amid unusually ordered pastures and ballooning trees. Was this Thrushcross Grange in *Wuthering Heights*? The location fitted, even if the interior was more likely to have been drawn from cosier timber-framed Shibden Hall, near where Emily worked as a governess in a girls' boarding school. The distance on foot from Ponden Hall to Withins matched Emily's four miles from Thrushcross to Wuthering Heights.

Beyond the reservoir, a wooden sign with Japanese translations pointed upward to Haworth and the Brontë Way. The track climbed steeply until it was a hundred metres above the reservoir, where there was a cross-tracks on the crest of the ridge.

Off to the right was the way to Withins; ahead, the track dropped into the little valley of South Dean Beck, where a canti-levered stone footbridge bearing a Brontë plaque arched over a peat-stained stream.

Close by, an enfeebled dribble fell from the moor. This was the waterfall that Charlotte walked to on 28 November 1854, the year she married her father's curate, Reverend Arthur Bell Nicholls. Charlotte had been about to sit down to write to her childhood friend Ellen Nussey, when Arthur called to her and suggested a walk.

They hadn't intended to go far since the weather was wild and cloudy, but half a mile or so into the moor, Arthur suggested that they press on to the waterfall, saying that it would look fine in spate with the melting snow.

'It was,' wrote Charlotte next day to Ellen, 'fine indeed – a perfect torrent raving over the rocks white and bountiful.'

But rain had come before Charlotte and Arthur left the water-fall, and the cold she caught contributed to her death the following March from *hyperemesis gravidarum*, excessive vomiting while bearing a child.

Eight years earlier, her greatest work had opened with the line: 'There was no possibility of taking a walk that day.'

Brontë Bridge and Brontë Falls are way-stations on the walk from Haworth to Withins and as I sat beside a silver birch, a constant trickle of coloured waterproofs passed by. Only the Brontës could have diverted so many from the funeral of a princess.

Withins was beyond 99. My path was steep and little trodden, climbing above the bridge to gain the moor. A more hideous land would be hard to imagine. Most Pennine moors have the capacity to suck light from the sky but those south of Withins were virtually black. Even the rock looked black; black enough for Charlotte, in *Jane Eyre*, to have mistaken it for granite.

Up here, before the rain came, I could see east to the fields and far-off roofs of Haworth and west to a cumbersome moor dimpled by a solitary speck of stone. Withins, if this ruined farm really was Wuthering Heights, looked appropriately adrift from the inhabited world – a place to brood on the 'horror of great darkness'. Pilgrims must be gratified to find the ruin conforming so closely to Emily's clues: facing south (ish) from the high, bleak place that still gets blasted by 'the north wind blowing over the edge'. From my viewpoint below Oxenhope Stoop Hill I could just pick out the drystone walls that the eighteenth-century tenant of Withins had used to enclose the land he'd tried to farm. His top pasture was more than 400 metres above sea level, marginal land pressed into service to feed the valley's burgeoning population of hand-loom weavers.

Beyond the hill an old boundary stone with a carved 'H' tilted from a pool of inky slime. Emily had written of swamps beside the path up to Wuthering Heights; the Ordnance Survey noted them too: White Swamp, Red Dike Swamp, Stairs Swamp. The rain raced in from the west as a silvery wall.

There were no paths over the moor and for an eternity I tripped and lurched through flooded peat and tussocks, face turned from the slash of the weather, too wet to care about boots topped with black ooze. The afternoon was late and I was on the highest part of the moor with three hours to the shelter of Calderdale. Ahead, a broken wall receded to infinity like a glacial scratch across the back of the polished bog.

This was Charlotte's 'golden desert', alive with lizards, bees and sweet bilberries, where Jane Eyre had lain on her ecstatic flight to the heights from the horrors of Thornfield Hall. Later, of course, the temperamental moor trapped Jane with darkness, bogs, rain and cold ('Oh, Providence! sustain me a little longer! Aid – direct me!').

The wall ended at Top of Stairs, the highpoint of the old cart-track from Haworth to Hebden Bridge. I turned to the right, following the track off the moor, out of the wind. It became a narrow road that dropped by wet farms. A Slurry Slave muck-spreader rusted in the mud. The rain smacked the flooded road and in spite of the blurring water I could sense that I was descending into a valley quite unlike the broad dales of the north. The map showed Calderdale to be a steep-sided canyon walled in woods and floored with buildings, roads, a railway and a canal. Crammed into the focal point of the Calder was Hebden Bridge, with its satellites Heptonstall and Mytholmroyd, fed by deep wooded clefts. The impression was one of secret collusion between moor and valley, of communities grown used to walls.

Hebden Bridge The kitchen of One Primrose Terrace was full of people talking poetry across mugs of steaming tea. Dropping my sodden rucksack in the hall I was waved to a chair and handed a mug. The bed and breakfast was run by a photographer and a painter, Claire and George.

Primrose Terrace was a typical Hebden Bridge double-decker, four storeys high, with numbers 1, 3 and 5 on top with their front doors facing the hill and numbers 2, 4 and 6 underneath, facing the town. The canal ran along one side of the terrace and the railway on the other. In Calderdale, space was tight.

An amiable hubbub bounced around the kitchen. Friends and neighbours were coming and going, borrowing pliers, planning readings. Amanda Dalton, a poet, was talking with Claire about a joint project on 'desire paths'.

Claire was photographing desire paths; Amanda was writing poems about desire paths. George was editing a 'Chaplin–Wenders' film about desire paths. Claire handed me a file of photographs, and a sheet headed *Desire Paths Mission Statement I*.

Desire paths, I read, were the imprints of 'foot anarchists', individuals who had trodden their own routes into the landscape, regardless of the intentions of government, planners and engineers. A desire path could be a short cut through waste ground, or across the corner of a civic garden, or down an embankment. They were expressions of free will, 'paths with a passion', an alternative to the strictures of railings, fences and walls that turned individuals into powerless, apathetic automatons. On desire paths you could break out, explore, 'feel your way across a landscape'. My own longitudinal path was clearly the opposite of a desire path. 'We shall make a journey of our own desire,' concluded the mission statement, 'stretching through village, field, suburbia, city to coast.'

Amanda was a co-director of a school for writers on the valley side above town. Lumb Bank, with Totleigh Barton in Devon and Moniack Mhor in Scotland, was run by The Arvon Foundation and it had helped turn Hebden Bridge into the cultural hot spot of the Pennines. Each year students flocked to the old mill-owner's house on the hill to learn how to put words on the page, stage and screen. Their tutors ranged from poets such as Simon Armitage and George Szirtes to Deborah Moggach and Debjani Chatterjee, author of *The Elephant-Headed God and other Hindu Tales*.

'Fill up?' asked George, wielding a teapot.

'We're half-way between Leeds and Manchester,' added Amanda's co-director, David. 'Bradford is close. And Halifax. Hebden Bridge is well placed; a gorgeous little town.'

A strategic location put Hebden Bridge on the map at the dawn of the Industrial Revolution. In 1768, the year that the Yorkshire explorer James Cook sailed for Australia, the Lancashire inventor Richard Arkwright set up his spinning-frame and created the 'manufactory', or factory. Arkwright's birthplace, Lancashire, became the world's first industrial zone, crowded with cotton-spinning mills spouting chimneys and spawning a new landscape of cramped housing, pubs and chapels.

So close to the Lancashire border, the confluence of Hebden Water with the Calder was an obvious target for the mill-builders; here in the heart of the Pennines there was abundant water to power Arkwright's new machines. Hebden Bridge became 'fustianopolis', a centre for fustian, the woven cotton fabric that took its name from the Cairo suburb El-Fustat where it was first made. The manufacture of corduroy, drills, cantoons, gabroons, diagonals, moleskins and whipcords swelled the town with cutters and dyers, finishers, seamstresses, sewing-machine makers and a host of supporting trades. Children as young as six worked seventy hours a week as 'bobbin-doffers'. There was an Empire to clothe. Hebden Bridge put the cords on railwaymen, dockers, farmers, navvies and steel-workers.

With so little space on the valley floor, the town clambered upward, with terraced houses built on top of each other and mills wedged beside 'cloughs', the streams that poured off the moor. Through the choked valley, engineers had to thread the canal, railway and road using aqueducts, bridges and tunnels. The railway was paced out by George Stephenson in 1836, shortly after his son had finished work on the Stanhope & Tyne line I'd crossed in Weardale. Only at Charlestown, a mile upstream of Hebden Bridge, were the railway-builders baulked. Loose shale forced them to abandon their tunnel and take the railway on a tight curve around a valley spur. It was on the Charlestown Curve in June 1912 that the Liverpool to Leeds express left the rails, killing four and shattering the coffin of a Mr Horsefield, whose corpse became pinned beneath the wreckage. To supplement the one-horse ambulance in Hebden Bridge, Sam Sunderland of King Street ferried victims to the infirmary in the carriages and landaus of his cab-hire business.

When the cotton industry collapsed, it was a local joke that the only smoke over the Calder was smouldering dope. 'The hippies moved in during the sixties and seventies, because property was cheap,' said Claire. 'We were a second phase of immigration; we arrived fifteen years ago.'

After the hippies, the eighties brought commuters from the boom cities of the Pennine fringe, who spotted that Hebden Bridge had scenery, community and communications. Meanwhile, the hippies had children, split up and re-formed. The epitome of confusion, I was told, is Father's Day in Hebden Bridge.

'Would you like,' asked George as the mugs were cleared, 'to come to our "E & C" evening?'

'E & C?'

'Eggs and chips. It's an antidote to pretentious southern dinner parties.'

The guests included a poker-playing Jewish actor, a scriptwriter, an ex-director of Lumb Bank and Mark Illis, novelist and scriptwriter for *The Bill*. It was one of the best evenings I couldn't remember: the eggs and chips, served by George in a green striped apron, came with mushy peas, beans, sliced white bread and sufficient wine to blot out all recollection of the conversations except an illustration by George of the difference between Hebden Bridge and its neighbouring mill towns.

There was, he said, a woman in Sowerby Bridge who left her husband by delivering to his local pub a typewritten list of all the men she had slept with. In arty Hebden Bridge, noted George, such a thing would never have happened. The list would have been handwritten.

After breakfast, George showed me his paintings and garden. The paintings were meticulous rural landscapes: a field of cut corn looking like hair; a distant house beyond a forest of green stalks, painted from the eye-level of a field-mouse. A smaller painting was a close-up of part of a combine harvester, hung with a labourer's cap and a shirt that had caught the wind. Full of sunlight and minutely detailed, their close-focus converted the ordinary into the extraordinary.

George's garden was a strip of railway embankment that he'd

bought for £200. We crossed the road and climbed the bank. 'I come here to find space. To avoid information pollution.'

Wild grasses waved in a wind full of butterflies. George had counted twenty species: Little Skipper, Small Copper, Red Admiral, Tortoiseshells, Peacocks, Painted Ladies, all the Browns and Whites. Birds sang; caterpillars stretched; sunflowers swayed. The railway began to tremble.

'It's guerrilla gardening,' he said quietly. 'I have to be surreptitious, else the kids will spot it and come and wreck it.' George's secret garden was like his pictures: framed pleasure. 'This is the nearest I can get to my paintings,' he said, pausing for a train to pass. 'I sit down and look at the grass and try to see the mystery.'

Rochdale Canal The canal-builders of the eighteenth-century dreamed with water. With the Rochdale Canal, they wanted to scale the Pennine watershed and link the Mersey with the Humber. They were not the first, of course, for the builders of the Leeds and Liverpool had been hard at work since 1777 on their northern route via Skipton. But a more southerly route through Hebden Bridge had the advantages of being shorter and of servicing the new cotton mills rising from the cloughs of the Calder.

Like the Leeds and Liverpool, the Rochdale had benefited from the intuitive brain of James Brindley, who had surveyed the route as early as 1765. Construction was delayed for twenty-nine years, till Parliament sanctioned the canal in 1794. The engineering challenge was awesome: to reach the 600-foot summit, 56 locks were needed on the west and 36 on the east. More than 100 bridges were built and 2 aqueducts. Each time a lock emptied, 70,000 gallons of water poured downstream; 8 reservoirs and 20 miles of drainage were required to keep the canal fed.

Opened on 21 December 1804, twelve years before the Leeds and Liverpool, the Rochdale Canal became the first to cross the Pennines. It was an immense success. Tunnels had been avoided, which had kept costs to £600,000, while the decision to fit the canal with large locks meant that a wide variety of boats could make the passage. At peak flow, fifty a day passed through Hebden Bridge, ranging from Yorkshire keels and fly boats to Mersey flats and narrowboats. An express service between Manchester and Sowerby Bridge could negotiate the thirty miles and ninety-two locks in thirty-six hours. (The same journey takes a modern truck using the M62 less than an hour.)

The canal thrived for forty years, until the next generation of engineers opened the Leeds and Manchester Railway: Brindley, the canal man, had to stand aside for the Stephensons and their railways. The railways had it good for a century, until the road engineers took over.

In September 1937 the last loaded barge travelled the Rochdale, and in 1952 it closed to navigation. Today, the canal is beginning its second cycle of life, open again except for twenty-two kilometres on the Lancashire side of the watershed. The plan is to link the ends of the Rochdale with the ends of its historic northern rival, the Leeds and Liverpool. A union between the two would create a navigable roller-coaster: the 'Pennine Ring'.

From Hebden Bridge I took the aqueduct over the Calder river, past the marina and its multicoloured narrowboats hanging at the bank like a shoal of tropical fish.

Ten minutes outside town, the open door of Walkleys Clog Mill beckoned. With cotton and canals, England was once big in clogs. This mill supplied clog soles to the entire British Empire at the rate of half a million pairs a year. Now it is a clog theme park, drawing 750,000 a year to its shops, café and demonstration workshop. The previous year, production had shifted to another mill at Elland, near the M62 outside Huddersfield, a move that was accompanied by acrimony and a clog war between the two mills. At the Elland Mill they still manufacture 20,000 pairs of clogs a year using copying-lathes to turn out soles in beech, sycamore, ash and oak. Clogs remain popular among production-line workers who have to stand for hours on cold concrete, and among steel-men who have to walk on hot metal.

Since the Romans brought them over as bath-house sandals, clogs have shown incredible longevity. The Lord Mayor of London still puts in a regular order.

Cragg Vale   The moment I turned out of the Calder valley into the deep slot of Cragg Vale I felt as if I was entering a confidence, a place that knew how to keep its own counsel. Dark woods fell sheer from the sky, and behind those dark woods lay the unseen lairs of the Cragg Vale Coiners.

The year that Richard Arkwright patented his cotton-spinning machine, excise man William Dighton arrived in Halifax to investigate the goings-on of a gang of counterfeiters based in Cragg Vale. By November of that year, Dighton was dead, shot through the temple with a home-made bullet.

The two assailants scaled a wall and walked back over the moors to Mytholmroyd, where they slept at the Dusty Miller Inn, then climbed next morning to their eyries in Cragg Vale.

Led by 'King David' – David Hartley – the Cragg Vale Coiners 'clipped' and filed gold coins and then melted and recast the filings into new coins. Local publicans laundered the forgeries. Tipped off by a gang member who had been promised 100 guineas, Dighton arrested King David. This did not amuse Hartley's brother Isaac, who matched the excise man's fee by putting up 100 guineas for anyone who could rid the region of Dighton. Contributions towards the expenses of topping Dighton were sought from other coining gangs in Lancashire and West Riding and, after three nights of lying in wait, the excise man was murdered. The repercussions were swift and severe. Investigations under the orders of the lord lieutenant of the Riding revealed that the Calder was riddled with counterfeiters; thirty in Cragg Vale, twenty in Sowerby, fifteen in Halifax, seven from Wadsworth and six from Warle and Midgley.

Dighton's murderers were hanged. So was King David. Thirty coiners were arrested. Isaac Hartley, the mastermind behind the murder, avoided conviction due to insufficient evidence and lived to the age of seventy-eight, dying at Mytholmroyd in 1815.

At the head of Cragg Vale, I lunched on Yorkshire puddings and Tetleys in the Hinchliffe Arms.

The pub was once owned by Hinchliffe Hinchliffe, the local mill-owner who used to pay his workers in tokens which could only be redeemed at the Arms. He avoided publicity and refused ever to have his photograph taken. When he eventually died in 1900, revenge was exacted on the picture-shy booze baron.

'Someone snapped him in his coffin,' nodded the barman, glancing at my rucksack in the corner. 'Are you a fell walker?'

'In a way, yes,' I replied, going on to describe how I was walking along a line of longitude that ran down the centre of the country. The line, I added, happened to pass right over the bridge outside the front door of the pub.

'This line,' queried the barman. 'You're saying it goes over the bridge? Here at Cragg Vale?'

'Yes. It goes right over the parapet.'

He thought for a moment. '*I've* never seen it.'

M62 It was a Sunday and I felt inclined to while away the day collecting stories in the Hinchliffe Arms. But the clear, sunny afternoon presented an opportunity to hurdle the fifteen kilometres of moors between Cragg Vale and Uppermill.

So I took the road up the head of the valley then peeled off on to a track which climbed on beyond the drystone walls to the moor and Great Manshead Hill, where, from a whisker over 400 metres, I could look north-west to the dark cleft of the Calder and see for the first time the black finger of Stoodley Pike, the millstone monument erected in 1814 to mark Napoleon's abdication and the Peace of Ghent. Further to the right rose a family of modern monuments, the masts of the wind-farm on Ovenden Moor.

The path dipped and rose over Manshead End, then fell back

down through the walls to the A58, the Rochdale Road, the Roman Road. For the second time, the meridian met the hoof-tracks of the imperturbable Celia Fiennes, who rode up here in 1698 en route for Rochdale. She was making the Pennine crossing on her way back south from Hadrian's Wall and was justifiably anxious about the descent over Blackstone Edge. Earlier that year, the diarist Ralph Thoresby had his leg crushed here when his horse slipped. Fiennes had chosen a bad day to tackle the Pennines; the mist and rain reminded her of the stories her father used to tell of his travels in the Alps. He'd died when Celia was seven.

From the Roman Road, the compass led me up on to Rishworth Moor, where, for the first time, I wished I'd brought binoculars.

To the south of the moor lay a very wide, undulating depression that was less of a valley than a sag in the moor. On the far side of this khaki waste, 2,000 metres away, was a thin line of shining specks. The M62. Beyond the motorway rose the steep black reef of Moss Moor.

This was always going to be a problem. Because England tilts on its axis, the meridian had not been running parallel with the Pennine watershed but slowly converging with it from the eastern side. Malignantly, the M62 chose to cross two degrees west at the same point that the meridian crossed the crest of the Pennines at their highest, bleakest point where there would be no reason to build bridges or underpasses.

From my vantage point on Rishworth Moor I could see where the motorway reached its highpoint a few hundred metres beyond the pear-shaped slip roads of Junction 22. If Junction 22 had been 280 metres further east, I'd have had no difficulty, but it was beyond the grid line 99. I would have to find a way over – or under – the motorway.

The volume of traffic was discouraging. My plan had been to wait behind the crash barrier and then sprint across when the opportunity arose. At this point on the moor, the two carriageways of the motorway were nearly one hundred metres apart. The slice of land down the centre would give me a respite before crossing the second carriageway. But even at a range of two kilometres, I could see that I'd need a jet-propulsion pack to cross the six lanes and two hard shoulders. I had two options: either I could lie up until the early hours of the morning and assume that the traffic flows would fall sufficiently to make a dash, or I could locate a feature on the map that seemed to indicate a culvert carrying one of the streams beneath the motorway from Moss Moor, and crawl through it.

The route to the motorway across the intervening moor took me across the dam of a reservoir and then along the bank of a pretty little gorge called Green Withens Clough, which grew into the deeper and oddly named Oxygrains and then met the A672, the old main road beside the motorway.

Darkness had fallen by the time I climbed up to the open aqueduct between the A-road and the motorway. Above me, I could now hear the steady rush of traffic. The aqueduct was fed by the steep little streams that passed beneath the motorway from Moss Moor. With the compass, my miniature torch and the map, I located the stream bed that would lead me to the culvert. I scrabbled up, slipping into unseen holes and checking the compass at every turn, until the stream petered out in a bog well below the motorway. Wet and frustrated, I postponed the culvert search in favour of a close-quarters peep at the motorway. Above the bog, I was baulked by an unscalable mesh fence, presumably erected to prevent animals mingling with the traffic. On the other side of the wire was the crash barrier, and beyond it, three lanes of flashing asteroids.

For five minutes I timed the gaps between headlights. Six seconds was the longest period of clear road. Assuming that I could climb the fence, I needed at least thirty seconds of grace to run from the safety of the crash barrier, across the hard shoulder and three lanes of motorway and then dive into the wide central reservation. Being caught in headlights would not be an option, since I couldn't predict what effect the sight of a sprinting figure with a rucksack and umbrella would have on a motorist in the fast lane. The M62 was the first impassable barrier I'd met on the meridian.

I slithered back down the bank and resumed searching in the dark for the culvert. Another look at the map by torchlight revealed that the stream bed I had followed from the aqueduct had bifurcated. The same stream had another tributary seventy metres to the west. I retraced my route to the stream and turned left, up another gully. This one too climbed towards the sound of the motorway, then appeared to fork again in a confused topography of hummocks and soggy dips. Floundering in the dark I pushed on upward, then saw it.

Right in front of me, penetrating the motorway embankment, was a black hole. Not a small black hole for drainage, but a thing big enough to take a bison. A very fat bison. A farm gate leaned across the entrance. Peering in, I could just see a pale dot at the far end.

Inside the tunnel, there was headroom to stand. The floor was hard beneath my boots. Concrete. It seemed dry. I walked slowly and carefully towards the spot of light. After about a hundred metres I began to sense a cool draught. After another fifty metres, the spot had swollen to a two-metre disc. I leaned over the gate and felt the cool rush of moorland wind.

There, in the tunnel under the M62, I pulled off my boots and unrolled my sleeping-bag.

The Pennine Way   A heavy truck woke me, rumbling overhead like a roll on a reveille drum.

Outside the mouth of the tunnel, wind-driven rain was flying from thick mist that had swamped the black cliff of Moss Moor.

While the commuters flew to and fro I packed away the sleeping-bag and mat, then left the tunnel with the compass set on south. The entire width of my 2,000-metre band was occupied by Moss Moor, which rose from the motorway at 350 metres, to an unseen crest in the cloud at 480 metres. Not one path crossed the moor. After twenty minutes of climbing through the bogs and tussocks I turned and looked back at the motorway, now a taut line over the moor, decorated with slow-moving fairy-lights. Ten minutes later I was in the cloud.

In one of the anonymous bogs off the back of Moss Moor my compass bearing met the black wound of the Pennine Way.

England's most famous long-distance footpath had shadowed

the meridian since I left Berwick. We had even touched for a few minutes two days earlier, where the Pennine Way swerved east to visit the Brontës.

The 417-kilometre National Trail runs from the Scottish borders to the Peak District and has a reverence at odds with its physical attraction. For dedicated National Trailers, knocking off the PW is a rite of passage akin to surviving the Somme. When my sister walked it with her boyfriend, they marked their graduation by getting married. Yet the Pennine Way is so popular that sections have now been laid with pavements to control the erosion caused by tramping boots. The Pennines are England's equivalent of the Rocky Mountains: our spine. Goal-inspired ramblers overlook the fact that the Pennines are probably the muddiest, wettest, most misted, featureless, environmentally ravaged range of hills in the world. I would have to be bound, gagged and strapped to a stretcher to endure the Pennine Way.

For a short while, along the millstone outcrops of Northern Rotcher, there was one of those convergences that is peculiar to watersheds; where the presence of a defined ridge separating two significant drainage basins attracts a variety of human lines.

Up here, it was not just the Pennine Way that ran with the meridian, but the county boundary separating West Yorkshire and Greater Manchester, and also the Roman Road that Agricola built to break the back of Britain in the early days of the invasion.

The coincidence of purpose didn't last; before I could reach the triangulation pillar on Millstone Edge, Agricola left the muddy trough of the Pennine Way and dived off the ridge to the Roman fort of Castleshaw.

Castleshaw Roman Fort For the young men of Bracara Augusta, Castleshaw must have been a shock.

Since 27 BC, Bracara Augusta, now Braga, had been the capital of Gallaecia, the province welded together by Rome from what is now Portuguese Minho and Spanish Galicia. It was a sunny, bustling commercial centre above the fertile floor of the River Cávado, at the focus of five Roman roads, with international trade links to Egypt, the Aegean and Germany. The young auxiliaries of the Third Cohort of the Bracaraugustani left this warm, hectic city for a small, wet fort above the treeline on a dangerous island at the northern extremity of the Empire.

Castleshaw was one of sixty or so forts that Agricola built from AD 79 during his campaigns to subjugate the tribes of northern Britain and it lay near the highpoint of the vulnerable trans-Pennine section of the road from Chester to York. The site was cleverly chosen to dominate the road as it climbs up from the south-west, while controlling the pass to the north-east too. A decade after it was built, the front line moved north and the fort was abandoned. Then, in about AD 100, it was rebuilt as a smaller fortlet, and occupied for another twenty years or so until tribal troubles and the building of Hadrian's Wall diverted military attention to the north again.

Nowhere is the British fascination with the Romans better illustrated than at this series of unremarkable turf embankments on a draughty Pennine hillside: 1,650 years after the auxiliaries marched away from their abandoned fortlet, Thomas Percival of Royton presented a paper to the Royal Philosophical Society describing 'a double Roman camp' which he had been 'well pleased to find'. Ammon Wrigley (whom I found described later that day in Saddleworth Museum as a 'writer, poet, archaeologist, historian, textile worker, artist, huntsman and lover of ale') showed up in 1897, digging trial holes and finding tile and pottery fragments. Over the next fifty years successive waves of enthusiasts dug trenches and added their own spoil heaps to the existing embankments. Coins, pottery and tiles were removed, maps drawn, photographs taken, reports submitted to august bodies such as the Lancashire and Cheshire Antiquarian Society. From the 1950s the site was excavated by Manchester University. Out of a pit that may have been the well, emerged leather sandals, more coins, a lead lamp holder, stamped tiles and a *pilum murali* – a defensive stake or lance that would have been carried in bunches of three by a Roman soldier. (That too was in Saddleworth Museum, looking like a piece of splintered stick, apparently the only *pilum murali* found in England.)

Two and a half centuries spent scrutinizing a minor fort have produced an extraordinarily detailed picture of its timber-built interior: a barrack block for eighty auxiliaries, officers' quarters, a hypercaust for heating, a latrine, a workshop with hearths for smithying and a *mansio* for official travellers. An unusually large granary for a fortlet measuring only forty-five by fifty metres aroused speculation that Castleshaw was a store base.

Underneath the Roman layers, the archaeologists found a late Bronze Age burial. In building their fort, the invaders had deliberately obliterated the grave of subjugated Britons.

Huddersfield Narrow Canal   From Castleshaw by way of Dirty Lane and Bleak Hey Nook to Diggle: from Imperial Rome to the Industrial Revolution.

Diggle snuggled into the head of a valley near the highest point of the district of Saddleworth, a string of villages which follow the River Tame from the Pennines down towards the Manchester suburbs. The meridian was now grazing the western edge of the range and for the first time the softer bumps of foothills met the moorland.

In Diggle, I found the western entrance to England's longest, highest canal tunnel, a tiny worm-hole in the hill, blocked by rusting steel gates.

The Standedge Tunnel was the crux of the Huddersfield Narrow Canal, an engineering feat that anticipated the financial and technical troubles experienced 200 years later by the builders of the railway between London and Paris. The canal had to burrow for an unprecedented $3\frac{1}{4}$ miles beneath the moor of Standedge. Water poured from the millstone grit and flooded the workings; long sections of friable shale had to be shored with brickwork and then a surveyor discovered that the two ends of the tunnel were out of alignment, and were not going to meet in the middle. As the costs escalated, investors panicked and forced the committee to scrap plans for a towpath through the tunnel, a decision that was to affect future profitability.

Just as the Rochdale Canal had sought to shorten the route taken by the Leeds and Liverpool, so the Huddersfield Narrow Canal sought to cut the bends out of the Rochdale. Work began in 1794, the same year that the first clod was cut out of the Rochdale, but boats didn't pass through the summit tunnel until 1811, by which time the Rochdale had been operating for seven years. A crowd of 10,000 gathered at Diggle as boats carrying the company managers, local dignitaries and a band entered Standedge Tunnel to the ponderous chords of 'Rule Britannia'. The eventual cost of the canal was more than double the £178,748 projected by its engineer, Benjamin Outram, while the five years he'd allowed for boring the tunnel had stretched to seventeen.

With no towpath, and therefore no horses or mechanical devices available to haul the narrowboats through the tunnel, propulsion fell to 'leggers', pairs of men who laid back on the barges, pushing for up to four hours with their feet against the tunnel walls. The record for legging through Standedge Tunnel was set in 1914 by David Whitehead, who pushed his narrowboat through in eighty-five minutes. Six hundred feet above the leggers, the towing horses were walked over the moor by a company employee who would make four trips a day. One of these professional walkers, a Thomas Bourne of Marsden, reputedly clocked up 215,852 miles between 1811 and 1852, the equivalent of walking the Pennine Way twenty times a year for forty-one years.

From the mouth of the tunnel I had the rare luxury of easy walking as the towpath stuck with the meridian for over three kilometres, falling in steps past locks that still bore their stonemasons' marks. Every turn produced ghostly whispers from that epoch of industrial purpose. Off on the right, stacks of new wooden pallets stood outside the old Dobcross Loom Works, which had once employed 500 and had its own branch line.

Downwind of Manchester, Salford and Rochdale, I was now in Lowry Country, the grimescape of smoking chimneys and faded white flake.

Saddleworth had landmarks that played allegorical roles in Lowry's oils: the stone obelisk to the fallen dominating the valley might have been 'The Landmark' (1936); the Loom Works must have known many a dawn when the incoming tide of coated workers funnelled through the factory gate as they do in 'Early Morning' (1955). The difference now is that Lowry's subjects have gone. The human minnows that swarm across his paintings travel in cars or not at all. There is little chance of seeing those Chaplinesque men in funny hats getting into fights, or being arrested. The children and gossiping adults, quaint invalid carriages and bikes, dogs and balls that Lowry employed to transform street scenes into fairgrounds have been cleared of human colour. Lowry's factory workers have gone the way of Breughel's animated peasants.

The towpath passed a milestone (12 to Huddersfield) and then toppled down a flight of locks to pass underneath the Saddleworth viaduct by way of a skew arch which gives the great spans a knock-kneed perspective from below. The viaduct was the scene of a ghastly accident on Christmas Eve 1866, when a passenger stepped out of his carriage unaware that the train had overshot Saddleworth station.

The macabre is a Saddleworth speciality. When Myra Hindley and Ian Brady committed the 'Moors Murders' in the 1960s, they were following a pattern. At Uppermill I left the canal for the museum and learned about the locally notorious Bill o' Jacks murders, the victims of which were landlord William Bradbury (Bill o' Jacks) and his son Thomas, bludgeoned to death at the Moorcock Inn on 2 April 1832. The murder was never solved, but the list of primary suspects makes a fascinating cross-section through the underclass of early nineteenth-century Saddleworth. The four contenders were: the 'Red Bradburys', against one of whom Tom was due to testify on a poaching charge; the Burnplatters, who lived in remote groups on the moor (Bill's dying word was 'Patts', or 'Platts'); three Irish strangers whom Tom had accused of stealing stockings; and a man who was later transported to Australia for stealing a cow and who apparently confessed to the crime, but was hanged in 1848 for a separate murder.

Standedge Tunnel also had a macabre history. In 1836 a

boatman screamed and disappeared overboard for no apparent reason. When the bore was drained to retrieve his body, a second corpse was found, of a young woman with a gashed throat. On another occasion a three-ton rock fell out of the tunnel roof on to a narrowboat; and the following year a gunpowder boat exploded. When regular traffic on the canal ceased, it became a conveniently isolated venue for suicides; between 1917 and 1936 an average of ten people a year died in this man-made Styx.

Returning to the canal, I walked on to Greenfield, the scene in 1797 of an explosion caused by bored miners from the tunnel who'd sought light entertainment by blowing up a huge boulder called the Raven Stone, killing one of their number outright and fatally injuring several others.

At Greenfield I left the water, and Saddleworth.

Alphin   The obvious walking route between Greenfield and the next village, eight kilometres to the south, was by way of public footpaths along the foot of the Pennines, but with characteristic perversity, the meridian ran a few hundred metres to the east, over the moors. For the first four kilometres there were no paths.

Crawling beneath a fence, I climbed through two fields, squeezed under more wire and reached Alphin's steep northwestern buttress.

To one side I could see across to Alderman's Hill and the Pots and Pans Stone – once believed to have been a Druidical altar – and the memorial to the dead of the First World War. Alderman's Hill and Alphin were old adversaries; it was a slinging-match between the two giants for the favours of Rimmon the water-nymph that left the valley strewn with rocks.

By the time I reached Alphin's 469-metre summit, the sinking sun had slipped behind a stupendous anvil of cloud and was loosing ray-bursts of light on to Manchester so that the distant city glittered like a scattering of broken glass. Alphin was on the edge, leaning over the flatlands of Lancashire that ran uninterrupted to Formby and the Irish Sea. West of Alphin there was no higher point until the Bens of Connemara.

At Alphin's triangulation pillar I met a man with a spade and a boy. They were looking for an American bomber. 'Came down here in the war,' said the man.

As I walked along the top of Alphin I met others, also with spades and metal detectors.

The south side of the hill was a wasteland of exposed peat that had dried into blocks and fissures. For an hour I blundered in the twilight on a compass bearing, keeping high to avoid the quarries, yet not so high that I would cross 01. In this trackless no-man's land, the usually resonant map names had been replaced by the labels of a ravaged landscape: Broken Ground, Irontongue Hill, Slatepit Moor, Turf Pits.

As darkness fell I crossed a dam between two reservoirs. I picked up an old cart-track that angled up to a dented ridge called Pack Saddle that overlooked a dark void spilled with jewels: sodium necklaces, villages twinkling like tiaras, emerald and ruby traffic-lights, solitary security lamps burning like diamonds.

In a small copse beside the track I unrolled my sleeping-bag while three inquisitive cows breathed heavily over a barbed wire fence.

At dawn, the cows were still there, staring.

Mottram in Longdendale The bins were being collected when I reached L. S. Lowry's home on Stalybridge Road.

Number 23 was a stone, semi-detached building in grey, slightly grander than its neighbours and disproportionately tall, as if Lowry himself had stretched its chimney and doorway.

It was not yet seven in the morning and the curtains were still closed. I stood on the far pavement, leaning on my umbrella ('Man Waiting', 1964, Oil on board), nonplussed by the ordinariness of The Elms. Yet in a backroom of this house had painted the man who symbolized the last days of the mill towns, whose work hangs in London and New York and whose life would soon be commemorated by the £64 million Lowry Centre under construction on Salford Quays, with a permanent collection, plaza, bars, cafés and restaurants (a good irony there, for a man who drank orange squash and favoured sausage, egg and chips) and a Hands-On Gallery.

Lowry had moved into the house in 1948, nine years after his mother died. He had no television, or phone or car; he didn't drink or smoke. He took his holidays in the Seaburn Hotel, Sunderland. Being alone sharpened his focus and placed him in a world of extremes, where there were not crowds but multitudes, and where a lone individual became a solitary lamp-post. Detesting Rembrandt for his realism (his own living room was lined with Rossetti drawings), he was able to invent composite industrial landscapes and cartoon portraits, a magic reality that was funny and tragic. He lived in Gogol's 'world of visible laughter and invisible tears', and died in 1976, never having been abroad, or been in love.

Mottram was a mess.

Since Lowry's time the stub of a motorway had been extended to the edge of the village, precipitating deluges of heavy traffic into streets scaled for horses and carts. The air shuddered with noise and grime and despite the thousands of passers-by there was no café.

In search of breakfast, I found myself looking at a plaque to another Mottram man, Lawrence Earnshaw, a weaver's son whose seven-year apprenticeship to his father was followed by four years as a tailor and then a dramatic switch to mechanical invention. In 1753 he designed a machine that could spin and reel cotton, then destroyed it in the belief that it would deprive the poor of work. Later, he invented an astronomical clock that was sufficiently successful for him to win many orders, including a sale for 150 shillings to Lord Bute.

Lawrence Earnshaw died in May 1767, four years after his namesake Thomas Earnshaw completed his watch-makers' apprenticeship and embarked upon his race against Harrison, Arnold and others for a method of measuring longitude. Thomas Earnshaw invented the first economic chronometer and won an award of £3,000 from the Board of Longitude, dying famous and wealthy, at eighty, in Chelsea; Lawrence Earnshaw died poor, at sixty, in Mottram.

One hundred years after Lawrence Earnshaw's death, a series of articles in the *Ashton-under-Lyne Reporter* prompted a public subscription for a monument to be raised in Mottram's cemetery.

In the absence of a café, I walked up to the weathered Perpendicular church to find shelter from the wind while I ate the bread and cheese I'd carried from Uppermill. The church stood on the crown of the hill in the path of the westerlies that gust off the Irish Sea towards the Dark Peak. Virtually every gravestone lay flat on the ground, as if swiped by a giant hand.

'It's Captain Whittle's wind,' nodded a bearded man walking his dogs. 'When Captain Whittle's gravestone blew over, he gave his name to the winds that hit Mottram.'

'The other theory,' added Graham McCarg, 'is grave-robbers. There was this local man who'd wait for a burial then dig up the body and take it down and sell it to the anatomical school in Manchester. Before he could do it, he'd go to the two pubs by the church to steal courage.' Eventually the body-snatcher got caught and thrown into a Manchester lime-pit.

Graham looked down at me huddled with my collar up in the lee of the tower (the church door had been locked). 'If you think this is bad, you should be here when there's a north-easterly down the Woodhead valley. I've been up here when it's been a typhoon.'

In 1891 the wind blew in the belfry window and stripped the village of chimney pots.

'This is called War Hill,' added Graham. 'There was a battle here in Anglo-Saxon times and after the dead were buried it became a Saxon shrine.'

New Mills   The Cyber Café in New Mills was still open when I walked into town late in the afternoon.

'It's quite cosmopolitan for a small town.' Ele handed me a plate of carrot cake and a mug of lapsang. At the back of the café, figures leaned at screens.

Looking for a place to stay, I called at a black wooden shack advertising organic food and, after a brief conversation with an ex-professional singer who claimed psychic powers, I was helped by the owner, Norman Eadle, who telephoned a neighbour.

Jilah Bakhshayesh, a half-Persian anthropologist, who played violin in a Jewish Klezma band, lived in a terraced house on the north side of town.

'Got to get my house in order,' she said, excusing the disordered living room. 'Need to get centred.'

Taking the arrival of a stranger in her stride, Jilah gave me a room upstairs and a bowl of organic soup.

New Mills is not what it first seems.

The town sits astride a 20-metre deep gorge – the Torrs – at the confluence of the Rivers Goyt and Sett. The Torrs were created by melting glacial water slicing through the sandstone. It is a town on two levels: up top there are the terraces, traffic and shops of a conventional mill town; down below there is a silent sun-dappled netherworld hiding mills, weirs and strange practices.

On my first descent of the pack-horse track into the Torrs, I was drawn by muffled voices towards the feet of the great viaduct where I found two young men practising 'direct action'. Between the trees they had woven a web of climbing ropes. Trussed in climbing harnesses and karabiners, the two of them were shuffling to and fro from tree to tree, high above the ground, training for an anti-road-building protest.

An 'Industrial Heritage Trail' had been created through the Torrs. Where Arkwright's disciples had built their mills on rock ledges above the water, there were now paths and viewing points, with an accompanying leaflet that told visitors where to find the weavers' cottages, the ruined (or vanished) mills, the sluices that powered the wheels and the stables that sheltered the 'chain horses' that were used to restrain the carts from running out of control on the steep descent from the town above.

On Jilah's telephone I called home and heard that Matt Dickinson, my daughter's godfather, was on his way to the Peak District to find me.

Matt arrived shortly before midnight. He had with him a copy of *The Death Zone*, the book which he'd written about the storm that had killed eleven climbers on Mount Everest the previous spring. Matt had reached the summit and descended with minor frostbite. He still looked haunted by the experience and we talked late into the evening. Like me, he'd grown up with Sir John Hunt's account of the 1953 expedition. Among mountains, Everest was unique for its ability to go on gaining allure after its first ascent. That is the way with shrines.

Jilah gave us a breakfast of wholemeal toast and coffee, then walked with Matt and me down to the Torrs and along the bank of the Goyt to the towpath of the Peak Forest Canal, where she waved us away southward.

We stayed with the canal for twenty minutes as it led us towards its terminus outside Whaley Bridge. The weather had improved; sunlight tinkled on the water and a broad blue sky promised a settled day. We passed a man who was quacking to himself and, five minutes later, another man face down in the nettles. We pulled him out and propped him on the towpath, where he continued chuckling quietly.

Approaching Furnace Vale, we came to a moored narrowboat. Horace and Margaret had sailed from Burton on Trent with a King Charles Spaniel, Lucky, by way of the Macclesfield Canal. *Avocet*, their 15-metre narrowboat, had been bought as a steel shell and the couple had spent a year fitting it out. Horace, combed and neat in an RSPB pullover, was a retired clock and watch repairer. Immaculate coach lines decorated the cabin, which had flower pots on the roof and a jaunty pennant. They travelled the canals for six or eight weeks at a time:

'Quite a few of us do it these days,' smiled Horace. 'Some people cruise from spring through summer to autumn, then lie up in a marina through the winter. They're called permanent cruisers.'

'Any problems?'

'The Ashton Canal can be tricky, into Manchester. They jump on the boats or put strings of supermarket trolleys across the canal and when you try to move them, they pelt you with stones.'

Shining Tor   Meridional cutoff meant we bypassed the centre of Whaley Bridge on a compass bearing through an estate of Tudor-beamed homes with double-glazed leaded windows and integral garages.

For most of the previous day, the meridian had played tag with county boundaries, twice leaving Greater Manchester for Derbyshire. Now it crossed to Cheshire. This new indecisiveness marked the beginning of the end of the Pennines. Beyond Whaley Bridge I had only to cross the western ripples of the Peak District before embarking upon Part II of the journey.

For once, longitude and landscape decided to harmonize: for five kilometres the meridian followed an exhilarating blade of millstone grit from Taxal Edge to Shining Tor.

Beyond Lapwing Farm a path left the road up Taxal Edge. Ahead, the ridge rose steadily southward as if rising to the heavens. On our right reclined a broad green valley dotted with farms and trees; on the other side rose the Peak District.

At Windgather Rocks we sprawled on warm stone and picnicked. Using a tube of rubber solution I'd bought in New Mills, I glued a large patch of canvas across the disintegrating seat of my trousers, which instantly solidified, giving the impression that I was wearing some kind of white latex protective device across my buttocks.

Beyond Cats Tor the ridge took a dip to a smooth saddle that rustled with the nylon wings of paragliders.

Steve Goodall, an instructor, helped a client into the air, then turned to Matt. 'I've got a project,' he said conspiratorially. 'Flying to France in the updraught of a Channel ferry. *Nobody's done it.* You'd need intimate radio contact with the captain, of course.'

He had another project too. 'It's the world distance record. At the moment it stands at 330 miles, done in the Rift Valley at 20,000 feet. I think it can be pushed up to 500.'

Shining Tor's triangulation pillar was erected in May 1948 for the relatively high cost of £10 8s 2d, a reflection of its inaccessibility. The brass top had been removed and the pillar adopted.

Ahead we could see the spines of the Roaches.

Cat and Fiddle Inn   'That's the last cutting of the grass this year.' The Cat and Fiddle had closed by the time we came off Shining Tor, but we found the publican at the back door.

Ian Ryder ran the second highest pub in England. It was built in 1800, on the pack road over the Pennines. 'In a way, we're really the highest *genuine* pub because Tan Hill doesn't open all the year round, whereas we do. And we live up here too. Till Tan Hill got its licence in the seventies, this was the highest fully licensed pub in England.'

In the bar, he spread photographs taken the previous winter, showing the pub looking like a Polar station, snow up to its windows and rimed with ice. 'We're often cut off till the snow-blower gets through. We've had the police staying here when they broke a half-shaft on their Range Rover.'

The police were up here a lot, trying to minimize fatalities. The road over the pass past the Cat and Fiddle is a motorcyclists' race-track. 'Two bikers died up here three weeks ago,' said the publican. 'Every night they race up here at six o'clock, after work. Up and down. Up and down. The outline of one of the bodies is still in chalk on the wall where he crashed.'

On the outside wall of the pub was a display cabinet recording casualties on the road. In the last three years there had been five deaths and twenty-three serious injuries. Nearly all of them had happened on Sundays.

'How long have you been here?'

'Ten years. I enjoy it. It's a way of life. It's had a lot of landlords this place, and they didn't normally stay more than a year. But I like it. I'm used to it.'

The Roaches Beyond the Cat and Fiddle we dropped with the setting sun into the deep cleft of the Dane.

This was like Northumberland again: soft voluptuous swells furred with bracken; tilted little lawns freckled with sheep; becks as blue as the sky; a sense of space and light.

We walked as far as Three Shires Head, where the county boundaries of Cheshire, Derbyshire and Staffordshire meet at a confluence of streams, which is itself marked by a stone-backed packhorse bridge and a dainty cataract. There is an inevitable potency about such nodes, especially when they happen to look like the backdrop to a fable; under the boughs the rocks were green with lichen. We slept beneath a tree on a mattress of fallen leaves.

Dawn, my last in the Pennines, seeped into the valley. I lay for a while in the bag. The valley swam with mist. Tiny water droplets fell against my face. It was chilly, almost autumnal. I turned over, and felt the tree root dig at my hip, then turned back, pulling the zip closer to my face.

Matt's head was by my feet. He was using the pillow he'd carried up Mount Everest. We were lying end-on-end behind a wall. The river was on the other side of the wall. It was the only level spot we could find.

'Brew?'

Matt had a small gas stove. For me, a luxury.

Ten minutes later my blackened steel mug was half-full of scalding tea.

Rain began to fall.

*

South into Staffordshire twisted the Dane, framed by the V of its walls, and then it was off to the west and we had to climb high around the side of Gradbach Hill to get on to the end of the Roaches.

Here, on the Roaches, I passed the mid-point on my journey down the meridian; 288.96 kilometres from the high water mark on the cliffs north of Berwick.

The crest of the Roaches is about 1,500 metres long, sheer on the west and easy-angled on the east. In the mist, it is a primordial place, strewn with blocks of millstone that are eroded into hooked beaks and reptilian heads. As a schoolboy Matt had learned to rock-climb here. 'Changed my life,' he laughed. The mist thickened until we were floating upward in a milky void, conscious only of the contours slipping by: 300, 350, 400, 450, 500 metres and then the dissolved form of the triangulation pillar, slowly hardening as we drifted up to meet the last summit of the Pennines.

Leek   Where the southern tip of the Roaches dipped beneath the cloud, we looked back and saw the angled prow of the Pennines streaming a misty wake, and looked forward into the sun where a rolling ocean of blues and greens filled the other half of England.

In stepping off the end of England's spine, I was crossing the Tees–Exe Line, used by geographers to separate England's Highland and Lowland Zones. It runs in a great diagonal from the Tees estuary in Yorkshire to the Exe estuary in Devon. North and west of the line lie the older rocks from the Pre-Cambrian and Paleozoic ages, folded and torn in the crustal shifts of the Caledonian and Hercynian, then heavily eroded. South and east of the line are the mainly sedimentary rocks of the Mesozoic and Tertiary ages, kinked into scarps and dips that resemble the grain in a well-worn plank of wood. The Tees–Exe also drew a line beneath the oat-growing lands of the cooler north and the wheat and root-crops of the warmer south.

It was coincidental that the Tees–Exe and the end of the Pennine backbone met the meridian at its half-way point, but it lent a pleasing symmetry to the line.

Our path cavorted down to lush green pastures where the grass looked as if it was washed and fed three times a day and the air felt fat and sloppy; too lethargic to work up a breeze. Drystone walls had been replaced by fences, and sheep by cattle.

By lunchtime the line had led us to the outskirts of Leek, the Victorian silk town that wove the 'Raven Black' worn by Queen Victoria after Albert's untimely death. Leek had restaurants, bed and breakfasts, a church by Richard Norman Shaw with Burne-Jones glass and James Brindley's mill – all of them out of reach. The only civic monument within meridional limits was the Kwik Save supermarket.

Beneath a poster claiming WE KUT THE KOST, we sat on a koncrete kerb in the kar park and toasted each other with karbonated orange juice. Then Matt rolled up the hat he'd worn on top of Everest, shouldered his rucksack, and left.

Consallforge   The meridian continued to avoid villages and towns. After three hours on field paths and minor roads, dusk was falling and so was rain.

The only feature on the map that hinted of shelter was 'Price's Cave', near a flight of steps called the 'Devil's Staircase' on the northern wall of the Churnet valley, a hundred-metre wooded gorge with a floor just wide enough to take the river, the Caldon Canal and a railway.

With rain drumming on the umbrella I reached the lip of the valley and began searching for the cave. The sodden sky and tree cover conspired with the failing light to turn the gorge into a dark, tentacled underworld of clutching briars, stinging leaves and unseen holes. Never has a cave been better hidden; I was looking for black on black. After rolling over a fallen tree then skidding on steep, greasy mud into a thicket, I gave up and returned to the Devil's Staircase.

At the foot of the steps, I came out on to the narrow, roadless valley floor of the Churnet at Consallforge. Off to the left was the 'PH' promised by the Ordnance Survey. Blurred by the teeming night, the ground-floor windows of the Black Lion glowed dimly like the saloon lights of a doomed river steamer in a tropical deluge. The aroma of burning coal seeped along the saturated valley with the creeping ground mist.

The four people in the bar looked up as I squelched through the door. A coal fire glowed and bar lights twinkled on horse brasses and beer glasses. I knew that I had to sleep in that pub, and I knew that pubs didn't take guests. That, I'd learned, was the difference between a pub and an inn, though I'd come across inns that didn't have rooms either.

The four were a customer called 'H', or Harry, who'd been an electrician with the National Coal Board for thirty-nine years, until they made him redundant; Maggie and Peter, the publicans; and Graham, who helped.

Peter went to make me a curry and I settled by the fire with a pint and asked Maggie if I could stay the night. Anywhere would do: the dog kennel, a shed. I'd pay. She said she'd speak to Peter. When she said that, I knew I'd be back in the rain. Peter seemed a prickly, sarcastic character and I couldn't see why he should complicate his life by accommodating a muddy itinerant.

Graham, a big, bearded man, had served twenty-two years in the Royal Navy. He'd gone in as an artificer apprentice and left as a senior maintenance rating, serving on *Hermes*, RFA ships, *Illustrious*, *Ark Royal*, *Invincible*. He'd gone through the Falklands War on *Invincible* as watch chief on 820 Squadron's Sea King helicopters.

'It was round the clock, keeping the aircraft in the air. There are moments of adrenalin when you're under attack. There's a missile coming in and you don't know whether it's for your ship or another. To be honest, you're shit-scared. It's incredible how people bind together. I had a couple of people below me who I'd always thought were time-wasters, but when the war started they were brilliant. Top stars.

'It was distressing too, especially when the bodies came in from *Atlantic Conveyor* and *Sheffield*.

'The homecoming to Portsmouth was fantastic. It was something you look back on and think "I'm glad I was part of it." '

The curry was hot enough to dry my clothes from the inside. Conversation turned to the Black Lion. H could remember coming to the pub as a teenager with his mates on Whit Mondays when the trains still ran up the valley.

'We took it on as a shell,' said Peter shaking his head. 'We thought that it would take £3,000 to do it up, but it went up to £20,000.' He pointed at the black timbers around the bar. 'We put the Tudor things on the wall.'

Now, steam trains were back in the Churnet, and soon they would come as far as Consallforge. Peter had plans to take his beer deliveries by steam.

They'd watched the funeral the previous weekend. 'To be honest, I didn't think one way or the other about her,' volunteered Peter. 'But then, all those people can't be wrong. It was very moving.'

While we'd been talking, Maggie had slipped upstairs and prepared a bed in the spare room. In the morning, when I tried to leave some money, Peter shook his head. 'It'll help redress the balance, Nicholas. I'm a nasty bastard sometimes.'

Caldon Canal For a kilometre or so I took the towpath through a dripping, misty slot that became so narrow that the canal, railway and river were squeezed bank-to-bank.

The River Churnet and Caldon Canal wove their own story across the meridian: the seventeen-mile-long Caldon had been opened in 1779 to bring limestone and flint from quarries in the hills to the factories of Stoke-on-Trent, drawing its water from Rudyard Reservoir, beside whose reflections John Lockwood Kipling proposed to his wife and after whose lucidity he named his first-born son. Further downstream, it was the Caldon (so it was said) that killed James Brindley. The great canal engineer had been surveying the last mile of the canal, and had been staying at the Old Red Lion in Ipstones, above Consallforge. The damp sheets gave him a chill from which he died.

The Caldon's riparian twin told a different story, rising beneath the Roaches, harnessed by the young Brindley for his mill in Leek and by Richard Arkwright for his mill near Rocester, then escaping into the Dove, and so to the Trent, which joined the rivers I'd crossed in Yorkshire – the Swale and the Ure, the Wharfe, the Aire and the Calder – to pour through the spout of the Humber Estuary into the North Sea.

Caldon Canal survived until the 1960s; the railway till 1964. Both have been resurrected for new careers with the leisure industry.

By Flint Mill lock, coal smoke trickled from the stove-pipe of a narrowboat and a path scrabbled from the gorge. Mist filtered through birch and sycamore, oak and hawthorn, parting for a moment to reveal interlocking spurs thick with tree-crowns and seething equatorial vapours. Staffordshire seemed to specialize in these kinds of tricks: serving slabs of raw countryside with a whiff of industry. Stoke-on-Trent was less than ten kilometres off to my right and some time during the following day I'd pass even closer to Stafford. For the next few days the meridian would sense the closing metropolis – a canal here, a factory there, a rising pressure on arterial roads – and then collide head-on with the West Midlands.

An hour after leaving the Caldon Canal, I emerged from the fields on Clemgoose Lane and turned along the verge of the A522 towards Cheadle.

Cheadle   It was a Friday, one of the three weekly market days, and the High Street was solid with cars and quarry lorries.

Cheadle was worn, grimy and friendly; over-familiar with making ends meet. For £3.95 I got a 'Workingman's Breakfast' (tea-cakes and jam extra) and then went in search of trousers. With the botched rubber repair and latticework of stitched rips, my existing pair were drawing stares. In an Aladdin's cave of army surplus water bottles and assorted hardware, I found a pair of 'Working-man's Trousers' for only £15.99. They were very thick and stiff, with a double seat, deep pockets and a curious sheen that hinted of steel fibres. They seemed ideal protection now that I was in a landscape of fences and hedges where maximum use was made of barbed wire.

Striding confidently in my glistening 'Cheadles' I walked along to the *Cheadle and Tean Times* (locally known as *The Stunner*) and asked the news editor, a young man with short hair and spectacles called Guy, what had happened to the shops in the High Street.

'I wouldn't say it's a thriving town,' he said. 'There are a lot of empty premises.'

The main local employers were the JCB factory and Alton Towers, Britain's biggest amusement park.

'Cheadle's been through the worst,' continued Guy. 'There are plans for a new supermarket, and a one-way system to deal with the Alton Towers traffic. But the roads depend on the supermarket being built, because the supermarket is paying a percentage of the road scheme. For Cheadle, it'll be the first step forward for ages.'

An amusement park and a supermarket; the roads to civic resurrection.

This was not the first time that Alton Towers and Cheadle had been locked in a mutually supportive embrace. Half a century before motor cars hit the town, the owner of Alton Towers bankrolled a young architect to create for Cheadle the most splendid parish church in the country. The 16th Earl of Shrewsbury had the money; Augustus Welby Northmore Pugin had the vision.

To Pugin, who converted to Catholicism in 1835, the decoration and architecture of the Middle Ages were the 'natural leaves and fruit of the Christian Tree', and he saw in the Gothic Revival the true expression of Christian symbolism: spires that reached towards heaven; three-part interiors to reflect the Holy Trinity; brilliant east windows and screens that separated laity and mystery, and which framed the liturgical drama.

The Earl of Shrewsbury wanted his church to rise above Cheadle in local materials crafted by local hands. Stone was quarried from his estate, oak and beech felled in his woods. Tiles were made by Minton and Wedgwood in the Potteries; glass by Wailes of Newcastle-under-Lyme. Denny, the foreman at Alton Towers, supervised the work and another local, Thomas Roddis, carved the altar, pulpit and nave-pillar caps. Construction took six years and costs rose from the initial budget of £5,000 to £40,000, an overspend that made the congenitally optimistic civil engineers of the time seem thrifty.

Such was the importance attached to this symbol of Catholic renaissance that the consecration in August 1846 was attended by most of the English episcopate as well as the archbishops of Damascus and Sydney, the Austrian ambassador, the Sardinian minister and the Pope's chamberlain, Count Datti. Pugin's own guests included Barry (with whom he'd worked on the Houses of Parliament) and the French Gothic Revivalists Didron and Gerante.

St Giles was empty when I pushed open the door and dropped my pound coin into the timed lighting machine. The effect of that church interior on a first-time visitor cannot be condensed into simple description; too much is happening. Everywhere there is decoration: gildings, carvings, paintings, in golds and reds, blues and ochres, foliar greens. Through the diaphanous tracery of the rood screen, Roddis's alabaster altar floats upon its plinth attended by angels; the sedilia's three seats are set in golden niches that are carved and painted with the symbols of the three officiants of High Mass. 'Cheadle, perfect Cheadle,' wrote Pugin to the Earl of Shrewsbury. 'Cheadle my consolation in all afflictions.' In St Giles the secular trinity of architect, patron and craftsman surpassed their own expectations.

Pugin's eccentricity ate him up. His preference for wearing second-hand, patched sailors' suits, oversize shoes (to allow room for his toes to spread) and coats with pockets big enough for sketchbooks and tails long enough to keep the rain off his legs, mutated into obsession: he wanted a 'real' Gothic wife, he had to have Gothic puddings and Gothic cheese. Married thrice, father of eight, aged only thirty-nine, he died insane in Ramsgate.

Symbolically, the meter controlling the electric lights in St Giles runs out before the viewer is ready for darkness.

Back in my High Street café, I opened the day's papers.

'Scotland says Yes.'

The beginning of the end of the United Kingdom had ousted

Diana from the front page: Scotland had celebrated the 700th anniversary of William 'Braveheart' Wallace's routing of the English at
Stirling Bridge by voting to return to an Edinburgh parliament.

Like the break-up of a great continental plate, the Empire had
fragmented and drifted away from the United Kingdom and now
the Union itself was cracking up. I found myself excited, sad and
frustrated. Dismantlement had to happen; the whole world was
reverting to tribal units. Scotland wanted to be a coherent entity,
like everywhere else. The English also needed a fresh start, led by
a generation who bore no imperial guilt or colonial responsibilities
and whose overseas adventures were limited to those of a paid-up
member of the humanitarian club. But the disbanding of one of the
most successful teams the world had ever known was a one-sided
affair. Great Britain had been a winner, dammit. I had liked being
British, too. At the end of it all, the English were helpless bystanders.
The tribe that had spawned an Empire had also exported its self-
will. All we could do was sit back and see what was left after the
Scots, Welsh and Northern Irish had deliberated. As I left the café
I drew strength from the absolute certainty that difficult journeys
are best undertaken alone.

Upper Tean Electronic surveillance signs warned me not to try a
short cut through the hospital as I left town by way of an alley in
order to keep west of 01.

On the truck-blasted verge of the A522, I walked south under
big-bladdered rainclouds until I met the Roman Road from Rocester
to Chesterton at Upper Tean. The T-junction was dominated by a
cliff of red brick that had once been one of Britain's first super-
factories, built in 1823 to manufacture tape. The new species of
factory sought to rationalize production by bringing all the workers,
machines and raw materials under one roof. The heart of the site
was the 217-foot, fireproof, steam-powered mill, twenty-seven bays
long and five bays wide, three storeys high. Hunched over their old
Dutch looms, the cottage-workers in the valley must have wondered
what was happening.

The *Cheadle and Tean Times* in my rucksack carried the 'shock news' that the factory, which still employed seventy and spun over one million metres of tape a week, was in trouble. The previous month had seen pre-tax losses of £5 million and the owners had accepted a takeover offer from a Swedish air-bag manufacturer. The site manager told the paper, 'I don't know exactly what is going on.'

Leigh Crossing   With rain pulverizing the gritty pavement, I dived into the inn opposite the factory and asked if I could stay the night.

'Don't do rooms,' shrugged the woman behind the bar.

'But you've got a bed-and-breakfast sign outside.'

'New owners,' she said, then suggested I try a place 'ten minutes' west of the village.

Twenty minutes later, soaked from the monsoon, I arrived at the bed and breakfast, a modern house set on a bank above the Roman Road. From the thighs down my new Cheadles were heavy with water. (I'd get straight into a hot bath then come downstairs for a pot of tea and biscuits.)

The woman who answered the door looked me up and down, scrutinized the wet walking boots. 'We're full.'

The presence of only one car, presumably hers, suggested that if she was full, her guests must have arrived on foot, by bicycle or by atomic re-materialization.

The rain ran off the brim of my hat, and now I'd stopped walking I could feel the chill of wet, clinging clothes.

'I'll pay to sleep in the garage.'

'We're not allowed to take paying guests in the garage.'

'I'll pay £20 to sleep in the garage.'

She shut the door.

My only way south was by farm track to the A50. After twenty minutes of being harried by heavy traffic, I reached a concrete bridge carrying another farm track over the main road. High up, where the embankment met the underside of the bridge, there was a crevice just deep enough to take a human body. I unrolled my sleeping mat, squirmed inside and waited for darkness.

Within minutes I was almost deranged. The crevice was reasonably comfortable, but the sudden explosions of tyre roar on the concrete slab road, the air rush and engine howl were amplified by the ceiling and walls of the bridge into screaming aural torture. How the hell did the homeless put up with it? I was reminded of a night twenty years earlier when I'd been caught by rain while cycling with a friend through Norfolk *en route* for Africa, and had slept inside a concrete pipe which had been of such a diameter that I spent eight hours with both arms stretched out ahead of me, in the high-diving position, emerging at dawn, deaf from traffic noise and covered from head to toe in black pitch. We'd laughed about it, then.

I dragged my kit back into the rain and for the next three kilometres battled southward over barbed wire, sodden meadows and ditches on a succession of public footpaths that had ceased through underuse to exist as imprints on the land.

By dusk I'd reached the deserted hamlet of Middleton Green, wet, covered in mud and still with nowhere to sleep. The rain had eased to drizzle.

I dumped the rucksack on the triangle of grass in the centre of the junction and waited.

Middleton Green seemed to have disconnected itself from the outside world. Its few houses were well-kept but showed no signs of life; dormitory hutches for commuters to Stoke or Stafford or Uttoxeter.

After fifteen minutes, a small car pulled up and a woman leaned from the window. 'Can I help?'

'I was wondering where to sleep.'

'Come back to my place. I'm sure we can sort something out.'

'Where exactly is your place?'

'Leigh Crossing.'

'Is Leigh Crossing within 1,000 metres of two degrees west?'

'Pardon?'

'I have to check the map.'

I opened the map at her car window. She was wearing brown shorts.

'I've been milking.'

Ruth's house at Leigh Crossing was 300 metres inboard of 01.

'I'd love to accept your offer.'

'Hop in.'

'I can't, but thanks. I like to walk.'

It took me twenty minutes to return the way I had come, then bear right along a narrow, puddled lane to the railway line at Leigh Crossing.

Ruth lived in a white cottage with black windows. A pretty garden opened on to fields. She made a pot of tea, found the biscuits and left me to bath upstairs while she went back to the farm. Outside the bathroom window, a train whooshed towards Stoke-on-Trent.

Up to my neck in tingling heat, I sipped tea and scanned *The Stunner*. The mayor of Cheadle, Mr Ron Locker, was pictured at the Annual Flower and Vegetable Show wearing a why-am-I-doing-this grimace and his gold chain, beside a row of missile-sized cucumbers; the Cheadle and District Summer Domino League pub fixtures were listed and there were reports and photographs from seven local weddings (honeymoons: Caribbean 3; African safari 1; Tunisia 1; Rhodes 1; Scotland 1).

I was sitting in an easy chair downstairs when Ruth returned.

'The cows were *awful* tonight. *And* they were kicking. Flies too.' The cows she was talking about belonged to John, her partner. John, explained Ruth, would call by later. 'He's moving drybags.'

'Drybags?'

'Milk cows who are having six weeks off milking before having calves.'

Ruth had lost her husband five years earlier. They had been on holiday in Scotland when he was stung on the chin in Tarbert and died of anaphylaxis. Ruth had pulled herself up; tragedy and two replacement hips had not taken the spring from her step.

John came in later, preceded by a bouncing dog called Jen who rolled straight on to her back to have her stomach tickled. John too was wearing shorts and he had a stringy athletic build that echoed Defoe's observation upon Staffordshire 'footmanship' – the county's ability to produce fleet-footed runners – which the eighteenth-century writer put down to hardy breeding rather than 'any particular temperature of the air or soil'.

Below the knees, each of John's legs was as white as a plucked chicken. 'Ah the welly line,' he laughed. 'The boots rub off the hair.'

He poured three whiskies and as we sat with the firelight playing on the amber glasses I saw this sad, wet bloke crawling with a rucksack and an umbrella into a concrete slot under a bridge on the A50. Glancing at Ruth and John, I couldn't think of a higher pleasure than to have been the recipient of an unexpected, incredible kindness.

Chartley   The public footpath across the fields south of Leigh Crossing had been obstructed by barbed wire, fences and finally a bull. So I emerged at a farmhouse in a mildly confrontational frame of mind. As I stalked through the farmyard a woman shot through a gate. '*Can* I help you!'

The aggressive landowner's rhetorical address to a stranger means the opposite of 'Can I *help* you?' and translates more accurately as 'Fuck off!'

'No. Thank you.'

'I saw you in the field. You know it's not a public right of way.'

'I was in that field because someone has put a bull in the field crossed by the public path.'

There was a moment's silence.

'It's not a dangerous bull.'

'How am I meant to know that?'

'If you knew about the countryside, you'd be able to tell.'

(*Long pause while townie breathes deeply*.)

'Weather's getting better,' I said. We talked about farming, BSE (all the fault of the media, naturally). I thanked her for the conversation and checked my map prior to walking on.

'You know,' she added, 'the lake by the hill is used by all kinds of wildfowl. It's a bit of a nature reserve really.'

I noticed that the public footpath passed within a hundred metres of the lake. The farmer's wife read my mind. '*You* won't be able to see the lake, because it's not on the public footpath.'

It was a day of cool clarity. The rain had rinsed the air and the sunlight painted black shadows under the billowing woodland. Summer was losing its warmth.

Being a stranger in my own land had been the plan, but I was increasingly an alien in someone else's land. These were the sorts of hedgerows and woods that I ran by as a boy, never thinking that they weren't mine. Now I lurked furtively in field edges.

Thirty minutes after my early-morning encounter with one of the countryside's genial custodians, I got lost.

The right of way I'd been following had led me through a wood and a field, to a minor road which passed a deserted hamlet called Fradswell, where I was forced to take to the fields again in order to keep within 1,000 metres of the meridian.

The fields were irregularly shaped and draped over muddling hillocks divided by dry valleys, and at some point I lost the line of the public path. Unconcerned cattle watched me pass to and fro on compass bearings. It was a difficult landscape; neither flat enough to see distant features, nor hilly enough to provide a helpful viewpoint. Almost anywhere, from the Gobi to the Andes, would have been easier.

This hummocked upland was described in 1868 by a writer who would be one of my most engaging companions over the coming days. The US consul to Birmingham, Elihu Burritt, visited on a day-trip. 'We came upon the wildest, boggiest, roughest stretch of land you could think possible to exist in the heart of a civilized county,' he wrote. 'One might well fear to wander deep into it, for it seemed endless and pathless, and fitted only for the lair of wild beasts.'

In this wilderness, the American was shown wild cattle, 'white buffaloes', whose raw steaks, he supposed, were supplied to Druids. These were the white cattle of Chartley, magnificent beasts with shining coats, dark ears and long, pointed horns. They came to a sad end. Thought at the time to have been brought over by Angles or Danes, they had survived till the Norman Conquest, when many became enclosed within royal forests. When the laws protecting royal game were repealed, revenge was exacted by the commoners. A few surviving herds were walled up by nobles in private parks such as Chillingham and Cadzow. The Chartley animals were rounded up in the remnants of Needwood Forest in about 1225 by William Ferrers, Earl of Derby, who drove them to Chartley. By 1899, fifty-five remained, but within years, tuberculosis hit the herd, reducing the number to eleven, who were offered for sale by auction in London. There were no takers. The Duke of Bedford acquired them by private treaty, but the train carrying them to Woburn Abbey caught fire and three more perished. In 1908 the thousand-acre park itself was destroyed by being put to the plough.

The Staffordshire Agricultural Society Ploughing and Hedgelaying Match was taking place in sight of the Earl of Derby's ruined castle.

In a vast field, squads of tractors and horses combed the soil before the watchful eye of stewards armed with tape-measures. Points were awarded for straightness, firmness, accuracy and something called the 'Ins and Outs'. A misplaced clod could lead to a point deficit. To an outsider, the classes were indecipherable: the category 'Best Ploughing With a Two or Three Furrow, One Way Plough (Traditional System)' carried a £20 first prize, with £5 for the second-best finisher under twenty-one.

Beside the tractors were the horse ploughs, teams of two beasts (Bosh and Bunter, Rosie and Jim, Lady Alison and Flash) leaning against the resistance of the curving share while the ploughman wrestled the long handles. Compared to the encased tractormen, the men who walked the furrows in thick cords were a convivial bunch, pausing now and again to wipe a brow, take a chat, discreetly knock a clod into place with the side of a boot.

For browsers, there were displays of baler twine and sheep pens, and a line of wheezing antiques tended by the Uttoxeter Vintage Tractor & Engine Club. Among them was a polished

Wolseley sheep-shearing machine made in Witton, Birmingham, in the 1940s, and an asthmatic Bamford running a water-pump off a long slapping drive-belt.

Phillip Hulme stroked his fleece-white beard as he sat in his immaculate red 1954 David Brown. 'I gave 240 quid for it when I bought it,' he said. 'As it is now it should be a thousand. It'll do about 32mph, on the road.' The tractor had once towed cargoes along the wharves of London Docks. He patted the cherubic bonnet of the David Brown. 'We've got five more at home. The wife likes tractors.'

Shugborough Two degrees west had seldom looked so trouble-free.

South from Chartley, the meridian was threaded with back-roads, towpaths, bridleways and footpaths which seemed to join end-on-end on a north–south axis as if someone had seen me coming and nudged the necessary bridges and public rights of way into a crooked, benevolent conformity.

For the next fourteen kilometres I could follow the sort of intuitive route that a walker might choose for its pleasing passage by canal bank and village to stately home and royal hunting forest. After the forest, everything would change, but that, for the moment, was a long way off.

Beyond a lampshade factory on the outskirts of Hixon, I joined the Trent & Mersey Canal. Thick unscuffed grass cushioned my footfalls on the towpath that Arnold Bennett had described in *Clay-hanger* as being 'a morass of sticky brown mud', his fictional narrow-boat hauled southward by a floundering 'unhappy skeleton' whipped around its crooked legs by a ragged bare-legged girl. Today, the canal is a picture of agreeable composure: beneath wind-tossed willows and a sky of tormented purple clouds, slid brightly painted boats, sunlit and dappled by turn, with fanciful names like *Dawdler*, *Little Otter* and *Chariots of Fire*; one with JESUS IS LORD on its windows. Polished brass portholes burned like giant gold gypsy rings and on the long roofs were coiled ropes, stacks of logs for wood-burning stoves, and Buckby cans hand-painted with dog roses and landscapes depicting canals snaking down from Alpine peaks past Lombard belfries to the industrial arches of red brick bridges.

The Trent & Mersey was James Brindley's most ambitious project, linking the two coasts of England in a 93-mile loop around the tail of the Pennines. Also known as the Grand Trunk Canal, it needed 76 locks and a 2,897-yard tunnel under Harecastle Hill. It was opened in 1777, well ahead of the three trans-Pennine routes further north. Financed by the Burslem pottery owner, Josiah Wedgwood, the Trent & Mersey was responsible for the industrial success of the Potteries. Freight continued to use its waters until the late 1960s.

Bascote No. 89, painted with poppy-red panels and elaborate scrolls, was headed south at walking pace. Julie and Peter were on their way home to Newbury. Julie wore black Doc Martens. Tresses of hair poured off her shoulders. She was an accountant.

'We sold the house,' she called across the water, 'thinking that we'd try a canal boat for a year or so. That was seven years ago!'

They spent the six winter months moored in Newbury, the six summer months cruising. This summer they had got as far as Chester; once they had reached Leeds, but that had taken them three months up and three months back. They had fitted-out the boat themselves. Through the open door mid-way along the hull throbbed an ancient Lister diesel, its copper and brasswork sparkling as if the boat's hold was loaded with precious metals.

At Hoo Mill Lock I left them, but they caught me again at Great Haywood, where I was sunning myself on the towpath bridge that spanned the junction of the Trent & Mersey with the Staffordshire & Worcester. Behind me, one of Brindley's great aqueducts opened the way to Wolverhampton. *Bascote No. 89* swung with the lazy turning-circle of a freshwater supertanker, off the Trent & Mersey and beneath my feet, headed for the Black Country and the distant south.

A few minutes down the towpath I left the canal and crossed the River Trent on Essex Bridge, a stone gangplank wide enough for one horse, with fourteen arches on cutwaters that sliced the current like a fleet of war canoes.

The path led through a wood to Shugborough Hall, the family seat of the Ansons. A Doric temple peeked from the trees. Ahead beamed the octagonal Tower of the Winds, copied from the marble original in Athens. Squirrels bounced on cropped lawns and sheep peered at the small-print of the pasture. Hall and park owe their treasures to two extraordinary Ansons, Thomas and his younger brother George, one a squire, the other an admiral. It was Spanish gold captured by George, then inherited by Thomas in 1762, which funded the park's collection of Greek Revival monuments. In a saga typical of so many great houses, a later Anson – the 1st Earl of Lichfield – squandered the family wealth, and in 1960 the estate was offered in part payment of death duties to the National Trust, whose tenant is currently the photographer and 5th Earl of Lichfield, Thomas Patrick Anson.

The triumphal arch that Thomas Anson built to commemorate the seafaring feats of his younger brother lay beyond my grid line, and so did the Lanthorn of Demosthenes, copied by the architect James 'Athenian' Stuart from a building of 4 BC in Athens. Where lawns ran down to the River Sow stood a crumpled ruin, with broken columns and truncated balustrades watched by an eroded Druid, and beyond it, a Chinese house copied from a sketch brought back from Canton by Admiral Anson, its parasol eaves reaching over a loop of still water. A swan dipped its head into the polished surface of the Sow, now marbled by clouds. The path led into the leaves, to the piece known as 'The Shepherd's Monument', where Nicolas Poussin's painting of 1639 had been carved beneath a Doric entablature. The sun slipped; the wind dropped. Deep in the foliage the shepherd traced with his finger the words *'Et in Arcadia Ego'*.

Great Haywood That night I slept in a lock-keeper's cottage beside the canal. The cottage had been converted into a holiday flat by a café owner, who let me rent it for the night.

Through the walls I could hear the rattle of rack and pinion, the rush of water through sluices and other miscellaneous sounds which could have come from any moment in the last three centuries: a man whistling, the whinny of a horse; the bump and grind of a narrowboat; the chink of a mooring ring.

Ships, and George Anson, came to mind. George had been born at Shugborough Hall in 1697. With the family seat due to pass to his older brother Thomas, George joined the navy and by the age of twenty-six was captain of the frigate *Scarborough*. By 1737, he was commanding sixty-gun *Centurion*, and it was in this ship, at the head of a squadron of six vessels, that George sailed three years later to harry the Spanish off south America. Two ships were lost rounding Cape Horn, then another three were sunk off Chile. With *Centurion* remaining and the crew cut to a diseased fraction of its original complement, George sailed on across the Pacific, captured the better-armed Spanish treasure galleon *Nuestra Señora de Cova-donga*, then returned around the Cape of Good Hope to England with £500,000 of booty. Later on the meridian, I'd meet another survivor from this epic three-year-nine-month circumnavigation.

The rush of falling water woke me, as the first narrowboat of the day passed through the lock on the other side of the wall. I pulled on my clothes, still wet from washing the previous evening. Full of water, the workingmen's Cheadles had a stiffness that made them freestanding. Incredible keks.

Little Haywood   Outside, dew still sparkled on the towpath grass. It was a Sunday morning. The sun blazed and by the time I'd reached Little Haywood my underclothes were nearly dry and bell-peals were bouncing across the rooftops.

Following the sound to its source, I came to the castellated walls of St Mary's Abbey as a congregation of nuns spilled into the sun.

'Would you like a cup of tea?' called a silver-haired woman with a soft Irish accent. She was with a black-clad priest and she led us both across the abbey drive to a modern house. Her name was Kitty, Lady Kitty Morrissey. Kitty's sister was the abbess.

'She's the baby of the family!' laughed Kitty, opening her front door. 'But she rose to dizzy heights.'

The three of us sat around her dining table with a view across the Trent Valley to the dark woods of Cannock Chase. Father Thomas was from Downside Abbey. 'On the Fosse Way,' he said, as if the last 2,000 years of road-building had passed him by.

I'd not intended to engineer morning tea in amusing company, which multiplied the pleasure.

Kitty and Father Thomas were old friends and both eighty-seven. They had the knack of pursuing their own conversations, alternately and with sudden switches of topic, so that I felt as if I was sitting between two radios, each set to change channel independently and without warning.

'I was converted to the Catholic Church in Paris,' said Father Thomas, 'when I was eighteen . . .'

'County Cork,' said Kitty. 'I was born in Cove . . .'

'. . . and joined the abbey a year after, 1929.'

'. . . and we had British sailors on the destroyers and soldiers in the forts so . . .'

'I left the Benedictines and tried the Cistercians.'

'. . . we were never short of a boy.'

'But that didn't work, and I thought I'd come to the end of my calling, then . . .'

'At school when I was fourteen,' chipped in Kitty, 'the nun said . . .'

'. . . I had an intuition that I must go to Lourdes.'

' "All of you put your head on the desk and those of you who'd like to, can pledge not to touch a drop of drink." '

'When I got to Lourdes, I spent three years working for the sick. Then I became director of the Knights of Malta.'

'And I did pledge, and I've never touched a drop.'

'I have a rule, not a vow, that if I'm drinking alone I never top up my glass.'

'More tea, Nick?'

'Thanks, yes.'

'Father Thomas?'

'Bless you. But after I left I kept up with the pilgrimages. Pilgrimages play a big part in my life.'

'All that travelling! He's a rich man!'

'I've made seventy-two pilgrimages to Lourdes.'

'Have you never had anything stolen?'

'I had my wallet stolen in Italy.'

'What do you carry all your money in?' asked Kitty.

'A money belt.'

'Money in a belt! Sacred Heart! He has money everywhere!'

'I was forty years a Catholic clergyman in Northampton. I built a church. St Gregory the Great's.'

Kitty left the room to answer the telephone and Father Thomas leant sideways. 'Do you know what kind of tea this is?' he whispered. '*Earl Grey!* Not my favourite.'

'I'm always grateful for a cup of tea.'

'Heaven forbid!'

The conversation turned to Diana. 'I'm very saddened,' said Father Thomas.

'Oh yes,' said Kitty, returning with the teapot. 'I was the same age as Diana when I got married, but I kept my thumb on my husband.'

'There seemed to be a week of hysteria . . .'

'His name was Finbar. Father, will you have another cup of tea?'

'. . . but at the same time the cries were self-controlled. People saw their future queen.'

'My son is called Finbar too. But we call him Barry.'

'Latterly she was a woman who knew her own mind . . .'

'Finbar is the patron saint of Cork.'

'. . . who cared for people in trouble. And that made people care for her.'

'Have another bun.'

In the distance, a long red train painted with the white word 'Virgin' slid silently up the verdant valley.

'What do you think of the spiritual state of the nation?' I asked.

'Rubbish!' said Kitty.

'I'd rather not say,' said Father Thomas, cautiously. 'It behoves us all to be hopeful.'

Cannock Chase   The meridian ran through the centre of Cannock Chase.

The rims of plateaux are like island coastlines: a meeting of mediums, land and water for an island, land and air for a plateau; a perimeter where man watches, builds and dies. If the meridian had skimmed the edge of the Chase, I'd have been able to visit Paget's deer park at Beaudesert or the Iron Age camp at Castle Ring, or the Katyn Memorial, or the birthplace of Dr Johnson, the Englishman who never fails to snag the nib of anyone writing a book about his native country. But meridians have no instinct. Straight-line walking is a triumph of faith over expectation; believing in the unexpected rather than expecting the unbelievable.

So I crossed the Trent and climbed through trees to the plateau at 200 metres above sea level. Sunbeams swivelled through passing stands of pine. I'd hoped for a retrospective view north across the Trent to the end of the Pennines but the conifers stood shoulder-to-shoulder as if they were in the Pindhos or Lévka Óri and I found myself using the compass to check my paths.

Bicycle spokes glittered through breaks in the ferns; a horse spluttered as it mounted a cut through Corsican pine. I caught glimpses of dog-walkers and day-packs. Pebbled paths wandered over the confusing topography of the plateau, meeting and veering at random. It was easy to imagine how folk could disappear on what the Celts called *cnoc*, hill.

'Kanck-Wood,' wrote Celia Fiennes during her 'Great Journey' of 1698, 'is but a barren heath ground but good wood.' The colonel's daughter was on her way north to Hadrian's Wall, but paused at Cannock Chase, where she praised the quality and price of Cannock coal, and wrote of the practice of harvesting the Chase bracken, which was being burned for its ashes, and then rolled into balls and used for scouring and washing.

Celia Fiennes had caught Cannock Chase at a mid-point in its shrinkage from a royal hunting forest of the Mercian kings to an Area of Outstanding Natural Beauty farmed by the Forestry Commission. A wilderness which once rolled from the Trent to Wednesbury now measures a mere sixty-seven square kilometres; the playground of kings is flooded with 2 million visitors a year. Cannock Chase is the smallest AONB in mainland Britain and the only one to lie entirely within green belt; it is the green lung of the West Midlands.

'We're very stretched,' the head ranger told me over coffee in the Visitor Centre.

Malcolm Hulme was one of seven rangers who looked after Cannock Chase. Surrounded by towns and cities, the Chase was a target for all kinds of illicit activities, from hobbyists with metal-detectors to model-aircraft flyers and off-road drivers. There were stories of IRA arms dumps hidden on the Chase. Someone had once taken a pot-shot at a courting couple. Where Henry II had galloped after deer, the herds were now being chased by mountainbikers. The rangers also had to keep an eye open for 'mining breaks', fissures that could suddenly open above abandoned coal mines. A boy had once been stuck in a break for three days. The rangers encouraged visitors not to stray off the paths, where they couldn't see what lay underfoot.

'It sounds like doom and despondency,' Malcolm corrected. 'But it's not.'

He was right. Considering how many used it, I was astonished by the tranquillity and good repair of Cannock Chase. The same seven rangers were also responsible for monitoring Staffordshire's public rights of way. 'We've got 4,000 kilometres of them. That's a greater distance than all the motorways in the country,' nodded Malcolm.

We swapped bull stories and compared notes on electric fences, broken stiles, sawn-off fingerposts and crops deliberately planted across paths and bridleways.

In Malcolm's office I heard my favourite arable parable. 'One of our rangers,' said Malcolm, 'was on a footpath talking to two farmers, neither of whom would admit to owning the field, so the ranger said, "I was only asking 'cos I've just found a fiver in the field."

'"That's mine!" said both farmers.'

For the rest of the day I made my way off the Chase in a series of loops and detours through the remains of military camps.

During the First World War, the Chase had been an obvious site for a training camp, on agriculturally useless land near to a mainline railway in the centre of the country. At the time, there were barracks in the UK for only 175,000 men, a fraction of the number required to field an adequate army for the war in France, and so camps mushroomed up and down the country, from Catterick to Crowborough. Further down the meridian, on the site of another of these camps, I was to connect poignantly with my own family.

On Cannock Chase, traction engines hauled twenty tons at a time to construction sites where 800 men laboured to lay sewage and water pipes, and to erect stables and messes, store rooms, offices and a fat factory where meat scraps, bone and fat were rendered into dripping. By March 1915, 500 huts were standing and the Chase was home to 40,000 soldiers. Later, a German prisoner-of-war camp was built up here too. After the Armistice, the weeds had hardly covered the remains of the camps when the huts, cinema and synagogue of RAF Hednesford, No. 6 School of Technical Training, sprouted up across another 250 acres of the Chase. The most conspicuous RAF leftover today is the officers' mess, now the Visitor Centre.

A path took me down through birch and pine and a calf-high froth of bilberry and heather, to the filter beds of the Great War sewage works. On the edge of a concrete tank sprouting with weeds, a German prisoner had chipped BUILT BY PoW 1916.

A little further I came to the site of the 1,000-bed hospital that had treated soldiers shipped home from the trenches with shell-shock and gas poisoning. The soldiers had planted laurel and rhododendrons along the road past the hospital entrance and eighty years on the shrubs now formed a tunnel through which I had to stoop, past the concrete plinth of the flagpole, the hut bases and an iron manhole cover cast by Ham Baker of Westminster. The hospital was a sombre relic, throttled with briars, twisted birch and bracken. 'This is a horrible place on the top of a hill,' wrote one First World War soldier of Cannock Chase. 'The cold is dreadful and always a wind blowing.'

Through the trees, I joined the track-bed of the railway the troops called the 'Tackeroo Express':

> Our Tackeroo Express, our Tackeroo Express!
> The scenery is wonderful, as you all confess,
> Everything is splendid, especially the Mess,
> From the sparks that fly as we pass by,
> On the Tackeroo Express.

Spaces for the sleepers still showed on the track-bed beneath my boots. The railway was standard gauge and laid by Irish labourers employed by the West Cannock Colliery Company at the beginning of the First World War. The railway led me off the plateau, out of the trees.

Valley Pit   West Cannock No. 5 is now a business park; Valley Pit is a heritage centre.

Valley became a working pit in 1874, when the Cannock and Rugeley Colliery Company sank its first pit on land leased from the Marquis of Anglesey. After extraction ceased in 1962, the pit lingered on as a National Coal Board training centre. The pithead baths, which had once washed 576 men at a sitting, were turned over to the Mines Rescue Service; the storehouse that kept corn for 200 pit ponies was converted to classrooms, a library and an office. Each morning, the trainee miners passed a large sign: 'This colliery is owned by N.C.B. – managed by the people on behalf of the people.' By 1989, Valley Pit was a museum.

The mining artefacts labelled and sealed behind the display glass recalled the camps on the plateau: men bunched shoulder-to-shoulder in black-and-white photographs wore the same expressions, frozen in youth, of the knots of chums departing for the Front. The mining pictures of buttressed walkways, duckboards, water and filth were images shared with the trenches, while their tools could also have been intended for the battlefield: the Casartelli anemometer (used for measuring air flow) looked like part of a field-gun and so did the improved mining aneroid, which had measured the depth of the workings. The electric shot firer could have been a piece of eccentric ordnance; miners' 'checks' – the pieces of metal stamped with their bearer's number – were like dogtags. Only the miners' lamps stood out as recognizable symbols. Up here in the daylight, polished for posterity, they lined up like mute icons, each bearing a number. The miners – like the men of the trenches – had become a generation of ghosts.

In a separate gallery the hardware of wives and mothers described a home-life as physical as pit-work. Here were the pots, tin baths, irons, mangles, sewing-machines and a Jiffy Automatic Clothes Washer (built in Accrington) which, despite its name, was operated by a heavy crank-handle. The bar of ' "Rub-a-Dub" Three Men in a Tub Carbolic' ('Gives a Mighty Lather' 3d) was a reminder that bathing was not a late-night leisure activity but a communal scrub.

Across the road from the Heritage Centre, the pithead baths had been transformed into the Lost Mine public house.

Behind the bar stood four pharaohs. A fake dinosaur fossil swam across one of the walls. From the shadows, two Inca gods watched American car-racing on a cinema screen. The all-over decor of sandy rough-cast completed the impression that Atahualpa had converted the tomb of Ramesses II into a Jurassic theme bar.

The pub had been created by the son of a retired miner. The other son had played guitar with Whitesnake.

Hednesford Behind the pub, a footpath climbed into Hednesford Hills, a promontory of heath between the pits and the town; perhaps the remnant of the 'fine wood called Hedgford' ridden through by Celia Fiennes in 1698.

Up here, miners had raced whippets and flown pigeons. Hoof-prints showed on the path that climbed through the heather and bracken. The rides had once been used to train racehorses. Three had won the Grand National.

Back to the north, Cannock Chase reappeared as a black forested rim on the skyline. All the other horizons were crenellated with dwellings and factories; a communications tower peered down from the evening sky. In the birch and pine on the highpoint I looked fruit-lessly for the cockpit where miners had once pitted their birds against each other while keeping an eye open for approaching police.

Hednesford exuded an air of weary insecurity. Road grime coated the houses on the hectic A460, and the first shop I passed as I crossed the main road into the village was Dobermann Securities, its windows stuffed with the wherewithal to convert a house into a panzer-proof redoubt. Having been warned off one pub 'because of the rockers', I continued down to the railway line, turned into Anglesey Street and pushed the doorbell of Number 24.

With net curtains facing the pavement, my room had been last used by chain-smoking stock-car racers who'd been competing at Hednesford Raceway.

'Were you brought up here, in Hednesford?' I asked Mrs Brown as she left the room.

'Hed-nes-ford?' she laughed, stressing the three syllables. 'Idiots call it "Hed-nes-ford"; new locals call it "Hensford"; old locals call it "Hedgeford".'

'Were you brought up here?'

'No,' she chuckled. 'Me? I'm a Black Country wench.'

'Wench?' I wondered.

'Woman. It's Black Country for a woman.'

*

Hednesford's *passeggiata* consisted of young men in small hatchbacks screaming repeatedly round the one-way system.

In the Balti restaurant I was the only diner. Ahmed Muhit, the manager, had come to Britain as a twelve-year-old in 1978, from Bangladesh. Like most of Britain's incoming Bangladeshis, Ahmed had grown up in Sylhet, underneath the Jaintia Hills. His family had settled in the Bangladeshi community in Smethwick, further down the meridian.

We talked about his country. In the mid-eighties my cousin Richard and I had ridden bicycles across Bangladesh and I had memories of being surrounded by an incredulous multitude each time the bikes stopped; of bending beneath a village pump and having a gang of boys crank torrents of cool water over our roasted heads; of being arrested for 'encouraging a riot' (our bicycle ride coincided with the end of martial law); of boats on the Ganges with sails so patched that a gust would have torn them to shreds; of paddies and pastures greener than any green I'd seen before; of poverty and cleanliness; of a bookshop in a bazaar crammed with English classics. Bangladesh was so fecund that a farmer could crop four times a year, and so crowded that even the countryside seethed.

In 1991 Ahmed returned home to visit his family. As the plane descended over Dhaka he saw that the land was brown. 'Only the runways were out of the muddy water. Driving from the airport, I saw that the water was full of bodies. Animals, humans.'

In one month's time it would be National Curry Day and Ahmed was going to give 10 per cent of his takings to Save the Children.

Heath Hayes Butting on to the south side of Hednesford was a model suburb for the new millennium, an eat–sleep zone of modern housing encircled by interconnected roundabouts.

Two cars juddered to a halt. The driver of the blue Escort yelped at the driver of the red Metro, who leapt out of his car, dropped something small and black on the road, scrabbled for it, then threw himself into the blue Escort, which whined off, leaving the Metro abandoned at the roadside.

I turned to the first house, rang the bell and used the telephone to dial 999.

The owners had moved in that week.

'It's lovely,' said Marie, who was the mother-in-law. 'They've got a garden and there are footpaths. The kids can walk to school. And you should see the supermarket. Very good it is.'

Twenty minutes later, two police cars showed up and I continued my exploration of Heath Hayes.

Brick-built terraces, det's and semi-det's with Georgian doors and plastic windows were planted along the verges of culs-de-sac and organically curved 'closes'. Heavily used desire paths tramped into the lank grass of a little valley between the houses converged on a feature marked on my map as 'District Centre': a gigantic Co-op superstore with a car park the size of an airfield. Inside, I could buy anything from brussels sprouts to a holiday in Florida.

Heath Hayes was a vision of the future, an instant, economic community clustered around a central warehouse that supplied every consumer requirement. Heath Hayes had no under-used church or idiosyncratic shops, wonky pub or skeletal post office. The Co-op dealt only in items that people needed or couldn't resist.

Leaning against the Co-op Superstore was a Raleigh All Steel Bicycle with an enclosed chain case, a three-speed hub gear with integral dynamo.

'I bought it in 1935,' said a tall man with a ramrod back, tie and tweed cap. 'It cost me £12 at a time when other bikes cost £3.' His name was Bill Rogers.

'It's the bike that keeps me going,' he said. He was seventy-five and lean. 'I was in the Guards. The Coldstreams.'

Bill had been working on bomb damage in Birmingham when he was called up in 1942. 'I was a gunner in a Churchill tank. We crossed the Channel five weeks after D-Day and went through France, Belgium and Holland. Overloon. That was a big one.' Bill hesitated. 'One man I'll never forget is Lieutenant Christie-Miller. All my life I've remembered him.

'We were lost in no-man's land, in Normandy. My commander, "Shiny" Shield, said, "Hold up, Tug – that was what they used to call me – there's a tank behind us."

'So this tank came up beside us. It was Lieutenant Christie-Miller. He says to Shiny, "What's up?"

'Shiny says, "We're lost, sir."

'"Don't worry, Sergeant," says Christie-Miller. "Follow me!"

'So Christie-Miller moves about twenty yards down the road and an "88" went through his tank and killed him.'

Bill shook his head. 'You see, we were between two apple orchards and there was a gap for a five-barred gate and that "88" was trained through the gate. They were waiting for us.'

Guardsman Rogers looked across at the Co-op, and the vast car park. 'I wake up every morning and think how fortunate I am. If Lieutenant Christie-Miller hadn't come up behind us just then, it would have been my tank driving past that gate. He saved my life.'

People like Bill came not just from another generation but a different place, an earlier England.

Bill's was a story that had a million duplicates. He'd been called up, done his bit, come home, and got on with life. There was no trauma-counselling, compensation, book deals or TV appearances. Bill returned to the Black Country, oiled his Raleigh, loaded his carpentry tools on the carrier, and went back to work. If I'd used the word 'hero' while we'd been chatting outside the Co-op, I'm sure that Bill would have been nonplussed. But of course he was a hero. They all were.

Months after meeting Bill, I traced the charge across northern Europe of the 4th Tank Battalion of the Coldstream Guards. Bill's battalion of fifty-eight tanks had driven their Churchills up the beaches of Normandy on 20 July 1944 and, eleven days later, were involved in the battle to capture 'Hill 309' that had cost Christie-Miller his life. By the time the 4th Coldstreams had fought their way across the lowlands of northern Europe to the Baltic, fifty-five of them had been killed and 177 wounded.

A letter of thanks from the commander of the US Airborne Corps, who had ridden on top of the Churchills from the Rhine, commended the Guardsmen for 'that atmosphere, that intangible something almost physical which only the finest troops create'.

Watling Street   Beyond the Heath Hayes estates stretched a ravaged no-man's land, a battlefield in the early stages of regeneration.

On the map were curious blanks where the contour lines had melted away. Entire hills had been rubbed out. Stains of grey stippling marked old tips, one of them a kilometre across; there were strange-shaped lakes where workings had flooded; blade-straight scars of disused railways, pylon lines and the dried canal; then the blood-red diagonal of the old border between the Danish north and the Saxon south – Watling Street, now the A5.

The map did not show what lay beneath the surface. The land here had been so burrowed that in July 1960 it sagged exhaustedly and the canal-bed fell twenty-one feet.

The only legal passage within my 2,000-metre band was a road that kinked south through the reclaimed land. In places, fields had been restored, but it was desolate and exposed and apart from the occasional passing car the only movement came from the scorpion-yellow earth-movers that prowled to and fro trailing droppings.

The road met Watling Street mid-point on a stretch where the Roman engineers had built the agger for five kilometres without a bend.

Lingering on the blasted verge, I remembered that I'd been here before: many years earlier I'd tried to ride a bicycle from London to Holyhead non-stop and I'd passed this spot as darkness fell. I'd been pedalling for ten hours and was still ahead of the 9½mph averaged by the Holyhead Mail the previous century, but as the orange fur of Cannock's street lights began to blur the horizon, I lost my night-sight to the streaking headlights and pedalled off the agger into the ditch.

When I came round and looked up at the traffic thundering past my head in the dark I laughed. What madness had made me think that I would survive a night on Watling Street? I'd been sharing one of the busiest A-roads in the country, at night, with two queues of traffic moving at seven times my own speed. Against the strobing headlights, my bicycle lamp looked like the glow of a distant cigarette. What I was doing was legal but suicidal. To a devotee of Betjeman's 'Centaur bike', this was a revelatory moment: England's 'open road' had become an illusion. In the years since I'd learned to turn a pedal, the number of cars on Britain's roads had tripled from 5 million to 16 million. Before the war, when my father took off as a boy to ride from Hertfordshire to Devon, he'd been sharing the roads with fewer than 2 million cars. By 2030 there'll be 33 million.

Traffic howled down the tapered straight. I waited for fifteen minutes, then ran across.

One day, a meridional walker will be unable to cross here, for this is the route of the 43-kilometre Birmingham Northern Relief Road. Relief for whom? Not the people along its course. When the road is open, 72,000 vehicles a day will pass over this sad landscape on a highway that has consumed 1,168 acres of agricultural land and £650 million. Its purpose is to relieve the pressure on the M6, which was built to relieve the A45 and A34, which were built to relieve the turnpike, which was built to relieve the original road that in Shakespeare's time linked the villages between Stratford, Coventry and Stafford. The Birmingham Northern Relief Road is the largest of the Tory bypasses to survive the Labour government's roads rethink.

Among the lobbyists for the new road were the industries and chambers of commerce in Birmingham and the Black Country, whose economies were being strangled by traffic. Wanting to loosen the knot they've tightened the noose.

Dark Lane 'Black by day and red by night,' wrote the US consul to Birmingham in 1868. 'It is a section of Titanic industry, kept in murky perspiration by a sturdy set of Tubal Cains and Vulcans.'

In calling up the images of Eden's iron-worker, Elihu Burritt MA was alluding to the birth of a new world. The Black Country, reported the consul to his superiors in the Department of State in Washington, 'cannot be matched, for vast and varied production, by any other space of equal radius on the surface of the globe'.

En route from Boston and Harvard to the Court of St James a few years earlier, Burritt's countryman Henry Adams was equally awed and wrote of 'The plunge into darkness lurid with flames; the sense of unknown horror in this weird gloom which then existed nowhere else, and never had existed before, except in volcanic craters.'

At the end of the following century, my Ordnance Survey maps showed the Black Country as a vast ash-grey shadow attached to Birmingham, a metropolis by default, a multiplicity of towns that had fused and burned hotter than the sum of their parts. Were it to have grown concentrically from an ancient kernel, with a single, centralized administration, the Black Country would have been England's second city instead of Birmingham. Not only was it bigger in area, but the Black Country's four boroughs exceeded the population of Birmingham by over 100,000.

This was the black hole in the centre of England, the furnace that sucked in sweat and ingenuity then spewed starbursts of products across the biggest Empire the world has ever known. At night the sky glowed with reflected flame; by day the air was dark with soot and smoke.

The Black Country had labour, location and iron, the substance regarded at the time as being most indispensable to the human race after air and water. The Black Country was at the centre of the nation, at the hub of the canal network, and surrounded by iron's raw materials: coal, limestone, iron-ore and sand. When Burritt took up his post in Birmingham, Great Britain was producing more than half the world's pig iron: 6 million tons a year. By 1907 production had risen to 10 million tons. Iron was the wonder-metal, abundant, strong and versatile: sudden cooling made it extremely hard, slow cooling made it soft and pliable. Iron could be made tough enough for bridges and rails, tools and machinery, or soft enough for horse-shoe nails which – so it was said – had to be so pliable that a smith could bend them on his forehead. The Industrial Revolution was the second Iron Age, the Black Country the crucible.

The Black Country was defined by its industrial fallout and by the fruits of its labours: keys from Wednesfield; horses' bits, harness fittings and saddlery from Bloxwich and Walsall; glass from Smethwick; anchors and cables from Tipton; springs from West Bromwich; nails and chains from Cradley; locks from Wolverhampton and Willenhall. The Black Country sold to an Empire that spanned five continents and contained over one-quarter of the earth's land area and population. Small metal parts were needed for an army in India, wars in Europe and the opening up by horse and rail of Asia, New Zealand, Australia and Canada.

Nowhere else on the planet was there such a concentration of mechanical endeavour. This was the flaming perdition beyond the imagination of all but the bravest investigators, the model for Nell's journey through hell in *The Old Curiosity Shop*, published in the decade in which Turner painted his flying hare being chased down by a predatory locomotive in 'Rain, Steam and Speed'.

Before the fires died and the collieries closed, there were some who could already see through the white heat of invention and technology to the shadows of environmental catastrophe:

Amidst these flaming, smoky clanging works, I beheld the remains of what had once been happy farmhouses, now ruined and deserted. The ground beneath them had sunk by the working out of the coal, and they were falling to pieces. They had in former times been surrounded by clumps of trees; but only the skeletons of them remained, dilapidated, black and lifeless. The grass had been parched and killed by the vapours of sulphurous acid thrown out by the chimneys; and every herbaceous object was of a ghastly grey – the emblem of vegetable death in its saddest aspect. Vulcan had driven out Ceres.

That was James Nasmyth, inventor of the steam hammer and pile-driver, writing in 1883. By the turn of the century, Muirhead's *Blue Guide* was warning readers away from the Black Country by describing it as 'a busy but uninteresting region of iron and steel works'.

Undeterred by the *Blue Guide* – on which he relied during his *English Journey* – J. B. Priestley trod where few travellers dared during the 1930s. The old soldier who'd survived the Western Front and seen what war could do to a landscape was appalled:

> Industry has ravished it; drunken storm troops have passed this way; there are signs of atrocities everywhere; the earth has been left gaping and bleeding; and what were once bright fields have been rummaged and raped into these dreadful patches of waste ground.

Twenty years later, when Ernest Homeshaw published *The Story of Bloxwich* in 1955, the fires were dying and the Black Country was

> characterised by drab industrial towns; new housing sites . . . spoil banks, shale, ironstone, and slag; some derelict canals . . . a profusion of strongly surfaced roads to carry heavy traffic . . .

The effect on any visitor, he added unnecessarily, was to make the aesthetic sense 'shudder'.

It was difficult not to be intimidated by the literature of the Black Country. My 1995 *Blue Guide* echoed Muirhead and wrote off the region as 'largely nondescript'. Lonely Planet's guide, *Britain*, did not mention the Black Country. Only the *Rough Guide* tackled the black hole head on, with a chirpy tour of a few industrial museums.

My sources could not agree on the geographical definition of the Black Country. Apparently there were folk in Bloxwich and Walsall who claimed not to be Black Country people, and Smethwickians who called themselves Brummies rather than Black-countrymen, yet all three 'towns' fell within most definitions of the Black Country. Most agreed (though not Burritt, who saw everything within a twenty-mile radius of Birmingham as Black Country) that the Black Country did not include Birmingham. If Walter Allen, whose book *Black Country* was published in 1946, had been accused of living in the Black Country, he would have been 'surprised, indeed indignant'. He was born in the grey zone, between Birmingham and Walsall. To Allen, the border was defined by dialect. On the Birmingham side people spoke with a 'slovenly tripe-tongued wretchedly articulated Brummagen accent' and on the other, Black Country side, they employed 'richer, slower, fuller tones' which he associated with country folk.

Bloxwich-born Homeshaw was emphatic, drawing a line around twenty or so towns from Bloxwich in the north to Halesowen in the south, but excluding Birmingham. The eleventh edition of the *Encyclopaedia Britannica* (usually a good arbiter in such matters) left off the northern and southern towns, all of which grew as suburbs after its publication.

It was tripe-tongued Walter Allen who presciently solved the problem by observing that the Black Country 'is never where one lives oneself but begins always at the next town'.

Today, the shame of bearing a sooty label has been replaced by a tentative pride in lost industrial might. The four boroughs of Dudley, Sandwell, Walsall and Wolverhampton (roughly equivalent to Homeshaw's Black Country definition) have combined to promote themselves as 'The Black Country, a unique area of the West Midlands, in the heart of England'.

On the far side of the A5, I crossed the county line from Staffordshire to the West Midlands.

Of the thirteen English counties that the meridian passes through, West Midlands has the smallest area but the largest population: 2.6 million people squeezed into 900 square kilometres, an average per square kilometre of 2,908 people. In Northumberland, the figure is sixty-one. Outside Greater London, the West Midlands is England's most densely populated region.

*

Dark Lane, now a footpath, writhed along field boundaries, through oak and hawthorn, ash, holly and sprays of hazel to the Wyrley & Essington Canal.

On a humpback towpath bridge, I was able to look back at the course of the old Lord Hayes branch of the canal, now stanked off – closed – and down the Wyrley & Essington towards the unseen suburbs. There was no sign of the towpath once trodden by the horses that hauled Cannock coal to Birmingham's furnaces. Reeds nodded at their own reflections in water that was as clear as glass.

'It's because there's no boats,' said an angler crouched by a tray of writhing maggots. 'The boats bring up the mud.'

The canal snaked towards a pair of tall shining blocks that rose above the distant trees like the rectangular towers of a Babylonian gateway.

As I closed on the urban fringe, the water grew a scum of weed and car tyres and polystyrene burger-cartons. A bridge loomed, and I turned on to a road past a chip shop and 1950s houses to the twin tower-blocks I'd seen from afar: Thomas House and Smith House. Tom Smith; Everyman.

'Everyman, I will go with thee and be thy guide. In thy most need to go by thy side.' The words of the Tudor morality play had a reassuring ring as I passed between the towers into the great metropolis.

Bloxwich   Flames licked from the mouths of hearths and the burning air was thick with the hiss and crash of two 400-ton presses punching soft metal into greased dies. The presses stood side by side, black and twice as tall as a man, each with a pair of spinning flywheels and a central screw thread as thick as an arm that caught the gleam of the flickering fires. Men with two-handed tongs lifted glowing billets of metal from the hearths and placed them in the presses, standing back to flick the lever that smashed the cold hard dies around the soft hot 'slug'. Through the spurting smoke of seared graphite grease, the upper die rose with the screw thread and the stamper's tongs wrenched the slug – now shaped into a door-handle for an ambulance or a light fitting – from the lower die, turned it over to check for flaws, then tossed it into a metal bin.

The chief stamper had worked on the presses for thirty years. Paul Knowles was a large man, stamped with tattoos and wearing a gold ring through his left ear-lobe.

'You get used to burns,' he shouted above the roar of his hearth. 'You don't feel it. You get toughened.'

Sometimes they cooked eggs and bacon on a shovel in the hearth. Brass needed to be heated to 560 degrees. Paul had no thermometer. 'You can tell by the colour,' he shouted. 'Copper goes blue then green then nearly white. Brass is ready when it's red.'

'What sort of red?'

He looked puzzled. 'I can't say, but I know.'

The trick was 'catching the blow', lifting the press just as the billet was struck. It required split-second timing. On a good day, Paul could stamp 1,500 pieces.

Hot-metal stamping had changed little over the previous century. Men still pushed wheelbarrows of billets from the saw-shop to the hearths, then barrowed the stampings back to a power press that would punch off the 'flash' – the wafer of metal formed where the two halves of the die had collided with each other. Afterwards, the semi-finished parts were 'barrelled' – chucked in a drum and tossed about to clean them ready for delivery to the customer. The presses had been built in 1936.

'There's nothing that would do a better job,' said the managing director in his upstairs office. 'They're fairly basic; the main running pieces are the screw and the bearings on the flywheel. There's not a lot to go wrong.'

Replacing one of the screws had just cost Richard Franks £25,000. Bloxwich Brass Stampings Ltd had, he said, a turnover of 'around half a million'. The presses occupied a set of low-roofed stables built the previous century for horses who used to pull the local railway trains; the offices were in a building that had been erected in 1918 for a drop-hammer specialist.

Richard leaned back behind a wooden desk piled with papers. His father, Norman Franks, had gone into metal-working in 1930, and the family firm had survived the war and the recession of the early 1990s.

'How are you doing at the moment?'

'We've got enough work. We're not so desperate that customers are shouting. It's a state I call "wonderfully average".'

'D'you feel part of a great industrial tradition?'

He chuckled. 'It all changed in the sixties. There's no sentimentality about the business now. Most days it's a bearpit.' He handed me a small piece of ribbed brass. 'Your friend's.'

On its flat side, the odd-shaped pressing was stamped with the letters LH.

Luke Hughes was one of the country's leading furniture designers. He was another friend who'd been to Everest, reaching the upper slopes before storms forced a withdrawal. The piece of brass in my hand was Patent Number 2272833. Luke had derived his invention from the kinds of small metal parts that had put the Black Country on the world map: his locking mechanism was adapted from that of a shotgun, while the mechanics of the release button had been modelled on the safety-catch of a 9mm Browning pistol. The invention was a locking catch for a folding table and it had already generated £2 million worth of business for Luke Hughes & Co.

Bloxwich, the meridian's gateway to the Black Country, went into the Industrial Revolution making the hardware for horse transport; Longbridge, at the meridian's southern exit of the Black Country, emerged from the Industrial Revolution making cars.

An 1813 survey of trades in Bloxwich put bit makers at the top of the list, then farmers, awl-blade makers, locksmiths, victuallers, stirrup makers, snaffle makers and coach bit makers. Apart from the steam engine erected on the road to Walsall by Mr Pratt, the miller, Bloxwich relied on muscle, family 'manufactories' tacked to the back of the houses. Boys shovelled coal and worked the bellows; men pounded anvils set on granite blocks; women filed and polished. Work ran from dawn till dusk, and by candlelight if the merchants and factors of Walsall and Birmingham demanded more.

A strong, skilled man could beat out 300 awl-blades a day. By 1834, when William White published his *History, Gazeteer, and Directory of Staffordshire*, the town of Bloxwich had become 'more celebrated than any other in the kingdom' for its awl-blades. It was probably Bloxwich blades that I'd seen on Josiah Thompson's 1882 warehouse inventory in Berwick.

But the bitties and tackies and awl-blade makers of Bloxwich got smothered by the march of the smokestacks. On the bank of the Wyrley & Essington Canal an iron and brass foundry appeared, and then a steam-engine manufacturer. Bloxwich men began to migrate to new coal pits and blast furnaces. In Birchills, just down the canal, George Jones employed 400 men to produce 20,000 tons of iron a year.

By the time the 1911 *Walsall Directory* was published, only seven awl-blade makers remained in Bloxwich.

Opposite the kick-boxing hall in the centre of Bloxwich, I took lunch in JJ's Café.

Out of the damp wind the café was muggy with steamed cabbage and smiling faces addressing each other as 'love' and 'pal'. For £2.85, the price in London of a cappuccino and a chocolate croissant, I got a heart-attack platter of roast lamb, baked potatoes, peas, carrots, gravy and a mug of tea.

Outside the rain-smeared window a girl wearing ear studs, a nose ring and a school uniform, sucked on a cigarette and laughed.

'It's a suburb of Walsall now,' said one of the waitresses when I asked about Bloxwich.

The notes were in my rucksack. When the industrial age ended, the suburban age began. Work no longer lay at the end of the street. First came the 1930s council estates I'd walked through on the way from the canal, geometric grids of red-brown brick with tiled or slate roofs, gathered in pairs or terraced batches of three and four, all set back a statutory twenty feet from the highway. Many carried the add-ons of the 1990s: satellite dishes, intruder lights, burglar-alarm boxes, plastic porches and fanlight front doors. Most still had the original crenellated front wall that delineated each suburban castle.

The last green belt on the east side of Bloxwich was gobbled up by the Ryecroft estates. To the west, Dudley's Fields and Mossley were built over after the last war, then Broad Lane. The building came to a halt when the fields were full.

The maps had changed colour when I entered Bloxwich. At arms' length, each sheet looked an indiscriminate monochrome mess. Closer to the eye, every kilometre square carried its own patterns: factory zones laid down like circuit-boards of computer chips; housing estates swirling and curling, repeating themselves, never identically, with tiny gardens that followed the dark spines of the terraces like fleshless dorsal fins.

Here were Alan Turing's reaction-diffusion equations applied to the urban miasma; spontaneous patterns created by chinks in the symmetry; perfect grids being interrupted by a hill-slope, railway, factory or cemetery, diffusing and reacting with geography to create at one extreme, simple forms like asymmetric pentagons and squashed ovals and at the other extreme, the patterns of animal hides and sea-shells that were too complex to have names but whose reproduced forms confirmed a secret rationale.

Cementing the whole fractured mosaic were the hot red roads.

This was the magical maze, the multiple-choice urban map. Here was a variety of routes that the countryside could never achieve. Lying on the line, I'd grown familiar with restricted options, but here was flexibility on a grand scale.

Yet the new freedom to move introduced a new anxiety: if every road junction was a crossroads, I would have to reject two roads for every one I followed. If each road I didn't take met another crossroads as frequently as the road I did take, there could be twenty-six complete routes I knew nothing about after my third crossroads. After my tenth crossroads, the unknowns could have totalled 59,048.

Omission had been a periodic frustration in the countryside. In the Black Country it would be continuous, and exacerbated by the way that the meridian missed places that would have given me a handle on a vast, unfamiliar conurbation. From grid line 303 to

275, two degrees west took a 28-kilometre cross-section out of the metropolis, missing Birmingham, of course, and the 'capital' Wolverhampton too. It also missed the Black Country's other main towns, Walsall, the birthplace of Jerome K. Jerome, and Dudley, the source of the Dauntless Rubberline Cistern. It missed Tipton, home of the All England bare-knuckle champion of the 1850s, the Tipton Slasher.

Of the various towns that had coalesced to form the Black Country, the only ones that the meridian hit with a bull's-eye were Bloxwich and West Bromwich.

At the bottom of Bloxwich High Street was the locked church, the boarded-up cinema and the war memorial.

Against the memorial slumped a scree of bouquets and stuffed animals. A green rabbit peered dolefully from its mattress of gritty cellophane. The wording on the stone ('Let those who come after see to it that their sacrifice . . .') was partially hidden by a framed portrait of the Princess, smiling in pink. In Bloxwich, it was flowers for the royal victim of a car crash which now obscured the memory of 316 local men who gave their lives at the call of King and Country.

Once, they were better remembered. On 5 November 1922, thousands stood along both sides of the High Street while the 5th Battalion South Staffordshire Regiment marched with its bands and colours to this cross of sacrifice. Present were the Bishop of Stafford, who would dedicate the memorial, the vicars of Bloxwich and Hednesford, the mayor, his aldermen and councillors, and the maces of the Borough and the Foreign of Walsall, the town clerk and the Labour and Liberal candidates for the forthcoming general election, Girl Guides, Boy Scouts, the Friendly Societies and the Bloxwich Male Voice Choir, conducted by Mr J. Bentley.

The regiment's wartime commanding officer, Colonel Williamson, unveiled the cross. One of those recalled was Harold Parry, Captain of School and the winner of an Open History Scholarship to Oxford. Second Lieutenant Parry thought often of Bloxwich during his days in the trenches, writing a poem called 'Beacon

Edge' that told of a walk with a loved one to Barr Beacon, the hill
that rose above the roofs on the eastern edge of the Black Country:

> But tell me, Love, what matters mud,
> What matters rain or sleet?
> My arms are round your good rough coat,
> I know that Life is sweet.

Harold Parry died in the mud of Ypres on 6 May 1917.

In the churchyard behind the war memorial was a contrasting epitaph, to Matthew Wilks:

> Here lies the body of poor old Matty,
> Better known as matty Watty,
> The devil he lived, the devil he died,
> And we'll leave the devil to belt his hide.

What had Matty done?

Walsall Canal   Rose of Bengal Tandoori, Bloxwich Wok Takeaway,
Blakenall Football Club, then right, over the railway into Leamore
and then down, below the rip-tides of traffic to the tranquil
netherworld.

Rushes pushed from each shore of the Walsall Canal. A long
red-brick wall on the far bank had been painted with a crude mural
of men in blue winching a locomotive wheel from a white-hot
forge.

If England's canals were the arteries of the Industrial Revolution, the Birmingham Canal Navigations were the capillaries that
supplied the heart: 160 miles of canal, 212 locks, 550 factory side-
basins, railway interchange stations, maintenance yards, pumping
stations, keepers' cottages, bridges, aqueducts and tunnels.

From the canal banks of the Black Country, a narrowboat could voyage north to Liverpool, Manchester and Kendal; west to Hereford and the Severn; east to Leicester and Leeds; and south to Oxford and London. So intricate was the BCN's infrastructure that the railway-builders found insufficient space to lay their lines and had to rely on the old narrowboats to feed their trains. As late as 1905, long after canals had gone into decline, BCN was still shipping 8 million tons a year. But by the 1950s the total was 1 million. By the 1990s it was virtually nil. National maps that had shown canals and railways before the First World War now showed only roads.

The dereliction was in the detail: the silenced foundry walls, leaning for want of mortar; rusty water; algae; barbed wire; empty yards; arthritic locks.

'It's a remainder waterway,' said Paul McIntosh, the custodian of the little museum beside Walsall Top Lock. A 'remainder waterway', he explained, was of a lower order than a 'cruising canal'.

Birchills Canal Museum was once the Boatman's Mission, a red-brick building with an upper floor distinguished by three pairs of arched-head windows graced with Gothic tracery. Inside were melancholy scraps of canal history: a cratch board painted in blue, yellow and white diagonals; a narrowboat rudder in gypsy colours; a podger bar that had once been used to break the floes around ice-bound boats and locks. Paul handed me a long tapering tiller, curved like a scimitar so that it could be flipped upside down in the rudder to allow crew the space to descend into the cabin.

We sat in the museum's replica narrowboat staring at the cast-iron stove with its little red electric light inside. Paul had crewed some of the last working-boats on BCN's canals. Nowadays he was lucky to get the odd request to do rubbish clearance. 'We find all kinds: beds, waggon wheels, toys, bikes, shopping trolleys. Handbags and safes.'

Upstairs, daylight flooded through the Gothic windows into a chapel that once had its own choir and marching bands. Up here presided James Brindley, painted with an unflattering complexion of pink blancmange, grasping the theodolite that he'd used to inscribe his lines on the landscape of England.

Birchills   In search of food, I climbed the brick ramp to street level, resurfacing in Birchills, a factory and terrace district on the side of Walsall. The middle of Walsall was 500 metres beyond the reach of the meridian, so I missed the new art gallery, with its Picasso and Modigliani.

Women fluttered by in saris. A newsagent advertised phone calls to Pakistan for 69p a minute, 55p to India.

The borough's Muslims were trying to build a mosque: 'In the Name of Allah Most Gracious Most Merciful,' read the signboard outside the building site. 'Please forward your donations to: Pakistan Muslims Welfare Association c/o Lloyds Bank.' The metal gates hung open, weeds struggled with the grit and ladders leaned against deserted scaffolding. The walls had crept up to ten metres.

Pleck Road   The Forge and Fettle Tap House told of the past; a garage called PURRFECT TUNE suggested a future. Pleck Road had lost most of its factories.

A hospital stood on the site of the Cyclops Iron Works, though the factory wall still ran beside the pavement, bearing the company's Roll of Honour: Josiah Priest, Levi Pascall, Fred Ford, Ernest Challoner. Old names from the old country. The survivors were small and specialized: a business that made tubes, valves and flanges; another doing galvanizing; a degreaser; an outfit called Wheelbase Alterations in Rolling Mill Street, its mills gone.

Pleck Road had become Walsall's ring-road, a conduit for people working in other places – in offices and schools and industrial parks scattered haphazardly across the West Midlands.

This was not a landscape to kindle passion. I'd caught the place between two revolutions, industrial and consumer, and the hiatus had left it with a personality disorder.

Priestley had been lucky: he'd had something physical to rub against. Where I had the 24-hour mutter of cars, Priestley had been deafened by screeching rolling stock and clanging mills. Looking down from Dudley's hill, he'd compared his view to a 'relief map of a heavy industry' that recalled the spectacle and inventiveness of the Great Exhibition of 1851. To the man from the mill country, the Black Country of the 1930s was a real-space exhibition of industrial prowess.

I'd hoped for something hideous, the Satanic carcass of the Industrial Revolution wriggling with cannibalistic maggots. Wrecking gangs. Racing architects. What I got was acres of grit, quick-fit tyre sheds, supermarkets, light industrial units, office blocks: symbols of function, consumption and efficiency, the architecture of facility rather than form. The most conspicuous additions to this post-industrial landscape were the roads and car parks; the blank lanes and blank spaces of the interconnected void.

Part-way down Pleck Road, J. C. Huskisson & Son ('Saddle, Harness and Horse Collar Makers') stopped me in mid-stride. Not quite believing that one of the founding businesses of the Black Country had survived, I knocked on the door.

'We make about 300 harness sets a year,' said Ian Huskisson, a smiling forty-year-old. 'We're the biggest harness makers in the country.'

Light from the windows facing Pleck Road played on a row of cast-iron sewing-machines with huge handles and foot-treadles. After seeing the sixty-year-old metal-bashing machines in Bloxwich, I shouldn't have been surprised by the use of museum pieces, but Ian noted my dropped jaw.

'They were made between 1890 and 1910 by British United in Leicester. You have to treat them with sympathy: when they don't work we give them a rest. The next day they're fine again.' Worn parts were replaced with cannibalized duplicates from other machines. 'We tried modern machines but they're not as good. The old machines are much better at pressing the stitching into the leather.'

Huskissons had been started in 1920 by Ian's grandfather, John Thomas Huskisson, who knew working horses from his years in the trenches of Flanders. They had seven full- and part-time collar and harness makers and had survived by concentrating on the top end of the market.

'Funerals are good for us. A four-in-hand funeral harness with all the decoration costs around £4,000. The bottom end of the market's been killed by cheap imports from places like Pakistan and Taiwan. They can sell a one-horse harness for £80.'

Raw materials were a problem. Ian pointed to a bench laden with strips of leather. 'It needs to be 4, 5, 6 millimetres thick. BSE affected us. Because the cattle were being killed young, the hides were smaller and thinner, so our curriers have been buying abroad. Sweden, Germany, France.'

Straw for stuffing the neck collars was also in short supply. 'It has to be long rye straw, which is difficult to get nowadays. Thatchers have the same problem. We like it six-foot long, and it has to be cut and thrashed the old way. Modern farmers like short straw with a high grain yield and they cut by machine. We've heard about some long straw in Poland and we're trying to put together a container-load with other companies.'

I asked about the rhythmic clank from the other side of the wall.

'We're barrelling chain,' said Ian, pushing open the door.

Inside was a workbench and vice draped with heavy chain, and on the opposite wall a revolving barrel. The floor was strewn with straw. A half finished horse collar stood propped in the corner. It was a scene from the previous century.

Huskissons cut and welded their own chain, then hand-twisted it with a bar so that each link would lie flat. Barrelling the chain cleaned the metal prior to plating it with chrome.

Ian hefted the collar. 'They were used for agriculture till machines took over after the Second World War. Now it's just a few people play-acting at agriculture, and people with coaches and gigs. Traps. It's not a huge business. There's only a handful of people in our line. It's a niche in the saddlery trade.'

Each neck collar took fifteen hours to make and would be sold with a harness for around £700 per horse. Harnesses for the big horses – the Percherons, Clydesdales and Suffolk Punches – cost up to £1,500.

Huskissons had supplied harnesses to most of the brewers. 'Hook Norton, Tetley, Sam Smith. They still like to do local deliveries by dray. And Wadworth.'

Wadworth were the only brewer on two degrees west, a few stops down the line in Devizes.

Pleck In one of those juxtapositions that makes urban hiking so pleasurable, Huskisson the horse specialist was next door to Reg Vardy's Ford car dealership.

Further down Pleck Road, I passed three white lavatories alone on the pavement outside a shop in the front room of a terraced house called Aqua Bella Bathrooms.

Down here, at the southern extremity of Pleck Road, I crossed the Walsall Canal again, into Pleck itself. 'Pleck', a shopkeeper told me, meant 'wasteground'.

Pleck had an unenviable location in the dip between Walsall and Wednesbury, a triangle of terraced housing bordered by the canal, the M6 motorway and the railway.

'Bangladeshis, Sikhs, Pakistanis, Kashmiris, Afro-Caribbeans, Iranian students, Punjabis. It's a mixed community,' said the public liaison officer with the Community Services Team at Walsall Operational Command Unit. He was a policeman and his job was to keep in touch with the locals. Pleck was peaceful he said. 'A few years back, during the riots at Handsworth, we didn't have a problem here.'

The police, he added, had got the measure of the troublemakers. The BNP had lost their meeting place in the Chimneys pub in Bloxwich and when they tried the Brownhills pubs, the licensees wouldn't let them in. Combat 18 and the National Front were lying low.

'You have to work at it,' said the policeman.

Pleck's shops could have been airlifted from the Indian subcontinent to Wednesbury Road. With the Pleck Balti was Sanaam Saree Centre, Sanam Balti Tower, Purnam Sweetmart, Chaudry Textiles, Shan-e-Punjab Sweet Centre and Sheeren Mahall Balti Centre. The most conspicuous indigenous shop was the Bankrupt Warehouse.

Amrik Singh ran one of the sweet shops. He'd come over from Punjab in 1979, aged twenty-six. 'I wanted to see this country. I read it in a book. It was a rich country.'

He had worked six days a week in factories while training to make sweets. The training took seven years. Then he got his own shop. Amrik smiled beneath his green turban. 'If you do very hard work, you do well.'

The shelves were piled with snacks and sweets: *kala kand, gulab jamun, alu tikka, channa bhatura*. He had four children and had been back to Punjab several times. 'When we first came to England, we felt cold. Now, when we go back, we feel hot.'

'According to the Home Office, we are the most disadvantaged ethnic minority in England.'

Mustafa Choudhury, community development officer, was sitting in a suit and tie behind his desk in the heart of Pleck. There were, he said, 300,000 Bangladeshis in Britain, 70 per cent of whom couldn't speak English.

Mustafa had been born in Sylhet and was fluent in Urdu and Hindi. He'd worked for Radio Pakistan in Karachi before being sent back to Bangladesh in 1973. In 1977 he'd come to England and spent ten years working at the Sonali Bank in Birmingham, then set up a laundry business which was destroyed by fire in 1995. The following year he began working at the Walsall Bangladeshi Progressive Society.

'There are 4,000 Bangladeshis in the neighbourhood, but we're here to help all ethnic groups. We advise on welfare rights, benefits, housing, education, help with their job-seekers' allowance. Many have language problems. We can write letters for them. We arrange courses in computer training and in food hygiene for those who work in restaurants.'

'Are there tensions between the ethnic groups?' I wondered.

Mustafa shook his head. 'I've no experience of racial problems. We are living as a harmony.'

While we were talking, a trickle of men and women, Sikh, Hindu, Bangladeshi, called to see their community development officer. One of them was Shamsu Miah, who'd been in England for twelve years but still spoke no English. 'I work in a kitchen,' he said through Mustafa. 'In a kitchen, you don't have to speak.'

Another visitor was Mustafa's son. Ruful Alam wanted to be a film actor. He was twenty-one and loved Pleck. 'I grew up here. It's my birthplace.'

During the day he worked for his father; each evening he worked in a restaurant in Cannock.

Ruful went to Bangladesh for the first time in 1992. 'It felt strange. As soon as I got off the plane I had people coming round. Beggars. I was really shocked. I'd never seen beggars.'

Ruful hadn't been to London.

'Pleck's changing. It used to be nice and clean but now it's a red-light district. And it's got the A–Z of drugs.'

Pleck's bye-law terraces had been immaculately crafted before the First World War, with deep-red brickwork, dentilled eaves and decorative string-courses; front doors on to pavements.

As I was taking a photograph, the door of the house in the viewfinder sprang open to reveal a Sikh in slippers. 'You want me to move the car?' he asked.

After he'd moved the vehicle out of the photograph, Darshan Singh asked if I'd like a cup of tea.

We sat side-by-side on the sofa while Darshan's wife Harjit brought a teapot, mugs and two yellow blocks of sweet Punjabi cake.

The ground-floor dividing wall that had once separated the front from the back room had been demolished by earlier occupants, leaving a single, thin room with two sofas along one wall and a small kitchen off the back.

There wasn't much else in the room, apart from an exercise bicycle beneath the window and a TV. An electric fan the size of a Dakota's propeller hung from the ceiling with gold patterns on its blades and a light bulb suspended from its boss. On the wall facing us were pictures of the children and the trophies they'd won at the temple for playing piano and *tabla*. Above our heads was a clock mounted between portraits of the first and tenth gurus, Nanak and Govind Singh. Darshan went to the temple every day.

Earlier, I'd called at the Nanaksar Sikh Temple, a windowless brick building shaped like a warehouse just off Pleck Road. I'd been handed a Duralex glass of hot sweet tea and a couple of syrupy *chum chums*, balls of milk pudding. The congenial calm inside the temple was a dreamy contrast to the frantic, clashing streetscape outside. In the main room, knots of men and women sat at tables or chatted, while the *Granth Sahib* – the Sikh Bible – was recited melodically over loudspeakers. In the entrance hall was painted the short history of Sikhism. Above the two wash-basins (women on the left of the hall, men on the right, with respective doorways through to the shoe-racks) were a series of pictures describing the trials of the Sikhs since the religion's foundation by Guru Nanak. He'd been born in 1469, fourteen years ahead of Protestantism's architect, Martin Luther. The pictures were not easy on the eye: Sikhism – like Protestantism – began as a revolt. Over by the ladies' basin queued men with severed heads on stakes, a scene, said the caption, from the 'rain of power' of Masa Ranghar the Tyrant of Jandiala, who'd hung Sikh heads on trees in a three-mile radius of Amritsar's Golden Temple. Another picture showed the babies of Sikh women who'd refused to accept Islam being tossed on to spears. Moving round towards the men's basin were gory depictions of a Mughal army massacring Sikhs, and Bhai Tasu Singh Ji, scalped for harbouring Sikhs. Above the doorway into the temple, the machine-guns of a contemporary atrocity spat fire at the shattered ruins of the Golden Temple. Finishing my last mouthful of sticky *chum chum*, I reached the picture of the great sufi Baba Sheikh Farid: 'Sweet are candy and sugar and honey and buffaloes milk yea, sweet are these but sweeter by far is God.'

On the sofa in Prince Street, my mug was refilled by Harjit. Darshan and Harjit had four children, Satveer, Herveer, Ranveer and Prabhjot. Darshan was an unemployed van-driver. He'd lost his job after contracting tuberculosis and drew £150 a week in benefits.

'Is it enough for you all to live on?'

'I'm happy with it,' he smiled through his immense black beard. 'I don't smoke or drink, and we're a vegetarian family.'

Later, Harjit made dahl and chapatis, which she brought with bowls of yoghurt to the low table in front of the sofa.

The family had arrived in England from the Punjab in 1978 and been in Pleck for ten years. 'I like it here,' said Darshan. 'It's a good community.'

They were going to send the children back to India to finish their education, away from the drugs and the other 'problems' in English schools. Darshan looked apologetic. 'Here, anything could happen.'

In Pleck, the Black Country began to make sense.

In looking for the kinds of physical drama that had inspired earlier writers to drag up images from Genesis to Vulcan, I was on to a loser. The industrial landscape – like the countryside – had lost its patterns of sound and colour. The weave of human movement had also gone: I saw relatively few people out on their legs; most were in cars or working indoors.

Travelling between the Black Country and the surrounding countryside, the American Henry Adams had written of 'the violent contrast between the dense, smoky, impenetrable darkness, and the soft green charm that one glided into, as one emerged'. A century later, Priestley had employed the same comparison, using the pleasures of the green belt to underline the horrors within.

Walking through at the end of the twentieth century, I found a flattening of physical extremes; field and factory had become variations in monotony. Diversity had moved indoors and had to be read in the software of homes and factories, churches and temples.

J9/M6   Between the Nanaksar Sikh Temple and Junction 9 of the M6, I spent the night in a roadside hotel which not only lay within my 2,000-metre band but had the distinction of being bisected by two degrees west.

When I checked in, conversationally explaining why I was carrying a rucksack through the West Midlands, the receptionist said, 'That's a coincidence. We had somebody here a few weeks back who was walking down a line of longitude. I'm sure he said it was two degrees.'

Palpitating, I took the key to my room and sagged weakly on to the bed. Impossible. It was absolutely inconceivable that anybody else should be walking this line. I hurried back downstairs in my socks.

'When did this other person come through?'

'Some time this summer. July perhaps, August.'

Then I remembered. I'd been asked on a radio programme to explain the line and had blabbed the whole thing. Clearly a listener had walked straight out of his door and got on to a train for Berwick. I'd been pipped to the post. Robbed.

'Shit.'

'Coincidence, I must say,' repeated the receptionist.

'What did he look like?'

'I don't remember meeting him.' The receptionist thought for a moment. 'We spoke on the phone, though.'

'The phone?'

'Yes. For ages. I remember he kept asking how many metres we were from Junction 9 of the motorway. He was a bit strange like that.'

Then I knew who this other walker was. Somebody sitting with an open map and a pair of dividers, plotting the exact location of the Abberley Hotel.

It was me. Back in London, I'd realized that I needed a better base-camp than a sleeping-bag when I reached Pleck, and had gone through accommodation lists phoning all the places near the meridian. The Abberley Hotel was the only one that I found on two degrees west. The receptionist had muddled a telephonic encounter with a real one.

'You don't know how relieved I am,' I gasped. 'I thought for a moment there were two of us.'

'That,' said the receptionist, 'would have been very weird.'

In the morning I took a pre-breakfast stroll in Pleck Park, an immaculate area of open space, with bowling greens, tennis courts, a football pitch and a children's playground running up to the stilts of the M6. The noise was staggering.

'Smell's terrible,' said a man walking his dog, 'especially when the wind's blowing this way.'

Above our heads crawled a slow-moving procession of heavy goods vehicles, their slab sides a non-stop commercial break across the sky: Great British Chips, Lucas, Sunpride, Radič Croatia, Exel Logistics, Kwik Save (It Makes Good Sense), Unilock, Hovis, P & O Ferrymasters, Bretagne Internationale and that liveried king among artics, Eddie Stobart.

The dog-walker pointed to a tree. 'Only time I heard a bird in here was when the IRA put bombs under the motorway and stopped the traffic. Lovely, it was. A woodpecker.'

The Abberley was a businessman's hotel. I knew this because my room came with a copy of *Big 'n' Busty* and breakfast came with the *Daily Telegraph*.

My fry-up also came with a cheerful cry of 'Good morning, young man, 'ow yer diddling?' They didn't get a lot of walkers.

At the neighbouring table was a civil engineer from the north who shared Priestley's views of the 'affected tittering South Country'.

'There's too much bias towards the south,' muttered the engineer, whose mental map of Britain was based on speed of communication rather than absolute space. 'London is inaccessible. No one can get there. The place is heading for a disaster. It's jammed solid. You can't move. As for Greenwich . . . It's totally cut off.'

The engineer's company was tendering for work on the Millennium Dome. 'It's a very sensitive project,' he muttered, going on to describe how the contaminated waste from the Millennium site, which had once been a gas works, was being shipped by truck to holes in the Home Counties. Some of the holes were at the old London Brick works in Bedfordshire. The civil engineer liked the logic of this. 'London came out of those pits; now it's going back into them.'

Five minutes after checking out of the Abberley, I was staring through the stained spans of the M6 at the sunlit spire of Wednesbury's church taunting me from its hilltop. Wednesbury (from Woden the Saxon god of war, and *beorg*, or fort) would have been as diverting as Walsall, but like Walsall, it was just out of reach of my 1,000-metre leash.

The motorway was the northern border of the Borough of Sandwell, the 'heart of the Black Country' and one of the four Black Country boroughs promoted as 'the heart of England'. Sandwell – covering an area of 21,000 acres between Birmingham and Wolverhampton – saw itself pumping the lifeblood of the entire country.

Of the various districts in the West Midlands, Sandwell was the most reliant on manufacturing, which provided 41 per cent of the borough's jobs. This was the home of Salter, the scale maker; of Bradfords Bakeries, who baked 43 million loaves a year; of Accles & Pollock, whose tubes went into nuclear power stations and jet fighters; of MCG Closures' tamper-proof plastic caps; of Darcast Components, who made 50,000 crankshafts a week; of legions of technicians turning out unglamorous components: scaffolding and chemicals, capillary end feed fittings, traps, wastes, interior trims and automotive castings.

Of Sandwell's population of 295,000, 15 per cent came from ethnic minorities and nearly half the homes were rented from the council. Nearly half the households had no car.

Black Lake   The rush-hour traffic was backed up on Wood Green Road as I climbed towards Wednesbury in the company of school-children, ties awry, shirt-tails flapping.

By the top of the slope I had reached the 99 grid line. The centre of Wednesbury was less than one hundred metres from where I stood, but I had to bear away to the left to dive beneath the Tame Valley Canal, one of the last canals to be built in Britain, completed in 1844, nearly a century after Brindley began his great works. Above the grey confusing streets was a ribbon of bright blue water fringed with green. It was as if somebody had laid a celestial canal across the sky. I could have escaped on that towpath, walking away from it all over the rooftops.

Back down below, the meridian took me to Black Lake, the mid-point on my traverse across the Black Country. Black Lake was a crossroads with a school, a church and cheek-to-cheek houses on top of a hill, but no lake. By the bottom of the hill I was beginning to lose the thread. Till now I'd managed to attach an identity to each urban region I passed through: Bloxwich had been an intact town swallowed by the metropolitan anaconda; Leamore was fac-tories and the canal; Birchills was Pakistani; Pleck Road had its factories; Pleck was Pleck; Mesty Croft and Balls Hill were inner-city suburbs. But at the bottom of Black Lake's hill two degrees west led me into a zone that defied categorization: a late twentieth-century estate built in Victorian red brick, with Tudor beams, Georgian up-and-over garage doors, leaded windows and infrared intruder alarms, with a rusting gasometer behind, a line of towering elec-tricity pylons looming over the roofs and an arterial road in front. Cartographically, I was between Wednesbury and West Bromwich; actually I felt lost.

Momentarily, I saw the Black Country through Priestley's eyes: 'The places I saw had names,' he wrote, 'but these names were merely so much alliteration: Wolverhampton, Wednesbury, Wed-nesfield, Willenhall, Walsall. You could call them all wilderness, and have done with it. I never knew where one ended and another began.'

*

Thankfully another canal (the feeder to Hateley Heath) allowed me to get a fix on the landscape. Just over its bridge I turned on a whim into the offices of the *Express & Star*.

Phoning upstairs from the front desk, I was put through to Anne Alexander, a news reporter on the *Sandwell Chronicle*, who said that she'd come down and join me in the foyer.

While I waited I tucked into the papers. The newspaper group covered an area of 5,000 square kilometres and had district offices in Dudley, Walsall, Cannock and Sandwell, each feeding in news items. That day's stories ranged from a Stafford pensioner who'd had her belly-button pierced with a navel ring to raise money for Age Concern to the mayor of Sandwell going down with diabetes. A car chase from Bloxwich to the M6 had damaged three police Range Rovers. Somebody wanted to build a £20 million cinema and leisure centre beside the M5 in West Bromwich.

'Yes,' said Anne when she came down. 'I'd say that's a fairly typical spread of daily news. We did have a good one recently about a guy in Smethwick who'd opened a horse meat shop.'

Anne's parents were from St Ann, Jamaica. Delzyn and George had come to Britain in 1962 and Anne had been born eight years later, in West Bromwich. I wondered whether she'd found it difficult as a black woman to break into the competitive world of journalism.

'It wasn't simple,' she laughed evasively, 'but I didn't have to face obstacles.'

She'd been a child through the mid and late 1970s when the National Front had been especially active. Things were different now. Tipton, she said, was the racial hot spot, where the Bangladeshi community was being provoked by Combat 18 and the British National Party. The latest Intelligence Unit report from West Midlands Police showed that there had been eighty-three racial incidents reported in Sandwell between January and August. The list of June's incidents included verbal abuse, graffiti, assaults and damage to property. Earlier in the summer, three youths were apprehended carrying offensive weapons which they claimed were for self-defence against a local Asian gang.

'It's better than a lot of the country,' said Anne. 'Most of the immigrants have been here for thirty years. The prejudice is there, but it's not really a problem.'

Anne had joined the paper as a trainee, and was about to be promoted from the *Chronicle* to the *Express & Star*. She was confident, ambitious and loved journalism. 'It's wonderful! It's great!' she laughed. 'One day I'd like to work on a national magazine. Features. I like being out and about and poking my nose in. Maybe I should be a travel writer.'

West Bromwich   The second of the two 'towns' that the meridian selected from the Black Country was West Bromwich, the civic climax of two degrees west.

With 154,900 inhabitants, West Bromwich was the largest population centre on the meridian, dwarfing by far Berwick-upon-Tweed (12,200), Skipton (13,200), Bloxwich (26,200), Devizes (10,600) and Calne (10,300). Only Poole, at 135,000, came close.

At West Bromwich too I crossed paths again with Charles Dickens. In a letter to his friend John Forster, Dickens mentioned that Nell's nightmarish flight in *The Old Curiosity Shop* had been drawn from a journey the author had made between Birmingham and Wolverhampton, via West Bromwich. So this was where 'strange engines spun and writhed like tortured creatures; clanking their iron chains, shrieking in their rapid whirl from time to time as though in torment unendurable'. Here, ruined buildings leaned against each other and 'women, children, wan in their looks and ragged in attire, tended the engines, fed their tributary fires, begged upon the road, or scowled half-naked from the doorless houses'. For Dickens, the road to Wolverhampton carried none of the wonder that the pre-industrial Americans, Burritt and Adams, had felt. This was environmental terror inflicted by the muzzles of chimneys 'never ceasing in their black vomit, blasting all things living or inanimate, shutting out the face of day, and enclosing in on all these horrors with a dense cloud'. Night brought no respite. Night was a diurnal mutation, a point on the clock 'when the smoke was changed to fire; when every chimney spirted up its flame; and places, that had been dark vaults all day, now shone red-hot, with figures moving to and fro within their blazing jaws, and calling to one another with hoarse cries'.

West Bromwich was in such a dire state when J. B. Priestley travelled this road in 1933 that, swore the author of *English Journey*, any attempt to use it in a novel would have risked accusations of Dickensian caricature: 'The whole neighbourhood,' he wrote, 'is mean and squalid.' Coming away from a steel warehouse in a street of crepuscular gloom which he dubbed 'Rusty Lane', the man who grew up below the chimneys of West Riding urged that the next imperial economic conference convene not in Mayfair, but in Rusty Lane and there be fed bread, margarine and slabs of brawn.

Sixty years after Priestley glowered at West Bromwich, I stood at the foot of a High Street walled with plate glass and back-lit plastic. In the sixteenth century, this was a three-kilometre strip of heath used by villagers for grazing and gathering fuel. The village of West Bromwich lay a kilometre to the north, around All Saints Church. As agriculture gobbled the rough grazing, Bromwich Heath became the largest surviving island of common land. Running through its centre was the coach road from Birmingham to Wolverhampton, on one of the routes from London to Holyhead. In 1727 the road was turnpiked, and in 1801 the West Bromwich Enclosure Act opened the way for Parliamentary Commissioners to enclose and subdivide 387 acres of the heath. Claims to common rights were assessed by the commissioners, who allocated plots and laid out a network of carriage roads, lanes and paths. A strip sixty feet wide was allocated for the turnpike. Shops and offices, workshops, factories, churches and pubs took root on the new plots along the turnpike, which became known as the 'Golden Mile'. A High Street was born.

The population of West Bromwich ballooned from 5,687 in 1801 to 65,175 by 1901. In less than a century, it doubled again. By the 1960s, congestion in the High Street forced planners to divert traffic on to a new circular 'ringway' and 'expressway' which swept along what was once the edge of Bromwich Heath, severing modern West Bromwich from its original village, now a suburb of terraces in a triangular sanctuary formed by the M5, the Tame Valley Canal and the expressway.

No other thoroughfare on the meridian could match the civic presence of West Bromwich High Street. It ran in a straight line for a couple of kilometres, a glittering channel flowing with counter-currents of commerce and local administration, progressing from the activities of the outer fringe to the architectural symbols of the civic gospel: from the Sandwell Confederation of Bangladeshi Muslim Organisations to a fish bar, a diner, an optician, the Marksman pub, a funeral parlour, the Old Hop Pole pub, a video rental shop, the Oddfellows Arms, Dial-a-Curry, Wing-Fat Chinese & Cantonese Takeaway, the offices of Medite Shipping, the Baptist Church, the DHSS office, an off-licence, the Rover car showroom, the New Hop Pole pub, West Bromwich Building Society, Sandwell College, the Job Centre, the town hall, the head post office and so to the library.

> Goo up the steps un thru' it's portals
> Look up un round at them immortals
> In cullerd glass abuv the doores
> Uz yoh walk in on terraza floores
> Shakespeare – Bunyan – Milton – Scott
> Browse awhile theer's such a lot
> Uv werks uv art fer all ter see
> Up theer in Bramwich Library.

The lines were Harry Harrison's of Tipton and I was shown them by the librarian, who brought me files and cuttings describing the library's opening by the mayor in June 1907. It was a grand occasion, and few locals would have been prepared for the library's exotic decor: a stained-glass portrait of Shakespeare above the door, mosaic floors, murals and a startling staircase glazed with green ceramic tiles.

With the town hall next door, and the post office opposite, these were the grandest stupas on the road between Birmingham and Wolverhampton, the twin engine-rooms of England and the Empire. Now, for the second time, the centre of West Bromwich had shifted and these Victorian shrines had lost their congregation: the head post office was now 'The Old Post Office Café Bar' and the crowds had moved off the High Street into the covered malls of the new shopping centre. In here West Brom lost its identity and became any English town, kitted out with the same Woolworth's, McDonald's and Dorothy Perkins. In W. H. Smith's and Boots I shopped for notepaper and film, and for a few minutes entirely forgot where I was. There would be no more towns on the meridian until I reached Calne in Wiltshire.

The Black Country of Dickens and Priestley had disappeared, yet it was still at the heart of the country's communications. The canals that radiated from the West Midlands had been replaced by motorways: the M54 west, the M6 north and east, the M42 north-east, the M40 south-east, the M5 south. All points of the compass were covered.

But there was a difference: the canals had focused on the Black Country because they were servicing the industries that fed the Empire; the motorways met here because the West Midlands happened to be a convenient node in the centre of the country. Instead of a terminus, the Black Country had become a plot in the centre of a gigantic roundabout.

A rough circle drawn through most of England's (and Wales's) important commercial centres – London, Southampton, Bristol, (Cardiff and Swansea), Liverpool, Manchester, Bradford, Leeds, Sheffield, Hull and Cambridge – had as its centre the Black Country and Birmingham. In the world of motor traffic, this was the country's true centre, England's Pole of Vehicular Communication, the eye of the storm.

In the back streets of West Bromwich I stumbled upon a sight so strange that I had to blink. Leaning over a bridge parapet expecting to see another abandoned railway or canal, I saw instead gangs of workmen laying a new electric railway and beside it, a cycle path. This, I learned, was to be the new Midland Metro line linking

Birmingham and Wolverhampton. Beside it was the West Bromwich Parkway cycle route.

For a few moments, till I got dusted by the next truck, I saw a utopian West Midlands criss-crossed with electric trains and spinning bicycle spokes.

Just down the hill I passed Skidmore Garage. Skidmore: a good name for a garage: more skids, more quids.

Galton Valley   Shattered glass rose in cones taller than a man, glacially green and weirdly translucent, as if lit by the memory of long-lost vision.

They were unnerving, those mountains that had once been windscreens, now reduced to icy sightlessness. Maybe it was their apparent coldness on a warm day, or maybe it was the nature of glass; the way that it is so absolute in its breaking. No half measures: it's either clear and miraculous, or splintered to commonplace fragments.

Beyond the glass recycling plant the stilts of another motorway shut out the daylight. Under the high concrete ceiling lay a still grey canal and a desert of dry grit. Through the stilts, mangled cars lay in careless scrapyard heaps; a ferrous slaughterhouse tactfully hidden from the vehicles flying overhead.

It was a sinister spot, a monochrome arena for nightfighters and underworlders. In my weaker moments I'd fantasized that my line would snap in such a place. I'd come to a canal with no bridge and have to wade through neck-deep water, snagging sunken supermarket trolleys, feet plunging through the chest cavities of rotting corpses, syringes bobbing at eye-level. Draped in fetid carrier bags and condoms, I'd make the far bank and look up to see a rank of insane faces punched with ear studs and cheek rivets, grinning as I tried to claw my way out of the slime.

The canal was Old Main Line, the motorway was the M5 and beside them both was a second canal – New Main Line – and the intercity rail line, all on different levels and all woven together in a tangle of road, rail and water.

Galton Valley was not a conventional valley but a line of least resistance spotted by James Brindley two centuries earlier. The valley had been cut into the high ground of Smethwick summit between the Black Country's right and left ventricles, Birmingham and Wolverhampton. In Galton Valley geography was to bring together some of the greatest names of the Industrial Revolution.

From Brindley's original contouring canal at 491 feet above sea level, Smeaton's corner-cutting Old Main Line of 1789 took it down to 473 feet, and Telford's direct New Main Line to 453 feet. Telford's dramatic ditch was opened a few months after George Stephenson's 30mph *Rocket* heralded the beginning of the railway era and the end of canals.

Brindley's canal had gone, but Smeaton's and Telford's were there, and, as I stared down from the road bridge, one of Richard Branson's red Virgin trains slid along Robert Stephenson's railway between Wolverhampton and Birmingham, opened in 1852, two years after he completed the Border Bridge at Berwick-upon-Tweed.

Making my way west beneath the motorway for about 500 metres, I came to an extraordinary intersection where I could stand on a cast-iron footbridge over Old Main Line, with Stephenson's railway above me and the motorway above that, while below me lay the Old Main Line that was crossing New Main Line on an aqueduct. I had to draw a sketch to figure out the various planes.

There was one other great name on this half-kilometre of semi-dereliction. The cliff of crumbling red brick that towered above my head as I walked along the towpath in Telford's canyon belonged to Chance's Glassworks, supplier of sheet glass to the Crystal Palace.

The Hyde Park centrepiece of the Great Exhibition of 1851 was conceived on blotting paper and completed eight months later. Following the fashion for Darwinian form, the architect Joseph Paxton copied the roof of his giant greenhouse from the water lily, *Victoria Amazonica*.

The plans for a glasshouse bigger than the palace of Versailles outraged *The Times*, who warned that the royal park would become the 'bivouac of all the vagabonds of London'. Predicting hordes of overseas visitors, the hereditary MP for Lincoln, Colonel Sibthorp, advised residents adjacent to the park to lock up their silverware and maids, and, referring to the sexual appetites of foreigners, warned the House of Commons to expect 'a piebald generation, half black and half white'.

On opening day, *The Times* changed its mind: 'They who were so fortunate as to see it hardly knew what most to admire, or in what form to clothe the sense of wonder and even of mystery which struggled within them.'

Prefabricated from 4,500 tons of iron, 600,000 cubic feet of timber and 293,655 panes of glass, the Crystal Palace floated in Hyde Park's greenery with impossible precision, delicacy and scale, spun seemingly by insects.

Disraeli thought it 'an enchanted pile'. The writer and politician, Thomas Babington Macaulay, was so amazed that he suffered an architectural short-circuit and drew two continents, three epochs and fantasy into his breathless comparison: 'a most gorgeous sight; vast; graceful; beyond the dreams of the Arabian romances; I cannot think that the Caesars ever exhibited a more splendid spectacle. I was quite dazzled, and I felt as I did on entering St Peter's'.

The opening ceremony on May 1st drew 25,000 spectators. A huge procession headed by heralds and Joseph Paxton entered the Palace, followed by ambassadors, commissioners and then the Prince Consort and Queen, and their complicated entourage, from Gold Stick in Waiting and Groom of the Stole to Lord of the Bedchamber.

'The arteries of the great city, surcharged with life, beat full and strong under the pressure of a great and hitherto unknown excitement,' raved *The Times* on the 2nd. 'Never before was so vast a multitude collected together within the memory of man . . . here was an occasion which might be celebrated by the whole human race without one pang of regret, envy or national hate.'

By the time the Exhibition closed in October, 6 million had passed through its doors. They left full of wonder, not just at Paxton's palace, but at the extraordinary exhibits inside. This was the world's first international exhibition, and it was full of curiosities: a rubber sideboard, a hat made from a cabbage, artificial manures (that foretold the fertilizer age), a Gothic bookcase from Vienna,

American machines with interchangeable parts, a penknife with eighty blades and gadgets, a jar of Greek honey from Mount Hymettus, mosquito nets from the nuns of the Convent of St Constantine, scientific instruments from chronometers and barometers to thermometers and urinometers.

The British stole the show with a celebration of skills and technology befitting an Empire that had mushroomed since 1800 from 1,500,000 to 4,500,000 square miles (and would more than double again by 1900 to 11,300,000 square miles). On display were guns from Birmingham, Staffordshire pottery, Lancashire cottons, a model of Liverpool Docks, knives from Sheffield, woollens from West Riding, Nottingham hosiery, lead from the Dales. The Black Country coalfield at Tipton sent a 6-ton block of coal and Chances themselves dispatched one of their 29-inch diameter lighthouse lenses, at the time the largest ever made. It was snapped up by the French government for £1,000. Just up New Main Line from Chance's, Fox and Henderson had contributed too: they'd cast all the ironwork that held the Palace together.

For the American consul Elihu Burritt, the Chance factory was the highlight of his tour through the Black Country and 'one of the most remarkable establishments in the world'. Here were all of the ingredients required of a Victorian industrial giant: fiery spectacle and mystical skill, brawny workers, mass productivity and a caring boss.

Then, the works was a small town of twenty-four acres, covered with spires and domes, turrets and warehouses, whose red brick glowed with the heat of furnaces and running glass to present 'a scene which Virgil and Dante would have described in terms and figures unsuited to modern conceptions or facts'.

To the American, watching circles of men stand around a Stourbridge fire-clay bowl filled with two tons of molten glass, dipping in their six-foot iron pipes and blowing cylinders 'as long as a two-bushel bag of wheat', the glass-blowing was 'magic' and the men themselves possessed of such supernatural lungs that they could blow 'a ship of the line across the Atlantic'. Burritt was delighted to discover that the mounds of offcuts from pane-cutting were not squandered but cut down further into photographic slides.

Wastage was minimized. With New Main Line running through the centre of the works, the score of company narrowboats imported raw materials and shipped out the finished product: window panes and stained glass, lighthouse lenses, telescope lenses, searchlight glass and the windows for the salon cabin of the Pasha of Egypt's state barge.

To Burritt's gratification, the 1,700 employees had access to a company library with 2,000 volumes and a company school for 500 children. All 'glass-house boys' under eighteen were expected to attend school three times a week, with a fine of sixpence a week for non-attendance; girls and young women went to evening school. Boys and girls awaiting employment in the works were expected to have a 'fair acquaintance' with reading, writing and arithmetic, and anyone hoping to work in the ornamental department had to master freehand drawing as well.

The school was built the year that Crystal Palace opened, and still stands. I found it in Crystal Drive on the corner of Sandwell Business Park, set back a few steps from Stephenson's railway, with steel security shutters on the door and windows and a car park where once there had been a playground. Chance House had become the offices of a civil engineering contractor. The little Gothic clock tower was intact and indeed restored, but where the glass factory had extended along the southern edge of the railway there were now neat industrial units with painted parking bays.

The three private bridges that linked the Chance's works each side of the canal still spanned New Main Line, one of them an elegant high-backed arch decorated with dimpled sandstone. Looking for a way into the old works, I turned into Palace Drive. Down here, one of the main buildings still stood, capped with a decrepit bell-tower and the word GLASS. Beside it was a row of derelict sheds with gaping doors and splintered windows. A roof had collapsed. In place of the furnaces, the elevated M5 strode across a bulldozed waste.

In the valley which had been hacked by Telford's navvies, a solitary narrowboat bound for Birmingham scratched short-lived ripples in the polished surface of the canal. Nobody trod the towpath. The glassworks that Burritt had marvelled at by moonlight and seen as a 'great nest of cathedrals and Turkish mosques' was derelict. Stephenson's railway line was woven with gantries and power cables for Branson's electric trains, and dominating the whole prospect, the concrete centipede of the motorway trampled the past underfoot. The most disconcerting aspect of this river landscape was the fact that I couldn't see a single human being.

To the eye this was the ugliest mess the meridian had thrown up, but there was a future buried deep in the stratified layers of function. Stephenson's railway still worked; both Main Lines were still navigable; the towpath below me would soon be 'Route 812' of the Sustrans National Cycle Network, linking Birmingham and the Black Country to mid-Wales by way of Telford's New Main Line. Chance's, though derelict, was a listed building in search of a tenant, and the glass it supplied to the Crystal Palace was still contributing towards the nation's culture: so successful was the Great Exhibition that an entity known as The Royal Commission for the Exhibition of 1851 still exists and has assets of £250 million and an annual income of £1 million. It owns the Albert Hall.

After the Exhibition, the Crystal Palace was dismantled and re-erected on Sydenham Hill, where it stood as a London landmark until a November night in 1936, when it caught fire and Chance's glazing melted back into the geology from whence it had come.

Londonderry   South of Galton Valley, the human landscape lost its form again.

My line was now tangential to anything that might make sense. I was between centres. No canals or major roads went my way, and neither were there any more urban nucleii.

Milestones became random: a cemetery; West Smethwick Park (deserted); a locality called Londonderry, with shops and a hair-dresser called Les Gentlemans. The road I took climbed (although I couldn't see the contours on the map for houses) past pebbledash terraces on Bristnallhall Road to another meeting of roads and a burned-out arcade, looking like a black-and-white shot of Beirut or Kabul; dog-shit heavy on the air. Up a hill, a pub called the Beeches, with no beeches; Bristnall Neighbourhood Office; a yellow and green Sandwell Borough van parked by two men mending a brick gateway.

A view: hills off to the right. The compass read 240 degrees. Not the Lickey Hills, as I had thought, but the Clent Hills.

A roundabout: a road with front gardens, off-street parking; Georgian extensions, security gates, a bungalow with Corinthian porch columns, another bungalow dwarfed by its double garage, a Neighbourhood Watch sign.

A dual carriageway, from Dudley to Birmingham, underlined on the map with the black dashes of a borough boundary. Administratively, this was the end of the Black Country, the southern perimeter of Sandwell. I ran between the cars.

Hurrying now to reach the edge of the map's grey zone, I registered the outer layers of the metropolis in a series of disassociated impressions: a primary school labelled 'Electronic Surveillance Equipment' and 'Guard Dog Patrol'; reggae from an open door; a black woman wearing a floral headscarf, breaking bricks with a hammer; trees beginning to appear at road junctions (the first intimation of *rus in urbe*); another arcade of shops (two mini markets, DIY shop, Iris Ladies Hairstylist); the Perry Hill Tavern, with parking for a squadron of heavy-lift helicopters; a country breeze (can't be long now); another dual carriageway, from Birmingham to Kidderminster, but this time there was a pedestrian underpass, painted with pastel whorls and urine; the first leafy street: Clydesdale Road, pollarded limes and cast-iron lampposts (the wind-rush of the M5 to my right); another dual carriageway, with trees and grass down the centre; Highfield Lane (a change of labelling here, from 'Road' and 'Street' to the rustic 'Lane'); a school; a path; a hedge.

A field.

Woodgate Valley Country Park   About 4,000 years before I got there, the valley carrying Bourn Brook was the home of early farmers who left behind a 'burnt mound' on the site of their sauna.

Boulder clay brought from the north by the last Ice Age left the valley with poor soil, and so it was used for grazing rather than crops. The names of the farms reflected the poverty of the land: Stonehouse Farm, Heathy Farm, Wilderness Farm, Broadhindley (heath clearing) Farm, Nonesuch (a mixture of rye grass and hop clover) Farm. Some of their hedgerows are now 800 years old.

Then came the Industrial Revolution. In 1794 the Dudley Canal Company began building a tunnel just south of the Bourn, leaving the spoil heaps across the valley. Brickmakers set up between the spoil heaps, using the boulder clay and building a tramway down to the canal. Then nailmakers came and built forges by their cottages. A tile kiln was erected in the field now known as Lower Tylers and an enterprising miner bored a 240-foot shaft into the valley floor in search of coal to sell to the brick- and tilemakers.

After the Second World War they all left, and the fields and wasteland became a popular belt of green space for the surrounding housing estates, which began to consume their own utility as they spread into the valley.

When, in 1979, the West Midlands County Structure Plan allocated thirty-eight acres of the valley for industrial use, serviced by a link road for heavy vehicles, 500 residents showed up at the public meeting, an action group was formed and a 5,000-name petition submitted.

Four years later the industrial plan was dropped, and in October the following year, 1984, 450 acres of the valley became Woodgate Valley Country Park. In its first year, this garden born of backyard passion was visited by 20,000 schoolchildren. Today, they come to learn how a river changes from its source to a confluence, to see meanders and bedrocks, to study hedgerows, to ride horses and to scrape away at the Black Country's industrial past.

Walking into the valley after crossing the Black Country on foot gave this green space the grace of an enchanted garden. Clear water bubbled in Bourn Brook. Hedgerows chattered with birdlife. A horse flicked its tail in a field. Children's laughter carried down the footpath. On the far side of the valley, at the top of a long gentle climb, I came to the Visitor Centre.

In olive green trousers and a cream safari shirt, the head ranger, John Price, made me coffee and gave me a chair. He'd been working at the Country Park for twelve years and smiled with the confidence of a man who has found a vocation. 'When I started this job, the valley was viewed by locals as the wasteground out the back. Now look at it!'

He explained how they kept much of the park as a working farm. 'It helps provide a traditional, diverse habitat for wildlife; there's not much unimproved farmland left nowadays. We've got a thriving colony of White-letter Hairstreak butterflies here, and wych elms. We've got wild orchids, the Common Spotted and the Southern Marsh, and we've got the only colony of Grass Vetchling in Birmingham and the Black Country.'

'What do you do with your hay?'

'We crop it ourselves. We get about 6,000 bales, which we use in our trekking centre.'

'Any problems?' I asked.

'We've got itinerants at the moment.'

'Gypsies?'

'We're not allowed to call them that. There are about fifty caravans. They've been here seven days.'

'Other problems?'

'We get a few burned-out cars. And rope swings, which we have to take down. There was a serious accident in the Lickeys.'

'Any more?'

'We get a bit of fly-tipping. Motorbikes. Sometimes people set fire to the hay. Considering we're an urban park surrounded by high-density housing, we get surprisingly few problems. We turned a corner recently. We're getting complaints about things in the park that are not right. If local people are complaining, they're caring.'

Frankley Beeches After the welcoming acres of Woodgate Valley Country Park I felt ambivalent about returning to the countryside, with its limited access, stressed wildlife and neurotic leaseholders. The Black Country and its pockets of public space had offered an exhilarating 'right to roam'.

These forthcoming difficulties became apparent ten minutes

after leaving the Country Park. As I cleared the last houses and reentered the world of commercial agriculture, the hundreds of optional routes that had existed in every urban kilometre now narrowed to one road and one public footpath, then thinned again to nothing: a white void on the map crossed by no roads and no public rights of way.

Late that afternoon, I walked up the hill to Frankley Beeches, climbed the bank and crossed into the trees.

I'd seen the copse months earlier, on the map. Frankley Beeches was marked as a lone green blob on a slice of white farmland between the grey maze of the Black Country and a scattering of grey blocks the shape of computer chips, marked 'Motor Works'. The blob was outlined in the National Trust's dark green and was perched on top of a pile of encircling contours, crowned by an Ordnance Survey triangulation pillar at 256 metres.

The trig pillar stood on the far side of the copse on a verge of silver-blown grass above a curve of ploughed red earth that led my eye down past six rectangular tower blocks to a wooded vale laid with vast shining roofs.

Herbert Austin had come this way in September 1905, leaning his bicycle against one of these beeches to study the unspoiled valley before him. He had been riding through the countryside south of Birmingham in search of a site for building cars. He needed clean air, for the slow-drying coach enamels he would use for painting his vehicles picked up dust and grit like flypaper. In Longbridge, ten kilometres from the centre of Birmingham and conveniently sited at the junction of the Midland Railway's line to Gloucester and a branch line to Halesowen, Austin came upon an empty tin-making and print works, on the market for £10,000. He got it for £7,750.

This valley and the surrounding hills became Austin's life. The valley filled with factory buildings and workers' terraces. In the hills Austin built a home, Lickey Grange, where one of his young draughtsmen, Stanley Edge, had sat in the billiard room sketching the shape of a new small car, the Austin 7. Stanley Edge now lay beneath my feet, his ashes scattered in Frankley Beeches.

The viewpoint invited lingering, but the sun was sliding into the Clent Hills and I was due to meet the night shift.

Longbridge Beyond Frankley Beeches I tried to push through a building site, but was turned back by a high wire fence.

Returning to the road, I was about to detour to the western limit of my 2,000-metre corridor in the hope of getting through a hospital, when a workman walking home told me of a short cut through another construction site. I emerged beside a new Safeways supermarket on the dual carriageway leading to the factory.

Late for my appointment, I covered the last kilometre at a jog, with the rucksack a bouncing rubber hump, umbrella in one hand, hat in the other and Black Country grime stinging my eyes.

Jill Howes was hurrying down the pavement outside K Gate. 'We thought we'd lost you!' she gasped, shaking my hand. I apologized and explained that Longbridge was cut off from the north, if you happened to be following two degrees west.

Jill, in a tailored red suit, was the press officer for Rover Group. She was accompanied by Anthony Osborne, the energy manager, who was also chairman of the Austin Ex-Apprentices Association. He'd signed on for a five-year apprenticeship in 1972, done his stint on the production line building engines and was now monitoring energy wastage in the plant.

'It's a historic site, Longbridge,' he said, leading us towards a fifties office block. 'This is the South Engineering Block. Built in 1957.'

Opening the building with an electronic pass, he led the way down the corridor to a locked door. 'The Shrine,' he announced. Inside was the office of the 1st Baron Austin of Longbridge. 'It wasn't always here,' began Anthony. 'When the original building was demolished, we moved his office piece by piece.'

The oak panelling, Persian carpet, banker's lamp, stationery tray and inkwell gave the windowless room the feel of a headmaster's study. The evidence that this was the throne room of a motor magnate was on the wooden panels. One of the pictures was a framed photograph of Henry Ford, signed 'From your friend'.

Austin's was an heroic dream. In his first year of production, 1906, he produced 120 cars. To do that, he'd had to spend £16,861 equipping the factory – twice what he'd paid for the buildings and land. By 1910 the workforce of 1,000 was working night shifts. In 1914 the company went public and was sold to the new Austin Motor Company for £339,993.

War turned Longbridge, and Austin, into symbols of patriotic defiance. During the First World War, the car factory turned out 8 million shells, 650 guns, 500 armoured cars and 2,000 aeroplanes, including the SE5a fighter. Austin himself became associated with the sacrifice when his only son, Vernon, was killed in 1915 by a sniper. At war's end, Herbert Austin was knighted. By 1936, he was Lord Austin of Longbridge.

Longbridge and Lord Austin were there for the Second World War too, mass-producing steel helmets, shells, ammunition boxes, fuel cans and 36,000 vehicles ranging from eight horsepower 'utility tourers' to four-wheel-drive trucks and ambulances. It was Longbridge that assembled the suspension and drive unit in the Churchill tank that Bill Rogers – the bicycling carpenter I'd met in Heath Hayes – drove up a Normandy beach in 1944. Longbridge also built nearly 3,000 Second World War aircraft, from Hurricanes to Lancaster bombers.

Lord Austin did not survive the war. After attending the funeral of workers killed in an air-raid on Longbridge, he caught pneumonia, and died on 23 May 1941.

On Austin's desk Anthony unfolded a map of the works. The site stretched for two and a half kilometres along the west side of the railway line.

The map told the evolutionary story of Longbridge. This was not a pre-packaged car plant that had been parachuted on to a green-field site by a Far Eastern investor in motor futures: Longbridge had spent nearly a century growing from a simple organism that had occupied the discarded shell of a previous business, to a complex body deformed by the constraints of building space.

The heart of the plant was hemmed in by housing estates

and the railway. Expansion had been opportunistic and not always ergonomic: the 'Old West' and 'New West' works had to hop over the Birmingham road; in 1993, the railway was hurdled and a field filled with a gigantic parts centre. The whole 430-acre site was held together by nineteen kilometres of roads, fourteen kilometres of plant railway and various strategic bridges. In an age of streamlined production, Longbridge's layout was perversely complex.

On to the map we drew the meridian and its 1,000-metre margins. Both the East Works and the North Works lay out of bounds, and so did the Cofton Hackett gearbox plant. But the remaining half of the factory was inboard of 99 and 01.

From K Gate, we crossed the Lickey Road and climbed a foot-bridge over a railway to a gigantic rectangular hangar: 'New West,' said Anthony. 'This is where we make the body shells for the Rover 400, 200 and 100 – the car that used to be the Metro.'

New West was opened by Prince Charles on 22 October 1980, and it was the first car works in the UK to pioneer robotic body-shell welding. The guinea pig was the new Mini Metro, the car that was supposed to replace Alec Issigonis's Mini. By virtue of its most famous owner, the youngest daughter of the 8th Earl Spencer, the Metro made its way straight on to the front pages of the world's newspapers. During her engagement to Charles, the photographers used to wait outside her flat for Metro shots. The year after Diana got her Metro, she married the man who opened the works.

Jill pushed through rubber flaps covering an outsize entrance. Inside was a parked train.

The statistics of that cavern emphasized its scale: its size was 70,000 square metres; the production line that made the body shell for the Rover 400 was 130 metres long and had 180 robots that made 3,640 welds every 60 seconds.

We climbed to an overhead walkway so that we could look down on the line. It was stationary and deserted but for three men scratching their heads in an avenue of frozen orange robots.

'It's the shift change,' said Anthony, explaining that the hours between the day shift and the night shift were an opportunity to service the machinery.

We went down to meet one of the recalcitrant robots, which

had names like Sinead, Debbie and Diane painted on to their limbs. 'Girlfriends. Wives,' grinned Jill. 'They can get quite sentimental about their robots.'

We walked on, past bins of neatly nested body panels.

'Generations of the same families have worked here,' nodded Anthony, whose wife, father-in-law and brother-in-law were Long-bridge employees. 'Most people in Birmingham know someone who's worked at Longbridge. There are 16,000 people here.'

As we walked up and down the lines I could only speculate on what New West looked like when the robots were firing. When it was on form, Longbridge was capable of coughing out a car a minute; 8,000 a week. In the financial year 1964–5, the year of their highest annual production, the factory made 345,245 vehicles. The total by 1992 was 12 million. With the other two factories in Solihull and Cowley, Rover was Britain's biggest car manufacturer and Longbridge was Britain's biggest car factory.

We left New West and walked back over Lickey Road and through K Gate to Number One Factory, a deserted brick shed in the heart of the plant. Number One was built in 1894 for the print works that had first caught Herbert Austin's eye.

'We use it for low-grade storage now,' sighed Anthony, as if he wished this historic shed to be resurrected for nobler roles. 'It used to be a mass of drive belts. We used it as a machine shop.'

We walked on, past the Fire Station, where a strange red Land Rover lurked, with six wheels and a ladder. ('Insurance,' grinned Anthony. 'You can get cheaper fire insurance if you keep your own fire engine.')

We passed the 'Kremlin', the 1948 administration block that became the headquarters of the British Motor Corporation, then came to another great shed. 'CAB 1. 1951.'

'CAB?'

'Car Assembly Building.'

Inside, painted body shells were gliding along production lines being dressed with all the underwear required to make them move. Engines dangled from an overhead conveyor; a team fitted wheels to Rover 100s.

In the lexicon of the line, I was looking at 'systems' that were divided into 'cells' comprised of 'stations' operated by 'production associates'. We paused at Line 1, cell 5 and Anthony introduced me to Kevin Meredith. Kevin had been with Rover for nineteen years. He was an area manager. Groups of four worked best, he explained. In an eight-hour shift, each person spent two hours on one job, then rotated. Short people got to do the jobs inside the cars, where space was tight. Beside me a woman curled into a foetal crouch around a handbrake, tightening nuts. Of the sixty or so on the line, about six were women.

The production associates in grey wore expressionless masks as they laboured, their movements automatic and repetitive, robotic. Rock music played from overhead speakers.

At the far end of CAB 1, complete cars rolled off the line, twinkling under the overhead lights as if they'd been dipped in glass. It seemed a shame to take them out into the dirt.

Anthony was at my side again. 'With the Channel Tunnel, we can get a car from Longbridge to Italy in forty-eight hours. In fact, within two weeks of a customer walking into a dealer, we can get them a car customized to their own specification.'

He talked about JIT. Just In Time. The new building, on the other side of the railway, was all about JIT. Into the 600,000 square-metre production components distribution centre poured 1,500 delivery vehicles a week, from 400 UK and European suppliers. Inside the centre, schedules transmitted electronically from the production lines would be made up into loads and moved to the appropriate cell, and a new order put out to the parts supplier. JIT meant less parts clutter on the production line, and therefore more space for more lines.

'What happens,' I asked, 'if the chap with the truckload of grommets falls asleep in a service station and arrives a day late?'

'Doesn't matter,' grinned Anthony. 'There's always buffer stock in the warehouse.'

Around a corner lurked a clutch of Minis for export. There was a Mini Cooper in jade for a Japanese customer, with electronic fuel injection, air conditioning and an engine compartment so stuffed with extra widgets that it looked like the inside of a watch.

'Japan is big on Minis,' said Jill. 'In 1990 we sold more Minis there than in the UK.' The car that was supposed to have been made redundant by the new Rover 100 outlived its replacement; 3.4 million Minis had rolled out of Longbridge.

We went back to Austin's office to collect my rucksack.

Into one of the oak panels was set a George V half-crown. After the First World War the company was on the verge of collapse and Austin had no money to pay the workforce. He tossed the half-crown in the air saying, 'Tails I close the works; heads I keep them open.' The factory stayed open and went on to build the small, affordable Austin 7, the car that turned England into a nation of motorists.

When Sir Michael Edwardes was shown Austin's office and told the tale of the half-crown, he fished a 50p piece out of his pocket and dropped it into the inkwell. It is still there.

The future of Longbridge was back in the air again. Since the last war the plant had suffered a string of civilian vicissitudes: a merger with the Nuffield Organisation; transformation into British Motor Corporation, which then merged with Leyland Motor Corporation. Then there was 'Red Robbo' and strikes costing £1 million a day, a tie-in with Honda and a buy-out by BMW. Longbridge had been rescued most recently by the great-nephew of Alec Issigonis, the BMW chairman Bernd Pischetsrieder. Thus did BMW take the driving seat of the British motor industry. As well as Rover, they controlled Land Rover, MG and Mini, and a clutch of extinct British marques such as Triumph, Morris, Riley, Austin Healey, the old sheep-shearing equipment company Wolseley and Austin. The efforts to make sure that Austin's coin always landed heads-up had been prodigious. Outside the factory gates, another 60,000 jobs depended upon Longbridge cars.

It seemed a bitter irony that the prosperity of the Black Country rested on the product that had turned it into a vehicular hell. One day, maybe, this eccentrically evolved factory would be the first to produce a car as perfect as the bicycle: clean, silent, simple, versatile and cheap.

It was late evening by the time I walked out of K Gate for the last time. I turned up the slope of Lickey Road, beside the factory railings. The factory seemed to run for kilometres. After some time I caught the red glow of cigarette ends through the railings, and peered between the bars. Two men in overalls were leaning on the corner of a building.

'What's it like,' I asked, 'working in a car factory?'

'Boring,' one of them replied. 'Bloody boring.'

Lickey Hills Lickey Road's street lights rose like beacons towards the black hills.

Chewing cod from a fish and chip shop at the crest of the climb, I turned up into the trees. The lights fell behind and the woods hissed in a rising wind. It was a night for Harry-ca-Nab, the Devil's Huntsman, who rode the Lickeys astride a wild bull when the wind blew raw. Or for the highwaymen who used to prey upon the coaches that creaked up the turnpike on the way to Worcester.

For a last look at the metropolis, I turned off the turnpike on to a path that climbed a spur to a stand of Scots pine. Back to the north, street lights glowed on the rise and fall of encrusted hills, the stars obscured by the glow of a million sodium hearths.

Balling the chip paper, I hefted the rucksack and picked my way over the pine roots and back down through the black trees to the turnpike. No lights burned at the Old Rose and Crown. I rang the bell for some time and eventually the door was swung open by a woman who led me into the hall, took my name and showed me through an inner door marked: 'Guard Dogs on Duty!'

'Everything around and in it was thoroughly English,' wrote Elihu Burritt of the Rose and Crown in 1846. 'The watering trough, the settle under the shade trees, the skittle-grounds, beer-mugs and all.' The US consul to Birmingham had stayed here on the eve of his great walk. Burritt had been dreaming for so many years of his first visit to England that he had already formed a picture of the perfect wayside inn, 'sketched by fancy'. His image of England as a Germanic-American hybrid extended to the landlady, 'a regular Saxon-faced and Saxon-haired woman, buxom, bland, and radiant'.

The woman who brought my Full English Breakfast next morning had worked at the Rose and Crown for twenty years. Marie Lees was the head waitress. She said that her Welsh grandmother

was related to a French countess and to the man who discovered
Nova Scotia. She was also related to a pirate whose brother was a
duke.

'It's all hearsay, mind,' said Marie, who lived in Rubery.

Burritt left the Rose and Crown in great excitement. For the American, this was Day One of a pedestrian odyssey that would take him
the length of England.

Such pilgrimages had been made fashionable among visiting
Americans by Washington Irving, the secretary to the US legation
in London during the early 1830s. Irving, the essayist and author of
A History of New York, by Diedrich Knickerbocker, was of the view that
'those who would form a correct opinion of the English . . . must go
forth into the country; . . . visit castles, villas, farmhouses, cottages
. . . and cope with the people in all their conditions.'

As I write *Two Degrees West*, the recently arrived US ambassador to the Court of St James, Phil Lader, is following the footsteps
of Irving, Adams and Burritt by making a 1,600 kilometre walk
from Land's End to John o' Groats in the kind of meet-the-natives
exercise that somehow seems inconceivable for a British ambassador
in Washington.

With splendid naivety, Burritt planned a rigorous daily schedule: spend night in hostelry; write newspaper articles and notes
until noon; take lunch in hostelry; buckle on knapsack and walk ten
miles to another hostelry; etc. This plan worked very well for the
first day. After that, unplanned diversions began to interfere with
his programme and his tour was not completed for eighteen
years.

On the American's second day out of the Rose and Crown he
was sheltering from rain in a nailer's shop and fell into conversation
over the anvil with the nailer and his smut-spattered nine-year-old
son. The boy couldn't read and neither could the father afford to
send him to school. 'I made a little martyr of him,' noted Burritt,
'and wrote my impressions of his condition in an article which had
a wide reading in the United States.' American children raised £30
to send the boy to school and another 2s 6d a week to compensate

the father for the loss of his son's labour. When the nailer's son grew up, Burritt employed him on his farm in New England, where he eventually settled, married and became the father of 'several happy children'.

In his books *A Walk from London to John o' Groats* and *A Walk from London to Land's End and Back with Notes on the Way*, Burritt often shows a Dickensian engagement with his subjects. He is still the only author to have devoted an entire book – the 448-page *Walks in the Black Country and its Green Border-Land* – to a hiking tour of the industrial West Midlands. When he left the Rose and Crown on his first walk, he presented the large Saxon landlady with his recipes for making bread, cakes and pudding out of Indian corn-meal.

Outside the front door, I shouldered my rucksack and took the path that Burritt had followed, into the trees of the Lickey Hills. For two centuries, Birmingham's green lungs have lifted the spirits of its inhabitants above the urban fog. They used to come in open-topped buses from Selly Oak to Rednal, then walk. When the new tram service opened in 1924, Easter Monday brought 10,000 customers to the Navigation Street terminus. The Lickeys still offer sanctuary to half a million urban refugees a year. To Burritt, the Lickeys were the best bit of the Black Country's green borderland, 'perfectly Scottish in cut and clothing', and ideal for 'airing one's body and soul'.

It was a glorious, balmy morning and I took the high ground through heather that cushioned the gaps between the pines and outcrops of rock, to Bilberry Hill where I met Bette Shellis and Edna Ward, sitting side-by-side on a bench with a balloonist's view over the roofs of the car factory to the blue puddles of the Bittel reservoirs.

'We're up here every week,' laughed Edna, 'summer and winter, rain or shine. We come every Wednesday, by bus.'

They had been friends for fifty-two years.

Bette and Edna gave me a bag of boiled sweets and directions to Icarus, a three-metre sculpture hewn from a tree trunk, spreading his wings on the end of Cofton Hill. From here I dropped into Lickey Warren and picked my way through the woods by compass, passing strange timber sculptures lurking in glades. One of these was a gigantic Green Man with a totem-pole head and cave-like mouth spitting tendrils of wooden foliage four metres long. Hands as tall as children emerged from the leaf mulch, ripping free of the underworld.

The Lickey Incline The Black Country slackened its grip on the meridian by stages: from suburb to green belt to commuter village; from the metropolitan county of West Midlands to the rural county of Herefordshire and Worcestershire. (In a reaffirmation of shire identity, the two counties were about to part company again.)

During this return to rurality, the meridian also lost height. Just as Cannock Chase formed a defensive bastion to the north of the Black Country, the Lickey Hills acted as a wooded wall to the south. From the Lickey Hills, the meridian would drop to the lowest point on its passage between the North Sea and the English Channel.

The public bridleway from Pinfield Wood took the tree-lined avenue that was bought in the last century by the Birmingham Association for the Preservation of Open Spaces for the use of day-trippers walking and riding hired donkeys up to the Lickeys from Barnt Green's railway station.

Barnt Green could have been lifted straight from the Surrey hills, complete with stockbrokers, second cars and a supermarket for residents who couldn't face the dispiriting descent into Birmingham; though it's unlikely that a Godalming deli could match the one in Barnt Green for Indian delicacies.

Loaded with samosas and onion bhajis for the days ahead, I pushed on south, under the M42 to fields of red earth and the symbols of the urban fringe: a golf course, a recreational cycle route and a remand centre for young offenders.

For a while my path grazed the Lickey Incline. Notorious among English rail ascents for its long, steep gradient, it has been immortalized by the artist Terence Cuneo and for over a century has been a pilgrimage site for train-spotters. The most famous of the 'Lickey bankers' was Big Bertha, the 73-ton, 1,800 horsepower Midland Decapod which used to drag the through-trains up the two miles of 1 in 37¾ climb from Bromsgrove towards Birmingham. Bertha was a monster. She had five pairs of 4ft 7½-in wheels powered by four great cylinders with Ramsbottom safety valves and a Belpaire firebox. Built in 1919, she was the only 0-10-0 in Britain at the time and enthusiasts came from all corners of the country to see her blast up the bank with her regulator wide open, thundering smoke and steam. Near the top of the incline I waited for fifteen minutes and was rewarded by a whirring three-car diesel.

A field path followed by a dash across the Bromsgrove–Redditch dual carriageway brought me at dusk to the Worcester & Birmingham Canal. On my left, the 535-metre Tardebigge tunnel bored through red sandstone en route for Bournville, Edgbaston and Gas Street Basin. To my right, a giddy flight of thirty locks stepped off the Birmingham plateau down towards the Severn. During the day I'd crossed a watershed; the meridian had left the North Sea for the waters of the Bristol Channel.

Above the canal, a footpath climbed to Tardebigge's hilltop church. *Tyrde Biggar* – Big Tower to the Saxons – had kneelers embroidered with canal boats and lock gates, and the torso of Henry, Lord Windsor, who lost his arms, legs and head when the tower collapsed in 1775.

At St Bartholomew's, I left the gingery blur of Bromsgrove's street lights and walked through the night until the glow behind me had faded to black.

On a hill I climbed over a gate into a stubble field and unrolled my sleeping-bag beside a hedge.

My ears were still ringing from the long clamorous cross-section through the Black Country and I lay awake for a while in the new white landscape, listening to the silence under the full moon.

On the threshold of sleep, contemplatively adrift but sensorily alert, I heard the voices of a man and a woman approaching along the lane. They stopped by my head, on the other side of the hedge.

'Do you really mean that?' asked the woman.

'Yes, yes I do,' replied the man, moving beyond the range of my straining ears.

When I woke, the landscape had swapped the sheen of moonshine for the milky light of day. Soaked in dew, I lay in the sleeping-bag chewing a Barnt Green naan. Far below, a line of pylons poked through the mist like marker posts on a tidal causeway.

Feckenham An old track marked on my map as 'Burial Lane' dived off the hill through holly and burrowed southward between tunnelled hedges. A pair of foxes paused in the fresh red furrows, then fled to the hedge.

At a cross tracks a mildewed cast-iron sign pointed to the Salt Way, presumably one of the routes from the salt springs at Droitwich. Off to the left, the bells of Feckenham's church clanged eight o'clock.

The church was locked. I sat on a bench in the Square while Feckenham woke up, the air busy with coughing engines and the crunch of rubber on combed gravel. Children waited by a tree for the school bus.

'It's a village of commuters,' shrugged Mick Wilson. 'It'll be empty in a few minutes. They'll all be gone till tonight.'

His garage was around the corner from the Square and I'd called in, having been told that he also sold food.

'Wanna coffee?' he asked. We sat behind the counter, clutching garage mugs.

'Tight bastards,' continued Mick. 'Millionaire came in here asking for a pint of milk and said, "Oh no! I haven't got any change."' There was, said Mick, a lot of money in the village. 'This is the only shop in the village. When I'm gone that's it. Two churches. Two pubs.'

Mick had served his apprenticeship in the same garage, when he was fifteen. 'I was on £4 a week, then I got offered a factory job for £100 a week. So I left. Dropped the apprenticeship.'

Mick had let one of his buildings to Saltway Mouldings, who

made sidecars and signs. 'That's what Feckenham's famous for,' he chuckled. 'You've seen those Jaguar signs at garages. Every one of those Jaguar signs came from Feckenham!'

Inkberrow   Where the Roman Road from Alcester to the salt springs of Salinae – Droitwich – passed Feckenham, vehicles screamed east and west along the straight, towing wallets of compressed smog that sucked at the foliage and had me tottering for purchase on the verge.

This was the threshold of Archer Country, the land of the long-running BBC radio soap whose stars are everyday farming folk. When I was a boy, the wireless made Archer Country seem as big as France. In reality, the village most closely associated with the soap, Inkberrow, lies at the centre of a 20-kilometre egg-shaped zone of rurality ringed with main roads and the six towns of Bromsgrove, Droitwich, Worcester, Evesham, Alcester and Redditch. The meridian formed the long axis of the egg.

South of the Roman Road, field tracks took me through to Withybed Lane, which was as close as I could get to Inkberrow and its pub, the Old Bull.

'That's right,' nodded a man with letters in his hand, 'Godfrey Basely lived in Bromsgrove, and he used Inkberrow for Ambridge. The Eddy Grundy Fan Club still hold their meetings in the Bull.'

He described the pub, timbered in black and white, tilting quaintly on the village green, with flagstones and brass and good food. (This was painful to hear, for the meridian had embarked upon one of its pub-impoverished phases.)

The church used for the wedding of Phil Archer to Grace Fairbrother, continued the man, was just up the road at Hanbury. 'When *was* that?' he asked himself.

I'd started listening to *The Archers* in about 1964. The wedding, he thought, must have taken place at least ten years earlier. 'I do know,' he said, 'that they recorded that particular programme in the church.'

As he left, he hesitated. 'You know, it is said that strange happenings in Inkberrow still have a way of finding their way into *The Archers*.'

It was a balmy morning and I was readjusting to a calmer rural pace. So I was still sitting on the verge of Withybed Lane when an elderly lady rode past on a 750cc Yamaha motorbike with *Easy Rider* bars and a teardrop tank. She was followed by a horseman and then a convoy of 4 × 4 vehicles towing horseboxes. One of the vehicles stopped beside me and its driver leaned inquisitively from the cab.

'I'm walking,' I called. 'How about you?'

'Worcestershire Hunt,' he replied. Tom Savage was a retired farmer. He'd been in London for the Hyde Park rally. 'The hunting people do a lot for the country,' he grumbled. 'Horse shows and all sorts. If the hunting goes, it all goes.' He shook his head. 'These "antis", as we call 'em. They're not anti-hunting. They're anti the people who hunt. It's class warfare. They don't realize that miners go hunting. And road sweepers. You just pay your subscription and join in.' He put the car in gear. 'It's putting country against town. It's not going to do anyone any good.'

Abberton   Withybed Lane led down to Piddle Brook and so to a deserted back road that climbed the hill towards the hamlet of Abberton.

It was a lovely road, steered by impenetrable hedges loaded with blackberries. Gaps in the thorn wall opened huge views to the crinkled blue ridge of the Malvern Hills, twenty-five kilometres away to the west. Beyond them lay the mountains of Wales. At every gap I paused and looked longingly at those forbidden, well remembered hills. Given the maps, I could sit down and recall every mountain I'd ever climbed. One of the first Welsh tops I stood upon was Pen y Fan. I must have been about ten, and I still have the piece of stone that I brought back from the summit.

Further up the hill, Rod Lloyd, a retired policeman from Redditch, was standing in the hedge holding a bag.

'Good blackberries,' we agreed. Both of us had hands stained purple.

Rod was a Welshman.

'Bad idea,' he said, when I asked him about the forthcoming devolution vote for Wales. He'd grown up in Bala, with Arenig Fawr on one side and the Berwyn mountains on the other. He still liked the hills.

Earlier in the year he had travelled to the Tatra Mountains in southern Poland. I'd been there too, trying to climb a peak which had been beset by mist and rain.

'Which mountain did you climb?' I asked.

'Rysy,' said Rod.

'Me too.'

Rysy is the highest peak in the country, Poland's Snowdon.

Abberton's handful of dwellings clustered around the crown of the hill below a church whose tower was taken off in the war by the Ministry of Defence. At the time it was regarded as a hazard to low-flying aircraft from nearby RAF Pershore, whose young pilot officers once managed to crash five planes in a single week. The ministry had paid the parish of Abberton generous compensation for the loss of their church tower, which was dismantled piece by piece and stored in a hangar at the airfield.

'They never put it back,' said the woman living in the converted barn below the church. Joan Swan poured me a mug of tea. 'I'll read you something,' she said, opening a book. 'It's by John Betjeman, "Diary of a Church Mouse".'

> Here among long-discarded cassocks,
> Damp stools, and half-split open hassocks . . .

Joan read while dust-motes slid down the sunbeams. When she finished, she slapped the book closed and laughed.

'*Those* are the lines that fit *our* church. I see that little mouse at Abberton, wondering why it is that the church only fills at Harvest Festival. Normally there are just four or so in the congregation, but the church is *full* at Harvest Festival and Christmas. John Harris makes punch. We all make mince pies. Then we all go to James's house, next door.' Joan shook her head. 'It only fills up for the pretty times, the nice times.'

There was a walking stick leaning against the stairs in Joan Swan's barn. At intervals down the stick's shaft, attached by metal clamps, were a bicycle bell, a toothbrush, a spoon and a miniature bottle of whisky. She saw me comparing its weight to that of my umbrella and laughed. 'It's a man-of-the-road's stick.'

From Abberton, the lone beacon of Bredon Hill drew me towards the Channel, only 180 kilometres to the south. As I came down the lane I had a flashback to the Catholic sierras I'd walked through five years earlier, and the solitary churches whose bells had called me eastward. England's bells were falling silent, and with them the music of the English village.

Since leaving Berwick (whose curfew bell was still rung each evening at eight), I'd come to rely on physical, rather than sonic, beacons. Most often these were hills: far views of the Cheviots, the Simonsides, Great Whernside, the Roaches, Cannock Chase and the Lickey Hills, Abberton's hill and now Bredon. Beyond Bredon, if the weather stayed clear, I would see the Cotswolds and then the Marlborough Downs, and from there the hills would be continuous companions as the meridian rode the troughs and crests of Salisbury Plain and Cranborne Chase to the Dorset foothills and Purbeck's downs. On the map, the remainder of my journey was a pattern of greens dissected by meandering blue threads. Compared to the Pennines, it looked like a big garden.

In Archer Country I ran out of water and called at a bungalow. It was a hot afternoon, and the front door was open. The cowman was sitting in a chair placed where the sun filtered through the grimy front window. He was, he said, seventy-eight, and had been a cowman since the age of fourteen.

In 1940 he'd joined the 12th Worcesters, but caught pneumonia sleeping in tents and so missed the trip to Norway. 'Only twelve of the battalion come 'ome, so t'was just as well I was ill,' said the cowman.

His pneumonia worsened while sleeping outdoors through the bad winter of 1941, and in 1942 the army let him go on the grounds of ill health. He took a job with a farmer near Evesham.

'Cows are dangerous,' he nodded. ''Ad me 'and broke when a cow dropped me across the manger.' He shook his head. 'That farmer, he used to go and buy anything at the market. All the rough ones. The bad cows.'

After that the cowman got a job with a good farmer. ''E was one of the best. Stayed with 'im rest of me time. And me sons. It's 'is house I'm in now.'

'A tied cottage?'

'Yes.' The farmer had built it for him in the fifties.

'Things have changed. We used to have good times and bad times. There's not a lot of hand-work now. As well as the cows I used to do ditching and hedging. It was hard work, skilled work. No one knows how to do it now. I used to plough with the horses. You've got to know what you're doing, especially when you've got four or six horses. Heavy earth round here. Clay. Ploughing could be pretty hard when the weather's against you, frosty or snowy. We could still use the horses if the snow wasn't too deep.' He looked out of the window. 'We used to get up at six in the morning and knock off at six in the evening. In summer we'd work till ten, bale-carting or whatever. A cowman might have to be up at midnight if a cow's calving.'

'What's the most important quality of a cowman?'

'To be on time. You've got to be there for the milking, three hours, twice a day. We used to do it by hand, me and a landgirl and two others. The farm had seventy Jerseys and Ayrshires. Young people aren't skilled like we were. They don't like work. You wouldn't get them doing the work we did in those days.'

The air in the cowman's sitting room was humid and laden with stale urine. He wore a collar and tie and stained trousers. Across his lap lay the racing paper. 'I have a bet on a Saturday. Had one or two good wins. I once won at Cheltenham. A pound each way, 20 to 1.'

The room was littered with the architecture of the cowman's life: a stack of old tabloids by the fireplace; a discarded jacket; two horse brasses; a fifties radiogram and a small transistor; two televisions, one facing the wall; a blotched telephone beside a couple of black-and-white prints of the cowman's retirement photograph. (He stands smiling, in broad braces, with one arm over a Jersey cow.) In the corner, china figures stared uncomprehending through the neglected glass of a display cabinet. Stacks of firewood lay on the brown floral carpet, thick with dirt. In the corner stood a plastic bucket of coal. On the brown walls was a small print of horses ploughing and six poster-size centrefolds from the *Sun* and the *People*, showing Pamela Anderson and the Spice Girls, milk-shed shots of distended pink udders.

'I get the *Sun* on weekdays and the *People* and *News of the World* on Sundays.'

The cowman had retired when he was sixty-five. He lived off his state pension.

'How much is that?'

'Seventy-eight pounds and a few coppers a week. Doesn't go far. You've got to get your electric and your food out of it. That coal is £6 a hundredweight, though I get a bit of coal at Christmas from the British Legion. It's hard work. You get used to it, though.'

'What do you watch on TV?'

'*The Bill. Home and Away*.'

'Do you always eat on your own?'

'I go over to the farm occasionally.'

The cowman glanced up at the far corner of the room where a spider had woven a nest that hung from the ceiling like a furry tennis ball.

'You never want to knock anything about. There's some big spiders in there. If I'm having a bath I always get 'im out and put 'im in the dry.'

I asked if I could fill my water bottle. The kitchen was down the corridor. I passed a lavatory, mottled, unflushed and reeking, then filled my bottle at the black, encrusted kitchen sink. The stench of excrement and rot in the hot unventilated space made me feel nauseous.

As I was leaving, the cowman put down his newspaper and fetched a small box from among the pill boxes and bills behind him. Inside the box was a bronze medal and ribbon presented to him by the Three Counties Cultural Society for long service. 'Forty-one years I did, and just after I retired, the wife died.'

Fladbury   A lane, a long-gone right of way by a field, a ditch, barbed wire, the road again.

Thus I teetered along the western limit of the meridian to the edge of Bishampton and a green lane past a piggery to the road that ran south over high land towards the Avon.

Up here, the orchards were ripening and the farms carried boards urging passers-by to pick up Worcester Pearmains, Coxes, Lambournes. Cookers. I turned into the Larches Farm where I found Mrs Hardy on her own. Frail and well ahead of eighty, she rootled in wooden trays, picking a couple of pears, for which I paid 20p.

Juice dripped from my chin as I watched the closing mass of Bredon Hill. Off to my right, the clouds had slipped down to touch the crest of the Malverns. It would rain in the night.

The road reached the edge of the Avon's river bluff and I peered at last into the Vale of Evesham, the armpit of mid-western England.

Fladbury, self-consciously affluent with its 4 × 4s and boats moored on gravel drives, was nervous of strangers. I asked a man polishing a pick-up truck whether there was anywhere I could stay in the village.

'Only the Chequers,' he sneered. 'It's expensive. You want to take the bus into Worcester.'

In the Chequers Inn that evening, a woman in the bar turned to me and said, 'You were with Mrs Hardy this afternoon.'

'How do you know?'

'She told me. And I saw you later, on the road. We all keep an eye on each other, you know.'

The landlord of the Chequers was Richard Alun Corfield. He was born in Wales, one of eleven children, all called by their second names. So Richard was Alun. His son was in the King's Troop of the Royal Horse Artillery. There were photographs of him on the pub wall.

Alun used to keep cockerels at the pub. He had fifteen of them. 'The "new people" in the village didn't like the crowing in the morning,' he said. 'One night someone let them out and the fox had them.'

'What did you do?'

'Bought a whole lot more.'

'Then what?'

'They got eaten again.'

'Did you give up?'

'No, I bought another lot.'

'Have you still got them?'

'They got let out again.'

The rain woke me and I couldn't get back to sleep. The room was cold and I was hungry. In the rucksack I found the last of the Barnt Green naans and lay in bed waiting for dawn, spilling crumbs on the pillow, listening to the falling water, glad not to be under plastic in a wood.

At 6.30 a.m. I turned on the bedroom's television. Wales had voted for their own elected assembly. Only one in four had voted 'yes', but it was enough. Scotland and now Wales; my English genes tingled with a guilty sense of liberation.

Photographs of Diana lying in the Mercedes had appeared on the Internet.

At nine o'clock I telephoned the RAF, the army and the Royal

Marines, each of them critical to overcoming the obstacles that were concentrated into the final fortnight of the walk.

At ten o'clock I left.

Cropthorne   The Avon was the journey's low point. Nineteen metres.

Water lay on the road as I walked down from Fladbury to the Jubilee Bridge. Between the salt-waters of the Tweed estuary and Poole Harbour, this was the closest that the meridian came to sea level.

On the far side of the bridge, the road climbed on to the bluff that formed the outward bend of the river.

Up here straggled the village of Cropthorne, its beamed black-and-white cottages telling of a time when oak trees were more plentiful than stone. The village took the first part of its name from Croppa's Land, and the second from the thorn hedge that used to separate it from its neighbour, Charlton. Of the nine villages along the Avon from Evesham to Pershore, Cropthorne had the most distinctive site, peering down from its high bank, midway between the two towns, with views of the intervening plain.

Offa, the King of Mercia, saw it as a strategic site when he gave Cropthorne to the Priory of Worcester in AD 786 and the village may have continued as a royal residence through to the reign of King Beorhtwulf, who was here in AD 841 when he signed and dated a charter giving land to Bishop Heahbeornt of Worcester. Two hundred years later, the Domesday Book recorded the parish appointment of a priest who was awarded one hide of land and a plough. By about AD 1100, the stones at the foot of the chancel arch in St Michael's were laid.

Inside the church I found the organist, Horace Lampitt. Horace had wanted to be a professional musician, but he was hit by a lorry when he was nineteen. 'It did me 'and in,' he explained ruefully. 'Knocked me through the floor of the lorry. I was in an awful state.'

Horace had a repertoire of ugly stories. 'There was a man at the end of the last century,' he began, 'called Bob Pulley. Pulley told his mates that he would meet a girl, and that she would two-time him, and that he would murder her on a particular date, and that they would find him hiding in a certain barn. Pulley told them the dates that he would be taken to the Magistrates Court and to the Assize Court, and he told them when he would be hung. You know,' said Horace. 'He got every detail correct.'

Horace's great-grandmother had walked down the lane just after the murder and had passed the dead girl but not seen her because she was lying in the ditch. The lane had become known as Bob Pulley's Lane. We looked at my maps, but Bob Pulley's Lane was out of reach of the meridian.

Horace also had a story about his great-grandfather, who had been a police officer in the Black Country. 'A chap let his donkey stray into town and steal vegetables from the stalls in the market. When my great-grandfather went to tell the chap to secure his donkey, he hit him over the head with a stone bottle and fractured his skull. Great-grandfather lasted fourteen months, then died in a mental hospital. Sad thing is, if he'd died in under twelve months, it would have been murder.'

Then, continued Horace, there were the Boswell brothers from Charlton, who were hung at Worcester for killing a gamekeeper. And Harry Stevens, whom Horace had met when he was a teenage evacuee during the war. Later, in the 1950s or 1960s, Horace had read in the *Daily Mirror* of a policeman called Harry Stevens who'd been shot in the mouth by a criminal. The bullet had hit a tooth and lodged in the roof of his mouth. Undeterred, Harry had chased his assailant over a wall and tackled him. Harry got the George Cross.

Talking about policemen reminded Horace of Stanley Woodward, who, like himself, had been born in Lower Moor, just across the river. Stanley had been shoved through a plate-glass window, with predictable results. The culprit was taken to Wormwood Scrubs and given twelve lashes with the cat-o'-nine-tails then seven years. 'You know,' mused Horace with wonder in his voice, 'he came out of prison as docile as anything. Never did harm again.'

The two steel donation safes in St Michael's had recently been smashed and raided, and a table stolen. 'We don't ask visitors to leave money in the church any more,' said Horace.

I was about to leave the church when Horace remembered the one about the officer at Pershore airfield who walked into a propeller that sliced off his face.

St Michael's will outlive this unholy age. These are old, old stones. Facing the door was an exquisite oolite cross-head from about A D 800, edged in a cable mould and carved with perched birds and foliage that swirled about the cross above a four-legged animal with zebra stripes and a griffon's head.

Two degrees west had once again contrived a coincidence that gave the line itself a pleasurable, if spurious, integrity. The birds and the inhabited vine-scroll on the cross-head had come down the line from Northumberland, whose manuscripts and carving style had filtered through the rest of Saxon England. Cropthorne's peculiar zebra-bird is related to similar beasts applied to purple vellum in a Northumbrian Gospel book now housed in an environmentally controlled vault of the British Library.

The Vale of Evesham had suffered the same erosion of services that I'd seen in the Pennines.

In Cropthorne, the combined shop and post office had been run by David and Sue Miller for fourteen years. 'There's not the loyalty to village shops nowadays,' said David, handing me my postcards. 'It's very sad, but it's a sign of the times. There's no way of stopping it.'

I asked about the other villages on the floodplain.

'The Combertons have lost their shop and post office, and Wick, and Elmley Castle. The village shop in Charlton closed two or three years ago and the 85-year-old lady who ran Charlton's post office packed up three weeks ago. She died a week later. Fladbury's post office closed a fortnight ago. Wyre Piddle's post office has gone. We're now the only village shop between Evesham and Pershore.'

'How long d'you think you'll keep going?'

'We'll stay till we retire, but we don't know if there'll be a business to sell by then. The big crunch came when Tesco in Evesham began sending a free bus three days a week.'

Ashton under Hill   With the turning of the season came the turning of the soil. The stubble fields were being sliced and folded into moist clods that shone like cut liver. The body of the earth sweated a slight mist.

The field paths I followed from Cropthorne wandered south through these vapours towards the solidifying form of Bredon Hill. Sadly, the viewpoint that William Cobbett described as 'a richer spot than is to be seen in any other country of the world' lay just the wrong side of the 99 grid line.

Beneath Bredon straggled Ashton under Hill.

The sub-postmaster spoke bitterly of the way the village was going. 'The pub's only just surviving. Rent increases, all that jazz. The shop closed twelve months ago; the supermarkets in Evesham did it.'

He described in incredulous tones how villagers had asked him to sell raffle tickets in order to raise money to buy a minibus so that elderly inhabitants could shop in Evesham. 'Incredible.' He shook his head. 'They really couldn't see that the raffle tickets they wanted me to sell would kill my own business.

'People don't even bother to come here for stamps now. They'll buy a book of first-class stamps from the garage while they're filling up, rather than walk twenty yards to my post office. Everything here depends on wheels. You won't get a job without wheels.'

Otherwise, he said, the village was doing all right. It had a cricket and football team. A tennis club. The Bredon Hillbillies were down to play a gig and line-dancing classes could be taken in the village hall.

'Is it a happy village?'

'There's not a lot of animosity,' he said. 'A little tittle-tattle. The usual.'

Chris performed the tasks expected of a village post office: keeping the chimney-sweep list and the phone numbers of reliable plumbers. 'I do the box office for the amateur dramatics too,' he added. 'I do it for the village, for nothing. But people still ring me up and are rude.'

As I was leaving, he handed me a leaflet issued by the National Federation of Sub-Postmasters headed BEWARE! The leaflet described how the Department of Social Security wanted to pressurize people into having their pensions and benefits paid directly into their personal accounts rather than allowing them the choice of collecting them at the local post office, then warned that 'thousands of post offices may have to close'. The leaflet's last bullet-point read:

> The community role of the local Sub Post Office is very important.
> It offers services, it is a vital part of a community, it encourages
> more people to shop locally.

It was true, but like all the other services that helped make rural communities function, nobody wanted to pay the extra premium.

Five minutes south of Ashton under Hill, I crossed the dismantled line of the Cheltenham to Evesham railway into Gloucestershire.

Gloucestershire and Wiltshire were the richest counties on the meridian. Both scored a gross domestic product of 114 per inhabitant, against a European Union standard of 100. Northumberland, the poorest county on the line, had scored 77.

Alderton   From Alderton Hill I could look down on the ploughed fields that spread for four kilometres to the dark rump of the Cotswolds. The village of Alderton looked like an island in a sea of mud. The meridian passed through the centre of the village.

Opaque mist rose to meet the drizzle. I walked down to Alderton to find food and a bed. The pub was closed. So was the post office.

As I was leaving, condemned to a damp bivouac, a van with

'Charlie's Chips' painted on its side pulled up near the pub. A queue formed so fast that, although I'd been there first, I was fifth in line by the time I'd got my wallet moving.

From the woman in front of me I learned that there was a bed and breakfast in the village. Clutching my hot paper parcel I made for the phone box, called directory enquiries and then the bed and breakfast, and was told politely by the landlady that there were no vacancies. Uncharitably, I wondered whether Alderton's Neighbourhood Watch had already frightened her with reports of a suspicious mud-spattered dosser.

As dusk settled, I sat on the parapet of a small bridge on the edge of the village eating cold cod while the commuters tore home to tea, telly and a warm bed.

Squinting at the map I saw a wood on the slope of the Cotswolds thirty minutes to the south that would offer some shelter from the rain, but I'd taken only a few steps from the bridge before I passed a solitary house with lights burning and a bed and breakfast sign on its outside wall.

Caroline Page was preparing supper for her children. I took a deep, steaming bath and came back downstairs to the kitchen for a mug of tea. On the TV the credits were rolling for *Flash Gordon's Trip to Mars*.

Caroline handed me a business card, and as I slipped it in my wallet I saw something odd. The address of the bed and breakfast was appended by a six-figure grid reference: SO997 327. For a few moments I savoured the expectation: I was in the home of an eccentric, or a surveyor.

'That's Keith,' laughed Caroline. 'He worked for the Ordnance Survey.'

Later that evening, when Keith came in from work, I told him that I was walking two degrees west. He laughed; we both laughed. For the first time, I didn't have to explain why the line of longitude that ran from Northumberland to Dorset, by way of Alderton, was the most important in the country.

'Is that why you're living here? To be on two degrees west?'

He laughed again. 'No. It's a coincidence.'

Keith, of course, knew all about the transverse Mercator projection, about Major General MacLeod, Davidson's committee and why two degrees west was the only line of longitude shown on the maps of the Ordnance Survey.

It all goes back to the Treaty of Tordesillas in 1494. Two years after Columbus sailed the Atlantic, the Portuguese and the Castilians divided the world into two; half each. Because the far side of the globe had yet to be visited and charted by Europeans, they used a map of the known world, drawing their territorial dividing line down the centre of the Atlantic.

The Treaty of Tordesillas was of course incomplete. The line needed to be continued around the globe so that the eastern and western hemispheres could be separated, like the splitting of an orange in two. The precise location of the other half of the Atlantic line was of immense commercial significance, since possession of the invaluable Spice Islands – the Moluccas – could not be settled until their longitude was fixed. The motive for completing the line was commercial; the method was mapping.

Magellan's voyage of 1519 was a multi-national, high-tech moonshot of an expedition, financed by Germans, piloted by a Portuguese, using German cartography, an Italian chronicler and flying the flag of Castile. On board the five ships were twenty-three charts, seven astrolabes, twenty-one quadrants, thirty-five compass needles, eighteen half-hour glasses and two planispheres.

This mass of navigational equipment was essential for mapmaking. Maps were the geopolitical currency of colonialism. They defined territorial control and were the oracle that guided military, commercial and political ambition. Maps were the arbiters of power, the key to the cosmos.

The Treaty of Tordesillas was settled by the ritual inscription of a map 'on which the said line shall be drawn in the manner aforesaid, and it will thus be agreed to as a declaration of the point and place through which the line passes'. The wording of the treaty reiterated the definitive role of the line – and the map.

Paid by acquisitive merchant-colonists, map- and globe-makers raced to chart the world's last coastlines. By 1529, Diogo Ribeiro had completed two exquisite world maps incorporating the latest exploration data. Months later, the geographer Gemma Frisius began five years of work on his great Louvain globe.

'The utility,' he crooned, 'the enjoyment and the pleasure of the mounted globe, which is composed with such skill, are hard to believe if one has not tasted the sweetness of the experience.'

A globe was still the only true model of the world, but it was cumbersome and its accuracy as a navigational tool was severely limited by its small-scale depiction of coastlines. Maps were not a reliable alternative because mariners were still unable to take a compass bearing from a map without being deflected from their sailing course by the curvature of the earth. The last great challenge was therefore to make a two-dimensional model of a three-dimensional sphere.

The solution was found in 1569 by the Flemish mathematician, geographer and map-maker who had engraved the segments of Frisius's globe.

Gerard Mercator's map, *Nova et aucta orbis terrae descriptio ad usum navigatium emendate accomodata*, depicted the longitudinal meridians running parallel to each other, rather than converging on the two poles, as they do on a globe. Compass bearings taken at sea matched those on maps, albeit at the cost of a world whose cartographic shape became increasingly distorted towards the poles.

For his prime meridian – the zero line of longitude that ran down the centre of the map – Mercator chose the mid-Atlantic line drawn seventy-five years earlier by the Portuguese and Castilians as they divided the world in two. The visual effect of Mercator's projection was to place Europe – and especially the British Isles – in the centre of the new world map.

The following 400 years were good for Britain. By the nineteenth century, the country was not only at the cartographic centre of the world but at the economic focus too. Britain became the world's leading maritime power and then solved the problem of measuring longitude. By the end of the nineteenth century, 72 per cent of the world's commerce depended upon sea charts whose prime meridian was drawn through Greenwich. Final confirmation of Greenwich as the starting line for space and time came in October

1884, when twenty-five nations met at the International Meridian Conference in Washington DC and voted 22 to 1 in favour of Greenwich being the 'initial meridian'. San Domingo voted against; France and Brazil abstained.

Britain's cartographers took fifty years to conform the country's maps to the new, universal longitudinal system. In the meantime, each British county was free to choose its own map scale and its own projection. The result was cartographic chaos: Britain was like a gigantic jigsaw whose fret-worked county boundaries could not be fitted together. No fewer than thirty-nine different projections were in simultaneous use.

In 1935, the year that Huxley launched *Geographical Magazine* with the cry 'Geography dictates!' (and the year that Brigadier MacLeod was appointed Director General of the Ordnance Survey and that Captain Hotine began work on the great retriangulation), seven men were charged with preparing a blueprint for the future of Britain's maps. Their chairman was the Right Honourable Sir John Davidson, MP for Hemel Hempstead and ex-parliamentary private secretary to Stanley Baldwin.

The Davidson Committee's most pressing task was to find a single projection for Britain. The priority was to minimize the distortion caused by converting a portion of spherical surface into a plane. They settled on the transverse Mercator projection, which is particularly suitable for tall, thin land shapes. Derived from Mercator's original concept, the transverse Mercator wraps the globe in a cylinder, then unrolls the cylinder. A centre line – the Central Meridian – is then selected, from which every point is measured.

Reviewing the options, Davidson's team recognized that the Greenwich Meridian was so far east that it would have distorted the mapping on the western part of the country. Of the other eight lines of longitude passing through Britain, there was only one contender. It lay eighty-six miles west of the Greenwich Observatory and it ran from Berwick-upon-Tweed on the Northumbrian coast to the Isle of Purbeck in Dorset. That line was two degrees west, the new Central Meridian.

Two degrees west became the line that changed the shape of Britain. Like the spine of a book, it bound the contents of the land to a single central axis. Of all the lines of longitude passing through Britain, two degrees west was thus the only one that could be depicted as a straight line on a map; the OS referred to it as the Line of Zero Convergence.

So why did this line – and not the Greenwich Meridian – come to be numbered on my maps as 00?

The answer is contained in the 'Ministry of Agriculture and Fisheries Final Report of the Departmental Committee on the Ordnance Survey', the document published by the Davidson Committee at two shillings a copy in February 1938.

Having recommended that the transverse Mercator be adopted as the new projection, the committee went on to describe how the projection should be overlaid by Britain's first unified grid, a mesh of metric squares that would allow any place to be given a unique grid reference.

There was of course only one meridian on to which the new grid could be aligned, since all the other lines of longitude curved towards the North Pole and could not correspond with the straight lines of the grid.

That line was two degrees west, the Central Meridian, the Line of Zero Convergence, England's Meridian.

'He was a radical,' said Keith. 'A very clever man. His revision was the Holy Grail.'

Keith had spent his working life on Davidson's revision. For twenty-one years he'd been part of the team that had surveyed the country, setting forth daily with his twenty-metre tape, 3H and 4H pencils, his scale, sixty-degree set-square, notebook, his 'Popeye' optical square and his aluminium-framed sketching case. He worked alone. His target was to survey a one-kilometre square, or plan, each week; forty-five plans a year.

'The Cotswolds were easiest: nice straight walls and big fields. Though once you've got slopes and woods it's slower.'

He'd been all over the country: from Yorkshire grouse moors to Gloucestershire farms. Gamekeepers, bulls – he'd seen and met the lot.

'The windy days were a pain in the neck: the case would come off your shoulder and smack you in the face. I spent twenty-one years in Wellington boots. I hate to get in Wellingtons nowadays.'

As I was eating breakfast next morning, Keith came into the room with something in his hand. 'I'd like to give you this.'

It was a flat, cream-coloured ruler, chipped and scratched and marked in sub-divisions that measured two metres on a 1:2500 map. It was his Ordnance Survey scale.

Gretton   Off to the south a feather of steam wafted across the Cotswolds.

From Alderton, the road ran across the arable flats through the hamlets of Alderton Fields and Gretton Fields, to Gretton itself, hunched beneath the railway on the sunless side of the hills.

The train blustered by again, trailing its rake of restored carriages and a cotton-wool cloud along a restored fragment of line that once carried the Vale of Evesham's apples to Stratford-upon-Avon and Cheltenham. The line closed in 1977, but volunteer enthusiasts have reopened an 11-kilometre segment which they dream of extending to its original termini.

Underneath the railway embankment, the door of Christ Church was open. Inside, Gwyneth Cocks was cleaning the floor. She was a member of the lay ministry.

'We're raising £200,000,' she said. 'We need a new entrance, loos, a lobby, a kitchen, a meeting room and a hall. We'll have a crèche and a Sunday Club for the children. We want the church to become the focal point of the village. This is our way of preparing for the millennium.'

A second woman paused in her sweeping and nodded towards Gwyneth. 'She's marvellous. *And* she does the cleaning.'

The church was Victorian Early English, built in 1868, said Gwyneth, by Emma Dent of Sudeley Castle. 'I've seen a note at the castle, in Emma's handwriting, saying that the money to build the church was from Uncle George of Macclesfield. It would be nice to know more about Uncle George.'

Gwyneth and her husband Colin lived in the oldest house in Gretton, a few minutes' walk from the church.

'It dates from around 1400,' explained Colin. 'Would you like a beer?' The house had been built beside the Norman church, whose ruined tower still peeped from the trees. 'It may have been the priest's house. We're not sure.'

The heart of the house was the cruck-beamed hall, unusual for the 2-metre high piers that had raised the beams high above the ground, clear of damp and free of rot. Around the massive ingle-nook were stones from Hailes Abbey, demolished during the Reformation. Three coats of arms had been built into the back of the fireplace, upside down. 'Inverting them symbolized their decon-secration. It seems that the locals rushed along to the abbey with barrows and helped themselves.' Upstairs, the walls were wattle and daub from the sixteenth century.

Earlier in its life, the house had been converted into three cottages, then used in the last war for refugees.

'It was virtually derelict,' said Colin. 'It was going to be demolished.'

They had bought the house twenty years earlier and had just added two extra rooms using English green oak, fitted together with mortise and tenon joints, pegged with dowel. 'You wouldn't expect to find carpenters who still knew those techniques. But we did,' said Colin pointing to the joints. 'They built the frame lying on the ground, then hauled the side of the house upright with ropes. It fitted together perfectly. It was beautiful.'

Leaving Gretton, I felt that a pattern was emerging. The plans for Christ Church, the rejuvenation of the railway line and the rising of a medieval house all required huge resources of motivation, time and money. But more importantly they needed passion. Like most passions, the belief was often more important than the need to know 'why'. The point was to recognize a quality of beauty, purpose or faith and to respond. Now, three-quarters of the way down the meridian, I could see that I'd come across countless examples, from Neil and his bird sanctuary in Coquetdale to volunteers who'd refilled canals and revived steam lines, to the postmistresses, pub-licans and farmers, to the Black Country community workers and whoever kept Pleck Park under the stilts of the M6 in such pristine condition. The instinct for pursuing ideals was alive and thriving. These were dreams with no unifying umbrella; they were apolitical and frequently uneconomic. They came from individuals. They just happened. Cumulatively, they defined everything that was good about England.

Cleeve Hill Behind Gretton, the contours crunched into the wrinkled brow of the Cotswold scarp.

The track I took leapt from 80 metres to 180 metres, rising above the Vale of Evesham until its odd sentinels, Alderton Hill and Bredon Hill, were molehills on the dim plain.

Standing on this spot 20,000 years ago, I would have been looking at the edge of the last ice sheet to smother Britain. At the time, Scandinavia and the Baltic were covered too, and the North Sea, Germany, Denmark, Poland and Russia. Britain north of the Cotswolds was an ice cap.

With the ice line, the meridian was about to cross another emphatic divide: the great diagonal that slices across the country from Lyme Bay to the Humber.

It's a line born of geology and nurtured by history, and it shows on geological maps as a banana-yellow band of Jurassic limestone. On a physical map it is the pale brown rumple of the South and North Dorset Downs, the Cotswolds and Northampton Uplands.

Before the great invasion of AD 43, the indigenous tribes do not appear to have used this line of intermittent upland to delimit territory. Rather than define boundaries, the limestone belt passed through the heartland of the Durotriges, and those of the Belgae, Dobuni and Coritani. But for the 40,000 Roman invaders of Aulus Plautius, streaming ashore on the island's south-eastern beaches, the great diagonal was the obvious bridgehead. It was where, after four years of fighting, Plautius called a temporary halt to the invasion and established a deep military frontier zone, a *limes* or buffer between the surviving tribes north and west of the Jurassic Rubicon, and the conquered province to the south and east. They built the Fosse Way along the limestone, and Cirencester (Corinium) became the most important node of radial routes outside London.

With time and the withering of the Roman Empire, the diagonal lost its meaning and became smothered by the silt of tangential histories: the Angles, Saxons and Jutes set up a north–south axis from the Firth of Forth to Ebbs Fleet (although for a while the West Saxons were bounded on their west by the Cotswolds and Dorset Hills). Then the Treaty of Wedmore split England down another, vertical axis, further west, to be followed by a latitudinal divide into the earldoms of Godwine and Leofric. Then, with William's invasion in 1066, England became a single geopolitical unit.

Two thousand years after the Romans used the Jurassic divide to separate civilization from the barbarians, it has reappeared as the country's greatest cultural battlement, dividing the 'south east' – the mythical land of plenty – from the 'provinces'.

On one side of the line, all roads lead to London; on the other are reemerging regional tribes convinced of their distinction and increasingly committed to autonomy from the capital. On one side is the city state and its symbiotic 'Home Counties'; on the other sprawls the island diaspora: Northumbrians intent on a Northern Assembly; Cumbrians claiming the special status of England's only mountaineers; Mancunians, Liverpudlians and Brummies talking up alternative urban foci; Celts beyond the Tamar whispering of secession.

The problem for England is the capital. London was in the right place for running a maritime empire and for keeping an eye on the continentals, but it's in the wrong location for relating to the north and the west of a country which now has to look to its own resources. Logic would suggest that the nation's political and economic powerbase should shift to the conurbation closest to the geographic centre of England, where it is best-placed to govern and to make efficient use of national communications. The Birmingham/Black Country metropolis is already at the heart of the country's road network. With the capital in the West Midlands, London could age gracefully into a sleepy backwater of museums and cafés, a Bonn to the risen Berlin.

*

So I turned my back on the Midlands and walked into clean round hills that could only belong to the south-east.

The sheep-cropped grass was as smooth as baize and absurdly easy to walk. Each stride felt 50 per cent longer than was imaginable on the gritty sponge of the northern moors. On well-drained limestone I would have no mud tugging at my ankles, or heather snagging my calves. Or bulls. (That week I'd read in the paper that Leslie Snowden, seventy-six, had been trampled to death by a bull on his farm near Corbridge.) In this soft, pampered land of vale and down the textures and contours were easy on the eye and kind to the sole.

A buzzard spiralled. Peeow! Peeow! A Spitfire bored east towards the Windrush.

From Winchcombe, snoozing in its blue vale, the sound of bells carried from the great wool church of St Peter's. I could just pick out its pinnacled tower rising above the pink-freckled town, set in the wooded scallop of the Isbourne. Henry Ford had wanted to buy St Peter's, then ship it to the USA.

The path skirted the stone wall of Postlip Hall, then climbed steeply beside 'The Washpool', a rugged gully eroded by water which long since found a more secretive route through the underground oolite. Higher up, braided paths threaded through the gorse on to the airy green cloud of Cleeve Hill, the watershed between the Severn and Thames, the Atlantic and the North Sea; the highest point in south-east England.

Cheltenham twinkled below the bald dome of the hill, and I lounged against the triangulation pillar that the Ordnance Survey had erected in 1936, the year after the Davidson Committee sat down to redraw England.

In the haze I tried to pick out the surrounding triangulation points that the OS had used for sighting from Cleeve Hill, from Hetty Pegler's Tump on its scarp above the Severn, to the Malvern Hills, to Broadway Tower (where they'd used a roof mark), to Rollright and Icomb Tower (another roof mark), to Wyck Beacon to the pair of trig pillars known as Ridgeway Base – White Horse Hill and Liddington Castle. Off to the west I could see the frown of the Black Mountains and the grey stain of Gloucester, with the M5 shining in the sunlight like a river of mercury, dribbling west towards Avalon and England's Celtic margins.

Lying on the grass with closed eyes, I could feel the breeze run its fingers through my hair; the colours on the inside of my eyelids swimming through Rothko tone shifts. The sounds of the hill, of the wind twisting in spirals and rotors through the coarse grass, were the sounds of black holes and of gliding atoms, of a bird on the wing. Adrift in an unmapped mind, I saw a hapless planet tumbling through the void, its air rank, its food tainted and its species in the throes of mass extinction. It wasn't much of a home to hand on to the kids.

Dowdeswell   The line unrolled south through empty hills, under an empty sky. Shotguns clanged in the woods, but little moved apart from occasional cars. The meridian touched only two villages as it crossed the Cotswolds. Once there were more. My strip maps were dotted with the shadows of former occupation: barrows and earthworks, the abandoned medieval villages of Whittington and Sennington (just off the meridian) and several sites of Roman villas.

Impermanence is a fact of rural life: Anglo-Saxons burned Roman villas, the monks of Winchcombe's Benedictine abbey (itself demolished by Lord Seymour of Sudeley in 1539) razed Saxon villages to clear the slopes for sheep, then the enclosures of 1755 parcelled land into rectangles rimmed with drystone walls and tree-belts to hinder the wind. Some places died of natural causes: the Saxon village of Coberley, 'Cuthbert's glade' (mistaken by Leland for being Norman 'Cow Berkeley') ran out of water when the springs dried up, and the inhabitants moved on.

Eventually the road leading south from Cleeve Common veered off the meridian and I took to the fields.

For a moment I considered a minor trespass down through Dowdeswell Wood, haunted – so it is said – by the last local to be hanged for sheep rustling, but just as I dithered at a gap in the drystone wall, the double blast of a shotgun shook the birds from the trees.

So I came down on a public footpath which brought me to the verge of the old coach road from London to Fishguard at the point where it hurdled the ditch of the Chelt, trickling uncertainly towards Cheltenham. Cars flew by in metallic blurs, sucking at my rucksack and sending my hat spinning into the oily grass.

Ten quick steps took me across the A40 to another field and the overgrown embankment that used to carry the Great Western Railway from Banbury to Cheltenham.

The door of Dowdeswell's church hung open.

A newspaper cutting in my rucksack told an odd story: inside the church were two galleries, built out of sight of each other and reached from the outside by two separate doors. During an argument in 1793 the vicar knocked off the hat of the squire, who sued. Thereafter the gallery at the west end of the church was the exclusive territory of the manor, and the gallery around the corner in the transept was used by the rectory.

Memorial slabs in the church recorded that the youth of this divided community died for their country at Suvla Bay and Ctesiphon and, in the next war, on the beach at Calais.

There was a burial mound on the hilltop above Dowdeswell and I lay under its trees with the last of Bette and Edna's boiled sweets.

The mound was a round barrow and occupied the highpoint on the eastern edge of Dowdeswell parish boundary. During the annual beating of the bounds, the words of St Paul used to be read from the mound, and for this reason it is marked on the OS map as St Paul's Epistle.

As I lay back against the mound with my eyes half-closed, a rustle made me look up at a young man wearing spectacles. He was the son of the farm manager. Andrew. He declined a boiled sweet. The land, he said, belonged to Mark Vestey. Four hundred cattle. One thousand sheep. Big. Andrew had a job in Gloucester and was serious beyond his years.

'Do you like living in the country?' I asked.

'I like the woods,' he said, and walked towards the trees.

River Churn   A narrow lane dropped into the valley of Hilcot Brook, following its meandering course as it unravelled around shaded bluffs towards its confluence with the Churn.

As the sun rolled along the horizon like a gigantic double Gloucester I came down through the fields to the deep-set valley where the River Churn slid beneath a bridge in the hamlet of Colesbourne.

The Churn would run on through Cirencester and Cerney Wick to the Thames by Cricklade and so to the tidal shores of London. Churn, Ciren and Cerne are derived from Corinium, the Roman sub-capital of Britain. The belief by locals that this stream is the true source of the Thames became sufficiently contentious that in February 1937 questions were raised in the House of Commons. Mr Perkins, the MP for Stroud, took the view that the Thames rose at Seven Springs, the source of the Churn; Mr W. S. Morrison, the Minister of Agriculture and MP for Cirencester and Tewkesbury, stated that it rose at Thames Head, south of Cirencester. In confronting the minister with his case, Mr Perkins asked, 'Is my Right Honourable friend aware that the source known as the Thames Head periodically dries up?' To which an Honourable Member was heard to mutter, 'Why don't you!'

Mr Perkins had a point: not only is the Churn the longest tributary, but its rising in the Cotswolds is much more romantic than the meadow at Thames Head. Were the Churn to be adopted as the true source, the Thames would win an additional literary association too, for Charles Lutwidge Dodgson, or Lewis Carroll as he is better known, used to stay with Alice Liddell's uncle, who lived one village upstream of Colesbourne. Maybe the make-believe woods in *Alice's Adventures in Wonderland* dappled the Churn.

Beside the Churn, I stayed in the Colesbourne Inn.

*

Bob and Elaine Flaxman had run the pub for twenty-one months and were beginning to relax. During the first three nights of their tenancy they'd fielded only eleven customers. Trade was picking up now. People were driving out from Cirencester and Gloucester to eat. They were thinking of live music.

The Flaxmans leased the Colesbourne Inn from the only brewery on the meridian, Wadworth in Devizes, who in turn leased it from the Elwys estate, one of whose earlier owners – Henry Elwys – had brought the first snowdrop to Britain and planted trees from the Himalayas and Rockies in this little Cotswold valley.

The Elwys estate once stretched as far as Coberley and Seven Springs, but the farms had to be sold, and then the land too, and even Colonel Elwys's foxhounds.

Later that night, when Wadworth's had blurred the limits of discretion, a local leaned across the bar. 'Elwys still owns the village,' he muttered. 'It's a *tied* village. We're living in the *feudal* age.'

Daglingworth   After breakfast I crossed the road in front of the pub and climbed a field while a tractor smoothed the worry-lines from the ploughed earth. Further up, where the slope became too steep, grass blew in the warm blue morning, giving the dome of Pen Hill the look of a tousled head.

For ten kilometres, the meridian was shadowed by a convenient sequence of footpaths, bridleways and minor roads, which gave a rare sense of legality to my progress.

Yet these hills were strangely deserted. The big combed fields and neat drystone walls were obsessively prim compared to the ragged pastures of the Pennines, while the absence of people and livestock added to the sense of sterile uniformity. Vast estates and efficient, mechanized agriculture had created a landscape as bleak and loveless as a Communist state prairie. Here was Sydney Smith's 'region of stone and sorrow'.

Beyond stone-walled Woodmancote, silent, trim and balanced on a hill crest above the Churn, a path dipped then climbed the great rib used by the Romans for the course of their highway from

Cirencester to Gloucester. Ermin Way, now the A417, was being widened with diggers and earth-movers.

Daglingworth lay in the valley floor below Ermin Way. Like Woodmancote, it had become a pretty dormitory: the police station had been re-badged as 'The Old Police Station', gabled, mullioned, with lichen-coloured drainpipes and a frothing front garden. Around the corner, clustered about a grit layby at the road junction called 'The Square', were the village services: a green plastic dust-bin, a lame wooden bench, a Sir Giles Gilbert Scott phone box, the bus stop, the red letter-box and the signpost to neighbouring vil-lages: the Duntisbournes and Sapperton. On the facing wall was the village noticeboard advertising the previous day's concert in Cirencester Parish Church by the Gloucestershire Police Male Voice Choir. Also posted were the dates of whist drives in the village hall, the bus times (two buses a week to Cirencester, two buses a week to Gloucester) and the visiting dates (alternate Thursdays) for the Five Valleys Mobile Library.

I sat on the bench for an hour, just in case anything happened. It didn't.

Daglingworth's Church of the Holy Rood slumbered at the back of the village. The graveyard was mown, the bench varnished, the gravel clean, the mortar sound. The stones of this church went back 2,000 years, their arrangement haphazard, as if a fossil bed had been thrown skyward and left hanging.

Of the many ages in these walls, it is the Saxon which is most remarkable, for Holy Rood dates from the beginnings of England, after St Augustine's landfall and before the Norman invasion, when towns had begun to make a comeback and when the first churches were being constructed from timber and stone. In Holy Rood can be heard the stonemason's blade, rebating the long and short quoins to form mock pilasters, and chipping the delicate channels in the sundial that sits above the door. The same Saxons took the Roman altar and cut it through with two little lancet windows which lit the east end of the chancel until it was moved to the top of the vestry wall. Saxons also carved the faces which stare from the nave and the north aisle: St Peter holding a key the length of a sword; Christ on the cross, flanked by Longinus and

Stephaton bearing spear and scourge, reed and sponge; Christ enthroned, with a deferentially tilted head and cross. In the crudeness of the expressions there is an enigmatic simplicity. These are the faces of compassion and of power, of frailty and strength, of youth and great age.

Before I left, I turned to the translation of the inscription found on the Roman stone on the vestry wall. The stone had been part of a pre-Christian altar, commissioned by a certain Junia and dedicated by her 'to the Mother and Genius of this place'.

Cirencester Park From Daglingworth, I followed a stony track bound for a distant line of woods bordered by a high wall.

Back in London, it had been impractical to seek permission from every landowner across whose land I planned to trespass, so I limited the requests to military sites, on the grounds that getting myself shot or blown up would have been inconvenient for the family. Although several large estates blocked the meridian, egalitarian logic suggested that there was no reason why a duke or an earl deserved to be consulted prior to a trespass, any more than the owner of a hill-farm. The reality was rather different: I'd discovered that my middle-class logic-board was fitted with a feudal circuit-breaker that made it harder to infringe the rights of the aristocracy than those of the 'lower orders'. Sneaking across a Pennine field was easier than doing a number on an inherited estate.

On this sunny morning in the Cotswolds, the entire 2,000-metre band was blocked by Cirencester Park, the ancestral home of the Earl of Bathurst. There were no rights of way across the park and, arriving from the north, I had no access to the park's main entrance or to its principal buildings, so I couldn't ask permission either.

For two kilometres, the track towards the park ran arrow straight for the trees and the wall. Beyond a polo ground, I came to a gate in the wall. Inside, I turned off the track into trees and bore south-east for Pope's Seat, the only feature in the park that I knew anything about. The poet used to come here as a guest of Allen

Bathurst, the Member of Parliament who built Cirencester House and its 3,000-acre park, and who became the 1st Earl three years before he died, in 1775.

After the Romans, it was Bathurst who put Cirencester on the map. With Pope, his friends included Jonathan Swift and John Arbuthnot, the physician to Queen Anne who wrote *The Art of Political Lying* and who Dr Johnson thought was 'the most universal genius'. Thomas Gray, the scrivener's son who wrote *The Elegy* and who declined the laureateship, was a visitor to Cirencester Park, and so was the literary politician Edmund Burke, and Matthew Prior, secret agent and author of *The Hind and the Panther Transvers'd to the Story of the Country Mouse and the City Mouse*.

Pope's Seat turned out to be a small stone neo-classical bus shelter. As I approached from the side, a voice from within said, 'Eh, love. Got anuvver with pickle innit?'

It wasn't the Earl of Bathurst.

Stepping into view, I startled a family of four.

The Park, said the man with the pickle sandwich, was open to the public, and he confirmed that all exits were beyond my range. The slight guilt I'd felt bypassing the Duke of Devonshire's 'Access Points' in the Pennines, now returned as I realized that the kindly earl who'd thrown open his park to the public was about to have one of his walls scaled.

With the compass I took the most direct route south, along a ride, through a fence and along a field edge, from where I saw a horseman in the trees to the west. The risk of being ejected from the park by an 'official' entrance left me with no option but to evade capture, so I ran as fast as I could, but not, I noted, as fast as a galloping horse. A slight valley ran down the side of the field, providing useful dead ground. At the foot of the field rose a dry-stone version of the Berlin Wall; much taller than myself, and bulging with age. The wall could be climbed, but a collapse would bring down several tons of stone, which would be bad for my health and for my relationship with the earl.

Taking off the rucksack, I pushed it through the barbed wire at the edge of the field, and crawled into the woods. My thought was to find a tree with a branch that overhung the wall, then climb the tree, snake along the branch until I was clear of the wall, and drop down on the far side.

Dead undergrowth crackled. The only way of moving silently through woods is very, very slowly, but I didn't have the time. At any moment, I expected the cavalry. Hurrying to a promising bough, I passed a gap in the wall and had to blink: there, hanging open, was an ancient wicket gate. I stepped through into the bright light of the outside world and the verge of the A419.

Now I was sandwiched between the park to the north of the road, and the estate of Cirencester Agricultural College to the south.

The college estate had no rights of way that I could use, and was surrounded by another high wall, but the main north entrance was only two minutes away, so I decided to walk straight in and then probe the estate's southern boundary until I found an exit.

Unfortunately, as I turned into the gateway I passed beneath a large sign warning that CCTV cameras were in operation. Already on film, I had little option but to pretend that I had pulled off the main road to re-tie a bootlace, which I did, then turned about and withdrew to the wood west of the entrance.

Three minutes later a man in a peaked hat and tie appeared on the edge of the wood.

With the benefit of hindsight, I should have continued through the gateway and negotiated a passage with the security men. Alerted, they were more likely to be suspicious than cooperative. So I had little option but to cross the estate beyond the range of eyes and cameras using the cover of walls and a wood, falling on to the Fosse Way knowing what a Romano-British fugitive must have felt during the early days of Saxon colonization.

The Fosse Way, now the A429, was a contraflow of hurtling cars and flashing ambulances. I waited ten minutes for a gap, then darted out of the Cotswolds into the lowlands of the Thames.

Twenty minutes south of the Roman Road, I came to a pair of late eighteenth-century barns that had been converted into a guest-house.

The Thames The Ordnance Survey placed Smerrill Barns 1,800 metres from the source of the Thames and 300 metres off two degrees west.

'This is the Heart of England,' Valerie Benson told me over breakfast.

Remembering that Sandwell Council in the Black Country had made the same claim, it occurred to me that the heart of a long, thin country can be many places at once. Here, the claim was based on the rising of the country's best-known river. In terms of scale, the Thames is unimpressive: it is shorter than the Severn and its drainage basin is smaller than that of the Yorkshire Ouse. Globally, it is a dribble: 268 kilometres from the source to Greenwich Observatory, compared to 3,688 for Europe's longest river, the Volga, and 6,516 for the Amazon. But Caesar's Tamesis is the river that flows to the capital. With rivers, size doesn't count.

The only other guest at Smerrill Barns was a walker from Luton. Angus was thin, with cropped hair, spectacles and a rucksack. He had already walked along the Grand Union Canal from London's Little Venice to Birmingham. Now he was embarking on a nine-day hike from the source of the Thames to its mouth, by way of the Thames Path National Trail. The trail had opened the previous year and Angus wanted to see it before it became as trampled as the Pennine Way.

Angus worked for British Telecom in Swindon, where he was involved with a computer system that stored phone calls. The system had a four terabyte memory. 'Tera', I learned, is ten to the twelfth power, formerly designated as 'megamega', and, according to Angus, allowed the system to store ten billion calls. 'Which is not big enough,' he sighed.

Angus had trained for his walk down the Thames by carrying a rucksack full of phone books.

After breakfast, the lane I was following towards the Thames passed a cottage called Ewen Wharf.

Scrambling up a bank, I was able to peer over the dilapidated railway bridge of the abandoned Kemble to Cirencester line, into the overgrown bed of James Brindley's Thames & Severn Canal. It wasn't a canal Brindley cared to recall: thirty miles long, messily financed and as leaky as a sieve (the two-mile Sapperton Tunnel lost 3 million gallons a day through its porous limestone bed), it never performed as well as the spectacular Kennet & Avon, which linked the Bristol Channel to the Thames by a more southerly route. In the Kennet & Avon's peak year of 1838–9 it moved 341,878 tons, compared to the Thames & Severn's total for that year of 60,894 tons. In 1927 the Thames & Severn closed.

On the edge of Ewen, a cow grazed in the centre of the Thames, so unused to water that its bed had become a shallow trough of turf.

Robert Gibbings had found forget-me-nots here, and watercress and deep pools. The first of his woodcuts in *Sweet Thames Run Softly* shows a pair of moorhens sailing over the reflections of water rushes.

Gibbings had walked down the Thames from the old ash carved with the letters TH – Thames Head – that used to stand beside the Roman Well on Trewsbury Mead. It was the last summer before the outbreak of the '39 war and Gibbings – engraver, travel writer and owner of Golden Cockerel Press – thought 'it might be fun' to explore the river in whose valley he'd lived for the last fifteen years.

At Lechlade he climbed on board *The Willow*, the flat-bottomed boat he'd built in the woodwork department of Reading University, and fitted with sculls and a locker for his microscope. It would be wrong to over-romanticize the voyage of *The Willow*, for there were aspects to the pre-war Thames that would cause national outrage today. At Chiswick, Gibbings passed children bathing in water the colour of beer and coated with sediment 'thick enough to be the beginning of a new continent'. The Thames is cleaner now, but there is less of it.

In search of water I walked 'downstream' from the bridge at Ewen. There was none at the spring below the village, and still none by the time I reached the 99 grid line and met a group of women who had walked up the Thames from Kingston.

'Have you seen any water?'

They thought for a moment. 'Not much today. The other side of Somerford there was some.'

On the way back to the bridge I called across the dry ditch to a man trimming a lawn with edging shears, 'Have you ever seen water in here?'

'I used to see the Thames,' he called back. 'It goes up and down. We'll maybe see some water in it before next Christmas. Can't say when it will run again.'

That the fount of our nation had dried up at the end of a millennium that had climaxed with so much environmental abuse seemed appropriate, and sad.

Poole Keynes Anthony Ponting was working in a garden in Ewen, dressed in large trousers, open shirt and a flat cap. He'd spent eighteen years on a farm and another eight delivering coal.

'Difficult to get gardening jobs nowadays,' he said, wiping his brow. 'They just don't pay the money.'

I needed a shop, for lunch.

'No, no shop in Ewen.'

'Poole Keynes?'

'No, no shop in Poole Keynes.'

'Oaksey?'

'No.'

'Upper Minety?'

'Don't know. There used to be. But I don't use it no more.' He lifted his flat cap and rubbed his head. 'I've got to be going. I'll be missing the Tesco bus into Cirencester.' As he turned away, he called, 'It's a free bus you know. They're good like that.'

Eddy Wood was mowing his lawn. He'd lived in Poole Keynes all his life. So had his father.

'My gramp too!' he twinkled.

'Where is everyone?' I asked, pointing up the deserted village street.

In a country whose open spaces are in short supply and of restricted access,
England's inland waterways act as precious channels of tranquillity.
Above, Coldgate Water in Northumberland;
below, the Trent & Mersey Canal in Staffordshire.

Hot-metal stamper Paul Knowles at his press in Bloxwich on the northern edge of the Black Country. A stamper judges by eye the correct heat of the billets in the forge, then lifts the red-hot metal into the press with long-handled tongs.

Rover's New West Works in Longbridge. This was the first car factory in the UK to operate robotic body-shell welders.

Galton Valley, in the south of the Black Country. The glass for Crystal Palace was made in Chance's works, seen here in ruins on the left of Telford's New Main Line Canal and Robert Stephenson's railway. On the left skyline is an elevated section of the M5 motorway.

A typical bed. With the approach of autumn, I slept fully clothed and woke wet with dew.

Harvest Festival at Wylye, beneath Salisbury Plain.

St Michael's church at Lower Dowdeswell, in the Cotswolds.

'There's quite a lot of us around nowadays,' said Ivor Franklin (above).
Ivor's Roman armour had been made in India and his Rover car in Longbridge.
Below, Phillip Hulme on his 1954 David Brown tractor.
'We've got five more at home,'he said. 'The wife likes tractors.'

'Keep Out' signs occurred frequently on the meridian. The two men at this airfield perimeter fence are military police from RAF Lyneham.

Rush-hour on Chapperton Down. The Salisbury Plain Training Area has never been subject to intensive agriculture and its rare species include the fairy shrimp, *Cheirocephalus diaphanus*, whose eggs are carried between flooded ruts on the tracks of armoured vehicles.

A final hurdle on the Dorset cliffs, part of 632 kilometres of English coast
that are protected by the National Trust.

The terminus of England's Meridian.
Above, one of the burial mounds on Nine Barrow Down and, below, the man-made rock-pool on the edge of Dancing Ledge.

'Working. Most people here are commuters. That's the trouble now. Villages are all the same.'

I asked Eddy who had the key to the church.

'You'll want Bob,' he replied. 'But he's out. Saw him go a while ago.'

We were still talking when a lone figure wearing a panama and a sleeveless grey pullover came up the slope towards the village.

'You're in luck,' nodded Eddy.

Robert Hiscock had large farmer's hands. He'd retired now that his son was running Church Farm and had been a church warden since 1932.

'When I was young,' recalled Robert, 'there used to be eight or nine in a family. When anyone moved into the village, it was a big occasion. They'd arrive with their furniture on a pram and a bicycle. If there was more than could be carried, the farmer who was going to employ them would fetch it in his cart. Now the newcomers arrive with two cars and a lorry.'

St Michael's would not have set Pevsner's pulse racing. Put up at the end of the eighteenth century on the site of an earlier church, it had a plain nave and chancel but a regular congregation of fifteen. The previous year the Queen had presented the church with a blue hassock embroidered with the royal coat of arms.

'She's the patron,' nodded Robert, 'of forty-two church livings in the Duchy of Lancaster. St Michael's is one of them.'

The hassock had been mounted in a glass-fronted frame on the wall. As Robert locked the door I saw that the Ordnance Survey had left their signature on St Michael's. Carved into the stone of the porch was a benchmark, one of the thousands of small levelling marks that the OS used for establishing heights above sea level. The last one I'd noticed had been chipped into a drystone wall near the 300-metre contour above Swaledale.

We strolled next door. Robert's son was the fifth generation of Hiscocks to live at Church Farm.

The old manor was a solid house of local oolite, with stone mullions and lofty gables. In its flecked grey face were the shadows of an old arch, and lost windows. Robert said that its predecessor had been listed in the Domesday Book.

'There's a story handed down the generations that Cromwell burned it,' said Robert. 'He came here after the Siege of Cirencester, when Royalists lived here, although Mrs Huxley didn't agree with me.'

Elspeth Huxley had devoted a chapter of *Gallipot Eyes* – her elegy to village life – to Robert's family, pointing out that Church Farm could not have been burned by Parliamentarians because Edward Poole, its owner, was himself a parliamentarian. Indeed Edward and his father Sir Nevill had collected Wiltshire's assessment of £725 a week towards the costs of the Earl of Essex's forces.

'She was a very intelligent woman,' conceded Robert. 'There's no two ways about it.'

Oaksey   Half-way between Poole Keynes and Oaksey the field path crossed Flagham Brook, out of Gloucestershire into Wiltshire, the least-populated county on the meridian since North Yorkshire.

The humid air trembled with aeroplanes: a pair of Hercules in line astern for Lyneham, lone roaming light planes, an AWACS burdened by its mushroom goitre, two helicopter bugs, a burbling biplane. In this inverted world, the land was deserted.

This was the road that William Cobbett had ridden in September 1826. A farmer's son and soldier whose principles put him in prison, Cobbett spent four years riding to and fro through southern England gathering information on the plight of a rural population he believed was being preyed upon by landlords and gamekeepers, 'tax-eaters', excise men and above all by the 'Great Wen' London.

The summer of 1826 had been fine and the fields running up to Oaksey had been thick with goldfinches feeding on thistle seeds. As the notoriously prickly author rode up the slope, the air filled with clouds of dancing birds, hectic with song and colour: 'I had,' he thrilled, 'a flock of ten thousand flying before me.'

Cobbett was en route from Cricklade to Malmesbury, gathering evidence against local parsons, who were falsifying their census returns by claiming that their churches were smaller than they really were, in order to create the impression of a recent population increase, and thereby to hang on to their tithes. Cobbett had been turned against tithes and the clergy during his time in America ('*Tithes* do not mean *religion*. Religion means a *reverence for God*') and what he saw in nineteenth-century England was the Church stripping the land of its 10 per cent; a tax on all regardless of spiritual inclination.

As Cobbett rode up to All Saints church in Oaksey, his belligerence, already ameliorated by the goldfinches, was eased further by singing that carried across the churchyard. He left his horse with a boy and went inside to count the pews, reckoning that, with the benches, the gallery and the unused spaces, All Saints could hold 2,500, somewhat more than the 200 claimed by the parson. He left the village with the mellow observation that Oaksey's quaint mathematics were 'nothing rare'.

Oaksey's oaks were reckoned by the seventeenth-century antiquarian John Aubrey to be the best in the county, though the oak is not the source of the village's name. This ribbon of dwellings on a ridge between Flagham Brook and Swill Brook has been variously written as Ocksey, Oxey, Okssey, Woxy, Oxhay and Wockes. In the thirteenth century it was Wockeseye; in the Domesday Book it was Wochisie, a derivation perhaps of Wuxi, a sheepfold made from wattles, or of Wocc's Eye, the island of Wocc.

To Aubrey, the people of north Wiltshire were a strange species:

> . . . the Indigenae, or Aborigines, speake drawling, they are phlegmatique, skins pale and livid, slow and dull, heavy of spirit . . . They feed chiefly on milke meates, which cools their braines too much, and hurts their inventions. These circumstances make them melancholy, contemplative, and malicious . . . they are generally apt to be fanatiques; their persons are generally plump and feggy: gallipot eyes . . .

Gallipot Eyes had been written by Elspeth Huxley while she lived in Oaksey. In her Preface, the author of *The Flame Trees of Thika* apologized for offering another 'village book'. But *Gallipot Eyes*, *Cider with Rosie*, *Lark Rise to Candleford*, *Akenfield* and the rest of them are testimonials to a way of life which spent thousands of years evolving, and fifty disappearing. Writing in 1974, Elspeth had been just in time to interview the last of the generation who had worked on farms before the First World War and who had actually *been* at Oaksey Races and *seen* Oaksey's silver band. That was also the year the elms died.

The village I walked into that lunch-time was dead. The church, where Elspeth's funeral had taken place earlier in the year, was locked. The Wheatsheaf Inn was closed (open evenings only). The post office had become 'The Old Post Office Cottage'. Nothing stirred. The new roundabout and traffic-calming chicanes suggested morning and evening rush-hours in a village that had only two cars when Elspeth arrived in the late 1930s.

So I met no Reg, standing at his gate to comment on the weather, or old Tom with his labrador, or Sid, digging his garden. Percy the beekeeper had long gone, and so had Charlie, who reared thirteen children on 30 shillings a week and whose catchphrase was 'Hard work never harmed anyone.' Neither would I meet Walter Sparrow the molecatcher who used to make waistcoats from the pelts and whose family had shown up on Oaksey's parish registers since 1670. The old-timers took Oaksey's oral history with them.

Out of Oaksey, the empty road to Upper Minety stretched for ever. I was hot, hungry and thirsty. Beyond Swill Brook the tarmac crept past the site of a Roman brick and tile kiln. The map marked a 'PH' in Upper Minety.

The church of St Leonard lay up a track at the north end of the village. Battlements and pinnacles rose above crazily tilted grave-slabs. Pevsner had liked the head-corbels, Mee the candelabra, Hutton the screens. A sign inside the porch read 'Welcome', but the door was locked. There wasn't even a note advising visitors where to find the key.

A few minutes down the road, Upper Minety's pub, the Old Inn, was closed too. I hadn't passed an open pub since the Colesbourne Inn on the A435, two days earlier, and the last shop I'd seen had been in a petrol station on the far side of the Cotswolds, four days earlier. During those four days I'd walked through eight villages.

But there was a post office in Upper Minety, and it was open. John Taylor was standing behind the counter.

'It's a waste of time really,' he said. 'We just struggle on. I've been here thirty-three years.'

He talked about village life. 'The allegiance isn't there. The villagers go through the motions, but it isn't there.'

A leaflet on the counter advertised forthcoming local attractions. If I hung on for two months, I could have a night out in the village hall listening to Fat Willy's Blues Band, who were coming to Upper Minety 'all the way from Surrey'.

John sold me the ingredients of a picnic from his shelves of groceries and then he showed me through to his garden, and a bench in the sun.

'What'll happen to the post office when you retire?'

'It'll close. It doesn't make money. Nobody will take it on. I do it because we own it and we don't owe any money. I couldn't sleep at night if I did.'

Walking out of Upper Minety, I tried to remember how many times I'd heard requiems for the post office and for 'village life'. The villages will survive, of course, reinvented as dormitories, retirement zones and home-worker sanctuaries. They'll exist because human beings seek solace in numbers, but they won't be tied to the land or the seasons. Lives won't turn slowly on an annual cycle that takes its cue from liturgy and field, but spin in a diurnal blur of desk and recreation. Shared adversities have been traded for individual struggles.

'The elms have gone,' wrote Elspeth Huxley at the end of *Gallipot Eyes*, 'and the fritillaries, and deeper things: the coherence of a small community whose members faced together the pains and dangers of the world.'

Sundays Hill   The meridian crossed another watershed, leaving the Thames for the Avon. The rivers I walked with from here would run west and south, to the Atlantic and the English Channel. Up on the watershed was the largest pond in Wiltshire, a still black pool surrounded by the dense trees of Braydon Wood, once part of a royal forest that stretched all the way to the Marlborough Downs. A century after Henry VIII hunted here, the forest was being raided by locals for firewood and timber. 'There are many greate spoyles, wastes and distractions made and commyted in our Woodes within our Forest of Braden,' wrote a Commission of 1611.

James I cracked down on the offenders, who had also taken to pasturing their cattle in the cleared glades. But it was too late; pressure for agricultural land was irresistible. Fodder for the deer herds was dwindling and profit for the King from the forest was negligible. In 1630 the Court of Exchequer disafforested Braden and the land was leased to three city merchants who sold the timber, then enclosed and sub-let the cleared land. Bereft of their common land, the locals rioted, and were jailed.

Walking through the trees, I wondered whether I might meet the current owner, a Belgian millionaire, but the house by the pond was silent, and the gamekeeper's cottage deserted but for aggressive dogs.

As I left the estate I noticed that the public footpath fingerpost by the gate had been rendered unreadable by a vehicle which had left the road and crossed the verge to strike the sign a glancing blow, accidentally of course.

Zig-zag lanes led over Sundays Hill and from up here I could see for the first time the northern rampart of the Wessex uplands, a long grey ridge with a rough crest like a coral reef, set above the floodplain of the upper Avon.

East and west England met where the headwaters of the Thames and Avon almost joined. All traffic looking for the lowest through-route was squeezed into a four-kilometre bottleneck. The motorway had used it and so had two railways, a canal and a major tributary of the Avon, Brinkworth Brook.

The public footpath crossing the first railway line was throttled with thorn. I crawled beneath the briars to the embankment and lay watching the track. Every few minutes a 125 express train hurtled from east or west. The trains exploded out of the sky, shaking the earth and filling the air with backwash and a clattering shriek. The aftershock of each passing train burned the senses like the retinal black-out that lingers after a flash-gun is fired. I could understand how people step in front of cars, or trains, without seeing them.

On the far side, I slashed through nettles and more thorns, then climbed a wire fence. Where the public footpath met Brinkworth Brook, the footbridge shown on the map had disappeared. The brook meandered through a field, buried in a deep ditch.

Leaping from a static start at water level, umbrella outstretched in pole-vault mode, I landed face down in the nettles on the far side, then hauled myself up the bank, gripped the fence and was flung back into the ditch. It was an electric fence. Climbing up again, I pushed the rucksack under the fence, crawled after it with water draining from my boots, and looked up to see a herd of galloping cattle.

Towing the rucksack and reversing rapidly under the electric fence, I paused and considered my options. Since I was already hard up against 01, my only exit was along the top of the ditch, westwards. Two hedges and several fields later, I emerged on to a road, muddy, sweaty, cursing, stung and tingling from electro-cution.

By now I'd been over-exposed to public rights of way which were often closer to military obstacle courses than to country walks. If I was honest with myself (which is not always a good idea until a journey is finished), I wasn't always enjoying the English country-side. Most country people were welcoming and generous, but they lived in a rigidly controlled no-go zone, stripped of species and dulled by factory farming. This was not the safe haven I'd known as a boy. Walking the wilder parts of the continent, I'd seldom come across blocked paths or been accosted by landowners. Neither had I been conscious of 'trespassing'. The English countryside was closed unless otherwise stated. Rustic enlightenment was tough on the nerves. When I wasn't breaking the law, I was confined to a grudg-ingly conceded line across somebody else's land.

English public rights of way were a historical anachronism. Many of the footpaths existed for reasons which were no longer valid, traipsing across fields rather than following their borders, or wandering aimlessly rather than providing through-routes or loops linking the kinds of places a country-lover might want to visit. Many were difficult to follow – even with a map and compass.

'There's a case for redrawing the network,' one park ranger had told me earlier on the walk, 'but officially we're not allowed to say that's a good idea.'

The network needed to be rationalized and made genuinely open to the public. On wilder uncultivated land – such as the moors, downs and mountains – the public should be able to wander at will. After weeks of walking, nothing could persuade me that small numbers of rambling humans could possibly match the damage inflicted on the landscape by pesticides, road building, mining or car use. Against the burned squares of the grouse moors and the gouges of mechanized agriculture, the imprint of a few shoe-soles would be imperceptible.

Neither was the landowners' argument that visitors drop litter and leave gates open supported by my own observations. Although I'd been walking during the height of summer, I'd seen few other walkers (except for those clustered around Grassington) and no loose stock. Most of the rural rubbish I'd come across had been agricultural, from animal carcasses to rotting farm debris.

Dauntsey Lock   Three kilometres across the floodplain, the wall of the Marlborough Downs looked close enough to touch.

The road kinked through scruffy farms to the commuter village of Dauntsey, where I turned to meet the M4. This was the last motorway that crossed the meridian. Beyond it lay older roads. Magnanimously (and unlike the malignant M62), the M4 provided me with a bridge. Below, traffic streamed like atoms in a particle accelerator. Ten minutes later I passed over the London to West Country railway, and beside it, the course of the old Wilts & Berks Canal.

The Wilts & Berks was not in the big league of inland waterways. Even when it was open to traffic, it was just a local delivery canal, built for £450,000 under an act of 1795 to carry coal to the agricultural towns and villages of the Vale of White Horse.

One generation's desecration is another's dream. Less than a decade after Cobbett raged against the 'accursed' Thames & Severn Canal, a young schoolboy on the towpath of the Wilts & Berks was gazing wistfully at the coal-barges, with their 'cosy little cabins' and steerswomen in printed headkerchiefs. To Tom, the dreamer of *Tom Brown's Schooldays*, in search of escape, a narrowboat was 'the most desirable of residences'. Born to the Industrial Revolution, Tom's countrymen had 'gadabout propensities' and his country was a 'vagabond nation'.

The Wilts & Berks closed in 1914, but beside Dauntsey Lock stood a late twentieth-century navvy: a yellow mechanical digger that had been clearing the canal bed of debris. One day, the Wilts & Berks will run with water again, reconnecting the Kennet & Avon Canal with the Thames. As each section of England's old canal network is laboriously restored, the country gets closer to reclaiming a system of waterways that will reach all three shores. The towpaths and the canal network provide alternative routeways for the recreational traveller, opening channels of tranquillity through countryside that is increasingly off-limits. The new cycle routes of the Sustrans national cycle network achieve the same end, and so do the National Trails and themed local walking routes. In the Age of the Car, there is no place on the roads for anyone unprotected by side-impact bars and air-bags. These alternative networks will breathe life into country and town.

In late afternoon sun I climbed the long hill up the scarp of the Downs to the village of Bradenstoke, perched on the edge of the plateau with RAF Lyneham to its back and a giddy view over the Avon. To the west, tail-lights curved like tracer fire along the M4 into the red hole on the horizon. It was the autumn equinox.

Bradenstoke

'On the other side of the Avon river I sawe Bradenestoke priory
ruines on the toppe of an hille . . .' John Leland, 1542

'No finer situation was ever chosen for a priory . . .' Edward
Hutton, 1917

'Bradenstoke Priory has perished before our eyes . . . a tale of
vandalism which should make an Englishman blush for very
shame.' Arthur Mee, 1939

'Little is left . . . substantial buildings were purchased in the 1930s
by William Randolph Hearst and taken to St Donat's Castle.'
Nikolaus Pevsner, 1963

Had they survived, the ruins of Bradenstoke Priory would have
been among the most romantic in the country.

The priory was founded in 1142 by Walter d'Evreux, whose
great-granddaughter Ela, Countess of Salisbury, was to found
Lacock and Hinton. Augustinian canons lived up here for 600 years,
drawing an income from their proximity to the London to Bristol
road, and from tolls on the steep slog up from Dauntsey to Bradenstoke.

Bradenstoke fell with all the other religious houses, surren-
dering to Henry VIII on 18 January 1539. Three of the monks were
found guilty of incontinence, while William Snow, the prior (a
traitor and a heretic, fumed Hutton), was appointed dean of the
new Protestant Cathedral of Bristol on a salary of £60 a year. The
dust would hardly have settled by the time John Leland looked up
at the priory ruins from the banks of the Avon three years later.

Over the centuries the surviving buildings passed through a
succession of owners until bought by the 67-year-old American
newspaper millionaire William Randolph Hearst, who wanted the
stone to extend his Welsh castle. Demolition was interrupted when
local labourers uncovered a seven-foot skeleton near the main
entrance. A chill settled over the site as villagers recalled the tale of
the giant 'Black Monk', whose secret trysts with one of Jane

Seymour's aunts at the Clack Hill toll gate threatened to bring disrepute upon the priory. Fearing retribution from Henry VIII, the prior entombed the Black Monk in a wall, alive, standing up.

By the time the labourers had finished, all that remained of Bradenstoke Priory was the tower and a pair of fourteenth-century undercrofts.

Not all of the priory ended up as part of Hearst's castle at St Donat's. Around 1930, the 104-foot tithe barn was dismantled and boxed-up in 109 crates, then shipped from its perch above the Avon, to La Cuesta Encantada, the Enchanted Hill, overlooking the Pacific north of Los Angeles. For nearly a decade, Hearst's architect, Julia Morgan, had been building a castle fit for a newspaperman. Behind an all-American façade of Mediterranean Revival Poured Concrete were 165 rooms containing the fruits of Hearst's European raids: Cardinal Richelieu's bed, a monumental sixteenth-century fireplace from a Burgundy château, Flemish tapestries, Roman columns, walls of Italian choir stalls, a cinema lit by gilded caryatids, flagstones from Siena, a ceiling from Spain, 3,000-year-old Egyptian statues and a zoo with ostriches, giraffes and a baby elephant. Into this world of cartoon antiquity came Bradenstoke's medieval tithe barn.

Hearst never saw his barn standing. Possibly he thought it was too dirty (his germ phobia was such that he put lavatory paper on the floor to prevent bugs being transmitted from the soles of visitors' shoes to his castle). Whatever the reason, Bradenstoke's barn never got unpacked. At the beginning of the Second World War, it was offered for sale, still in its numbered crates, through one of Hearst's papers, the New York *Journal*. There were no takers.

Then, in June 1960, the Hearst Corporation found a buyer in Alex Madonna, the owner of the Madonna Inn (100 Madonna Road) in San Luis Obispo, an agricultural market town famous for opening the world's first motel.

The new owner of the barn was the local pioneer of Civic Pink Style. Alex Madonna had painted his Madonna Inn pink and installed it with matching notepaper and urinals like whales' mouths. Each of the 109 rooms had a different theme; he'd created a caveman room, made entirely of rock, a love-nest and a Swiss chalet. Sadly for Madonna, the city authorities refused to grant him permission to erect his new acquisition on the grounds that it was not earthquake proof. So Bradenstoke's tithe barn still lies in its crates. According to a letter written in 1990 by Alex Madonna to one of Bradenstoke's residents, some of the stone has been stolen.

The village once boasted a blacksmith, a fishing shop, two cobblers, a baker, a dentist, a builder, a clock mender, a pub and an inn. The doctor used to ride over from Wootton Bassett on his horse. Now Bradenstoke has one shop, which also serves as the post office.

There used to be two pubs, the Jolley Trooper on the main square, and the Cross Keys near the shop. Historically, there was always a degree of competition between the two pubs and each had its own loyal customers. When the owner of the Cross Keys bought the Jolley Trooper and closed it down, the Trooper's customers were outraged.

'This is a village split in half,' I was told. 'Half the village doesn't speak to the other half.'

Sheila and Arnie Robinson hadn't known about the feud when they bought the Cross Keys earlier in the year.

Arnie had been born in Armagh and had just come out of the RAF. He'd been a cook. He'd cooked by numbers: for hard-working recruits, 6,000 calories per man per day at a maximum cost of £1.10 per man per day.

'It was a good life,' he recalled handing me a pint of Archers. 'But now the RAF has been civilianized, it's taken the life out of the camps. There's no sense of community any more.'

The Cross Keys was one of the locals used by personnel from the 3,000-strong airbase behind the pub. Later in the evening, Arnie introduced me to Flight Lieutenant John Rowland.

'The jet pilots call us truckies,' smiled John. He'd been a pilot for forty years, twenty-six of them at the controls of a Fat Albert.

Fat Albert (the person) was a chubby camouflaged creation in a Bill Cosby TV cartoon called *Fat Albert and the Cosby Kids*. Fat Albert (the plane) was a four-engined Lockheed C-130 customized for RAF use with powerful Allison engines, and British avionics, then renamed Hercules. They came to Britain in 1967, the year the Beatles released *Sergeant Pepper*.

RAF Lyneham had the country's entire population of Fat Alberts: fifty-two of them in four squadrons. In thirty years of operations, RAF Fat Alberts had been to the extremes of the earth, pulling troops out of a desert oasis in Aden one year, and resupplying the British TransArctic Expedition the next. In the Falklands War, when Alberts were flying non-stop round trips to parachute supplies to the ground troops, Flt Lt Locke set a Hercules world endurance record of twenty-eight hours and three minutes. Fat Alberts were the first RAF aircraft into the Gulf and by the end of the operation they'd flown 12 million air miles. Fat Alberts dropped famine relief into the Himalayas and earthquake relief into Nicaragua; they took medicines to Kampuchea and seed to drought-stricken Mali. In Saigon they'd flown out embassy staff under mortar fire; in Sarajevo they delivered 28,300 metric tonnes of supplies and brought injured Bosnian children back to Lyneham.

Fat Albert is a contradiction, a humanitarian Trojan Horse capable of dropping eighty-eight heavily armed paratroops from 1,000 feet at night for a high-explosive surprise attack and of delivering 42,000 lbs of essential food to starving refugees the next morning. Fat Albert is night and day, evil and good, black and white. Fat Albert is everything contemporary civilians want of the military hardware they buy with their taxes: a benign combatant.

Later that evening the telephone in the bar rang and Arnie handed me the receiver. It was an officer from the airfield, arranging an RV for the morning. Although they didn't usually take in guests, Arnie and Sheila made up a bed for me in a room above the bar.

'You'd like breakfast before you cross the airfield,' grinned Arnie at closing time. 'An RAF breakfast.'

*

The meridian was embarking upon a martial chapter.

Since leaving Berwick, two degrees west had made frequent contact with England's military past. In many villages, the sole remaining community symbol was the war memorial, while wartime veterans were among the most engaging conversationalists I'd met. They were used to spinning yarns. My journey was just in time to catch the last survivors of the Second World War and I was conscious that the oral record of millions of unwritten episodes was disappearing fast. Most weeks *The Times* and the *Daily Telegraph* carried the obituary of another war hero.

The military have always liked Wiltshire. The county has the UK's largest training area, huge camps, airfields, discreet storage facilities and a retirement population who choose to spend their twilight years on the playground of their youth.

So for a while, the armed services took over the line. In part it was a voluntary digression, for I'd come to see that England's martial heritage was mine too.

'Every man,' observed Doctor Johnson, 'thinks meanly of himself for not having been a soldier or not having been to sea.'

In my case the list was a lot longer. I thought meanly of myself for not having been a pianist or a painter; climbed Mount Everest, been a teacher or a hydrologist; run a sub-three-hour marathon or stood for Parliament.

But Johnson, as always, had a point. Soldiering and the sea were rites of passage; initiations into manhood; the obligatory social hurdle that required every boy to accept risk, overcome fear and then to live with success and failure. Initiation rites seem as popular as ever, but now they are likely to be chemical.

Sergeant Ali Macdougall was wearing a pair of waterproof mountaineering gaiters. 'I've walked across airfields before.' Macdougall had with him a car with stripes and a corporal.

'We'll drive round to the crash gate,' said the sergeant, opening the car door. 'Hop in.'

'I can't do that. I have to walk everywhere.'

He told Corporal Webb to drive the car through the village to the crash gate. The sergeant and I walked through Bradenstoke, the military man in his uniform and gaiters, the civilian swinging an umbrella. Mist oozed between the houses. It was too early for anyone else to be up.

Macdougall was born in Aberfeldy in the Grampians and joined the forces at eighteen. He had a bristled scalp and moustache and wore big black boots and a zipped black jacket. A radio aerial poked from one shoulder. His worst posting had been to Greenham Common, defending the airfield from 'smellies'. He was forty-five and would be retiring from the airforce in sixteen months. 'Airfields are always in wet, windy places,' he grimaced. 'I'm going to the sun. Cyprus. Got friends there. People I can do business with.'

We reached a side road leading to a crash gate set in the airfield's perimeter fence. The gate had a low-resistant latch that would snap open when hit by a fire engine. Corporal Webb was waiting for us in the military car.

The two men opened the gate. On the far side, a sign read: THIS IS A PROHIBITED PLACE WITHIN THE MEANING OF THE OFFICIAL SECRETS ACT. UNAUTHORISED PERSONS ENTERING THE AREA MAY BE ARRESTED AND PROSECUTED.

'If I'd climbed over the fence last night, how far would I have got?'

'You wouldn't,' grinned Macdougall. He was one of four sergeants running airfield security. They had dogs.

Corporal Webb left, to drive the car around the airfield to a crash gate on the far side.

The mist could have been imported from the Grampians – heavy, wet and utterly impenetrable. Smeared on to the non-existent topography of the airfield, it had created a world with no edges. We were suspended in an opaque soup with not a landmark to be seen. Sergeant Macdougall pulled on a green reflective jerkin.

We began walking along a concrete taxiway, then crossed the end of a runway, on to grass. The grass was long and wet, and as the water seeped into my socks and trouser legs I saw why Macdougall had dressed in gaiters. Somewhere close by, turboprops chopped the mist.

We seemed to be veering slightly to the left and I began to worry that we would get drawn too far east and stray across 01. Sergeant Macdougall's stride slowed a little. We crossed more concrete. Macdougall stopped uncertainly. 'Do you have a compass?'

I fished the tiny black Silva Type 23 from my pocket and showed the sergeant. 'As fitted to the survival kits in Tornados.'

Unamused, Sergeant Macdougall continued, on a bearing of 180 degrees. The roaring grew louder. Lights began to glitter through the murk. We came to the main runway, and stopped.

Macdougall spoke into his radio. 'Cabin Zero Five. Are we clear to cross Active?'

The radio muttered intimately. 'Clear to cross. Report when clear.'

Remembering my 'Green Cross Code' from childhood, I looked right, then left, then right again. There were no aeroplanes coming.

At a brisk walk we set off across the main runway. It was remarkably wide, a road built for a colossus, with a white line down the centre. I paused for long enough to look each way along the enormous avenue of lights and in that instant I knew what a hedgehog would feel like stopping for a breather in the middle of a motorway.

At the far side, the sergeant spoke to the control tower again. 'Cabin Zero Five. We're clear of Active.'

Walking on, we quickly made visual contact with the south side of the airfield. There were hangars, fuel-storage areas, explosives dumps. A yellow four-wheel-drive jeep raced past.

'The BCU,' nodded Macdougall. 'Bird Control Unit.' The BCU, he explained, toured the base letting off flares and broadcasting amplified bird calls. Earlier in the walk, a Geordie had told me that security units at Newcastle's Metro Centre used the same tactic, broadcasting Delius's symphonic poem *Sea Drift* to drive away hooligans.

Off to the left, the aircraft squatted on the ground like fat grey ducks. We passed beneath the control tower, isolated inside its own stockade of barbed wire.

Corporal Webb was waiting at the crash gate with the car.

Sergeant Macdougall shook my hand and opened the gate. 'I enjoyed that,' he said, unconvincingly.

A public footpath followed the southern perimeter fence, and as I made my way along the narrow gap between the woods and the chain link, the mist dissolved to reveal a vast absolutely smooth plain, with a single grey aeroplane suspended, apparently weightless, above a runway.

The plane didn't land, but skimmed the airfield then banked into the blue. Beyond the chain-link thundered an Allison T56A-15 that had been bolted to a steel frame, the unsilenced pistons pummelling the rising mist, the propellers a manic windmill. Engineers watched from a cabin, heads squeezed by ear-protectors. I pulled off my wet boots and socks and sat on my sleeping-mat propped against a field gate while Lyneham went to work. Every few minutes a Hercules drifted over the trees, almost silent on landing, roaring fit to bust on takeoff. Olive-green helicopters came and went. The Allison by the fence did its best to tear its frame from the ground, and from Salisbury Plain, south down the meridian, came the distant crump of heavy artillery.

The wooded vale beyond my feet woke to another day of peacetime.

Lat 51°28′N   An hour's walk south of Lyneham's perimeter fence the meridian crossed the latitudinal parallel of the Greenwich Observatory, 139 kilometres to the east.

In an abstract way, it was a pleasurable little encounter, like seeing your own home from a train window.

The landscape artist Richard Long had once used the Greenwich Meridian for one of his 'walking works', setting out at sunrise westwards from 0 degrees along the shore of the English Channel, while a friend followed a simultaneous course along the shoreline of France. I'd been fascinated by Richard's walks for many years, and before embarking upon the meridian, I'd gone to visit him at his home on the edge of the Cotswolds. He'd just returned from making a twelve-day, 360-mile circular walk called 'A Circle of Middays'.

'The geometry of distance!' he urged, after describing another walk that had covered 1,000 miles in 1,000 hours.

Richard's boots stood in a row by the door: boots for mountains, boots for roads, boots for art galleries, boots for private views, boots from Italy, boots from Iceland.

Some of Richard's walks were short, like the small, precise path called 'Boot Circle' that he trod into the dust of New Mexico. Some were long, like the 1,000-kilometre hike he'd made across Spain in 1990.

Some were straight.

'Walking Without Travelling – The Sahara 1988' was a straight line trodden into the desert grit, leading towards a distant mountain. The line stopped and started nowhere, as if the boots that had formed the pale prints had materialized from the empty sky; a brush coming from nowhere and sweeping a single pure stroke across an empty canvas. 'Going nowhere,' he'd explained. 'It's another aspect of walking.'

Calne   From latitude 51°28'N, I took a footpath and then a lane over Fisher's Brook into the northern housing estates of Calne, 'the vile rotten borough' that Cobbett targeted for especially incandescent invective: 'I could not come through that villainous hole, Calne, without cursing Corruption at every step; and, when I was coming by an ill-looking, broken-winded place, called the town-hall, I suppose, I poured out a double dose of execration upon it.'

Calne has known better times. Once it had twenty weaving mills. Once it was a stopover on the main road from London to Bath. Once it was Britain's bacon capital. Now the mills have gone and traffic has switched from the A4 to the M4. Harris's Bacon factory, which took out a patent for curing pork in 1864, and which once employed 2,000, was closed in 1983. Now, the town's largest surviving business is a sheet-metal works employing only 150. I found the church chained and padlocked and the Lansdowne Strand Hotel (once the coaching inn) deserted. The new focus of Calne was a vast supermarket, rising from the site of the bulldozed bacon factory in the centre of town. Sainsbury's would open in time for the tidal surge of incomers headed for the 1,100 new homes planned for the fields on the northern edge of Calne. England, the nation of shopkeepers, has matured into an economy of supermarketeers.

Stockley Lane   Where the railway and motorway west from London had taken the easy ground through the Vale of White Horse and Avon valley, the Roman Road, the coach road and the A4 took the high, dry route over the Marlborough Downs.

The Roman Road crossed the meridian half an hour's walk south of Calne. West, it ran to Bath; east, it led past Silchester and Heathrow, along Oxford Street (past the front door of James Smith's umbrella emporium) to the steps of the forum.

Where it met the meridian in Wiltshire, the Roman Road had survived as a long straight hedgeline, as the parish boundary between Calne and Heddington, and as a public footpath.

This, perhaps, was the line that Richard Long had walked two years earlier when he created 'Walking Stones'. He'd been walking at right-angles to the meridian, across England from west to east. Each day he picked up a stone and carried it through to the next day, then swapped it for a new stone. Thus did the Atlantic shore lose a stone and the North Sea gain one. He'd covered the 615 kilometres in eleven days, an average of fifty-six kilometres a day. On 'Two Stones', a walk of Richard's that the meridian had crossed in the Pennines, he had averaged forty-nine kilometres a day. Richard was a prodigious pedestrian.

'You're a writer,' he'd told me in his home before I'd started walking, 'and I'm an artist. Your work is like a big representative painting; mine is abstract.'

Oliver's Castle As the setting sun picked out the folds on the downs I paused at a thatched inn in Heddington for a pint of Guinness, then took a short cut over a field recommended by the inn's only other customer, a local who'd been waiting with his newspaper for the door to unlock.

There was a new chill in the dusk and the wintry whine of a chainsaw sent a shiver up from the village.

A track curled around the foot of the downs until it met the old London to Bath coach road. Centuries of wheels and hooves had chewed the chalk track-bed into a greasy gully up the front of Beacon Hill, rising 100 metres in a kilometre, a sweat for horse or man, an epic struggle for a loaded coach on a dark, wet night. Impassable in snow. The highwaymen had easy pickings.

From the top, the old coach road unrolled over the swell of Roundway Hill. It was open country, cavalry country. Royalists under Henry Wilmot, Earl of Rochester, had cantered across here in 1643 to relieve Lord Hopton, cooped up by Sir William Waller's Parliamentarians in Devizes and so short of match for his guns that he'd ordered all the bed-cords in town to be requisitioned and resinated.

The indefatigable Waller – survivor of Venetian and German wars, husband of a Devonshire heiress and MP for Andover – met Wilmot where the track up from Devizes joins the coach road. On the hard open turf of Roundway Hill, Wilmot and his Royalist horses hit Waller like a battering ram, scattering the Parliamentarians west towards the ramparts of the Iron Age hill-fort, perched on the brink of the hill.

When I reached the fort, the first stars were pricking the sky. It stood on the western extremity of the Marlborough Downs, triangular in plan, set like a ship's prow above the lowlands of Avon. A few wind-torn trees clung to the site. Over this prow fled the Parliamentarians, followed by Wilmot's horses, who were chasing so hard that they too could not stop. Roundheads and Cavaliers tumbled in shrieking confusion down the sheer face of the hill, to die in the ditch at the bottom. Leaving my pack at the fort, I slithered down the grass and sat for a while on the bank of 'Bloody Ditch', listening to the wind pour like water through the black trees.

It was the Ice Age that sculpted the precipitous tip of the Marlborough Downs. On the way from Beacon Hill, I'd walked up and down the dry gullies that had been cut by meltwater into the slope of the Down. In the Alps these gullies are still stone-filled and loose; on the Marlborough Downs they have been softened by time into smooth waves reflecting off the great promontory behind them.

Microscopic lights twinkled in the darkened vale. With beer and cheese from Calne I lay at the western apex of the fort, on dampening grass that hid the memory of earlier passers-by.

Beaker and Bronze Age people left shards of pottery on this hill, and hearths, flint scrapers and arrowheads. Haematite-ware from the early Iron Age was uncovered below the rampart, where perhaps it had been flung one dusk 2,000 years ago, by a woman who'd stumbled and broken her cooking pot. Or maybe it was slung over the side as a piece of old rubbish by 'late-phase' Iron Age workmen building the rampart that still surrounds the $3\frac{1}{2}$-acre site.

William Cunnington, the ailing linen draper who took up archaeology after being told by his doctor to 'ride out or die', was one of the first to dig here, in 1907. He exhibited his finds in a moss-lined summer-house.

A red-winking light moved out of the south, level with the hilltop. As it reached the fort, it swung abruptly overhead, momentarily shutting out the stars, then touched down at the corner of the wood behind the fort. As I scrambled up the rampart, the helicopter lifted, twisted then spun into the night. An hour later as I lay in my sleeping-bag, sheltered from the wind by the Iron Age bank, the red-winking light came back, and the thudding rotor. I slept badly.

Roundway Hill Covert   Light returned like a reluctant promise, sidling into the day with little conviction and no warmth.

The wind was still wild and cold. I lay for a while, too chilled to be comfortable but not cold enough to want to leave the sleeping-bag. Getting up required only the lacing of boots, since I'd slept in all my clothes. The temperatures had plummeted since the night

I'd spent on Hadrian's Wall. Over the rampart, the vale below was filled with racing milky mist.

Curiosity pulled me back from the rampart towards the corner of the wood, Roundway Hill Covert, where the helicopter had landed in the night. Unsurprisingly, there was no sign of odd nocturnal happenings, but there was an enticing stile into the Covert.

Day had barely broken. The air in the wood was damp and stilled by the trees. Somebody had coppiced the hazel and elder. Young beeches had been planted and there was box too, put down by a long-gone gamekeeper to provide cover for his pheasants. A new path led through the trees. I moved quietly along the path, hoping to come upon deer, or a fox hunting an incautious breakfast, but instead met a tall, slender man in Wellington boots and a bow-tie.

Dr Colin Hallward and his wife Diana often visited Roundway Hill Covert before breakfast. Sometimes they walked up from Devizes; this morning they had travelled by car. The Covert, they explained, had been planted by Lord Roundway and was currently leased by the Merchant Venturers of Bristol to the Forestry Commission. The wood was protected by English Nature, who'd designated it a Site of Special Scientific Interest, to be enjoyed by the public on a path built by Devizes School and the Wiltshire Wildlife Conservation Corps, supported by the Wiltshire Trust for Nature Conservation. Life was so much simpler when a tree was a tree.

'You must come for breakfast,' said Dr Hallward after we'd checked the proximity of their house to the meridian. 'We'll see you in Devizes in an hour or so.'

Devizes Below the Covert, I picked up a footpath which led to a minor road marked on the map as Consciences Lane. Off my route, this connected intriguingly with another path called Quakers' Walk, sadly on the wrong side of 01.

Gazing at the sixty-four square-kilometres that filled the eight-kilometre gap between Calne and Devizes, I was struck by the poetry of the place names that happened to fall in this random block of Wiltshire: Rough Leaze Farm, Ox House, Clayhole Cottage, Withybed Wood, Consciences Bridge, Cuff's Corner, Clinghill Wood, King's Play Hill, Green Lanes, Provender Mill, Mother Anthony's Well, Blacklands Crossroads, The Splatts. They were old names, each of them conjuring up an image from an age when man and land were intertwined. In the same rectangle, the modern additions to the landscape read with the baldness of a spare-parts catalogue: Reservoir. Rifle Range. Sewage Works. County Police Cemy. Dismtd Rwy. Wireless Station. Golf Course. Picnic Site. Sports Ground.

Consciences Lane led me to Iron Peartree Farm and a public footpath through the fields to Devizes, high on the watershed between two Avons: one flowing south through Salisbury to Christchurch and the English Channel; the other, grander Avon pouring west through Bath and Bristol to mix with the Atlantic. The land bridge at Devizes links the Marlborough Downs with Salisbury Plain, connecting the ridgeways that run from the Thames at Goring Gap with the henges of the Wessex downs. The town takes its name from the Latin *ad divisas*, 'on the boundaries'.

Red House was a solid red-brick Georgian home set back from the traffic with a gentle lawn running down to the calm surface of the Kennet & Avon Canal. Through the kitchen window, I saw that Dr Hallward and Diana were already at breakfast.

'No no, don't worry about those,' ordered the doctor as I tried to pull off my boots (I'd already washed the mud off in a stream). 'Come and eat. *Eat!* It must be *months* since you've had a breakfast.'

Colin's swept silver hair gave the impression of a man used to creating his own slipstream. His father had been an accomplished RAF flier who'd competed in the Schneider Cup.

'Built in 1767,' he said of Red House over a bowl of fresh raspberries. 'Alec Clifton Taylor came here once and *insisted* that we replace the ground-floor windows with original Georgian frames. Cost was *enormous*. Had to wait until we'd finished educating the children. But we did it, eventually.'

Pevsner had awarded Red House a seven-word entry. The Hallwards loved their house. They had built another house in Cornwall, where their neighbour had been John Betjeman.

'We were very careful with materials; we used local slate. Betjeman was insistent about the windows. Have some toast.

'When he came to lunch with us in Devizes we were rather looking forward to hearing his views on Red House. But he was far more interested in the Victorian convent that you can see across the canal from the bottom of the garden. Betjeman loved Victorian architecture.'

Colin was company physician to Wadworth the brewers. 'You are going to visit the brewery, aren't you?' he said, heading for the telephone before I could answer.

Henry Alfred Wadworth – 'Harry' to those who loved him – was the first man to ride a bicycle from London to Bath, a feat accomplished in two and a half days balanced upon an imported French machine with iron tyres.

Harry was also into hot-air ballooning. On August Bank Holiday 1875, the year he bought his brewery, he rose to 6,000 feet above Wilton Park and flew south-south-west for three hours until the prospect of ditching in the English Channel forced him down outside Poole.

'I know little about the business,' wrote the 22-year-old to his mother, shortly after establishing Wadworth & Company. A photograph of Harry shows a man with an elongated head, muttonchop whiskers and bulging cheeks. He hunted twice a week and began work every day at 5.30 a.m.

Harry was a brilliant brewer. Other brewers in Devizes such as Blencoes, Humby's and Tylee's were bought up or went bust and, by the mid 1880s, Wadworth & Company had run out of space. For Harry it was the moment to make his mark: he designed and oversaw the construction of the red-brick brewery that still looms over Devizes.

Through an introduction by Dr Hallward, I was taken on a tour of Harry's shrine by the head brewer, Trevor Holmes. Behind the neat rows of white-painted Victorian windows was a series of caverns filled with pipes and steaming vats. From the ground floor, where the beer was injected into bottles and barrels, flights of steps led up to huge coppers where the hops were added and the wort boiled. In the adjacent tun room stood a row of stainless-steel tanks the size of mini-submarines. On the next floor up were gigantic fermentation vessels frothing with brown shampoo, and a cold storage tank for the chilled beer. More steps climbed to a floor bearing the mash tun, where the starch in the grist was converted into sugar, to produce the wort. The mash tun and the nearby collecting vessel (into which the yeast was added) were fed from the floor above, which had the grist case, full of milled malt and the wort receiver which pumped unfermented beer through a heat exchanger. From up here, fifty feet above Devizes, a final ladder led up to a hatch, and a small platform surrounded by a railing.

Beyond the roofs I could see Roundway Hill and my bivouac site on the edge of Oliver's Castle. To east and west of the brewery the Kennet & Avon Canal was marked by a slender line of trees. Below lay the Market Square, seething with slow-motion pin-figures and toy cars. Where the meridian cut the southern horizon rose the abrupt scarp of Salisbury Plain.

The all-round aerial view and the small basket-shaped railing made me feel as if I was in a hot-air balloon, which was presumably Harry's intention.

Down below, in a workshop cluttered with barrels and tools, 34-year-old master cooper Alastair Simms was pulling an adze along a stave.

He was a big man, built like a boxer, with a broken nose and forearms as thick as thighs, one stamped with a large blue tattoo. Over his '6X' T-shirt he wore a leather apron that reached to the wood-shavings scattered on the cooperage floor. 'You need it: if a hoop breaks, it can slice your leg.'

Alastair was born in Masham, below the eastern shoulder of Great Whernside. There were only twelve brewers' coopers left in the country, seven of them Yorkshiremen.

'My dad wanted me to go into bricklaying,' he said, shaking his head. Instead Alastair signed on for a four-year apprenticeship with Clive Hollis at Theakston. 'Clive was patient and understanding. He never lost his rag with you. If you did something wrong, he'd talk you through it rather than shouting and bawling. He told stories, and the stories helped the learning.'

From apprentice to journeyman, Alastair had become a Master Cooper in 1990. His tools were treasured and many had been inherited from other coopers. 'The tools mould to the cooper's hands,' he said hefting an antique adze. 'They are very individual.' Each tool had a block mark identifying its owner. The block marks, he explained, were introduced in 1213, before coopers could write. Some of the tools on his wall had three or four block marks. 'That makes them at least 200 years old,' he nodded, showing me his own block mark, made up from the letters ADS.

The diversity of tools used by a cooper seemed far in excess of the number required to make a wooden barrel. Over 150 were listed in the current catalogue of Burton Wood Turnery and their names had the onomatopoeic resonance of the Middle Ages: jiggers, scrapers and buzzes, crozes, bick irons, timber scribers, stoup planes, shive plugs, dip rods, tenter hooks, chime beaters, coopers' devils, flagging irons, bung floggers and boring bits.

The barrels themselves also came from another age, sized according to ancient, pre-decimal tradition, from the 32-gallon ale barrel and 36-gallon beer barrel to the 16-gallon ale kilderkin, 18-gallon beer kilderkin, 8-gallon ale firkin and 9-gallon beer firkin. A firkin is half the size of a kilderkin, which is half the size of a barrel. Mostly, Alastair made firkins.

'Polish oak is superb,' he said, handing me a stave as smooth as ivory. 'It works like butter. No knots. German oak is knotty and American oak has too many tannins.'

In the days of piece work, coopers worked in pairs, making 120 firkins in ten days. Flat out on his own, Alastair could make seven casks a week.

Shaping the staves was exceptionally laborious, each one being individually cut down and tapered in two planes with a coopers' axe. Then they were steamed for forty minutes and set over a charcoal fire.

'The finishing of each cask is done for pride,' concluded Alastair. 'There are a different number of staves in each cask; it's not repetitive.' The staves were fitted to the cask ends and the chine hoops hammered into place. Each cask was finally stamped with his block mark.

'What do you think Clive Hollis would say if he saw you now?'

'I think he'd be pleased.'

Head brewer Trevor Holmes pulled me a pint. 'IPA is my favourite,' he sipped. 'Golden, well balanced with a long aftertaste. It's been called biscuity. Very popular as a session beer.'

'A session beer?'

'You can drink it all night without getting legless.'

Trevor had an MSc in Brewing Science from Birmingham University and had been brewing for thirty-one years. In his button-down collar and tie, white lab coat, silver hair, clipped moustache and silver-rimmed spectacles, he gleamed like a new scientific instrument. He'd learned his craft with Wilsons in Manchester.

'What's the difference between a northern beer and a southern beer?' I wondered.

'The local beers down here are a lot sweeter than northern beers. Ours have less head. Yorkshiremen like head; Wiltshiremen like full glasses.'

Trevor led the way through the building to the sacks of hops. 'Fuggles is what we use most,' he said, sifting a mound of hop leaves. Dried and broken, they looked like sackfuls of locusts. 'Dr Richard Fuggles bred it in Kent in 1875. Now it comes from the West Midlands, Herefordshire and Worcestershire. The hops are the herbs and spices that make the taste. You tell the taste by rubbing the dry hops between your hands, then smelling your hands. We mix different hops to create blends.'

One brew used $6\frac{1}{2}$ tons of malt, 24 pounds of hops and 1 pound of liquid yeast.

'Sevens,' continued Trevor. 'Brewing beer works in multiples of seven. A complete brew takes seven hours to make 300 barrels; the beer takes seven days to ferment and then another seven days for maturation, warehousing and delivery. Then the beer has to be used within twenty-eight days of it being put in the barrel.

'We only make traditional English ale, and 90 per cent of it is real ale; cask ale, a sediment beer. Cask ale is a unique English style; the final fermentation occurs in the cask. It takes two days after the cask is delivered to the pub for it to clarify, and it comes into its best ten days after it's been put in the barrel. It's a unique non-pasteurized living product. Like champagne.'

In the lexicon of English real ales – which includes alarming labels like Wreckless Eric's Recked-em, Hogsback Ripsnorter and Titanic Wreckage – the Wadworth beer names are mild-mannered and allude to rustic good health: Farmers Glory (named after a book written by the Wiltshire writer and broadcaster A. G. Street), Old Timer and Easter Ale. Only Summersault (a pale 4.5 per cent beer made from Saaz hops from Bohemia) with its implication of involuntary gymnastics carries any suggestion of side-effects.

As had been the case with the brass-stampers I'd met in Blox-wich, Wadworth's strength was the inherited experience of an age-old process. They still used one of the original coppers installed by Henry Wadworth in 1885 and they still had their own stables, four horses and two drays (using harnesses from the workshop I'd called at on Walsall's Pleck Road). Their market was on the doorstep: Wadworth's 230 pubs were all within a 100-kilometre radius of Devizes. On the way down to the street, I asked, 'Is there still money in beer?'

'We pay 31p a pint excise duty, and pass that cost on to the publican who passes it on to the customer. A publican selling a pint at £1.70 is making less than half that amount after he's paid VAT. The retail margins don't exist to support pubs, and excise duty is the cause. The customer pays seven times as much as the French and six times as much as the Germans. In Europe, only the Danes charge more. Business is not brilliant. We're working hard to keep up. People are drinking wine, and there's cheap beer coming in from the Continent.'

'What d'you think will happen to pubs?'

'There's going to be fewer of them, but they'll be better. There's got to be a big shake-up in the way pubs operate. If pubs are going to survive they have to be made a destination venue; a place to eat and drink, with family facilities. The drink and drive legislation puts people off; they don't risk driving to a pub. People are spending more on other things – TV, video films, going to sports centres. They don't spend the evenings in pubs any more.'

Market day in Devizes was like market day in Berwick, Skipton and Cheadle. On display were the same racks and trays of acrylics and Yangtze plastics I'd seen further north, although the ornamental reclining pigs seemed peculiar to Wiltshire. England doesn't have France's painterly mountains of seasonal vegetables, wicker pens of rabbits or baskets of quail eggs, and there's no demand for the hardware of rural self-sufficiency – horse tack, goat bells, cheese-making cauldrons, shotgun cartridges – that can still be seen on market stalls from the Carpathians to Portugal's Tràs-os-Montes. Like Berwick, Devizes had an adjacent flea-market that provided a few gems, among them Charles Hadfield's *British Canals*, *The Right Way to Keep Hamsters* and *Pub Games of England*. When Celia Fiennes rode by at the tail-end of the seventeenth century, she found a 'very neate little town' with a market thriving on the clothing trade.

The market square is the largest in the west of England, with a fountain and a market cross carrying a salutary tale about a local woman who swore she'd drop dead if she was found to have cheated over a sack of wheat (she had, and she did). A century before Ruth Pierce expired in public, Lieutenant General Cromwell fired his heavy artillery from the square at Devizes Castle, and a century before that the market crowd watched a tailor called John Bent from Erchfont burned to death for denying transubstantiation. Spectacles (discounting the second-hand ones in the flea-market) are nowadays absent from Devizes market.

Inevitably, I ended up in the Bear, the black-and-white coaching inn that dominates the market square. Ale has been served in the Bear Hotel since at least 1599, when John Sawter was granted a licence, but it was another two centuries before it achieved a notoriety beyond its regulars, and the custom of King George III and Queen Charlotte, various archdukes, duchesses and princes.

In Sawter's time, the 107-mile journey from London to Bath

could take six days over roads which were often less than six feet wide and flooded to eight inches in mud, with a sting in the tail where the old road climbed over the exposed downland west of Marlborough.

In the 1660s the service was revolutionized by the introduction of 'The Flying Machine', a coach carrying only six passengers, which increased the daily mileage from twenty to thirty-five and reduced the journey to three days ('if God permit', qualified the advertising poster). The Flying Machine left the Bell Savage on Ludgate Hill at 5 a.m., three mornings a week, and terminated its journey at the White Lion in Bath. The fare was one pound five shillings; fourteen pounds of luggage could be carried free and excess baggage was charged at three halfpence per pound of weight.

The condition of the roads was still appalling. In 1668 the Bath Flying Machine stuck fast and needed four borrowed cart-horses to haul it from the mire. Then there was Claude Duval, the miller's son from Normandy, whose habit it was to delay with a blunderbuss the Bath coach as it crossed Hounslow Heath. A highwayman of style, Duval was eventually arrested in the Hole in the Wall on London's Chandos Street, executed at Tyburn in 1670 and then carried in state to the Tangiers Cavern in St Giles, where he was laid out in a black-clothed room surrounded by eight wax tapers and a flock of tall gentlemen in black cloaks. The heavy rain that fell that night was said to echo the tears of many young women.

Highwaymen preying upon the new élite bound for fashionable Bath led to the abandonment of the lonely crossing of the Marlborough Downs in favour of a southerly detour through Devizes. The Bear was suddenly on the national map, with up to thirty coaches pulling up outside the inn each day.

The landlord at this time was Thomas Lawrence. Writing in 1780, a Miss Burney described finding one of Lawrence's beautiful daughters playing the overture to Piccini's opera *La Buona Figliuola*. 'But though these pretty girls struck us much,' she noted in her diary, 'the wonder of the family was yet to be produced. This was their brother, a most lovely boy of ten years of age, who seems to be not merely the wonder of their family, but of the times, for his astonishing skill at drawing.'

At five, young Thomas could stand on the dining-room table and recite the verse of Milton and Collins. Travellers diverted to the Bear in Devizes to see the boy, who would dash off pencil sketches for amazed guests. The actor David Garrick became a regular. By the age of twelve, Thomas had his own studio in Bath and at twenty he painted the portrait of Queen Charlotte which now hangs in the National Gallery. Thomas Lawrence the innkeeper's son was knighted in 1815, became president of the Royal Academy and was buried in St Paul's.

Lunch in the Bear was a sociable affair. The basement buffet was packed with elderly market-goers queuing for steak and kidney pie ('+ 2 veg + potatoes') for £2.95. To fit more customers into the room, tables had been pushed together, and I found myself opposite an elderly, slightly deaf gentleman who opened a conversation by shouting, 'It's not raining!'

'It isn't,' I yelled back.

'Always rains on a Thursday, market day,' bawled my companion. 'Not raining today!'

In the best tradition of English conversation, we talked rain for ten minutes and then I asked if he'd like me to fetch him a Bakewell tart (+ custard).

'No thanks!' he shouted. 'I'm dyslectic. No, not dyslectic. *Diabetic.*'

He was collected shortly by his wife.

On my left, Ronald Brinkworth began to chat. Ronald had been in the Ordnance Corps in the war, working as a 'checker' at HQ 28 ASD, an ammunition supply depot in the Forest of Dean. 'My job was checking in the ammunition,' he recalled over the hubbub. 'We used to build elephant shelters for it.'

Once, he had been detailed to dig holes and bury several tons of mustard gas in galvanized five-gallon containers. 'We didn't have any bleach, which you're meant to bury with mustard gas to make it safe. We were told to bury it anyway.'

'Where is it now?'

'S'far as I know it's still there, in the Forest of Dean.'

Ronald's grandfather and uncle had spent their lives on Salisbury Plain, one as a shepherd, the other as a dew-pond maker.

Over coffee (free) my neighbour on the other side described his medical history. He'd been queuing for a cataract operation since the previous December, and been told that the waiting list ran till next June.

'Then my doctor said that I couldn't drive until I'd had the op. And my hip needs doing too. I feel helpless. Someone has to take me everywhere.'

Each week he played the Lottery. 'If I win I can go private and pay for my operations.'

A360 For the eight kilometres to the foot of the Plain, the A360 clung to the meridian. Impatient cars and no pavement turned it into the most unpleasant road I'd walked in the six weeks since leaving the Northumberland coast.

Deer once leapt in the valley to the right of the road. On the Ordnance Survey map, the stubby hachures of ancient embankments were labelled in Gothic script 'Park Pale'. Within the embankments were 'Lower Park Farm' and 'Old Park Farm'. In word alone this was the relic of one of the great Norman deer parks that dotted the country between the twelfth and seventeenth centuries, providing venison, buckskin and sport at a time when feeding cattle and sheep all winter was impractical through lack of fodder. Wiltshire may have had as many as 100 deer parks, covering 2 per cent of the county.

Eight hundred years ago this valley would have been a garden of mixed woodland and 'laundes', the grassy glades that in later centuries were manicured into 'lawns'. Around the park ran the fence of split palings, the 'Park Pale', and just inside this was a ditch, whose spoil was piled on the outside of the palings; wild deer could spring from the top of the embankment, over the palings into the park, but the depth of the ditch and height of the palings prevented a return journey. The ditch was known as a 'lypiatt', or leap-gate (the word survives as a place name, as Nether Lypiatt in Gloucestershire).

When John Leland passed through Devizes in about 1545, on what was to be his last journey, he noted this as a 'fine park'. Today, the Park Pale encloses the town sewage farm, a disused railway line, workers' terraces and a rectangular grid of arable fields.

Thirty minutes down the A360, I took a break from the traffic in the village of Potterne, a once lovely spot on the prow of a hill.

Inside St Mary's church, the stepped east window was divided by slim pillars of Purbeck marble that had been quarried from the end of the meridian, only a week or so to the south; and below the west window was an unintentional epitaph to the wildlife that once leapt through the surrounding woods: an Anglo-Saxon font shaped like a vast stone bucket, with the words of Psalm 42 around its rim: 'Just as the hart desires the running brooks, so longs my soul for Thee, O God.'

West Lavington   Where the A360 collided with the wall of Salisbury Plain I found the house whose address I'd been given. The village of West Lavington would be my jumping-off point next morning for a critical rendezvous with the army.

Dominique Bull lived at the end of a dirt road in a Queen Anne house beside one of the streams that trickled from the spring line along the northern slope of the Plain. She was a neighbour of Guy, who knew Hector, who knew me. I couldn't stay with Guy, because he lived a few metres outside 01, so he'd telephoned Dominique and asked whether she could provide a roof for a man walking from the North Sea to the English Channel by way of the longitudinal line of two degrees west.

Dominique was from Belgium. 'You would not be able to make this journey in my country, you know.'

'Why is that?'

'A Belgian would not understand the necessity to walk in a straight line. In England this kind of thing is quite normal. But in Belgium it would be very strange.'

For Guy, whom I met in the pub later that evening, my hike was a fairly routine exercise.

Guy was tall and dark, with the gentle manner of a specialized soldier. Guy had met Hector on their SAS selection course in a wet wood near Hereford.

Hector, who was on his first outing with the SAS, had showed up with no knife, torch or cord. Guy, who'd been before, helped Hector 'get sorted' and build a 'basha'. They had been friends ever since. Hector was going to join me for a day on the meridian, but he'd fallen out of a tree and broken his ankle while teaching a godson how to climb.

Their world was one I could never share. Guy and Hector had operated during the height of the Cold War and had a highly developed sense of understatement and evasiveness which, to a harvester of stories like myself, was deeply frustrating.

'Great days out,' smiled Guy over a pint, when I asked about SAS selection. 'The scenery was lovely. *Big* views.'

Unlike a few of their colleagues, Guy and Hector had no need to share their histories. In an age when talking about the deed was often bigger than the deed itself, these two saw *not* talking as the bigger deal.

Guy's soldiering had come to an end one night over the Surrey Hills when, strapped to 100 pounds of equipment, he was dispatched from a Fat Albert at 500 feet and hit the ground harder than intended. Landing some distance away, Hector had heard his friend's bones snapping.

Salisbury Plain   It was a classic Wessex morning: dew drops glinted around the rims of chalk-flecked fields, a wood pigeon swooped in a dappled copse and the air flexed to the thunder of heavy artillery.

Everything about that late September Saturday felt good: it was sunny and I was about to visit a unique tract of English countryside. The 1:25 000 maps promised 90 per cent of the day out of sight of roads and I had a rucksack stocked with food and water.

The sound of the guns swelled as I climbed a gently angled

ramp of short grass up the side of White Hill, marked on my map with the warning DANGER AREA.

The rendezvous with my army escort was for 1000 hours at Highland Cottages, an isolated cluster of buildings on the road over White Hill. In Devizes, I'd taken the precaution of buying a military haircut. (Years earlier I'd been sent by a magazine to learn free-fall parachuting with the Parachute Regiment and the theme of the non-stop abuse from the training corporal had been the length of my hair.)

At 0930, killing time in a field, I was spotted by a military Land Rover. From the passenger seat jumped a camouflaged officer wearing captain's pips on his chest. 'Ah! Mr Crane!' He pumped my hand. 'Thought I'd pop up here and see if you'd arrived early. We've got a bit of a battle going on behind that hill. I've got to check a few things and I'll be back at the RV by 1000 hours.'

Captain Edmund McMahon Turner of the 32nd Regiment, Royal Artillery, executed a brisk U-turn and disappeared.

Highland Cottages had been turned into a military redoubt, with bricked-up windows and a barn converted into a tank-hide. While waiting for the captain to return, I opened the maps. The meridian cut across Salisbury Plain just west of centre, running over West Lavington Down, Chapperton Down and Berril Down. The straight-line distance over the firing ranges, from Highland Cottages to the outskirts of the village of Chitterne, was only six grid squares, six kilometres. Given the heavy firing to the south, I wondered how much trouble I would have persuading my military escort to stay on the line.

On the dot of ten o'clock, the firing subsided and three vehicles pulled up outside the cottages. McMahon Turner, flushed from his battle, said that he was going to walk with me. So was the training area marshal, Warrant Officer John Roessler of the Royal Tank Regiment, and his black labrador Megan. Roessler would make sure that we did not step on anything explosive. With him was the conservationist for the ranges, Paul Toynton, bearded, in a baggy blue jumper and an embroidered Moroccan skull cap, and Ian Barnes, Archaeology Officer, Defence Estates Organisation (Lands) (South West).

To my military escort were added the occupants of the third car, Chris Brasher, inventor of my Brasher Boots (and of the *trilbava*), and the mountain photographer John Cleare. Chris was going to join me for a night up on the Plain; John had spotted an opportunity to photograph a rarely accessible part of England's countryside.

With Megan the labrador leading the way, the two army officers, Olympic runner, mountaineer-cameraman, conservationist, archaeologist and myself set off past a sign saying MILITARY FIRING RANGE KEEP OUT towards the still-smoking battle-field. After so long on my own, I now found myself overwhelmed by conversationalists.

'Forty per cent of unimproved chalk grassland in Britain is here on Salisbury Plain,' enthused the army's conservationist. 'It's the largest area of chalk grassland in north-west Europe: 40,000 hectares ... 20,000 hectares of it is an SSSI – a Site of Special Scientific Interest ... It's an incredibly diverse habitat ... plants, insects, birds. The centre of the Plain has not been grazed since the forties ... In the last fifty years about 80 per cent of Britain's chalk grassland has been lost to agriculture ... compare this to the Marlborough Downs, which are as flat as a pancake now ... it's the deep ploughing and fertilizers which do the damage ... you look at a square metre of Salisbury Plain and you'll find thirty-five or forty different species.'

The stream of biogeographical titbits was interrupted by Ian, the archaeologist, walking on my other shoulder. 'The SPTA ...'

'SPTA?'

'Salisbury Plain Training Area. It has 2,300 archaeological sites ... from Neolithic barrows through to medieval strip lynchets ... 551 of them are scheduled monuments ... the amazing diversity of the sites is because the landscape was fossilized when the military took over at the end of the nineteenth century ... huge areas were saved from the destructive effects of ploughing ... it's an island of archaeological remains.'

'Ah!' interrupted Paul as we neared the top of the Down. 'We're crossing from improved grassland to unimproved. Look!' He bent and pointed to the tussocks of thin, hairy-leaved grass through which we were now wading. 'Upright brome. *Bromopsis erecta*. Very common on the more intact parts of the Plain. You get this where there's been no ploughing or re-seeding or use of fertilizers. This grass shelters lots of herbs and the herbs support insects . . . This is *such* a rare place . . . quite mind-boggling . . . Every day that I come to work I think that I've got the best job in the world.'

My notebook filled with pages of scrawl as I strived to keep pace with the fusillades of data illustrating the Plain's unique state of preservation.

The army had invested well in Toynton and Barnes. The Salisbury Plain they described was a unique natural park, not the shell-pocked mudscape of my imagination. After ten minutes in their company I was persuaded that all of Britain's uncultivated country-side and national monuments should be handed over to the Ministry of Defence for safe-keeping. There was no litter, no vandalism (excepting the explosive kind), no unsightly car parks or street lights, and a diversity of flora and fauna that made many National Parks look impoverished.

Speculation was interrupted by the conservation officer calling us to a pair of deep puddles.

'Brilliant examples of how tanks help to propagate a fragile species. Look!'

We crouched over two water-filled ruts cut by tanks. In the murk hung a tiny translucent crustacean. '*Cheirocephalus diaphanus*,' called Paul. 'The Fairy Shrimp! Its eggs can survive for six or seven years in the mud. They get picked up on tank tracks and carried across the Plain, then dropped in another puddle. We've got Britain's biggest population.'

Indeed, it appeared that the shrimp *needed* tanks in order to survive, for *Cheirocephalus diaphanus* could not live in permanent ponds. It depended upon its armoured fifty-ton host to carry it to its next temporary pool.

We walked on, past a deserted breeze-block house, with frameless windows and bullet-chipped masonry.

'You'll have to make it clear in your book,' intervened Warrant Officer Roessler, 'that this area is closed to the public. We don't want people walking into firefights.'

'In the postglacial period,' added the archaeologist, 'Mesolithic men were up here hunting. We've found their flint tools on the Plain.'

Roessler dropped into a trench and pulled back a curtain in the end wall to reveal the habitat of another of the Plain's limicolous inhabitants.

'A command post. Normally we bulldoze them after an exercise, but this one is used regularly.'

Inside, it was surprisingly comfortable, with wriggly-tin walls, a strengthened roof and a dry floor. Crouching in the dark, I pondered ruefully that this was just the kind of five-star bivouac that one never finds on a rainy night.

Walking on over the Plain, I realized that I was not going to find craters and burned-out vehicles. The most serious environmental damage we passed was a fifty-metre band of mud ploughed by tanks, a sight which triggered a virtuous dissertation from Toynton upon the measures already in hand to guide the tanks between new belts of trees. He called it 'traffic management'.

We stopped for lunch on top of a grass bump raised like a cartoon bruise from the smooth skull of Chapperton Down.

'Kill Barrow. It's an Early Neolithic long barrow,' said Ian, '4000 to 3000 BC.'

To deter tanks, the barrow had been encircled by a palisade of concrete 'dragons' teeth' pillars, one of which had been sheared in half. The archaeologist nodded approvingly at the concrete stump. 'It knocked the sprocket off a Warrior.'

The barrow had never been excavated. Beneath us lay the bodies of England's first farmers, men and women who had come to the Plain because the chalk was the lightest soil they could find. As the new concept of working the land moved northward through Europe, the Plain would have been one of the first areas of England to have fallen to arable agriculture.

Later, Bronze Age farmers had worked the same fields, leaving one of their round barrows on the other side of Chapperton Down. The Iron Age settlers who'd built the monumental forts along the edge of the Plain above the Wylye valley had grown their grain on Chapperton too. The previous month an archaeological team at Battlesbury had unearthed a coral bead that had made its way from the Mediterranean to Salisbury Plain well before the Romans made the same journey.

In the gentle rhythm of the Plain's silver waves there was no hint of distant shores. The opaque sky and steppe met at a barely divisible horizon. Only in the south-east was there any sign of life, where silent flashes and drifting smoke marked a clash of unseen forces.

Roessler pointed out the far-off freckles of what appeared to be a village. 'For training,' he explained. 'FIBUA – Fighting In A Built-Up Area. It's a complete central European village.'

Almost invisible beneath the waving grass, another, much older village ran over the down beside us. 'It's Romano-British,' said Ian. 'Farmers who used to grow grain for the Romans. The south of Britain was one of the Empire's main areas of grain production.'

There was a theory, continued the archaeologist, that the village on Chapperton Down was a 'workers' settlement' for a Roman villa in a valley below the Plain.

The village was over a kilometre long. Down the centre ran a 'hollow way', still a metre or so deep. The farmers who'd scraped out the bed of the way to keep it passable had piled the spoil in a heap that now formed the highest point on Chapperton Down, marked on the Ordnance Survey map with a 152-metre spot height. During the Second World War, the hollow way was used by tanks for cover during exercises.

'It's protected now,' said Ian, pointing to a sign that also forbade soldiers to dig trenches in the area.

When the Romano-British villages on the Plain were abandoned, sheep moved in and stayed for 1,500 years. On the waterless chalk, the shepherds had to be as hardy as their sheep. To provide puddles of surface water, dew-ponds were dug to gather mist, rain and runoff from the grass. Construction of the ponds was a curious science. Once the pit was dug and its surface beaten to make it watertight, a variety of linings were added. Some of the last to be dug on the Plain used a layer of soot and chalk to keep out the worms, then a final coating of straw and clay to give the lining of the pond a cool surface, though the reason for this is a mystery, since condensation of night moisture would have been insufficient to contribute to the pond's depth. Sometimes the ponds were called cloud-ponds or mist-ponds; the word 'dew-pond' did not appear till 1877, and may have been derived from the reputation of Mr Dew, the pond maker to George III.

One of the last shepherds to have worked on the Plain must have been the grandfather of Ronald Brinkworth, the old soldier I'd shared lunch with in Devizes. Ronald remembered childhood visits to his grandfather at Tilshead. With two dogs, he used to look after 1,000 sheep. Ronald's great-uncle had been on the plain too, working as a dew-pond maker, and his mother had been born up here, at Imber ('You know what they said about Imber,' Ronald had chuckled. 'Imber Imber on the Down; seven miles from any town'). Imber's residents had been evacuated in 1943 and the village still stands empty in the midst of the military training area.

After the war, the advent of piped water rendered the dew-ponds redundant and the sheep ceased to suffer from liver fluke contracted by drinking the habitat of water-snails.

'Tea, anyone?'

On top of the burial chamber, Chris Brasher was crouched over a tiny titanium cooker that he had imported from Sweden. As an ardent advocate of the Eric Shipton travel-light/travel-far principle, Chris was passionate about saving weight, comfortably.

The last drink I'd shared with Chris had been a mug of Macallan's single malt whisky on top of a mountain in the Transylvanian Alps, so it didn't seem strange that we should now share a mug of Lapsang Souchong, harvested in the tea-fields of China's Fujian province and brought across two continents to a Neolithic barrow in the middle of a firing range. Chris had remembered a fresh lemon to slice into the tea.

The military expedition that had embarked so energetically on a traverse of Salisbury Plain three hours earlier had mellowed into a sleepy picnic: John Cleare, who'd done his National Service as an officer in the Royal Artillery, was reminiscing with Warrant Officer Roessler; Captain McMahon Turner was on the phone to someone; Megan the dog stood sentry.

Peace was split by a frenzied engine roar as a large armoured vehicle burst from a line of conifers.

'I'll 'ave 'im!' yelped Roessler, leaping to his feet. 'He's speeding.'

The warrant officer set off at a gallop. Like the student dissident who stood in front of a tank in Tiananmen Square, Roessler lifted his hand in the path of the tracked monster, which skidded to an abrupt halt.

The exchange which followed was out of earshot, but when Roessler returned, he was grinning. 'He won't be doing that again: a Warrant Officer One Range Marshal was the last thing he expected to meet.'

It was late afternoon now, and a Friday, and we found ourselves caught in rush-hour traffic heading back to barracks.

A gang of armoured personnel carriers charged past tailed by bouncing Land Rovers. Flat-bed trucks and armoured cars wallowed by, many of them speeding. Roessler dashed hither and thither.

The dust eventually settled, leaving a solitary APC lurching along, intermittently coughing. Like a crippled beetle, it stopped, then staggered a short way, slewed slightly, and stopped again, its engine dead. A dust-caked helmet emerged from the turret. 'It's had it,' said the head, looking down at us.

Conversationally, I asked which unit he was from.

'Gunner Dickinson, 47th Regiment, Royal Artillery, sir.'

'Are you having trouble?'

He looked slightly dazed, as if he'd been over-indulging in a particularly destabilizing fairground ride.

'Been playing-up all afternoon, sir,' replied Gunner Dickinson, under the impression that the man with the trilby and umbrella was a high-ranking officer in mufti.

'What have you been doing?'

'Guarding a bridge against air attack, sir.'

'What happened?'

'We held them off, sir. But right at the end, we got hit, sir.'

'What sort of planes were they?'

'Tornadoes, sir.'

('Damn fine show!' I wanted to say.)

'How are you going to get home?'

'Dunno, sir.'

'Good luck.'

'Thank you, sir.'

Gunner Dickinson was last seen standing on the turret of his APC, staring wearily across the interminable Plain.

Chitterne We came off the ranges into the village of Chitterne, where my military escort climbed into waiting Land Rovers and left.

A ribbon of cottages, each connected to the road by a bridge over a desultory stream led past a phone box on the green, a shop, and battlemented All Saints with its chequered walls of stone and flint.

In All Saints there was a reference to an earlier point on the meridian. A memorial relief on the wall depicted two men-of-war shrouded with cannon smoke. They were the ships *Centurion* and *Nuestra Señora de Covadonga* and the remembered moment was George Anson's capture of the fabulous Spanish treasure ship off Cape Espirito Santo in 1743. Two weeks earlier I'd passed the Ansons' family seat in Shugborough Park; now I found myself at the resting place of one of Anson's captains, Matthew Michell of Chitterne. Michell had gone to sea at eight years old and was thirty when he joined Anson's epic circumnavigation. Off south America, with four of the fleet of six sunk, Michell's ship *Gloucester* eventually rotted beneath his feet and was scuppered in the Pacific. Nearly four years after sailing from Spithead, Michell had been one of the few survivors to return on the treasure-laden *Centurion*. Chitterne must have glowed for years with reflected glory.

Chris Brasher and John Cleare chatted over pints on a bench outside the King's Head.

They belonged to a generation of Englishmen who had inherited the will to succeed from the servicemen of the Second World War. They were the civilians who'd gone on winning medals. Chris had helped to pace Roger Bannister to the first four-minute mile and then won a gold medal for the steeplechase in the 1956 Olympics. John had led the first British ski ascent and descent of Muztagh Ata, and put up pioneering rock climbs on Purbeck's cliffs – coincidentally where the meridian fell into the sea. As a journalist, Chris won the 'Sportswriter of the Year' title twice. John had filmed Clint Eastwood hanging off rocks in the movie *Eiger Sanction*. Chris became sports editor of the *Observer*, set up the London Marathon and founded a trust that helps to protect wild country. John was a vice-president of the Alpine Club and had created the UK's leading library of mountain photographs. Both were in their sixties. Chris was about to run in a ten-mile race. John had just returned from a camel trek in Australia's Great Victoria Desert.

Theirs was an era of great British firsts: Hunt's Everest, Chichester's circumnavigation, Moorhouse's Saharan crossing. I'd grown up with stories (at home we had no television) that epitomized my version of Englishness: soloists were self-reliant (no helicopter rescue or satellite navigation), leaders were decisive and selfless, teams were loyal. Discomfort and danger were part of the package; giving up was not.

While I was researching the meridian I found in one of my boxes of newspaper cuttings some yellowing pages which I must have torn from the *Radio Times* in 1971. The article described the ill-fated international Everest expedition that had attempted the south-west face. The BBC had sent a film crew. One of the three cameramen was a youthful John Cleare.

'Those ten days in Camp 2,' John had told Peter Gillman in *Radio Times*, 'were the worst, the most miserable ten days I have ever spent in my life. We ran out of food. We ran out of drink. We had one book to read.'

The book was *Three Men in a Boat*, the classic warning to those who attempt goals in groups bigger than one. John went down with pneumonia and glandular fever, coughing till he cracked a rib. The '71 expedition ended in recrimination and disaster when Major Harsh Bahuguna died caught on the rope less than half an hour above the tents.

'Morale just had to suffer with your mate hanging up there,' John told Gillman.

I told John of the cutting I'd found, and asked whether he'd ever thought of giving up mountaineering.

'Good Lord no,' he said, shaking his head. 'Sitting in a wet tent with your friend dead outside is one of those things you have to go through. Like being in a trench in the First World War.'

East Codford Down　A shroud was pulled over the shadows and sunlit stubble. Dusk settled, damp and still. An owl slid silently along a fringe of black trees. At the top of the slope, where our field path crossed another, the street lights of Chitterne faded. Night fell.

In the dark, Chris and I settled into the corner of a copse. I cleared the knee-high grass of sticks and flints and laid out my short, thin sleeping mat. Jupiter winked into life. There would be no rain. It was a good night for sleeping beneath the stars.

Chris had brought a lightweight one-man tent, but in his haste to leave home, he had picked up the wrong bag and was laying out the components of a complex Scandinavian invention which required a trigonometry degree to assemble. The first erection produced an object like a dustbin sack stuffed with broken sticks. The second time we got it up, the door was in the side. 'Deliberate,' said Chris, unconvincingly. 'It's a new design.'

That night I was an itinerant on parole: as well as his high-tech stove, Chris had brought sachets of freeze-dried food and a flask of Macallan's.

Our bivouac lay near the centre of the largest 'tranquillity area' that the meridian had sliced through since the Pennines. The south of England had not scored well on the tranquil area maps drawn by the Council for the Protection of Rural England. Their criteria for measuring disturbance, from road noise to light pollution, left an area centred on Salisbury Plain relatively clear. It was nothing like the size of Northumberland's tranquil area that I'd walked through at the top of the meridian, but it was a lot better than nothing. That it existed at all was due to a happy conjunction of the Salisbury Plain Training Area with two Areas of Outstanding

Natural Beauty: the North Wessex AONB to the north, and the Cranborne Chase and West Wiltshire Downs AONB to the south. Around us was the tightening urban noose of London, Reading, Swindon, Bristol, Bath, Bournemouth and Southampton.

Yet, even up here, Chris and I had to wait until 10 p.m. for absolute peace. On both sides of us, farmers were ploughing by headlight, raking the sky as they turned chalk once trodden by Mesolithic explorers. When they eventually switched off, the silence of the Plain was crushing. A shooting star streaked and the diaphanous limb of the Milky Way pointed to lost heavens.

For breakfast Chris produced a foil sachet labelled '*Petit déjeuner énergétique*'. In the bag was a mixture of coffee, muesli and milk – all the ingredients for a classic breakfast – mixed for convenience outside the stomach. Chris had bought it in Chamonix in pursuance of his quest to shave a few more grams off his rucksack weight.

'All you do,' he said, flicking open a Swiss Army knife, 'is cut it open and add boiling water.'

Inside the sachet, a sinister brown sludge bubbled like bacterial mud from a tropical swamp. Chris reeled backwards. 'Blimey!'

Wylye Valley   We came down from Salisbury Plain through a pig farm to Fisherton de la Mere, a forgotten hamlet on the shadowed side of the Wylye valley with a church cared for by the Redundant Churches Fund.

The stones of St Nicholas dated back to the Norman colonists, who added the 'de la Mere' to the old manor of Fisherman's Town. The church was rebuilt in 1833, with walls decorated with chequerboard flint like those of Chitterne.

Inside, the Churches Conservation Trust had left a pile of green leaflets printed with a selection of Saints' prayers and a fragment from T. S. Eliot's *Four Quartets* that put words to my own pilgrimage:

> We shall not cease from exploration
> And the end of all our exploring
> Will be to arrive where we started
> And know the place for the first time.
> Through the unknown, remembered gate
> When the last of earth left to discover
> Is that which was the beginning;

These lines were one of those titbits thrown to lone travellers whose isolated preoccupations include a quest for universal truths, the sparks of knowledge that come from who-knows-where and which spell a sudden understanding. With Eliot's seasonal poem came the reassurance that there was no such thing as a solitary pilgrimage, but a migration of kind; that a line was a circle and must end where it began; that the point of a journey may not be to arrive but to pass through that 'unknown remembered gate'.

From Fisherton de la Mere we followed a path along the bank of the Wylye, the river that gave its name to Wiltshire ('a horrible county', the intemperate Cobbett had spat).

William Cobbett had liked the Wylye but didn't rate it as highly as the Avon, whose deep incised meanders charmed him more than these softer upstream slopes. But the Wylye wasn't bad. 'Here are watered meadows nearest to the river on both sides,' he noted appreciatively, 'then the gardens, the houses, and the corn-fields. After the corn-fields come the downs.'

The stream slid without a ripple beneath tresses of arching willows. Trout hung in the clear water and the warm morning shuddered with motor traffic, the howls of cars punctuated by crashes as heavy trucks hit the expansion joints on the concrete bridge carrying the A303, the way to the West Country. We used to do the 303 as kids, three abreast on the hot leatherette seat of the Morris Oxford, past Stonehenge and Wincanton, then hours in sizzling jams waiting to get through Honiton while Mum strung out the I-Spy in a vain attempt to fend off back-seat fisticuffs. Since then, the A303 had thickened and shifted out of the village.

Our riverside path met the old road. Between these winding verges Cobbett had ridden in 1862, on a humid afternoon that had been 'Hotter, I think, for a short time, than I ever felt it in England before.' Under brooding thunder and plagued by flies, his humour had been worsened by the sorry state of Wylye, 'a gay place when I was a boy'. He found the village 'in a state of perfect carelessness and neglect' and blamed the rector. 'They seem,' he fumed, 'to be a sort of creatures that have an *inheritance in the public carcass*, like maggots that some people have in their skins.'

Wylye's church was rebuilt twenty years after Cobbett came by and stands at the focal point of the village, between the shop and the pub. Flint-chequered cottages faced the church across a deserted street, an intruder alarm peeking coyly from beneath the thatch. In the shadow of a great yew that was planted in 1636, crowded gravestones and tombs cut from the bedrock of nearby Tisbury and Chilmark. A lone figure wearing a Royal Artillery tie limped purposefully past the churchyard wall towards the Bell Inn. It was opening time.

Major Burroughes remembered a boy who walked to school in Wylye each day from Imber, a round trip of fifteen miles across the Plain. 'He must have been about six or seven,' recalled the major. 'His name was Hubert Colburn, although his brother used a different surname, Colbourne.'

The major had walked to school too, from his home off Piccadilly, where the Hilton now stands, to Mr Gibbs' Prep School at the bottom of Sloane Street.

The major and his legs have an extraordinary relationship. At Eton they carried him to victory on the running track. In London they conveyed him around the triangular perimeter of Hamilton Gardens playing hide and seek with the Royal Family. 'One afternoon I was inveigled into being "he" while the two Princesses Elizabeth and Margaret, and their notorious nanny, and their Mum and Dad, the Duke and Duchess, all hid. I counted to one hundred and ran off round the edge of the gardens. The first people I found were the Duke and Duchess, hiding behind a clump of holly trees.

"Home" was a park bench fifteen yards away, under a mulberry. One of them shouted "Look out! Here he is!" and they started running.

'Now, I was faced with an awkward problem: who should I chase? The Duke or the Duchess? I decided that the least offensive option was to chase the Duke, so I ran after him fast, but slowly, because I thought it tactful not to catch him.

'Later, the Duke pointed to the members of the public climbing on the garden railings trying to see what was happening and he said to me in that awful stammer: "Young mmmmman . . . we're like mmmmmmonkeys in a cccccage. Ddddd'you know where there's a hose, bbbbbecause I'd like to ttttturn it on them."'

On 29 September 1939 the major sailed across the Channel on *Royal Daffodil* with some six-inch howitzers left over from the previous war. On 29 May 1940 he was back on *Royal Daffodil*, going in the other direction, without the howitzers.

Dunkirk was chaos. He had arrived with his men at the besieged port on the night of the 28th and had commandeered a motorbike in order to search for the officer who would direct his unit to their point of embarkation. 'Couldn't find anyone,' said the major, putting down his pink gin, 'and when I got back to my chaps, they'd vanished.'

Their truck however was still loaded with rations, so he filled his bag and made his way towards the sea.

'There were great queues on the beach. Ships coming and going, machine guns and the rest of it. I met an infantryman friend and we sat down and waited. While we were chatting I was scooping the sand with my hands, as you do when you're on the beach, and I uncovered part of a dark cylinder. "Oh my God!" I thought. "I'm sitting on a shell!" I carefully scraped away the rest of the sand and saw that I was sitting on an unopened bottle of champagne. So the two of us sat on the beach having a picnic of issue biscuits, bully beef and champagne.'

When *Royal Daffodil* eventually returned home with the major, he was put on a train to Gloucestershire, where Queen Mary, who was living nearby at Badminton, visited the Dunkirk survivors.

'There were forty officers and 600 or 700 men from many differ-

ent regiments, all drawn up in ranks on a field. But just as the
Queen's Daimler drew up, a Harvard Trainer flew over, making the
same awful screaming sound that the German dive-bombers had
made in France, and the entire parade fell flat on its face in the field.'

After a spell as an instructor at Larkhill on Salisbury Plain, the
major helped to train the 3rd Division for D-Day. As gunnery liaison
officer with the Canadians attacking Juno Beach, his job was to
control the field-guns firing from the landing craft as they
approached shore. 'It was the last fire support the infantry had
before they hit the beach. We had to land the shots 800 yards ahead
of them. We obtained a fairly good level of precision.'

Some way off shore the major's landing craft hit a sandbank,
and they had to wait until the tide rose sufficiently for the craft to
float free and continue. When the ramp came down the major took
off his boots, socks and gaiters, rolled up his battledress trousers
and pulled on a pair of plimsolls, then climbed on to his Jeep. He
reached France with one wet foot.

The major's war ended in the debris of an observation post,
twelve kilometres inland from Juno. It was the first of two incidents,
fifty years apart, that left him at the top of a flight of stone steps,
with legs that did not work.

'I was in my tank, a Sherman, when I got a call over the radio
that German 88s were holding up the attack. We were at a place
called la Bijude, north of Caen. There was a rise ahead of us, and
each time a tank reached the top of the rise there was a bang and it
was knocked out. The only way I could see where the shells were
coming from was to climb into the upstairs of a big stone granary,
but the Germans had already been there and they knew that it was
the perfect observation post. I set up the radio and started "ranging". The shots began to fall each side of the 88s. The Germans
knew that it was an observed shoot. And they knew we could only
be in the church tower or in the top of the granary.

'I'd just finished ranging and was about to give the "Fire for
Effect" order when one or two of the 88s hit the granary. A great
chunk of stone came down and put a dent in my tin hat. The radio
was smashed and so I had no communication. I decided to crawl
out, across this wonderfully polished floor; you know how grain

polishes the timbers of a barn floor. Then I had to crawl down the stone steps. I got half-way down and got stuck. I couldn't reach the next step. My leg was all mucked up and I just couldn't push myself down. One of my chaps came up and whipped out a field dressing and turned me the right way up. I've still got a chunk of German steel below my knee.'

Fifty years later, the major was bell-ringing in the church tower in Broad Chalke in the Ebble valley when the bell-stay broke and the bell flipped right over, dragging him up into the tower. 'As I looked up, I saw that the diameter of the hole in the ceiling through which the bell-rope passed was considerably smaller than the diameter of my body, and I realized that my best course of action was to let go of the rope.' The impact broke both his heels.

For the second time in his life, the major had to negotiate a flight of steps without the use of his legs. 'Fortunately,' he laughed, 'the other two bell-ringers were a fireman and a retired naval commander who had escaped from Colditz.'

'He is marvellous. I absolutely adore him!' We were standing in the garden of Wylands Cottage and Sue Burroughes was speaking of her husband, the major.

Both cottage and garden might have been constructed for a Thomas Hardy film set. There was not a right-angle, or straight line in sight. Blossoms and frothing foliage billowed around a sloping lawn which rose from the cottage's crooked stone and timber walls.

'It was our first cottage. We had no money,' laughed the major's wife, leading me past neatly tilled ranks of vegetables. 'Army pay wasn't up to much. It was 1953 and an aunt gave us £100. A lot of money, then. We had to choose between going to the Coronation, and buying a fridge.'

'You went to the Coronation.'

'We bought the fridge!'

Unable to join the Coronation, the major put on his top hat and tails and ceremonially planted a copper beech in the back garden. Today, forty-four years later, that sapling was a full-grown tree, blazing pyrotechnically.

There was no television in the cottage and no central heating. Neither were there any valuables, for all had been stolen during the spate of burglaries that had cleaned out Wylye a couple of years back. The walls were lined with paintings of the cottage and family portraits. Mike and Sue Burroughes had eight great-grandchildren. Buried behind the plaster in the hall wall was an emptied Scotch bottle refilled with the family archive.

The Burroughes family had become a part of the cottage, as it had of them.

Nadder Valley   Chris and I walked out of Wylye along Teapot Street, then turned up Wylye Cow Down Bottom, a broad bowl of cropped grass ulcerated with molehills and protected from the plough (according to a signboard) by English Nature.

Up on the chalk ridge that formed the high-level route from Salisbury to the West Country, we passed through a gap in Grim's Ditch, the Iron Age boundary of a sixteen-square-mile enclosure built to retain the stock of one of Wessex's more powerful tribes. The ditch was throttled with vegetation and the banks that had been raised each side of it had long been ploughed to oblivion. A few steps beyond the ditch we crossed the line of the Roman Road that once carried lead pigs from the Mendips to Sorbiodunum, Old Sarum, Salisbury.

Ahead rolled the emotive mouldings of Hardy Country and off to the right (thankfully out of bounds, for few footsteps are as demoralizing to follow as Jude's) the 'down and turnip-land' where Jude and Sue sought shelter in a shepherd's cottage during their spontaneous hike over the chalk from Wardour to the Wylye.

Their shepherd ('Don't 'ee mind I . . .'bide here as long as ye will') was one of the high-level loners, along with the cowherds, gamekeepers and others, who provided the seasonal human link between the upland and the valleys and who were always there for the succour and curiosity of passers-by. To Sue, these exotic uplanders were 'outside all laws except gravitation and germination'.

In a wood by Teffont Magna, Chris broke free of the meridian and walked out to Tisbury for a train back to London.

Beyond the wood, I lay on the grass of a public bridleway, snacking from my rucksack.

A Land Rover clattered across the field. 'Can I help you?' demanded the driver.

'No, thanks. I'm just fine.'

The gamekeeper glanced at my rucksack. 'You haven't been interfering with the pheasants?'

I wondered how long he had been watching me.

'I'm eating an apple.'

He looked long and hard at the symbol of alien effluent that had come to rest so untidily on his master's land. 'Why can't you eat your apple somewhere else?'

The cucumber sandwiches and bone china were on the table when I knocked at the door of Hyde's House.

George, the young, charming tenant of Hyde's House, was a friend of Luke Hughes, the furniture designer whose patented table-catches I'd seen being made in Bloxwich. Luke had asked George if he wouldn't mind providing a bed for a passing itinerant.

The house that was the birthplace of Edward Hyde, the first Lord Clarendon, Chancellor of the Exchequer and adviser to Charles II, is now in the possession of the country's third largest landowner, the National Trust. (Ahead of the National Trust are the Forestry Commission and then the Ministry of Defence.) Owner of a quarter of a million hectares, 880 kilometres of coast, 60 villages and hamlets, and 7,000 properties, the National Trust has 1.45 per cent of England. Hyde's House is not one of their grander properties, and Hyde himself does not have the pulling-power of, say, Stephenson or Wordsworth, whose very ordinary birthplaces have been turned into tourist sights by the Trust. Impeached for high treason, Hyde died in Rouen, an exile. His house is not open to the public.

'A noble edifice, somewhat Palladian, presented itself, with a magnolia pinioned to its yellow stone walls,' wrote Cecil Beaton while house-hunting in the forties. He dismissed Hyde's House as 'altogether too grand for my taste or my pocket' and settled instead at Broad Chalke, one valley south.

It's a warm house, sunny side to the Nadder, with Ionic columns astride the door and formal gardens tended by George's partner, Chris, a trained horticulturalist from Queensland. To one side, terraces ascend to an elevated pasture planted with a circle of limes around a single lilac.

'On a clear day,' said George, pointing up the Nadder valley, 'you can see the spire of Salisbury Cathedral.'

After Charles had refused to let him come home from France and die in his own country, Edward Hyde must have thought often of this prospect.

Fovant   Only the English countryside knows how to be so exquisitely wistful on a Sunday morning; sometimes it seems as if Constable's byways and cornfields are threaded with a melancholic carnival of haymakers, war poets and rusty knights.

In the field beyond Hyde's House a family drifted by, a straw-haired girl borne on waxed-cotton shoulders above the inked shadow of a black dog.

Another stile opened the way to a field that sloped to the Nadder: a wood, the crunch of boots on railway ballast and the river, shallow and clear, and beyond it a turfed rib running across the hillside. This was once the branch line to Fovant Camp. Had I been here eighty years earlier, I'd have seen a holly-green Pecket and Sons saddle-tank engine called *Westminster*, sparkling with copper and brass, burst from the trees towing wooden carriages full of soldiers, among them my great-uncle Reginald, en route to the trenches.

Beyond the trees, Fobba's Spring – the Saxon village of Fobbanfunta which became Fofunte and then Fovant – appeared to have drifted into deep sleep.

In the tight valley only the stream moved, flowing down the side of the village street from its spring at the foot of Cranborne Chase. Brick bungalows and weathered stone cottages rubbed shoulders, their summer blooms faded. A sign reminded visitors that Fovant had once won the 'Annual Award for the Best Kept Medium Village in Wiltshire'.

The silence was broken by the distant thud of a single-cylinder motorbike. For the next twenty minutes an intermittent cavalcade of black-and-chrome motorcycles puttered by. Middle-aged men in pilots' goggles and pudding-basin helmets clung thin-lipped to juddering bars as they steered through the sunlight towards the downs: an AJS, Nortons, a BSA, Ariels, Triumphs, all British, pistons thumping like distant mortar fire.

They built the camp above the village on Fovant Plain, a kilometre-deep terrace between the scarp of the chalk downs and the drop-off to the Nadder.

Compared to the camp I'd passed through on Cannock Chase, Fovant was lower, warmer and less draughty. The Garrison Cinema ran twice-nightly shows, with Buster Keaton and Charlie Chaplin. There was a church and chapel, hospital, post office, water-pumping station and power station for electricity. Farm buildings were adapted for use as a general store and Vic East, with his wife and mother-in-law, opened the Tipperary Tea Rooms.

One of the units to arrive early in the war was my grandfather's regiment, the London Rifle Brigade. In 1916 soldiers of the LRB began cutting an immense replica of their cap badge into the scarp of the chalk down above the camp. The task was of sufficient importance to make its way on to the Daily Routine Orders sheet ('working parties will muster at 0500 hours').

Drilling beneath the great white badge of the LRB encouraged other regiments to shoulder picks and shovels and trek up the turf of the down. My great-uncle Albert's regiment, the Machine Gun Corps, cut their badge, and so too did the Royal Army Service Corps and Queen Victoria Rifles. The badges got bigger and bigger. The 6th City of London regiment spent three months hacking out a badge 150 feet high. By the end of the war, there were at least twenty badges and emblems on the slope.

Twenty years after the Armistice, my grandfather Stanley

used to halt the family car on the A30 and point out the LRB badge.

My great-uncle Reginald's train pulled into Fovant early in January 1916.

Reg had joined the Post Office Rifles in June the previous year and spent a month at Fovant with the 8th Battalion before sailing for France. He must have been training hard in Fovant, for a letter he wrote on 27 January 1916 to his sister Gwen asks for 'a pair of rubber shoes size 8', explaining: 'You can imagine that when we do get the chance we are glad to get into our shoes for a rest, especially after a long march.'

The morning after he wrote that letter, Reg was on the train down to Dinton and Southampton, without the rubber shoes. He sailed for France on 1 February.

The letters to Gwen continued to flow. Her replies have not survived, but Reg's letters, in neat pencil on small sheets of War Office paper, were carefully saved, each one full of brotherly love for a younger sister whose only two brothers were in the trenches. Reg gave little away, and the censor prevented him from revealing his location or much of his circumstances. There are references to tent life, to sleeping in freezing barns, endless marching, the digging of trenches and dugouts. By the end of April 1916 the two pairs of gloves that a girl called Rose had given him were covered in patches and Reg was asking Gwen to send a replacement pair.

On 2 May 1916 he wrote an uncharacteristically short note to Gwen and on the 14th dashed off a longer, barely legible letter that ended: 'We often see the sunrise & sunset in France, especially when we are in the trenches. Well now it is almost dark & I can't see & so must say goodbye . . .'

That was the last letter Gwen received from her brother. The following Sunday the Germans launched a devastating bombardment against the British trenches on Vimy Ridge, then attacked. Reg was reported 'missing after action'. His body was never found.

*

Stanley Crane, whose regiment had been the first to carve its cap badge on to the down above Fovant, had joined up in the same year as his north London neighbour Reginald.

By 1918, Stanley was a second lieutenant in the 2/4th Londons, but on 20 March that year, the Germans launched the second Battle of the Somme. The attack began at 3.30 a.m. with gas, artillery and *minenwerfer*, followed at 9.40 a.m. by waves of infantry. The Germans took 90,000 prisoners, among them Stanley, who spent the remaining months of the conflict in a prisoner-of-war camp called the Citadel, in Mainz.

Only the British could have converted the horrors of the recent past, and the numbing sense of defeat that had followed capture, into the optimistic, comic spirit that existed in the Citadel.

The formula involved entertainment, education and competition. A monthly magazine, *The Queue*, was launched, carrying jokes about sauerkraut, satirical essays and cartoons of plump guards. The Mainzprings put on musical comedy and pantomime; the camp Dramatic Society staged *Arms and the Man* and *Mr Wu*. Captain Maurice Besly, Royal Engineers, lectured on *Tristan and Isolde*, while Second Lieutenant Burton of the Norfolks sung the *Liebestod*.

A Future Career Society was formed, offering advice on architecture and building trades, banking, insurance, languages, law, medicine and, under Lt Col L. N. Finch of the Cheshires, 'Training & how to keep fit'. A Library Committee was created, and 1,200 books accumulated.

For competition, there were inter-block eight-a-side football tournaments (twenty minutes each way), with cigarettes for the winners, and a Sports Day, with events ranging from Finding the Ham (the only event won by a private) to the One Mile, Putting the Weight, the Block Relay Race and the 100-yard Sprint, with separate events for officers and orderlies. There was an Arts and Crafts Exhibition with fifteen categories from Watercolour (From Memory) to Chip Carving, Regimental Crests and Needlework. An essay competition was held, with an entrance fee of 20 Marks and a choice of six subjects ranging from 'Hitching one's wagon to a star' to 'Rupert Brooke' and 'The merits and de-merits of town and country life as affecting the lower classes'.

When they ran out of ideas, a competition was held to find more competitions.

At the Armistice, the German guards fled and Stanley walked back to the English Channel, found a ship and returned to London, where he married Gwen Brown, the girl who'd corresponded so lovingly with the brother who disappeared on Vimy Ridge.

Above the village I climbed a bank and looked across Fovant Plain to the scarp of the downs.

Where the camp had once sprawled, the Greensand terrace had reverted to a level prairie of pale dry mud, ruled into arable blocks, but the badges were still there, paraded across the 100-metre wall of turf.

To foil Luftwaffe reconnaissance planes during the Second World War, the badges had been left to grow over, but after the war, local volunteers had dug out the channels and refilled them with chalk carried in tin baths from pits.

Thanks to them, Second Lieutenant Stanley Crane's London Rifle Brigade badge was still there, shining like the one he'd worn in his cap before leaving for Picardy.

On the far side of Fovant Plain, a lane cut a switchback up the steep scarp to the ancient drove road that ran along the northern crest of the downs.

For a kilometre or so I followed the track, past Fovant Hut, the only house on the Ridgeway, standing like a coastguard's cottage above a misted swell that receded north across Fovant's fields and the Nadder to the hazy island of Salisbury Plain.

Uncle Reg had surely marched this way in 1916, his boots splintering frozen puddles, wondering what lay ahead. 'I am so glad that Rose came to see you,' he wrote to his sister Gwen from Fovant. 'Would you write to her sometimes if you get any special news of me.'

Who was Rose, I wondered, and did Gwen write to her when she got the 'special news' from Vimy Ridge?

Cranborne Chase   For the rest of that afternoon and into the evening,
I crossed Cranborne Chase, the last major range of hills on the
meridian.

These high chalk downs had an eerie, colourless air at odds
with their richly woven past. When William the Conqueror gave a
tract of prime southern upland to his Queen, he created a royal
hunting forest and a wildlife sanctuary that would survive for 800
years. Just as military rule protected Salisbury Plain, the extreme
regime of Chase law created an island of silviculture while all
around fell to the axe and plough. So strictly protected were the
deer that it was an offence to interfere with the vegetation on which
the animals fed.

Some of the bloodier clashes between gamekeepers and
poachers were recorded by the man Sir Walter Scott described as 'a
Parson mad upon sport', the Reverend William Chafin. In 1818
the galloping vicar (who finally gave up hunting at eighty-three)
published his *Anecdotes and History of Cranbourn Chase*. In it, he
describes the December night in 1780 when a gang of deer-rustlers
attacked gamekeepers with 'swindgels', lethal weapons resembling
threshing flails. One keeper suffered a broken knee-cap; another,
broken ribs, from which he later died. Attacking with 'hangers' –
short swords – the keepers hacked off the hand of one of their
assailants and cut up the gang so severely that they surrendered.
In Pimperne churchyard, the severed hand was buried with battle
honours.

Chafin – who survived being struck by lightning while writing
his short history – knew the Chase in its dying days. A decade
before William Cobbett railed at the industrial age in *Rural Rides*,
Chafin recorded that the old royal forest had shrunk to an area
'about fourteen miles in extent . . . on an average about one mile
and a half wide'. Yet this limited area was the scene of extraordinary
diversity. People came to hunt truffles and to coppice the woodland
for fences, hurdles and thatching spars. Each autumn they camped
in glades during the hazelnut harvest, some staying on through
winter to raid the hoards buried by mice. 'If the Chase was to be
destroyed,' warned Chafin, 'what distress and misery would it not
therefore bring upon these poor commoners, to be deprived at once

of all their worldly dependance!' Twelve years after *Anecdotes and History* was published, Parliament abolished hunting rights on the Chase and the felling began.

By the 1890s Thomas Hardy was writing of the Chase as a historic remnant: 'one of the few remaining woodlands in England of undoubted primeval date, wherein Druidical mistletoe is still found on aged oaks, and where enormous yew trees, not planted by the hand of man, grew as they had grown when they were pollarded for bows.'

Crossing the same hills a century later, I saw no trace of the great forest. Where kings and queens had galloped and bowstrings twanged, there was now smooth earth. Yet it was the clearing of this southern rampart of Wessex that revealed to General Pitt-Rivers the prehistoric mounds and banks of the first inhabitants of Cranborne Chase. Pitt-Rivers's scientific approach to the digs he made on the Chase led to his identification as the father of modern archaeology.

All afternoon I saw no other pedestrian. Or deer. The one village I passed – Ebbesbourne Wake – snoozed around a closed pub and locked church.

Losing height down the southern slopes of the Chase, I came to a belt of trees that hid the massive embankments of a long-lost hill-fort. Beyond its southern ditch, the land sloped down into Dorset, the last county on England's Meridian.

History had endowed the meridian with a progression of criminal species: border raiders and salmon poachers in Northumberland; murderers in the Pennine mill valleys; highwaymen on the Wessex coach roads; deer-poachers in Wiltshire's royal forests; and now smugglers, whose kegs and bales could be spirited up from the Channel to the hidden glades of Cranborne Chase.

From the Chase to the sea, the meridian would cross many a smuggler's trail.

Sixpenny Handley The Saxons felled a glade they named 'seaxa pen' (hill-top) 'hean leah' (high clearing), which mutated into the medieval hundreds of 'Sexpenna' and 'Hanlegga' and thus to Sixpenny Handley, which had been shortened to 6D HANDLEY on the signpost I passed as I walked into this bustling village on the sunward slopes of Cranborne Chase.

Through a stone-tiled Norman porch, buttressed as if to withstand meteorites, the door of Saint Mary's was open and the tomb of John and Dorothy Alie piled with the fruits of a contemporary harvest: Jaffa Cakes, Heinz tomato soup, Marks and Spencer marmalade, Safeway tinned peaches, Batchelors Cup-a-Soups, Happy Shopper tuna chunks, McVitie's digestives, Tesco plum tomatoes, Kwik Save chocolate chip cookies.

Harvest Festival came to Sixpenny Handley barcoded in a supermarket trolley. There was a time when deer-poachers used to hide carcasses in one of St Mary's' empty tombs.

The 9 a.m. rush had filled 6d Handley's narrow main street with impatient traffic. Since leaving Berwick I'd hardly come across a village with so many surviving services. W. S. Clarke & Sons, Family Butchers, had a noble shopfront with two enormous carved rams' heads and the date 1896. Half-way down the street was Handley Hair Shop. There was a hardware and garden shop, two newsagents and two pubs. Kevin's Cars had a (very) used Nissan in the forecourt, for £200.

'Not what it used to be,' recited the woman in the upper newsagent. 'We used to have a greengrocer, two bakers, a haberdasher's. The man who used to run this shop could order anything from shoes to a television.'

She paused to serve another customer. 'In the old days my mother only went shopping in Salisbury once a year, on Christmas Eve. Now villagers dash to and fro every day.'

A glance at the map revealed why 6d Handley was still a commercial hub: a fifteen-kilometre radius around the village was entirely empty of towns. For a village in southern England, it was surprisingly remote.

It was isolation that attracted one of Dorset's most celebrated smugglers to settle at Thorneydown, just outside the village on the Blandford–Salisbury road. In 1768 Isaac Gulliver married the innkeeper's daughter and stayed for a decade, wittily changing the name of the Blacksmith's Arms to the King's Arms.

Gulliver was the archetypal lovable rogue, claiming never to have killed a man in his life. After taking the tenancy of the inn, he seems to have operated with his father-in-law on the shore between Poole and Christchurch. Evidence of Gulliver's activity is largely circumstantial: in 1778, nine casks of spirits and $^3/_4$ ton of tea seized by excise men at Thorneydown were 'liberated' by a gang of pistol-firing smugglers on horseback, who donated two of the casks to spectators and rode off with the rest. Gulliver died in 1822, free and wealthy.

Ten minutes out of Sixpenny Handley I passed the distant roofs of Thorneydown and crossed the Salisbury Road at Endless Pit. Ahead lay the way to the sea.

The Dorset Cursus 'The Roman Road runs straight and bare/As the pale parting-line in hair.'

Perhaps Thomas Hardy was describing the Imperial way from Old Sarum to Badbury Rings. It was the most impressive Roman Road I'd met on the meridian, surfaced with beaten earth and so close to a southerly bearing that I was able to stay with it for three kilometres.

A side track led up Gussage Down to the Ordnance Survey triangulation pillar (June 1939; £4 2s 8d). For thousands of years, man has been drawn to this gentle dome between the sea and the Wessex uplands. On and around the hilltop were barrows and tumuli, the curvilinear banks and ditches of an Iron Age settlement, the Roman Road and the Dorset Cursus, one of England's most enigmatic monuments.

Had I been walking the meridian 5,000 years earlier, I would have found the Cursus entirely blocking my route, a wall of chalk two metres high, running for ten kilometres across the valleys and downs to the south of Cranborne Chase. Had I scrambled on to the wall, I would have seen that a second wall ran parallel with the first, one hundred metres back. At their termini, the two were connected by end walls, forming an enclosure whose interior was entirely hidden from the outside world. There were only two entrances, close together on the north side of the Cursus.

Today, the walls have gone, although their course is still marked on Ordnance Survey maps, and aerial photographs clearly show the enclosure as a pair of pale lines across the hills. The Cursus was the most extraordinary antiquity I'd met on the meridian.

In my axial world, other lines had come to assume an almost cosmic significance. They'd taken many forms, from wall lines and production lines, to contour lines and railway lines. At night I'd slept beneath a sky that was cross-stitched with satellite tracks and cyber highways. I'd trodden path lines and crossed art lines. I'd steered between grid lines.

Long, narrow and designed to confine, the Cursus was uncannily similar to my own meridional corridor. Its purpose was a mystery, and its construction a staggering physical feat. At the time, this was the biggest linear earthwork on the island. While their Neolithic cousins were carving cup-and-ring marks into the bedrock of the Cheviots, an army of excavators in the south was spending half a million worker-hours shifting 232,000 cubic metres of soil – enough to fill 40,000 builders' skips – from two exterior ditches to the adjacent walls.

While the walls and ditches have disappeared, the burial mounds associated with the Cursus have survived. Some of the barrows were oriented towards the Cursus. One of them stood inside it, on what is now Gussage Down. The barrow rose beside my path, smoothly humped like a pregnant belly, a shape, say some, which links Neolithic culture to worship of the Earth Goddess. Gussage Down barrow rose at the highest point of the Cursus, and was visible from both its ends, silhouetted on the skyline about three-quarters of the way from the north-eastern terminus. Significantly, the Gussage Down barrow – and the Cursus – were oriented towards the midwinter sunset.

To Neolithic farmers, the darkest moment of the year would have symbolized the death of the land on which their survival depended. To have linked this temporal nadir with the burial chambers of their own ancestors would have reinforced the sacred unity of sky and earth.

Standing by that barrow on Gussage Down, I saw the two gleaming walls tapering away in both directions, so high that I could see nothing but sky. What went on within the walls? Processions perhaps? Initiation rites that involved the exhumation of ancestral bones? Astronomical observations? Whatever occurred was shielded from non-participants.

The archaeologist Richard Bradley – who excavated here in the 1980s – called this place a 'British Avenue of the Dead'.

River Allen   Back on the Roman Road, I almost broke into a run.

No path I'd trodden had been so suited to the meridian. It was dry and firm and traffic free and for half an hour it went with me towards the sea. In places the agger rose above the fields like a dyke intended to hold back the tide. The contrast between this monumental way and the spectral Devil's Causeway that I'd failed to follow from the Tweed could not have been greater.

The Roman Road took me down to a tributary of the River Allen and the village of Gussage All Saints, where the door of the Drovers Inn gaped like a Venus Flytrap. Over a pint and a bowl of soup, I spread the maps.

Seventeen kilometres down the line lay the last – and largest – obstacle on two degrees west: Poole Harbour. According to the Poole tourism office, it was the second-largest natural harbour in the world. Crossing it required three boat rides, since a spit of land intervened and I also wanted to call at the only island on the meridian. To complicate matters, shallow water and deep mud necessitated a specialized craft and accurate synchronization with high tides. From the telephone on the bar, I called the number given to me in London by the Royal Marines, scribbling into my notebook RV times and grid references: 00509275 for 1100 hours on Tuesday; 99759005 for 1000 hours on Wednesday.

At Amen Corner on the edge of the village, I embarked upon

a final struggle with the English countryside. For ten kilometres from the foot of Cranborne Chase to the twin towers of Wimborne Minster, the meridian was constantly snagged by barbed wire and the meanders of the River Allen. Five times I crossed the river, once in the grounds of Crichel House where the track I'd been sent along by a helpful farmer cleared the trees to reveal a crescentic lake and the ivory rectangle of a neo-classical country house. Like the barrow blocking the Dorset Cursus, Crichel House obstructed the meridian – a final symbol of Englishness that required a pause.

Crichel had cropped up earlier, on the day I'd waded the Tyne. The obituary was in my rucksack, torn from the *Daily Telegraph* and folded for safe-keeping. It was a long obituary, for it not only described the robust war record of a naval lieutenant-commander, but it recalled the infamous Battle of Crichel Down.

The son of a distinguished vice-admiral, George Gosselin Marten spent the war in destroyers, escorting Atlantic convoys and serving as a first lieutenant on *Penn* during the infamous Malta convoy that saw nine merchantmen sunk and the battered tanker *Ohio* creeping into Grand Harbour with her vital cargo of aviation fuel. It was Marten who led the boarding party from *Penn* on to *Ohio* to take the stricken tanker in tow.

Marten came out of the war with a DSC and a second battle on his hands. Back in 1937, the Air Ministry had compulsorily purchased 300 acres of hilltop to the west of the house, for use as a bombing range. At the end of the war, Whitehall gave Crichel Down to the Ministry of Agriculture rather than offer it back to the original owner. This was a mistake. Marten's campaign of lobbying forced the Conservative Minister of Agriculture, Sir Thomas Dugdale, to order a public enquiry. Published in 1954, the report condemned the civil servants for their 'regrettable attitude of hostility' towards Marten, which, they stated, was 'engendered solely by a feeling of irritation that any member of the public should have the temerity to question the acts or decisions of officials'. The minister resigned and Crichel Down was returned to the Martens. Lieutenant-Commander Marten had died on the same day of the year that *Ohio* had berthed in Grand Harbour.

After a pig farm and an unfortunate accident in a ditch I'd not seen when I jumped out of a hedge, I crossed the River Allen for the last time and entered Wimborne Minster.

Wimborne Minster   That night the BBC Big Band were playing at the Tivoli Theatre. At my bed and breakfast I buffed my boots with lavatory paper, combed my hair, chipped the cow turd off my Cheadles then joined the throng of barathea blazers and twinkly earrings in the theatre foyer. The expectant buzz was as palpable as the fog of aftershave and perfume. It had been a long time since the BBC Big Band were in Wimborne. 'Friday December 20th 1996. Nine months ago,' noted a silvery retiree in spit-and-polish slip-ons; 'Well nine months one week.'

Sitting at their instruments, the band gave the initial impression that we were in for an evening of sedate melodies. Then Barry Forgie stepped forward, raised his hands, glanced at the brass, and the ceiling seemed to cave in. Decibels and adrenalin hammered at the auditorium walls. The volume was incredible, the band and the audience impassive. Barry ripped through numbers by Benny Goodman, Stan Kenton and Count Basie. We had 'Tiger Rag', 'American Patrol', 'Skyliner' and – of course – 'MacArthur Park'.

During the intermission the audience chucked back pre-ordered gins and Scotches, and when the show resumed with 'Boogie Express' the man in the service tie beside me was loose enough to tap his knee. Jeff Hooper had to come on stage to slow things down. Jeff was short and shiny and born in Llantrisant. He did Frank Sinatra and Lou Rawls and finished by announcing that he was going to introduce a special guest. 'You'll never guess who is here tonight! Yes! Sitting here in the audience is Reg! Reg flew with the Dambusters! A big round of applause for Reg!'

It was a wild evening.

The old part of Wimborne Minster slumbered twenty metres above sea level on a finger of land between the converging rivers Allen and Stour.

The town sat roughly equidistant from the two ends of the English Channel. To the east, buildings straggled almost uninterrupted to North Foreland on the corner of Kent; to the west the coast was protected by AONBs for most of the way to Land's End. The Allen was the Rubicon that defied the westward march of the hod-carriers.

On the south coast's dividing line between the built and the un-built, Wimborne Minster stood as a symbol of what there was to lose; a picture from a scrapbook of old English market towns, with a sunny street of Georgian houses, apparently thriving shops, the theatre and Holy Communion three days a week.

In the minster was the history of Wimborne, layered so richly that it was possible to believe that the place would always be there, a great hunk of architectural coral that will accrete a little each century as generations pass through. It was not a conventionally handsome church: Pevsner complained of its spotty complexion, the 'uncouth' crossing tower and a lack of balance only partly due to the collapse of the spire in 1600. But it was an imposing pile that had gathered sufficient curiosities over nearly 1,000 years for the faults of form to be forgiven.

Inside were fragments of Roman mosaic, Norman arches and a brass that once covered the grave of King Ethelred, dead from wounds after fighting the Danes on the downs in AD871. His young brother Alfred stood in this place, a king at twenty, then beat the Danes, signed a truce and saw them return and burn the minster where he'd buried his brother. In a side chapel stood a Saxon oak chest rescued from a nunnery that was also burned by the Danes.

There were echoes here from other points on the meridian. Dickens, whose path I'd crossed in Berwick-upon-Tweed, at Dotheboys Hall and in the Black Country, is fondly thought to have taken Snodgrass and Wardell for *The Pickwick Papers* from names in the minster, and in 1542 the travelling antiquary John Leland – who'd also been with the meridian since Northumberland – had stood in the minster at Ethelred's tomb. Purbeck stone from the end of the meridian had been quarried for Ethelred's slab and the Norman font, and under the floor lay two of Daniel Defoe's daughters,

Hannah and Henrietta, the latter having married a local excise officer who was a contemporary of Isaac Gulliver the smuggler. Gulliver's gravestone was in the minster too. A 'venerable piece of antiquity,' wrote Defoe of the minster, before he knew that his daughters would be buried here.

Inside the West Tower hung an astronomical clock, showing the sky, sun, moon and stars revolving around a centrally placed, fixed earth. The clock was built at the end of the 1300s, over a century before Nicolas Copernicus proved that the sun, not the earth, was the centre of the universe.

Time and space were the twin architects of my meridian. I was walking a line devised to measure space, derived from a line that defined time.

When Davidson committed England to the transverse Mercator projection, time and space were measured from Greenwich. Both have moved on.

Time has moved to Paris, where it is calculated by the International Earth Rotation Service, who take Universal Time (derived from observations of the earth's rotation) and International Atomic Time (from atomic clocks), then use computers to generate a compromise called Universal Co-ordinated Time. It is UCT that triggers the pips on the radio.

Space is measured from space. Coordinates supplied by the satellites of the Global Positioning System are the standard for air navigation and one day will also be the standard for maps and charts. The US military satellites that feed GPS with data are zeroed on a line 102 metres east of the brass meridian strip in the courtyard of the Old Observatory.

Our fate is back in celestial hands: we wait to see which way the wind blows, hot or cold. They say it's more likely to be a hot wind; a globally warming three-degrees-a-century wind. Then a cold wind. If they're right, the minster could be lapped by salt-water before its astronomical clock reaches its 1,000th birthday.

Corfe Hills   The mist was lifting from the water-meadows of the Stour as I stood pressed against the parapet of Julian's Bridge trying not to be smeared on to the 400-year-old stone by the riptide of ill-tempered commuters.

Across the floodplain the meridian rose to a hill crest where Romans once fired pottery and a fingerpost read 'Footpath to Happy Bottom'. In a couple of strides I regained the sanctuary of a path which twisted through woods in sparkling sunlight until it found the road built by Vespasian's engineers 2,000 years earlier.

The Second Augustan Legion had waded ashore at Hamworthy in AD43, striking north from their bridgehead along a hastily built road that they used as a supply-line for subduing the Durotriges. Like the Roman Road I'd followed the previous day, this too connected to Badbury Rings, the Iron Age hill-fort that Rome turned into a road junction. Again, the meridian exceeded all past records, coinciding with a long, straight track that would take me all the way to salt-water. For the next five kilometres, two degrees west and Vespasian's road ran side by side.

Between Berwick and Hamworthy I'd steered a truer course than any Roman surveyor could have imagined possible. A legionary making the long march from the Tweed back to the bridgehead at Hamworthy would have walked far further than I had. Once he'd turned his back on Oceanus Germanicus he'd have headed south through Alauna to the ford at Coriosopitum and a long eastward dogleg through the Pennine margin of the subjugated Brigantes, from Vinovia to Cataractonium, Eboracum (occupied by Vespasian's nephew Quintus Petillius Cerialis) and over the estuarine mud at Petvaria to Lindum, now Leicester. Here he would have turned south-westwards down the Fosse Way through Ratae and the tribal lands of the Coritani to Corinium, where another eastward kink would have taken him over vale and downs to Cunetio, Sorviodunum, Vindocladia and so – along the very road I now trod – to a beach on Oceanus Britannicus.

Vespasian's road still ran true. By turn gravel and sand and beaten earth, it cut through the woods and heath of the Corfe Hills until it ran into a housing estate on the northern fringe of suburban Poole. Between bungalows, the Empire's supply-line had been laid with bitumen and given the street name 'Roman Road'. A side turn was 'Caesar's Way'.

For the final descent to sea level, the estates fell back and the old road thinned to a silvine avenue as it dropped down beside the bracken of Upton Heath to a roundabout on the A35.

The line of the Roman Road continued into Upton Park and past its sprawling nineteenth-century house. As I was passing the public lavatories, a Roman Legionary exited the gents with his hand on his gladius. He was gone before I could bridge the neuro-logical gulf between incredulity and speech. He'd been dressed in body armour, helmet and studded sandals, bearing a spear, a sword and a dagger. I caught up with him in the café, where he was leaving the counter with a cup of tea and a piece of fruit cake.

Ivor (Second Augustan Legion) was the personal bodyguard to Vespasian, conqueror of southern Britain, and lived at Fairview Crescent, Poole. With a military spine and a face straight off Trajan's Column, Ivor spent his working hours with Securicor and his leisure time as Gavius Silvanus, clanking about schools and fêtes and Upton Park, where he was resident Roman in a reconstructed Romano-British thatched farmstead behind the car park.

India, he said, now supplied the Roman Army: £300 for the cuirass, £250 for the helmet and £150 for the sword. The bits of Ivor which weren't armoured were tattooed: Fleet Air Arm on his arms, Roman on his legs.

In the car park, Ivor loaded his weapons into the boot of his Longbridge-built Rover 213S, removed his helmet and unbuckled his cuirass. 'You know,' he mused, 'there's quite a lot of us around nowadays. Us Romans.'

Holes Bay   Sea water had last been in sight of the meridian from Tosson Hill, several days' march north of Hadrian's Wall. Now it reappeared as a silver lake seen through clapping leaves.

Holes Bay is about 2,000 metres long and 1,500 metres wide, cut in half laterally by a railway which runs along an embankment. Two cuts, bridged by the railway, allow water through into the inner, northern half of the bay. Beyond the bridges lie the town of Poole and, beyond there, the main part of Poole Harbour and Green Island. I planned to spend a night in Poole, then cross to the island at high tide the following morning. The island was uninhabited, but the owner Jo Davies had agreed to meet me there and show me its secrets.

The Royal Marines had warned that crossing Holes Bay by boat would be a 'poor shout', a reference I presumed to a drowning man gagging on harbour silt. They said that they'd try, but that they could not make any promises. If they couldn't reach me, my fallback plan was to trespass along the western shore of the bay, climb the railway embankment, cross the lines and then drop down into the back gardens that – residents permitting – would give me access to Hamworthy and then to Poole. The map made the land route look more problematic than an attempt at crossing Holes Bay by boat. When I reached the shore of the bay, I changed my mind.

The rendezvous the Marines had given me was a concrete culvert carrying a small stream into the bay. The tide was in, but the water was too shallow for anything but bath toys. Beneath the surface, the mud looked as soft as chocolate blancmange.

When the distant dot of a small boat appeared under the eastern of the two railway bridges, I watched in helpless fascination as it hit mud and then began probing for alternative routes across the bay. The likelihood of the boat reaching the RV receded with the tide. Finally, after thirty minutes of struggle (during which I thought I saw one or more of the crew go over the side), the boat extricated itself from the bay, slipping back under the bridge, out of sight.

Following the fallback plan, I pulled on the rucksack and began rehearsing what I'd say to the homeowners whose back gardens I was about to infiltrate. But as I retraced my steps into Upton Park I passed a map on a signboard and saw that a new public footpath had been built around the western shore of Holes Bay. It appeared to pass beneath the railway embankment about eighty metres inside Grid 99, then enter Hamworthy.

For the first time, the Ordnance Survey had been left behind by current events. My triumph at finding a flaw in the system (and in avoiding a complicated trespass) was muted by a reminder that maps were indeed fallible; maps were not reality.

With all the distortions created by projection, scale, choice of material and medium, I had now stumbled across humdrum outdatedness. Earlier in the journey, I'd also discovered deliberate falsifications by the Ordnance Survey in order to hide militarily sensitive sites, places that the OS privately calls 'secret installations'. One of the sites I'd passed further north had been an extensive area of tobacco-coloured warehouses surrounded by security fences. It was marked on the map as fields. The OS also censored place names; removing from the landscape (and therefore from common usage) labels deemed too vulgar for printing. So Ring Bum Gardens, Smoking Hole, Scratch Arse and Shit Yallery Hole, all of them quarrymen's vernacular for locations on and around the meridian's Purbeck terminus, did not appear on the map in my pocket.

Manipulating maps is an old game. But in a world of distortion, they're still the primary source.

Poole   Blue sparks of oxyacetylene flickered from the deck of a freighter called *Sand Skua* as I walked across the lift-bridge that spanned the narrow channel separating Holes Bay from Poole Harbour.

Under a late summer sun the old seaport stirred in the last hour of the ebb tide. Two men peered into a hatch on the aft deck of the lifeboat. A dog-owner shuffled while his pet defecated on the cobbles. A woman in a leopard-skin coat and sunglasses slowly turned a page of the *Guardian* at an aluminium café table outside the Custom House, the scene in 1747 of a raid by sixty armed smugglers who battered their way into the building to recover tea that had been seized from the lugger *Three Brothers*. Later, the two-man escort to a witness of the break-in was murdered by the smugglers, several of whom came to a premature end on the gallows.

Longitudinal constraints limited me to the western 800 metres of the old town, a promontory that included the quayside that had dispatched Poole's fishermen to the cod banks of Newfoundland in the wake of John Cabot. In June 1944 the same waterfront was cluttered with khaki as the largest of the invasion fleets – eighty-one landing craft – assembled in Poole Harbour prior to sailing for the beaches of Normandy. Today the quay is punctuated by an Anthony Caro sculpture that climbs in semi-clefs of curved blue steel against the multi-filament pyramids of yacht rigging.

Daniel Defoe included Poole in *A Tour Through the Whole Island of Great Britain*, but his powers of invention failed to rise to the occasion. Poole, he noted blandly, was 'a considerable sea-port, and indeed the most considerable in all this part of England'. He offered no incidents, or insights, or flights of fiction, just a pair of paragraphs on the fishing industry, which could have come from an eighteenth-century Chamber of Commerce press release. 'Tis observed,' he wrote, 'more pearl are found in the Pool oysters, and larger than in any other oysters about England.'

To its association with cod and oysters, Poole can now add Tim Berners-Lee, who worked here before creating the World Wide Web, and crispbread, which is produced in such prodigious quantities that the output from the local Ryvita factory could encircle the world six times a year.

In Poole I saw the last of Defoe and of his sixteenth-century predecessor, John Leland. The orphan who became a scholar to Henry VIII noted how Poole had prospered with the silting-up of Wareham at the head of the harbour. The port, he wrote, had 'much encreasid with fair building and use of marchaundise'.

In a modern townhouse shoe-horned into the crooked architecture of Church Street, I found a room for the night.

'I don't usually take single men,' warned 76-year-old Mrs Pat Parish, relenting when I explained that hers was the only accommodation address in Poole that lay between the grid lines of 99 and 01.

Self-adhesive labels instructed guests how to work the lighting, the television and the illuminated fish tank. Pat had lived in the house since it was built, and when the builders moved out they told her that they'd bricked-up a Roman well in the garden. To help to pay her grandson's school fees, Pat had opened her front door to paying guests. One of these recently stole her silver.

'He was tall and blond, middle-aged and full of himself,' recalled Pat without rancour. 'I went to my insurance company, who I'd been paying for fifty years, but they said that it wasn't burglary. There had been no breaking and entering, so I got nothing.'

Hamworthy The family I'd last seen standing on the banks of the Tyne outside Corbridge had told me that they lived on Poole Harbour.

Digging my early notes from their protective plastic bag at the bottom of the rucksack, I recovered the Sullivans' phone number and called them up from Pat's house. 'Oh yes,' laughed Elaine. 'We remember you!'

They lived in Woodlands Avenue, about two kilometres from Poole and well inboard my graticular corridor. By the time I had walked back out to Hamworthy and found their house, evening had fallen and Bryan had left for skittles. We drank orange juice in the sitting room and looked through the photographs which Bryan had taken of the Tyne crossing nearly six weeks earlier. There was, in these riverside snapshots of a man with no trousers draped in footballs and wearing a child's rubber ring, a rucksack and an inflated bivouach bag, the hint of some kind of bizarre immersion ritual – or of a man suffering from an agoraphobic condition that precluded the use of bridges. I could see why Bryan had shielded his family.

One of the footballs I'd given the Sullivans at the Tyne sat on the sitting-room floor amid the dinosaurs and books.

As I walked back through the darkened streets of Hamworthy, over the harbour bridge and past *Sand Skua*, sleeping at the wharf with her night lights on, I realized how the strange constraints of my linear world had created that essential catalyst for human exchange: curiosity. Curiosity is the traveller's calling card, but in this age of commonplace journeys it's often unrequited. It's difficult to imagine anyone in the world – from an Amazonian hunter-gatherer to a Saharan hermit – who hasn't clapped eyes on a foreigner. In photogenic hotspots from Zermatt to Grassington, visitors overwhelm the locals. I was lucky. By virtue of my line, curiosity was reciprocated. Curiosity had opened hearts and doors. Most of the places I passed through were not used to visitors, especially those who were wading streams and hiking through housing estates in order to stay within a pair of invisible lines. To many I met, I had no past or future. I was the perfect confidant: eager to listen and of disposable judgement – the ultimate throwaway friend. I'd been the recipient of extraordinary kindnesses, usually from people I'd never have met had I been following habitually trodden paths.

Green Island   Grid reference 99759005 was a small promontory on the southern edge of Hamworthy Park, just behind some bathing huts.

Arriving fifteen minutes ahead of the 1000 hours RV with the Royal Marines, I settled down in the sun with the *Daily Telegraph* while a bunch of schoolchildren scuffled on the seawall. Poole Harbour was calm; the visibility perfect. At 0959 and 50 seconds a small black craft travelling at inconceivable speed came tilting out of the west. I had no time to fold the newspaper. A figure in camouflage standing in the bow shouted: 'Jump!'

I leapt off the groyne and was shrugging off the rucksack as the boat reversed from the shore, then swung about and surged forward.

The officer shook my hand and helped me on with a life-preserver. Three others were on board: the helmsman, standing in a cockpit at the craft's stern, and two men perched on the pair of 'saddles' that ran the length of the forward part of the hull. Griz, Jock and Matt wore dark blue one-piece suits with watertight rubber cuffs.

'How fast does it go?'

The helmsman pulled the throttle levers and the Rigid Raider skidded across the sea.

'Twin engines. Both inboard,' shouted the officer. 'Thirty-five knots. It's the new model.'

The boat streaked quicker than I could think. Weeks moving at 4 kph had slowed my mind. If I wanted to check my position I'd often look for a grassy bed, lie down, take off my boots, open the map, tinker with the compass, make some notes, unpack the rucksack in search of a photocopied extract; doze; wake; then reverse the entire process.

Barely a minute seemed to have passed before the boat slewed up to an island. Green Island was small and wooded and surprisingly high, with a long wooden landing stage. Two people were waiting.

Jo Davies – silver-haired and laughing, in a leather waistcoat and postbox red trousers – welcomed us to her island. With her was her cousin, the Reverend David Pain, vicar of Billingshurst. The men in one-piece suits solemnly shook hands and we walked ashore.

There were red squirrels on the island, and owls and pheasants, but no rabbits. Or snakes. It was twenty acres only, arranged around a little hill twenty metres high.

A fawn froze in the birches, heart thumping. Our breath held and the world stilled, as the young beast stood painted into a frame of leaf and lawn against a backdrop of cerulean blue sparked by a solitary sail.

A breath. A falling leaf. The fawn sprang and the chronometer came back to life.

Green Island cast its spell. Paths twisted through trees, teasing with snatches of sea and sky, and revealing the island's special places: a timber bench angled to admire the passage past Poole Harbour's islands to the English Channel; the sunny plot where an islander had grown figs and raspberries back in the thirties; the old Morello cherries, once part of an avenue from the water to a vanished wooden bungalow. I longed to linger on this viridescent isle; to stay all winter and to lie on its southern slopes in springtime and feel the bracken shoots rising against my skin.

We climbed to a lawn which looked down upon this

water-circled rock. Islands spread before us: Brownsea and Furzey, Long Island and Round Island. To the north lay the low, grey harbour rim around Hamworthy; the other way, over the blue channel of South Deep, lay the Isle of Purbeck and the end of England's Meridian.

As we looked down the line, a seal surfaced in South Deep and slid with the leaving tide towards the open sea.

A young man with a mane of blond hair and an austere frame joined the view.

Until recently, Matt.Hew had been the island's lone resident. For two and a half years he slept by day in the tent-shaped timber house, working by night with clay in a cabin down in the woods. Matt.Hew was Jo's son. 'Mum and Dad said that I could choose my own middle name when I was eighteen. I became Matt.Hew.'

His early work – scarified and broken amphorae – lay in the undergrowth, artistic complements to the island's archaeological sediment. It was fragments of much older amphorae found here that suggest a pre-Roman wine trade between Green Island and the Continent. Other finds tell of Iron Age armlet makers living on the island, and Roman potters who may have made the black burnished ware that was favoured for its durability among the garrisons on Hadrian's Wall. Before Matt.Hew, Guy Sydenham lived and potted on the island for twenty-five years. It was Guy who taught Matt.Hew how to throw pots. Green Island – like England – got its beauty from geography, but its identity from human continuity.

The island's latest kiln was rising from the leaf-mulch in the woods, built of brick, with two chambers and a neck which reached through the leaves of the surrounding trees. Matt.Hew was constructing a strange and unique hybrid, a marriage between the Japanese Anagma climbing kiln and the English Bourry Box, that would allow him to develop his tall, wood-fired salt-glazed works. Beside the kiln rested a stack of fuel: rhododendron timber cleared from the upper slopes of the island, where it had rampaged since the fifties (an aerial reconnaissance photograph taken by the Luftwaffe in 1942 showed Green Island entirely clear of its leathery invader).

We sat with coffee at a wooden table in the sun and Jo talked of the Green Island Holiday Trust, a charity she'd formed that provided holidays on the island for disadvantaged and disabled people. Often in wheelchairs, they'd come for a week at a time with carers.

'I see a lot of spiritualism on this island,' said Jo. 'Especially from the carers. It's not spiritualism that's necessarily under the auspices of the church. It's care. Love.'

The vicar put down his mug. 'They're Christian principles.'

The men in waterproof suits reappeared. We had to cross South Deep before the tide towed all the water from Ower Bay.

Green Island shrank upon the stern wave of the Rigid Raider. The crossing of South Deep took less than a minute.

The helmsman brought the craft to a drift in the narrow channel entering Ower Bay. At the bow, Griz and Jock unlashed the small rubber inflatable Gemini and lowered it over the side.

Griz climbed from the Rigid Raider into the inflatable. My rucksack followed, and Jock. Griz yanked the toggle to start the Gemini's motor and we crept across the bay towards the shadowed rectangle of Ower Quay Cottage, the terminus of the track over Newton Heath.

The motor died. Griz pulled off his boots and slid over the side. I followed him towards the shore, boots swinging, the stones and slime categoric between my toes. The spell of the sea was broken. I was back to the confinement of paths.

Shin-deep in the warm water, I handed back the olive-green life-preserver and watched Griz wade back to the Gemini, then pull himself on board, a sock of mud on each foot. They heaved the small rubber boat on to the deck of the Rigid Raider, then motored out of South Deep as three other identical craft came creaming out of the east. Griz and his crew tagged on to the flotilla and were soon black bouncing specks receding to invisibility.

Ower Ower Quay Cottage looked locked but well kept, with climbing roses and the melancholy echo of lost custom.

Ower or Ore, wrote John Hutchins in 1773 in his *History of Dorset*, was 'formerly a manor and hamlet, now a farm and tything . . . the chief, if not the only key [quay], for exporting stone, which has been neglected since 1710 . . .'

It is possible too that the Romans had used Ower, for they had favoured Purbeck marble for mortars and for inscribed tablets. They liked the contrast between the flecked rock and their cinnabar lettering.

As the tide ebbed, recollections of that industrious era emerged from the water: seaweed-draped blocks of Purbeck marble that had fallen from barges and two rows of rotted stakes that must once have been the footings of a landing stage.

By the time Hutchins reached this spot towards the end of the eighteenth century, Swanage had eclipsed Ower as the entrepôt for Purbeck's stone, and the turnpike trusts had opened up the roads connecting the Isle of Purbeck's quarries with the 'mainland'. Had Hutchins been a century earlier, he'd have found this remote bay seething with activity. Back in the days when flat-bottomed boats and stone-carts met at this water-margin, Ower Quay Cottage was an alehouse where quarrymen could rehydrate before the homeward haul inland to Purbeck's dusty villages. Beneath the brick upper floor of the cottage, I could see courses of Purbeck stone, perhaps the walls of the original alehouse. Over the very spot on which I now sat had passed the stone for Salisbury Cathedral, Westminster Abbey and the tomb of the Black Prince in Canterbury Cathedral.

Once a year, on Shrove Tuesday, the Ancient Order of Purbeck Marblers and Stone Cutters still make their annual pilgrimage to Ower. Beforehand, they convene in the Fox Inn in the village of Corfe Castle, where apprentices are vetted for possible induction into the Order. To be considered, each apprentice has to bring to the Fox a small loaf of bread, a quart of ale, 6s 8d (or its decimalized equivalent) and a record of apprenticeship. At noon, on the ringing of the curfew bell from the church opposite, the Order crosses the street. In the upstairs room of the smallest town hall in England, a secret meeting begins. Centuries ago this meeting would have fixed the price of stone for the following year; today, only the freemen know what is discussed. The meeting lasts an hour or two, and then the freemen emerge on to the street and ritually kick a football down West Street, up an alley, across the fields and then back down East Street to the town hall, whereupon one of the freemen sets off with one pound of peppercorns to Ower Quay Cottage.

The peppercorns are a rent and annual dues payable to the owner (now tenant) of the cottage. The ritual has continued for hundreds of years, although the details have changed slightly. Back in 1773, Hutchins records that the ritual took place on Ash Wednesday, and that the payment was 'one pound of pepper and a football to the lord'. What the lord did with all his footballs is unclear.

Today the dues are paid not to the lord (or to Ower Quay Cottage) but to the tenant of Ower Farm, a secluded house I passed ten minutes inland. The previous year, the pepper was delivered in a glass coffee jar, conveyed by red Ford Fiesta.

Nine Barrow Down   Nine grid squares remained out of the 578 that separated the Northumbrian coast from the English Channel.

The day was bright and the forest soft with resin and an infant breeze. From Ower Quay, the quarrymen's track cut through the conifers, then emerged on to open heath beneath the rampart of Nine Barrow Down. A Hercules aircraft turned in the warm air, the lugubrious lower lip of its tailgate hanging open. I fancied for a moment that the Fat Alberts of Lyneham had followed me down the meridian and were staging a fly-past for the finish of the journey. As each plane lumbered over the coast, figures fell then blossomed into mushrooms that drifted down towards the water of Studland Bay.

Looking back, I could see how the blue lagoon of Poole Harbour had severed two degrees west and how it connected with the sea to surround the Isle of Purbeck with water on three sides. In his *Blue Guide* of the 1920s, Muirhead had called it a 'bold promontory'. For England's Meridian it formed a fitting conclusion.

A track angled up on to Nine Barrow Down, a dramatic blade of chalk that reappears from beneath the sea twenty-five kilometres to the east as the Needles on the Isle of Wight. On the crest of the down, grave-diggers from the Stone Age and Bronze Age had left a cluster of seventeen round barrows and one long barrow, among them – so it is said – the resting-places of nine kings who died in battle.

At the other end of the down, the Ordnance Survey had erected the last triangulation pillar on the meridian. It stands at 199 metres, cast in concrete at a cost of £10 8s 6d on a cold January day in 1936. Up here an OS observer had lifted his 'Tavi' theodolite on to the top of the trig pillar and bent to the eyepiece, searching for dots of light on a semi-circle of hilltops from Lyme Bay to the Isle of Wight. One of those hilltops – Win Green – I could see now, poking above the downs of Cranborne Chase. In the opposite direction was a long brush-stroke of consistent blue. The sea, at last. In 1965 the OS erected a temporary thirty-metre steel tower above the trig pillar on Nine Barrow Down so that observations could be made across the Channel to a 120-metre hilltop above the French hamlet of Digulleville on the tip of the Cotentin peninsula. Off to the east, the Needles gleamed like a silver cutwater below the Isle of Wight's chalk cliffs and to their left, mists smudged the New Forest, hiding Southampton and the headquarters of the Ordnance Survey. On this down I bade farewell to the map-makers who'd converted a three-dimensional globe into a two-dimensional picture that fitted my pocket.

On this down too, I left Celia Fiennes, the indomitable rider I'd met first on the Tyne. My walk through England had taken place on the 300th anniversary of her first great journey, when she'd ridden north from London, to beyond the Wharfe and the Yorkshire Moors. One of her earlier explorations had taken her west to the Isle of Purbeck, where she'd climbed the down above Corfe Castle and looked at the view I now shared: 'From this ridge you see all the Island over, which lookes very fruitfull, good lands meadows woods and inclosures.' She'd liked it, and so did I. There's a sense of place about islands – even when they're semi-detached – that sets them apart from continents.

The meridian dropped from the trig pillar to the foot of the down and crossed the narrow lane that Richard Long had walked for one of his 'Dorset Song Lines'.

As I sat with the landscape artist over toasted Stilton in his home before taking the train north to Berwick-upon-Tweed, he'd suddenly leaned forward after explaining the fascination of line-walking: 'The symmetry,' he reminded me. 'The geometry!'

Langton Matravers   The pavement slabs of Langton Matravers were silver in the low western light as I walked up the hill past St George's Church, its squat tower hunched below the roofline as if ducking the sea draught. One of the many local smugglers' tales claims that the choir were once singing 'And Thy paths drop fatness', when the roof collapsed under the weight of hidden kegs. The church was on the direct route inland for smugglers using Dancing Ledge.

Beyond the church I turned for the sea, past Langton House, where the first man I'd met on this journey had been to school. Back in Berwick-upon-Tweed, when Gavin Douglas had spoken of learning to swim in a rock pool on Dancing Ledge, I'd been incredulous, for Dancing Ledge was where my line ended.

Not for the first time, I was struck by the connectivity that two degrees west had often contrived. Frequently an aspect of a person or a place had recurred later on the meridian, sometimes in circum-stances that appeared to stretch the parameters of coincidence. What, for instance, was the mathematical probability of meeting on the meridian in Northumberland a family whose home was on the meridian in Dorset?

'Your 2,000-metre band is about one-hundredth the average width of the country,' explained my father Hol, who had reappeared with my mother on the Isle of Purbeck. 'So for everyone you met who didn't live on the part of the meridian you were on at the time, there was one chance in a hundred they'd live somewhere else on it. Assuming,' he added carefully, 'that your cross-section has the same density of population as the rest of England.'

Such coincidences became a pattern when someone or some-thing recurred repeatedly along the line. Patterns emerge wherever we stop and look. The country is thickly stratified with references to our lives; our history and culture. Every day we unknowingly miss these connections. (I once hurried past my own father in a London street.) We have traded local interest for global unfamiliarity.

Dancing Ledge   South of Langton House the tarmac ended and a track ran up to the cottages of Spyway Barn. Less than 1,000 metres remained.

On the edge of the land a grass amphitheatre framed the English Channel. A path cut downwards then faltered at the brink of a short cliff. At its foot lay a terrace of rock similar to the one I'd hopscotched across nearly two months earlier. According to my eighty-year-old *Blue Guide*, Dancing Ledge took its name from 'the motion of the waves of the making tide'. The tide was indeed rising.

I left my clothes beside the rucksack at the cliff foot then slipped into the rock-pool on the edge of Dancing Ledge. On one side, the pool was open to the waves, which surged over its lip, aerated and eager. I lay in this watery sarcophagus, lifting and falling on the ebb and flow of memory, until the sun set and the sea turned black.

Index